D1192643

Cognitive and Instructional Processes in History and the Social Sciences

Cognitive and Instructional Processes in History and the Social Sciences

edited by

Mario Carretero
Autonoma University
Madrid, Spain

and

James F. Voss
University of Pittsburgh
Pittsburgh, PA

Routledge
Taylor & Francis Group
NEW YORK AND LONDON

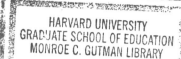

First Published by
Lawrence Erlbaum Associates, Inc., Publishers
10 Industrial Avenue
Mahwah, New Jersey 07430

Transferred to Digital Printing 2009 by Routledge
270 Madison Ave, New York NY 10016
2 Park Square, Milton Park, Abingdon, Oxon, OX14 4RN

Library of Congress Cataloging-in-Publication Data

Cognitive and instructional processes in history and the social sci-
ences / edited by Mario Carretero and James F. Voss.
        p.   cm.
        Papers presented at a conference held Oct. 1992, at the
Autonoma University, Madrid, Spain.
        Includes bibliographical references and index.
        ISBN 0-8058-1564-3. -- ISBN 0-8058-1565-1 (pbk.)
        1. History—Study and teaching—Congresses.   I. Carretero,
Mario. II. Voss, James F., 1930–   .
D16.2.C64   1994
907--dc20   94-39611
                                                                CIP

Publisher's Note
The publisher has gone to great lengths to ensure the quality of this reprint
but points out that some imperfections in the original may be apparent.

Contents

Preface   ix

Chapter 1.   Introduction   1
James F. Voss and Mario Carretero

Part I.   Cognitive Developmental Processes   15

Chapter 2.   Young People's Understanding of Politics
and Economics   17
Adrian Furnham

Chapter 3.   Children's Understanding of the Concept
of the State   49
Anna Emilia Berti

Chapter 4.   Stages in the Child's Construction
of Social Knowledge   77
Juan Delval

Chapter 5.   Dimensions of Adolescents' Reasoning about
Political and Historical Issues: Ontological Switches,
Developmental Processes, and Situated Learning   103
Judith Torney-Purta

Discussion of Chapters 2–5: Cognitive Development
and Representation Processes in the Understanding
of Social and Historical Concepts   123
J. Linaza

Part II.   Teaching and Instructional Processes in History   129

Chapter 6.   Learning to Reason in History: Mindlessness
to Mindfulness   131
*Gaea Leinhardt, Catherine Stainton,
Salim M. Virji, and Elizabeth Odoroff*

Chapter 7.   Understanding History for Teaching: A Study of the
Historical Understanding of Prospective Teachers   159
G. Williamson McDiarmid

Chapter 8.   Constructing the Learning Task in History
Instruction   187
Ola Halldén

Chapter 9   Controversial Issues in History Instruction   201
Carole L. Hahn

Discussion of Chapters 6–9: What Do People
Consume History For? (If They Do). Learning
History as a Process of Knowledge Consumption
and Construction of Meaning   221
Alberto Rosa

Part III.   Learning from History and Social Sciences Texts   235

Chapter 10.   Outcomes of History Instruction: Paste-up Accounts   237
Isabel L. Beck and Margaret G. McKeown

Chapter 11.   How Students Use Texts to Learn and Reason
about Historical Uncertainty   257
Charles A. Perfetti, M. Anne Britt,
Jean-François Rouet, Mara C. Georgi, and
Robert A. Mason

Chapter 12.   Contextualized Thinking in History   285
Samuel S. Wineburg and Janice Fournier

Discussion of Chapters 10–12: Promoting Narrative
Literacy and Historical Literacy   309
Maria José Rodrigo

Part IV.   Complex Processes in History and Social Sciences   321

Chapter 13.   Struggling with the Past: Some Dynamics of
Historical Representation   323
James Wertsch

Chapter 14.   (Re-)Constructing History and Moral Judgment:
On Relationships Between Interpretations of the
Past and Perceptions of the Present   339
Bodo von Borries

Chapter 15.   Historical Knowledge: Cognitive and Instructional
              Implications   357
              Mario Carretero, Liliana Jacott, Margarita Limón,
              Asunción Lopez-Manjón, and Jose A. León

Chapter 16.   Historical Reasoning as Theory-Evidence
              Coordination   377
              Deanna Kuhn, Michael Weinstock, and
              Robin Flaton

Chapter 17.   The Collapse of the Soviet Union: A Case Study
              in Causal Reasoning   403
              James F. Voss, Mario Carretero, Joel Kennet,
              and Laurie Ney Silfies

              Discussion of Chapters 13–17: The Cognitive
              Construction of History   431
              Angel Rivière

Author Index   445

Subject Index   453

Preface

The chapters that appear in this book are the product of an international conference held at Autonoma University of Madrid, Spain, in October 1992. The main purpose of the conference was to bring together a small number of scholars from Europe and the United States to discuss their ideas and research about cognitive and instructional processes in History and Social Sciences, with the focus primarily on History.

It was hoped that the seminar would help to initiate and/or strengthen the development of the cognitive study of History and the Social Sciences. As far as we know, this seminar was the first of its type, that is, in which cognitive/instructional approaches to the problems of understanding historical concepts, texts, and problems were discussed. Thus, although considerable progress has been achieved in the cognitive study of domains such as physics or mathematics, little work has been carried out in the field of social sciences and even less in the field of history. The seminar was designed to help bring via cognitive analysis a better understanding to the processes of learning and reasoning in these disciplines.

ACKNOWLEDGMENTS

The conference was made possible via the generous support from the USA–Spain Joint Committee for Scientific and Cultural Affairs, the Spanish Ministry of Education, and the Autonoma University of Madrid. Other contributing institutions were the Comunidad Autonoma of Madrid, the Deutsche Institute, the British Council, and the Faculties of Psychology from Autonoma University and the UNED, both of Madrid. We want to thank these institutions for their valuable support and would especially like to thank two people who were the first to put trust in this project, perhaps because both of them are historians, J. Ordonez, Vice President of Autonoma University, and J. Prats, Assistant Director for Teacher Training at the Ministry of Education.

A number of individuals also made valuable contributions to the planning and detail work that is so necessary to have a fruitful scientific meeting. We therefore want to thank the local committee: M. Asensio, L. Jacott, J. A. Leon, M. Limon, A. Lopez-Manjon, and J. I. Pozo. All of them did a wonderful job making possible four days of human and scientific communication at Miraflores de la Sierra where the conference was held. We also want to thank Joyce Holl for her time and effort in performing the task of preparing the chapters of the manuscript for publication.

Finally, the idea of this conference and its preparation was conceived during a sabbatical leave of the first editor at the Learning Research and Development Center of the University of Pittsburgh (Grant PB91–0028-C03–03). He would like to express his gratitude to this Center for offering him a very stimulating and fruitful period.

1 Introduction

James F. Voss
University of Pittsburgh

Mario Carretero
Autonoma University

As mentioned in the Preface, this book is about cognitive and instructional processes in history and social sciences, with an emphasis on history. Why a book about these topics? Is history an important topic for people who are not historians or history students? Does history deserve the interest of cognitive and instructional researchers? We think it does, even though until recently there has been a scarcity of such studies. Looking at the mundane, we find that best-selling novels in many countries are historical, and these novels frequently became movies, movies that indeed may distort history. Also, the industry of tourism, which has grown so much since World War II, may in part reflect an interest of people to look at their past. From a religious point of view, Christians and Jews visiting Israel, and Muslims visiting Mecca, and other cities may be providing such a meaning.

What about the teaching of history? Assume that an academic goes on sabbatical to an African or Asian country. If her children attend a local school in that country, the history lessons are probably quite different from those found in Europe and the United States. Indeed, with different European countries the contents of history may differ as well as even within different regions of the United States. Moreover, not only would the lessons differ in contents, they would also likely differ with respect to the role that history and social sciences play in the school system as well as in the state. The nature of both history and history teaching thus becomes a function of context.

Let us take another example. Are monuments always viewed in the same way? The Roman forum was totally forgotten as an important historical site until the 18th century, and then it became as important as the Alhambra

1

palace in Spain, which was rediscovered by Washington Irving. Thus, for some extended periods of time, monuments are considered as something old that cannot be used for any productive purpose, but at other times, monuments have been considered as ancient and valuable sources, representing a memory of a society. History, when considered a necessary and important activity of a society, involves a desire to understand the past, frequently viewing the past in relation to the present.

This volume is concerned with several questions pertaining to how individuals learn and process complex information about history and the social sciences and how instruction can facilitate such processes. Questions addressed include: How do students represent social and historical concepts? How do such representations vary with grade and knowledge? How does such reasoning differ, if it does, from that found in other domains such as the natural sciences? How can instruction facilitate learning in history and social sciences? How do students acquire information from history texts, and how may such texts be improved? What factors do people think cause historical events? Continuing with a consideration of these issues, however, we turn to some characteristics of history as a discipline that need to be addressed as general background.

A BRIEF HISTORY OF HISTORY

When, as a discipline, did history begin? Before the reader responds, we present some historical questions. When and why was the use of dating from the birth of Christ introduced? What kind of historical knowledge was produced during the Renaissance period? It was probably not produced until the early 6th century A.D. when Dionysius Exiguus introduced in Rome this way of dating, and it was not until the 8th century that it became successfully popularized by the English historian Bede. With respect to the second question, the reader perhaps may surmise that during the Renaissance intellectuals were producing historical research and studies as substantive as some work in other fields. However, although the Renaissance was influenced by the Roman and Greek classic periods, there was not much progress in history during the Renaissance because its immediate past — medieval times — was considered as something without any interest. As a matter of fact, some authors confused Roman authors with contemporary writers.

These two questions were presented as examples of the idea that historical knowledge develops across centuries. Are history teachers aware of that process? Do they introduce historical content as something that is not definitive but mutable according to various times and interpretations? Most of science educators would probably agree that science should be presented to students as something that is a product of a research process, and therefore its conclusions could be reinterpreted on the occurrence of new theories or new methods.

On the other hand, is history a collection of stories, in which narrative form and contents have no limits, or is history a hypothetical-deductive activity similar to science, at least to some extent? Interestingly enough, romanic languages, such as Spanish, French, and Italian, use just one word for "history" and "stories" (i.e., *histoire* in French or *historia* in Spanish). Thus, the word has two different meanings, representing a serious and documented academic discipline or representing a kind of tale or narrative (see Rosa, this volume, for a discussion of the different meanings of *history*). It is important to keep in mind that these two ways of looking at history have been present in the discipline almost from its onset. It is generally considered that history as a discipline was started by the Greeks, with, in fact, the word *history* coming from the greek verb *historeo*, which means "investigation," with the meaning of the verb referring to looking for vestiges and testimonies of the past. Herodotus and Thucydides are considered the founding fathers of history because they were able to present an organized corpus of knowledge about past times, and their work influenced most of the subsequent historiographical production until the 18th century. It is important to mention that the main reason for this is that these authors tried to distinguish facts from fiction, even though they were not really able to fully accomplish it. The knowledge of the past accumulated by other societies different from Greek (i.e., in Egypt, Babylon, etc.) consisted mainly of a series of genealogical records, myths, and fictions, and that stored information was rather unmodifiable precisely because there was no historical knowledge.

Nevertheless, this pioneer work was criticized because of its methods. The work of Herodotus and Thucydides was primarily based on personal experiences and testimonies whose final product was a narration. Aristotle, however, had a different idea of what history was. He strongly criticized the narrative approach and refused to consider it as a science. Instead he argued for what was called *antiquarian research*, which involved the use of data from auxiliary sources such as topography, geography, or philology.

If the goals of history existing between Herodotus and the present were defined, most historians would probably agree that they would be twofold. One goal would be to provide precise information about how our ancestors lived, and the other would be to offer multicausal explanations of change and development. It can be said that in general terms most of the Roman and medieval historians accomplished the first goal as much as the Greek historians did. A number of Roman historians are considered much more subjective than the Greeks, especially in the use of sources, and later medieval historiography was influenced by the idea that history was shaped by God's plan. This lack of improvement in historical knowledge makes greater the work of Ibn Khaldun (1332–1406), an Arab historian who is considered one of the most important and original thinkers in history and social sciences of any time. One of his main contributions consisted of raising the issue of causal mechanisms and processes in producing historical and social events. In fact, he wrote several volumes about general sociology, politics, urban life, economics, and education, always from an historical point of view. For example, one of his conclusions about the decline of some states was based on his concept of "social cohesion," a force determined by a number of social and historical variables. According to him, if this aspect of social groups suffered a process of weakening, then it produced a decline of states or empires. In this respect it can be compared to a physical force because Khaldun considers historical issues as problems in which the essential variables are beyond specific persons. Thus, historical knowledge was presented by Khaldun in a way that was not essentially a narrative, but instead took a position that searched for general principles or laws in order to explain sociological, political, and economic processes.

As is well known, during the Enlightment period a number of ideas appeared that had an enormous influence on historiography. Among them are the following: the idea of progress, the existence of a rational plan for history, the interrelationship of the different aspects of social reality, and the idea that scientific ideas could be applied to the study of history. The development of these ideas, the improvement of different historiographical methods, and the availability of different and more refined sources, that is, more archives were opened for historians, produced a more sophisticated historical knowledge than was present before the 18th century. Thus, history was influenced by the advance of social sciences as empirical and systematic intellectual endeavors. Sociological, political, and economic concepts, which at present have empirical support and a coherent theoretical background, were applied to the study of history. For this reason, historiographical efforts of the last two centuries were interwoven with the contribution of social sciences. For example, Marxism, which appeared as a political and economic theory, had a significant influence on the European historians from the beginning of the century.

On the other hand, it can be said that not only social sciences but social and political events also have an enormous influence on the way history is being conceived at the end of 20th century. The critical events of these last decades have had an impact on historiography, and a crisis of history is commonly considered in journals and publications (see Rivere's chapter, this volume). Of course, we cannot go through an analysis of this impact, but it might be interesting to suggest a few reasons for this crisis. General theories about historical phenomena, as for instance with Marxism, were abandoned; the inability to predict the future, or at least to provide a direction for history, was observed; and, there was dissatisfaction that occurred with studies that produced an unlimited number of regional or local "histories." In this context, it is interesting to observe the opinion of one historian in relation to the goals of history for the next decades. According to Stone (1993), the goals would be: (a) to provide a more convincing explanation about change through time, (b) to connect economic and social history to cultural history, (c) to understand the role of religion, (d) to use microhistory in relation to the general past periods, and (e) to give a clear role in history to the exceptional individuals, a factor opposed to looking for the supposed scientific laws of history, or, "real human beings with their contradictory complexity should come back to history from where vulgar Marxism, estructuralism and quantification expelled them" (Stone, 1993, p. 8).

In summary, we think there are a number of issues that have been essential in the development of history, and it would be important to consider them in relation to its teaching. These include: sources as essential data in history, the objectivity versus subjectivity in the use of sources, the existence of causal regularities in historical processes, structural and narrative methods of investigating the transmission of historical knowledge, and the role of historians.

THE STUDY OF HISTORY AND THIS VOLUME

History and Social Sciences as Forgotten Subject Matter

In recent decades considerable research has been devoted to understanding how students learn and solve problems in mathematics and in the physical sciences, especially mathematics and physics, with much of this work conducted in a cognitive context. The research has advanced our understanding of how individuals reason in these domains and how instruction can be modified to enhance math and science understanding. But similar research in the domains of history and the social sciences has been almost nonexistent.

One may of course speculate about why history and the social sciences have not received greater attention. One reason is that, for economic and military reasons, governments are quite interested in advancing technology and therefore spend considerable amounts of money on research and development projects within these domains. Also, from the point of view of investigators, the subject matter of math and science is in many ways more tractable than that of history and the social sciences. Nevertheless, despite the general lack of research commitment in history and the social sciences, we feel that enhancing learning and understanding in these domains is extremely important, and some reasons why this is the case are now considered.

First, although mathematics and science education have captured the forefront of research interest, and the technological nature of contemporary society reinforces this position, we, nevertheless, more than ever before, are being confronted with problems that to a substantial degree have been created by scientific advancement but that cannot be solved solely by further scientific accomplishment. Scientific research may help produce a solution, but the problems of hunger and homelessness, ecology and the destruction of the forest and living species, war-producing nationalism, religion differences, health and welfare, the expanding population, quality of life, North-South global differences, and strife based on racial and ethnic differences are problems that require reasonable human judgment and good policy decisions, decisions that often are better informed if the decision makers are aware of historical factors as well as many contemporary political, cultural, economic, and geographical issues. The 19th-century faith in the ability of science to bring the good life has given way to the 20th-century realization that science has brought with it not only the curing of diseases and the enrichment of life via new media, technologies, and transportation, but also has helped to produce diseases, such as pollution-based cancer, nuclear weapons and waste, and other destructive mechanisms. It is at least in part through the appropriate study of history and the social sciences that hopefully we may become better able to address problems of such proportion, gaining a broader perspective and insight, thereby helping policymakers formulate, generate, and execute wise choices.

A second reason why history and social science research is important is to develop greater literacy and understanding of the subject domains in question, expanding student knowledge in depth and breadth. What can we learn from the problems of ancient Greece? What can we learn from the Gulf War? Understanding the past can help us to understand the present, and vice versa, and understanding the present also can help students achieve a better appreciation of not only one's own country but also how one's own country is a player in the increasingly broader global perspective. Enhanced learning in history and the social sciences thus should help students become familiar with not only one's own community but with other communities, and something can likely be learned from how other communities have dealt with their problems. On the other hand, history, as well as the social sciences, can be used for the purposes of political indoctrination, for giving answers without raising questions, and for promoting one-track thinking rather than freedom of inquiry. The issues of history thus require examination (see chapter by Rosa, this volume).

A third reason to study learning and reasoning in history and the social sciences is to provide a broader understanding of human thinking processes and the extent to which such processes are domain specific. Is reasoning in physics the same as in history? What are the similarities and differences? Will the same theoretical formulation apply to thinking in both domains? These are cogent questions to the task of developing a better understanding of thought processes.

A fourth and related reason to study learning and reasoning in history and in the social sciences is simply to improve instruction in these domains. Studies in the United States have indicated that student knowledge of history and the social sciences is often quite poor, whereas a study in Spain has shown that among secondary school students history is judged to be the most difficult topic. There seems to be little question regarding the need for improvement in instruction.

Finally, a fifth reason to press for research in history and social sciences is simply to encourage investigators to pursue interesting research questions on these topics, to generate interest among the uninitiated, and to indicate to the interested that other people share their interest. In other words, a reason to study history and social science understanding is because research questions of general theoretical interest remain to be defined and addressed. The questions are "out there."

Given the concerns stated here, we felt that an important step was to have a conference of individuals interested in how people think and learn in history and social sciences, not only to obtain an idea about what was happening in research in these domains and to transmit the work via this volume, but to bring together individuals who were somewhat varied in their own interest and approach to the subject matter and who could become acquainted with research perhaps unfamiliar to them that was related to their interests.

Conference Considerations

In planning the conference, a perusal of the literature suggested that there were a relatively small number of investigators studying issues related to the purpose of the conference, although we realize that our searching procedures may have been faulty. We defined the research of interest in a relatively amorphous way. We were primarily interested in people with a more or less cognitive orientation, but we did not want to limit the conference to such individuals. We also wanted to include investigators who had a genuine interest in learning and thinking in history and/or social sciences, regardless of whether the interest was in a classroom context or in a more general framework.

We also thought it essential to have the participation of scholars from different countries, not only because of the general enrichment obtained from such contact, but also because history, as noted in the initial examples in this chapter, is not taught and understood in the same way in different societies (see also chapters by Wertsch and Rosa, this volume). The contributors to this volume thus come from Italy, Germany, the United Kingdom, Spain, Sweden, and the United States. Of course, we think this range should have been broader, and in any future meetings of this type we would hope there would be greater variety.

In addition to the matter of potential contributors, we needed to face the question of the extent to which we should emphasize history or social sciences. The decision was made to focus more on history, for two primary reasons. First, history is taught in elementary and secondary schools more than any of the social sciences, and our concern with instructional improvement led us to believe that a focus on history was reasonable. Second, with the exception of economics, in which work is being carried out such as that found in the *Journal of Economic Education*, there was more research being conducted in history subject matter, or at least so it seemed to us. Given these two factors, the reader will find that this volume indeed is more about work in history than in the social sciences.

Organization of Conference and This Volume

The subsequent conference, as well as this volume, were organized in terms of the following four topics. The first topic in this volume involves the relation of developmental psychology to the learning of history and social science subject matter. The second topic is that of how instruction-based research can influence learning in the domains in question. The third is the nature of history text and how individuals learn from such text, whereas the fourth is how individuals reason in history and the social sciences. Certainly there may be better ways to organize the work, but this categorization seemed to be reasonable, based on research that had been conducted and the interests of the contributors. Although presumably each of these topics had a particular set of issues associated with it, it also is the case that the four sections are highly interrelated. An overview of each of the four parts is now presented.

Developmental. Furnham describes research that has been conducted on the economic and political socialization of children, considering theoretical approaches that have been employed, including the notion of developmental stages. Berti and Delval each employ a Piagetian framework to discuss the child's development of the concept of a state and of the growth of social knowledge, respectively. Torney-Purta takes a cognitive perspective, considering the conceptual restructuring of political and social concepts and how instruction relates to such change. Along with the comments of the discussant, Linaza, the series of papers, taken as a whole, revisit the developmental psychology stage issue, as it is found in historical, political, and/or economic contexts. Cogent questions are raised about how concepts are acquired and how they are modified, the extent to which children's knowledge is adult-like in nature, and, to some extent, what constrains a child's learning and understanding of history and the social sciences. Both Berti and Delval show that children's representation of social and historical concepts are rather primitive, generally demonstrating a lack of knowledge about these matters. Childrens' concepts about the mechanisms of how a society works tend to be concrete and static. If we compare these results with those described in other chapters (Carretero et al., Kuhn, and Voss et al.), it seems that adolescents and some adults have limited knowledge of this kind. Linaza's discussion of the first group of chapters provides an examination of the study of concept development and the use of stages as explanatory devices.

Teaching and Learning.   The chapters on instruction in history and the social sciences address instructional matters from both a teacher's and a student's perspective. The Leinhardt et al. chapter considers explanations in history in three contexts, from a variety of theories dealing with the nature of historical explanation, from interviews with historians about the nature of history, and from classroom performance. Leinhardt et al. point to how historical knowledge requires teachers and students to be "mindful" rather than "mindless," in the sense of providing integrated, historical meaningful explanations rather than viewing history as an unintegrated series of events. How this may be accomplished in the classroom is considered. Leinhardt's conceptualization of student representations of historical concepts is not unrelated to Torney-Purta's conceptual structures, both essentially use the node-link structures found in cognitive psychology.

McDiarmid has studied what potential student teachers learned in an undergraduate course in historiography, investigating the question in the broader context of whether teachers should have more specific subject matter courses, as in history, as opposed to teacher education courses. McDiarmid obtained somewhat disjunctive results, indicating that although the potential teachers learned more about history and the methodology thereof from the historiography course, such learning seemed to have little effect on their views of teaching and learning, that is, the methods and problems they used seemed to have little impact on their conception of classroom teaching.

Hallden employed classroom cases to study how students develop their ideas about what constitutes an appropriate course of historical events, that is, what goes into the construction of a narrative. Hallden points out that in

Swedish classrooms this goal is often accomplished by student discussions, termed *shared reasoning* by Hallden, with the discussion guided by the teacher. Hallden points out that a problem is that a student needs to know what narrative is being constructed, or what "voice" (see chapter by Wertsch, this volume). This includes moving toward the goal or event the narrative is being constructed to explain, as well as considering how detailed the narrative should be. Hallden points out that the issue is not only related to the teaching method, but to the nature of history itself and how organization of historical concepts takes place, especially as related to causation (cf. Voss et al., this volume).

Hahn's chapter is concerned with conflict as an instructional tool, especially as it relates to the good citizenship goal of history instruction. Citing a number of studies from a number of countries, Hahn notes that topics producing conflict in the classroom are better learned. Hahn relates such findings to what practices historians and expert teachers follow. Interviewing four teachers, Hahn also determined some factors mitigating against the employment of conflict as an instructional device.

In a thought-provoking discussion of the chapters of the instruction section, Rosa considers why history is taught, beginning with notions about how America seems to have the ability to bury the past, whereas some other countries use the study of the past to emphasize the past. History as a political tool is thus considered. Rosa discusses the similarity of individual memory and history and notes how the concepts of involuntary and voluntary memory seem to apply in both areas. Rosa also addresses a problem often raised in science education, that is, whether students should be only consumers of the knowledge of the domain, or whether they should also have "hands on" experience with respect to what the historian does. Rosa opts for the latter, in part so that the students gain a better understanding of how historical accounts are constructed. The use of history to construct the past is noted by Rosa in relation to the Russian half-joke, "The past is unpredictable."

The section on instruction thus raises a number of important problems about the contents and methods of history instruction, the beliefs of teachers about such instruction, problems confronting students, and the role of conflict.

Text Comprehension.   Concerning the role of texts in the teaching and learning of history, the research presented primarily addresses two issues. In the Beck and McKeown chapter, the content and coherence of history textbooks is considered, and from previous work these authors conclude that difficulties of student comprehension relate to a student's prior knowledge, inadequacies of text consistency, and a lack of text coherence. Studying the same students in fifth and eighth grade, having instruction in

American History in both grades, the authors found relatively little difference in student outcome for fifth- and eighth-grade instruction, a result the authors relate in part to the textbook contents. To remedy the situation, the authors suggest the need for more coherent texts, the need for discussion to utilize text information, and the importance of covering material in greater depth.

The Perfetti et al. chapter considers learning from a history text in relation to psychological research on the causal structure of narratives, that is, story understanding. Studying how individuals process the contents of texts that have differing perspectives on a given issue, they found that students are sensitive to the different text orientations. Thus, in this case, the conflict was in the texts (see Hahn, this volume). Perfetti et al. also report the results of work involving student use of documents, that is, use of primary and/or secondary documents. Again, students were sensitive to content differences, as well as to bias.

Wineburg and Fournier consider the role of documents, primarily the accounts of the Lincoln–Douglas debates, in studying the question of whether Lincoln was a racist. Their analysis readily portrays the difficulties in interpreting "source" texts and the problems that arise in establishing "facts." Rodrigo, in discussing the chapters on learning from text, points out that not only is textbook improvement and instruction needed, but so also is the assessment of historical literacy. Different levels of narrative representation can be discerned, Rodrigo notes, and it is important that an appropriate level of literacy is established. Rodrigo also notes that narrative literacy constitutes a relatively low level, but necessary, facet of learning history, and also mentions that modification in teaching instruction is needed as well for greater literacy of history.

Reasoning Processes in History. The chapter by Wertsch focuses on narrative structure and in particular the representation of agents and to a lesser extent the representation of events, the analysis existing within the framework that historical narrative constitutes a cultural tool. Wertsch notes that such narratives may be "multivoiced," that is, viewed from more than one story line. Wertsch presents data indicating that when asked to write essays on how the United States began, college students generated "unvoiced" text, focusing on the Euro-American version of pilgrims landing, considering Native Americans in a secondary role.

One of the points in emphasis of von Borries' chapter is the role of values and moral judgment in examining historical events. Using a large sample survey procedure, von Borries used the First Crusade to examine the motivational and emotional factors as well as values that students of different grades used to evaluate the Christian and Moslem positions.

The chapter by Carretero et al. presents a number of theoretical issues about history as a discipline that are relevant for the cognitive research about complex processes in this domain. Thus, the importance of ideological and political values is raised as well as how those values could affect the whole process of historical cognition. The authors also present an empirical study about how students of different ages and expertise view historical causation. Some of the results indicate that in general adolescents and adults tend to consider personalized agents as essential in producing historical events, whereas historians tend to consider abstract and structural agents such as political and social causes as more important.

Using juror reasoning as a case study, Kuhn discusses the relation of a person's theory about an event and how the individual evaluates evidence concerning the evidence. Kuhn includes consideration of the epistemology held by different individuals, focusing on the extent to which individuals vary from certainty, to complete subjective opinion, and to the evaluation of both sides in evidence.

In the Voss, Carretero, Kennet, and Silfies chapter, individuals were asked to write an essay on the fall of the Soviet Union. The essays were examined for causal structure and the role of conditions and actors. Subjects were then provided with potential causal factors and asked to draw a causal map of the collapse. Subject essays ranged from quite simple to highly developed, taking the form of multiple-branching structures. Psychological conditions were regarded as important as well as economic and political conditions, and the role of individuals such as Gorbachev were included to a lesser degree. The collapse thus was viewed as having multiple causes. Riviere's discussion of this section establishes a number of relations between the mentioned issues and some aspects of the philosophy of history, on the one hand, and some cognitive psychology distinctions on the other.

Instructional Implications

From the point of view of the relation between developmental psychology and instruction, a number of implications appear. It is clear that historical contents are much more difficult for children than social contents, and thus it appears difficult to maintain that history should play an important role in elementary school as Dewey suggested many years ago. But it is also true that the teacher should not wait until the student is spontaneously able to understand social sciences contents. On the contrary, he or she should try to foster historical understanding. In order to do this, he or she could present some social science contents in a historical perspective. In order to achieve this goal, it may be reasonable to present historical events in a personalized manner (specific persons should play an important role in the teaching of history), that is to say, specific persons could help the children in acquiring a better understanding of history. And probably this is also true in the case of adolescents.

Much of the research about social concept representation has been carried out in a developmental framework. Unfortunately, this type of research suggests a limitation for instructional purposes, namely, these studies usually only examine subjects up to approximately 12 years of age, and the teaching of history properly speaking is not a usual practice until adolescence.

Concerning the role of texts in the teaching and learning of history, the research presented in this volume is about two different topics. On the one hand, contexts and coherence of textbooks are analyzed (Beck). This analysis has a number of instructional implications, but history textbooks are often just a summary of historical events. If a constructive understanding is pursued, then it is clear that the goal of teaching history is not only to present a collection of historical events, but to present it as a discipline in continuous progress and needing different interpretations. Thus, from an instructional point of view, it is important to take into account this distance between the discipline and the textbooks contents.

On another point, if causal reasoning analysis of historical situations is an instructional goal, we need much more research on how students understand causality in history. Some of the data in this volume show that subjects tend to give more importance to immediate causes than to remote causes. But remote causes are essential for historical explanations. On the other hand, it is also important to consider that historical causality has rarely been included as an educational goal. For example, if we examine history textbooks of many countries, we find out that "causes" and "consequences" of historical problems are offered to the students as recipes and not as something to think about.

A Look at Outcomes

A fair question to ask is — given that the conference was held and this volume was published, what should be the nature of another conference and volume if it were to occur? We asked the conference participants this question, and from their answers as well as our own thoughts, we believe the following points require consideration. (Incidentally, we would welcome from the reader any comments on this question or on any other issue found in this volume.)

First, there needs to be a greater emphasis on the question of the goals of history and social science instruction. What should be taught? What skills should be acquired? What appreciations should be fostered? Second, in a related manner, there should be a need to consider to a greater extent the epistemological basis of history. Third, it was deemed desirable to extend the cross-cultural study of history, asking how and why is it taught in different countries. A fourth observation is that there should be a need for more historians than were included in this conference. So, if there is another meeting and volume, such suggestions would be taken into account. But, as for now, there was a conference, this volume was sent to the publisher, and, as they say, "the rest is history."

REFERENCES

Stone, L. (1993). Las tareas en las que se deben empeñar los historiadores en el futuro [Tasks to be accomplished by future historians]. *El Pais, 29,* 8.

COGNITIVE DEVELOPMENTAL PROCESSES

2 Young People's Understanding of Politics and Economics

Adrian Furnham
University College London

Socialization is generally defined as a process through which individuals learn to interact in society. It concerns learning social roles and acquiring the knowledge and skills related to them. So far comparatively little research has been done on economic and political socialization than on other aspects of social development (e.g., moral development). Still less had been done on *how* knowledge and beliefs are acquired as opposed to the *content* of the knowledge base (Berti & Bombi, 1988; Haste & Torney-Purta, 1992). Furthermore, it has not been until comparatively recently that researchers have looked at young people's reasoning about economic and political issues (see Torney-Purta, this volume).

A detailed examination of the economic and political socialization of children and adolescents is of both academic and applied interest. In Great Britain, in 1990, 14- to 16-year-olds had nearly £10 per week in disposable cash. In West German 7- to 15-year-olds received 7,5 billion DM of pocket money and monetary gifts in 1988, and the spending power of 12- to 21-year-olds even amounted to 33 billion DM annually. And of course in most Western democratic countries teenagers of 18 years are allowed to vote in local municipal and national elections. Young people have both political and economic power.

Many different aspects of young people's understanding and perception of the economic and political world, their attitudes toward money and possessions, and their spending and consumption habits are relevant to the teaching of economic principles in schools as well as to the research of psychologists, educationists, marketing people, and even to economists (Furnham & Stacey, 1991).

THE DEVELOPMENT OF ECONOMIC AND POLITICAL
IDEAS IN THE CHILDHOOD STAGES

What do children know about economics and politics? How and at what age do they acquire their knowledge? To what extent are there differences of knowledge and belief regarding gender, age, nationality, socioeconomic background, and experience with money? These are some of the early questions researchers concentrated on in studies examining children's and adolescents' cognitive development related to economics and to a lesser extent politics. For many years research was predominately concerned with attempting to describe the stages children went through in the development of specific concepts. Stagewise theories and descriptors are currently out of fashion but often retained for heuristic purposes (see Delval, this volume).

Strauss (1952) is among the first to examine the development of money-related concepts. In his study he interviewed 66 children of both sexes between 4½ and 11½ years old and classified the answers into nine different developmental stages that reinforced the Piagetian idea of the child's advancement by stages rather than by continuum. According to Strauss the content of the child's concepts undergoes systematic change as it moves from one level to the next, which depends on the child having understood the respective prerequisite notions. Each level of conception though not only signifies a different degree of intellectual maturity but also a different level of experience, perception, and values. This regarded children of different levels as different "beings" rather than simply possessing different degrees of knowledge. Six years later, Danzinger (1958) asked 41 children between 5 and 8 years old questions about money, the rich and the poor, and the "boss" to examine whether the development of social concepts in the child could be applied to Piaget's theoretical model of cognitive development. From the results he drew up four different stages in the development of economic concepts:

(a) An initial pre-categorical stage occurs when the child lacks economic categories of thought altogether. There is no special realm of economic concepts differentiated from social concepts in general. (b) At the second, or categorical stage the child's concepts appear to represent a reality in terms of isolated acts which are explained by a moral or voluntaristic imperative. (c) At the third stage the child becomes able to conceptualize relationships as such, by virtue of the fact that a reciprocity is established between previously isolated acts. But these relations are in their turn isolated and cannot be explained in terms of other relationships. (d) Finally, the isolated relationships become linked to each other so as to form a system of relations. We then have a conceptualization of a totality wherein each part derives its significance from its position in the whole. At this point a purely rational explanation becomes possible. (Danziger 1958, pp. 239–240)

Danziger believed that firsthand experience enhances the advancement onto the next level of conception. The children in his study appeared to be at a higher level in their understanding of economic exchange than in production, and he attributed this to the fact that they had experience of buying, but none of work. Since then this firsthand experience of the economic world through part-time work, buying and selling, children's games, and so on, has attracted a good deal of research, particularly among cross-cultural researchers.

Sutton (1962) interviewed 85 children between 6 and 13 on money and the accumulation of capital. Irrespective of age, intelligence, and socioeconomic background, the majority of replies were in the beginning stages of conceptualization, thus emphasizing the importance of firsthand experience in the development of economic concepts (63% of the answers were to be found in the second of the *six* stages she codified from the 1,020 replies).

Jahoda (1979) conducted a study that comprised a role play in which 120 working-class Scottish children between 6 and 12 played the role of the shopkeeper and the interviewer that of customer and supplier. Answers were grouped into notion (of profit) absent or transitional and notion present according to whether the difference between buying and selling price had been realized. The results suggested that most children did not begin to understand the concept of profit until about the age of 11. The interview that followed showed that the development of the understanding of the concept of profit passed through three stages: (a) no grasp of any system — transactions conceived of as simply an observed ritual, (b) two unconnected systems — shop owner buys and sells at the same price, and (c) two integrated systems — awareness of the difference between buying and selling price.

Burris (1983) found general compatibility with the Piagetian view that knowledge develops through a sequence of qualitative cognitive stages from the answers of 32 children at each distinct stage (preoperational, concrete operations, and formal operations). More recently Leiser (1983), Schug and Birkey (1985), Sevon and Weckstrom (1989) supported these findings. Schug and Birkey (1985), like Danziger, also stressed that children's economic understanding varies somewhat depending on their own economic experiences, though the quality of the evidence they acquired is debatable. Sevon and Weckstrom characterized younger children's perception of the economy as from the viewpoint of *homo sociologicus* (driven by moral and social norms) and the one of older children more as of *homo economics* (striving for personal hedonic satisfaction). Of the three age groups — 8-, 11-, and 14-year-olds — the youngest group, when asked about the thinking and acting of economic agents, first felt the need to decide whether these agents would become happy or unhappy before thinking about why this was the case (e.g., "The shoe retailer would be happy about the reduction in shoe prices because 'people can save their money'"). The answers of the younger children thus described *moral* or "Christian" thinking (concern for other people or other people's approval or disapproval of own behavior important) rather than *economic* thinking (viewing other people as means, constraints, or obstacles to personal satisfaction). Some of the older children, however, saw the economy more as an instrument and the action of the individual as led by the search for opportunity to increase his or her own wealth. This is partly due to their increased ability to think more abstractly, but as adults also sometimes argue from a moral viewpoint, intellectual sophistication cannot be the only explanation. Family values and socialization clearly play a part.

Although most researchers largely seemed to agree on the Piagetian view about the development of economic concepts in the child, they apparently have found a different number of stages. This might be due to several reasons: the age ranges of the subjects were different, the number of subjects in each study was different (sometimes perhaps too small to be representative), and each researcher's precision in the definition of where one stage ends and the next starts and the methodologies used were different in precision. These are possible explanations although they do not all necessarily have to be true for every single study.

Table 2.1 shows that there is disagreement about the number of stages, points of transition, and content of understanding at each respective stage. The trend among the more recent studies though seems to be that the number of (sub-)stages are summarized, and three broad main phases are defined: (a) no understanding, (b) understanding of some isolated concepts, and (c) linking of isolated concepts to full understanding. By no means do these stages suggest though that the child's understanding of different economic concepts always advances simultaneously. As Danziger (1958) stressed, a child's understanding of buying and selling, for example, may be more advanced than his or her understanding of work, as he or she might have had experience of the former but not of the latter. It would therefore be of great interest to further investigate if and what other factors, such as parental practices and social class, actually tend to speed up or perhaps slow

TABLE 2.1
Summary of Studies on Developmental Stages

Researcher	Year	Subjects	Age Range	Stages
Strauss	1952	66	4.8–11.6	9
Danziger	1958	41	5–8	4
Sutton	1962	85	Grade 1–6	6
Jahoda	1979	120	6–12	3
Burris	1983	96	4/5,7/8,10/12	3
Leiser	1983	89	7–17	3

down the transition from one stage to the next. Furthermore, it would be interesting if these stages replicate across understanding not only of economics, but also of politics and history (see Berti, this volume).

Nearly all the relevant research consists of self-report studies using interviews. Most Piagetian work is task-based (role play, games), and it may well be that experimental studies on economic concepts would yield clearer, more interesting results. Also, most of these studies have been conducted in Western, industrialized, capitalist countries and, if economic education and experiences are relevant to the development of economic concepts, studies need to be done in Third World or socialist countries. Furnham and Stacey (1991) concluded:

Frequently rather different stage-wise models compete in the description of a phenomenon. Yet there are a number of characteristics common to all stage-wise theories: (a) A stage is a structured whole in a state of equilibrium; (b) Each stage derives from the previous stage, incorporates but transforms the previous one and prepares for the next; (c) Stages follow in an invariant sequence; (d) Stages are universal to all human at all times in all the countries. (e) Each stage has a stage from coming-into-being, to being.

All stage-wise theories appear to have a number of implicit assumptions; *that the sequence of development is fixed that there is an ideal end-of-state towards which the child and adolescent inevitably progresses* and that some behaviors are sufficiently different from previous abilities that we can identify a child or adolescent as being in or out of a stage. Non-stage theories do not see people progressing inevitably to a single final stage since environmental forces are given more power to create a diversity of developmental responses. However, rather than portray the stage-non-stage approach to development as another manifestation of the famous heredity-environment, nature-nurture maturation-learning debate, most would argue that this is a false dichotomy and a non-issue. Most researchers would be interactionists, at an intermediate point on the extreme or strict stage vs. non-stage (or process) approach. A second assumption with which most would agree is that the young play an active part in their own development, that is, young people construct an interpretation of the information that they selectively attend to, based on their previous experience, maturation, and indeed momentary needs. The moderate novelty principle applies here which states that young people attend to and learn most from events that are mildly discrepant from (as opposed to very different from or identical to) their current level of conception about the social world. (pp. 192–193; emphasis in original)

Webley (1983) and others have criticized the application of the standard Piagetian approach and argued in favor of looking for what is distinct about economic concepts instead of treating economic cognition as just another area in which general principles of cognitive development apply.

He reproached researchers for their use of a static standard approach toward the investigation into children's development of economic thinking and regretted that no attempts have been made to "produce a characterization of the environment which might allow variations in the development of economic thought apart from social class distinction" (p. 3). What is special about economic factors such as property is that they form the basis of power in society and interpersonal relations, and the concepts or ideology a child develops are therefore of vital concern. The need to relate to the economic structure of the society—an idea more radically expressed by Cummings and Taebel (1978), and the importance of characterizing a child's environment, such as exposure to the child's own economic experience, are therefore aspects that might distinguish the development of economic concepts from other types. In this sense the understanding of economics, history, and politics is different from that of physics, chemistry, and meteorology. Social values and ideology are intricately bound with the former and not the latter and can influence understanding profoundly.

Without exception all studies agreed that there are changes in economic reasoning with age. But not all agree which changes or how much the factors that covary with age have a major influence on economic understanding. These factors include: (a) accumulation of knowledge and experience from primary and secondary socialization and education, (b) increasing of general ability to complex reasoning, (c) diminishing egocentrism, (d) change in role behavior, that is, with increasing age children assume more of adult behavior in the economy. It is impossible to compute how much cognitive development can be attributed to each process, and others, as they are interdependent and vary with each individual.

Research on the Development of Economic Thinking

Although numerous studies of children's understanding of different aspects of the economic world have been carried out, it appears they have concentrated on some topics rather than others (Berti & Bombi, 1988). Relatively few studies exist on young people's knowledge of betting, taxes, interest rates, the up and down of the economy (boom, recession, depression, and recovery), or inflation. This might be because such concepts are considered to be too difficult for children to understand, although in a study in Yugoslavia by Zabukovec and Polic (1990), the children's answers clearly reflected aspects of the then-current economic situation, such as inflation, a result showing that the "difficulty" always depends on the circumstances (exposure to the economic world). There is, however, failed, detailed, and replicated research on topics such as possession and ownership, wealth and poverty, entrepreneurship, prices, wages, money, buying and selling, profit, and the bank. Because the common denominator to all economic interactions in the Western World obviously is money, its understanding is therefore a prerequisite for all other concepts.

Money.   As money is the basis to almost all economical actions, its full understanding clearly is a prerequisite for other, more abstract concepts. Children's first contact with money happens at quite an early age, as when children watch parents buy or sell things, but research has shown that this does not necessarily mean that although children use money themselves they fully understand its meaning and significance. For very young children, giving money to a salesperson constitutes a mere ritual. They are not aware of the different values of coins and the purpose of change, let alone the origin of money. Children thus need to understand the nature and role of money before being able to master more abstract concepts.

To investigate children's ideas about the payment for work, Berti and Bombi (1979) interviewed 100 children from 3 to 8 years old regarding where they thought money came from. Four categories of response emerged. At level 1 children had no idea of its origin: The father takes the money from his pocket. At level 2 children saw the origin as independent from work: Somebody (a bank) gives it to everybody who asks for it. At level 3 the subjects named the change given by tradesmen when buying as the origin of money. Only at level 4 did children name work as the reason. Most of the 3- and 4-year-olds' answers were in category 1, whereas most of the 6-, 7-, and 8-year-olds' answers were in category 4. The idea of payment for work (level 4) thus develops out of various spontaneous and erroneous beliefs in levels 2 and 3 in which children as of yet have no understanding of the concept of work, which is a prerequisite for understanding the origin of money. Although at that level they did notice occasionally that their parents take part in extra-domestic activities, children did not call them work or even saw a need for them.

Two years later Berti and Bombi (1981) undertook another investigation (80 subjects between ages 3 and 8) of the concept of money and its value. Building on the work of Strauss (1952) and others, they singled out 6 stages: Stage 1: No awareness of payment; Stage 2: Obligatory payment — no distinction between different kinds of money, and money can buy anything; Stage 3: Distinction between types of money — not all money is equivalent anymore; Stage 4: Realization that money can be insufficient; Stage 5: Strict correspondence between money and objects — correct amount has to be given; and Stage 6: Correct use of change. The first four stages clearly are to be found in the preoperational period, whereas in the last two, arithmetic operations are successfully applied. Strauss (1952) found 9 stages in the child's understanding about money, ranging from the first stage in which the child believes that any coin can buy any object to the last one in which correct understanding is achieved.

Pollio and Gray (1973) conducted a more "practical" study with 100 subjects, grouped at the ages of 7, 9, 11, 13, and college-aged students, on "change-making strategies." They found that it was not not until the age of 13 that an entire age group was able to give correct change. The younger subjects showed a preference for small value coins, with which they were more familiar, when making change, whereas the older children used all coins available. More recent studies have looked at such things as children's actual monetary behavior. For instance, Abramovitch, Freedman, and Pliner (1991) found 6- to 10-year-old Canadian children who got allowances seemed more sophisticated about money than those who did not. Clearly, understanding of the origin, function, and meaning of money in young people will attract a great deal of further research as it remains unclear what factors influence these various cognitions (see Delval, this volume).

Prices and Profit.   Buying is one of the earliest economic activities of a child. There are a number of prerequisites to buying and selling. A child has to know about function and origin of money, change, ownership, payment of wages to employees, shop expenses, and shop owner's need for income/private money that altogether prove the simple act of buying and selling to be rather complex. Furth (1980) pointed out four stages during the acquisition of this concept: (a) no understanding of payment; (b) understanding of payment of customer, but not of the shopkeeper; (c) understanding and relating of both the customers and shopkeeper's payment, but not of the shopkeeper; and (d) understanding of all these things.

Children in stage 2 saw change as the source of customer's money: "Sometimes he gives you 4 pence for the sweets back and sometimes he gives you more when you want some bigger things. The money doesn't stay there all the time, because the shopkeeper forgets which money it was . . . and then he gives the people the money" (age 6.8; Furth, 1980, p. 14). They don't pay for the goods, "No, cos' they have the shop, they wanted to do a shop . . . the money the lady collects, she gives it to the blind or something, the poor people" (age 7.7; p. 15).

Jahoda (1979), using a role play in which the child had to buy goods from a supplier and sell to a customer, distinguished between three categories: (a) no understanding of profit—both prices were consistently identical, (b) transitional—mixture of responses, and (c) understanding of profit—selling price consistently higher than buying price. The fact that in this study there is one stage less than in Furth's may be due to the fact that it only was concluded from the ideas of profit, and whether or not a child was credited with understanding was not actually examined. Furthermore, the child was already told to buy from the prices given. The child was also told to buy from a supplier, therefore he or she knew previously that the supplier had to pay him or her (which in Furth's study was not the case).

Supporting the idea of gradually integrating subsystems, Berti, Bombi, and de Beni (1986) pointed out that the concepts about shop and factory profit in 8-year-olds were not compatible. Despite improving their understanding of shop profit after receiving training, the children were not able to transfer their knowledge onto factory's profit, thinking that prices were set arbitrarily.

Berti et al. (1986) showed that by training, children's understanding of profit could be enhanced. Both critical training sessions stimulated the children to solve solutions to contradictions between their own forecasts, and the actual outcomes and ordinary tutorial training sessions (information given to children) that consisted of similar games of buying and selling proved to be effective. However, the results of the posttests also showed that neither kind of experience was sufficient in itself to lead children to a correct notion of profit, partly due to a lack of arithmetical abilities. Nevertheless, the authors suggested that although arithmetical abilities are essential, "making children talk about economic topics they have not yet mastered, far from being an obstacle to learning may contribute to their progress, constituting in itself a kind of training, as Jahoda (1981) also found in different circumstances" (p. 28).

In a recent study with 11- to 16-year-olds, Furnham and Cleare (1988) also found differences in understanding shop and factory profit: "Of 11-12 years olds, 7% understood profit in shops, yet 69% mentioned profit as a motive for starting a factory today, and 20% mentioned profit as an explanation for why factories had been started" (p. 475). The understanding of the abstract concept of profit, which depends on the previous understanding of the basic concept of buying and selling, grows through different phases. Young children (6–8 years) seem to have no grasp of any system and conceive of transactions as "simply an observed ritual without further purpose" (Furth, Baur, & Smith, 1976, p. 365). Older children (8–10 years) realize that the shop owner previously had to buy (pay for) the goods before he or she could sell them. Nevertheless, they do not always understand that the money for this comes from the customers, and that buying prices have to be lower than selling prices. They thus perceive of buying and selling as two unconnected systems. Not until the age of 10–11 are children able to integrate these two systems and understand the difference between buying and selling prices. Of course, these age bands may vary slightly among children (or cultures) as experiential factors play a part in the understanding of economic concepts. Because of the obvious political implications of the ideas of profit and pricing, it would be particularly interesting to see not only when (and how) young people come to understand the concepts, but also how they reason with them.

Banking.   Jahoda (1981) interviewed 32 subjects each from the ages of 12, 14, and 16 about bank's profits. He asked whether one gets back more, less, or the same as the original sum deposited and whether one has to pay back more, less, or the same as the original sum borrowed. From this basis he drew up six categories: (a) no knowledge of interest (get/pay back same amount); (b) interest on deposits only (get back more, pay back the same); (c) interest on both, but more on deposit (deposit interest higher than loan interest); (d) interest same on deposits and loans; (e) Interest higher for loans (no evidence for understanding); and (f) interest more for loans — correctly understood.

Although most of these children had fully understood the concept of shop profit, many did not perceive the bank as a profit-making enterprise (only one-fourth of the 14- and 16-year-olds understood bank profit). "They viewed the principles governing a bank as akin to those underlying the transactions between friends: if you borrow something, you return the same, no more and no less — anything else would be 'unfair'" (p. 70).

Ng (1983) replicated the same study in Hong Kong and found the same developmental trend. The Chinese children however were more precocious, showing a full understanding of the bank's profit at the age of 10. From the same study he discovered 2 more stages — 0 = funny idea stage, 2b = interest on loans only, unrelated to profit — in addition to Jahoda's original 6. A study in New Zealand by the same author (Ng, 1985) confirmed these additional two stages and proved the New Zealand children to "lag" behind Hong Kong by about 2 years. Ng attributes this to Hong Kong's "high level of economic socialization and customer activity, and the business ethos of the society at large. . . . Their maturity represents, in short, a case of socioeconomic reality shaping (partly at least) socioeconomic understanding" (pp. 220–221). This comparison demonstrates that developmental trends are not necessarily always similar throughout different countries, although they may prove to be so in many cases. A decisive factor seems to be the extent to which children are sheltered from, exposed to, or in some cases even take part in economic activity. In order to evaluate the impact of the latter, it would be necessary to examine exactly what kind of experiences influence the understanding of which economic concepts at what age. This means that there sometimes may even be greater differences within the same country than between different countries, depending on the way parents raise their children and explain and show them how banks operate. Furthermore, different banking procedures and laws, as in Muslim countries, could account for such differences.

Possession and Ownership.   The topic of possessions and ownership is clearly related both to politics and economics, but has been investigated mainly through the work of psychologists interested in economic understanding. Berti, Bombi, and Lis (1982) conducted research on children's conceptions about means of production and their owners. They interviewed 120 children between the ages of 4–13 in three areas to find out children's knowledge about (a) ownership of means of production, (b) ownerships of products (industrial and agricultural), and (c) product use. From the answers they were able to derive 5 levels, each having two parts. The first level includes: (a) owner of means of production is a person found in spatial contact with it (bus owned by passengers), and (b) industrial and agricultural products are not owned by anybody, anybody could possess them. The second level includes: (a) owner is the person who exercises an appropriate use of or direct control over object (factory owned by workers), and (b) owner is person closest to using or constructing object. The third level consists of: (a) owner uses producing means and controls their use by others ("the boss"), and (b) product ownership is explained through ownership of producing means ("boss" must share produce with employees). The fourth level consists of: (a) differentiation between owner (giving orders) and employers, and (b) product belongs to "boss." And the fifth level includes: (a) distinction between owner (top of hierarchy) and boss (between owner and worker), and (b) products belong to owner of means of production and employees are compensated by salary.

Children's ideas about ownership of means of production develop through the same sequences but at different speeds. The notion of a "boss-owner" for instance seems to occur at 8–9 years of age for the factory, 10–11 years for the bus, and 12–13 years for the countryside, perhaps due to the fact that 85% of the subjects in the study had no direct experience of country life. Although very few had direct experience of the father's working environment, they heard him talk a lot about his work and thus acquired their information. Cram and Ng (1989) in New Zealand examined (172 subjects of 3 different age groups: 5–6. 8–9, 11–12 years) children's understanding of private ownership by noting the attributes the subjects used to endorse ownership. Greater age was associated with an increase in the endorsement of higher level attributes and in the rejection of lower level attributes, but there was only a tendency in the direction. Already 89% of the youngest group rejected "liking" as a reason for possessing, which increased to 98% in the middle and oldest group, whereas the differences on the other two levels were more distinct. These results indicate that, surprisingly, 5- to 6-year-olds are mainly aware of the distinction between personal desires and ownership. This does not necessarily contradict earlier work, but makes it necessary to interview children younger than the ones in this study to find out whether and at what age egocentric ownership attributes are endorsed during earlier stages of development.

Furnham and Jones (1987) studied children's views regarding possessions and their theft. One-hundred and two subjects aged 7–8, 9–10, 12–13, and

16–17 years old filled out a questionnaire based on work by Furby (1980a, 1980b) and Irving and Siegal (1983). Results indicated that, as hypothesized, views about possessions become more sophisticated and "realistic" with age. The favorite type of possessions proved to be age dependent, varying from toys to sound and sports equipment, computers, and clothes. The younger groups showed no preference for the means of acquisition of an object, whereas the older groups attached great importance to self-bought and individually owned objects motivated by a desire to effect and control their environment. As with increasing age, the child's self-concept gradually depends more and more on his or her possessions, and reactions toward theft become harsher and empathy with the victim increases, even under mitigating circumstances. Most of the younger subjects simply demanded a return of the stolen object, citing mitigating circumstances as poverty or unhappiness, even where there were none, whereas older subjects demanded conditional discharge or prison sentences of different durations as a punishment. Although the oldest group was relatively stringent in its actual demands for punishment, in moral terms the group was rather lenient. This is understood as a pragmatic acceptance of the need for law and order to provide general safety.

For children of all ages the element of control over their environment seems to be the most important characteristic of possessions. For older children who are more active consumers themselves, possessions often imply power and status and an enhancement of personal freedom and security.

Concepts relating to means of production seem to develop similarly to those of buying and selling. They also advance through phases of no grasp of any system, to unconnected systems (knowledge that owner of means of production sells products, but no understanding of how he or she gets the money to pay the workers) and to integrated systems (linking worker's payment and sales proceeds), depending on the respective logic-arithmetical ability of the child. Although these concepts seem to follow the same developmental sequence, it cannot be said whether, to what extent, and how the same factors (experimental, maturation, educational) contribute equally to the development of each concept.

Poverty and Wealth.   In 1975, Zinser, Perry, and Edgar conducted a study to determine the importance of the affluence of the recipient to preschool children's sharing behavior. Most of the children favored sharing with poor recipients over rich recipients. They were also more generous with low-value items than with high-value items equally,and these findings were consistent across all three (4–6) ages. There are two possible explanations for this behavior: (a) societal values, in that society already has communicated to these young children that poor people are more deserving as recipients of sharing than rich people, or (b) empathy, that is, perceived need arouses affective reactions in the children that motivate sharing, which in turn reduces affective reactions.

Winocur and Siegal (1982) asked 96 adolescents (12–13 and 16–18) to allocate rewards between male and female workers in four different cases of family constellations. The results indicated that concern for need decreased with age. Older subjects preferred to distribute rewards on an equal pay for equal work basis, whereas younger subjects supported the idea that family needs should be reflected in pay, but there were no sex differences in the perception of economic arrangements. This confirms Sevon and Weckstrom's (1989) suggestions that younger children judge from a *homo sociologicus* and older children from a *homo economicus* point of view.

Leahy (1981) asked 720 children and adolescents of four age groups (5–7, 9–11, 13–15, 16–18) and four social classes to describe rich and poor people and to point out the differences and similarities between them. The answers were grouped into different types of person descriptions: (a) peripheral (possessions, appearances, behavior), (b) central (traits and thoughts), and (c) sociocentric (life chances and class consciousness). The use of peripheral characteristics in descriptions decreased considerably with age. Thus adolescents emphasized central and sociocentric categories, perceiving rich and poor as different kinds of people who not only differ in observable qualities but also in personality traits. Lower class subjects tended to refer more to the thoughts and life chances of the poor, taking their perspective, and upper middle-class subjects tended to describe the traits of the poor, perceiving them as "others." On the whole, there was a uniformity across class and race in the descriptions and comparisons of the rich and the poor.

To explain these findings, two theoretical models are conceivable: (a) a cognitive developmental model, suggesting that later adolescence is marked by an increased awareness of the nature of complex social systems; and (b) a general functionalist model, suggesting that socialization results in uniformity among classes and races as to the nature of the social class system, thus retaining stability in social institutions. As there has been no research on this topic in other societies of historical periods, it is not possible to exclude the second model, although the way studies have been conducted and interpreted so far, results (understanding of all concepts reached through gradual advancement by stages) favor the cognitive-developmental model of class.

Stacey and Singer (1985) had 325 teenagers between the ages of 14[00ab] and 17 years from a working-class background complete a questionnaire, probing their perceptions of the attributes and consequences of poverty and wealth following Furnham (1982). Regardless of age and sex, all respondent groups rated familial circumstances as most important and luck as least important in explaining poverty and wealth. With internal and external attributions for poverty and wealth rating moderately important, these findings differ slightly as compared to Leahy's (1981) results, because in this case adolescents clearly thought sociocentric categories to be more important than the other two. A reason for this difference might be that subjects were from a working-class background, and as Furnham (1982) found out, subjects from a lower socioeconomic background tend to attach more importance to societal explanations than subjects from a higher socioeconomic background, who tend to offer more individualistic explanations for poverty such as lack of thrift and proper money management.

Most studies in this field have tried to describe the levels that children go through in their development of certain economic notions. The occasional disagreement as to the number of levels and points of transitions is probably mostly a matter of methodology, and because results had been interpreted within the Piagetian developmental idea. Whether this is justified or not is subject to debate. Webley (1983), for instance, who put into question whether the Piagetian approach is applicable for economic concepts, favors a social learning model. Furthermore, most of the researchers already agree that external stimuli, such as socioeconomic environment, personal experience with money, formal teaching, or parental practices, have great influence on the child's development of economic thinking and may contribute to premature knowledge. For instance, Wosinski and Pietras (1990) discovered in a study of 87 Polish subjects of ages 8, 11, and 14 that the youngest had in some aspects, with respect to the definition of salary, better economic knowledge than the other groups. They attributed this finding to the fact that these children had been living under conditions of an economic crisis in Poland. These children had experienced conditions of shortage, increases in prices, inflation, and had heard their family and TV programs discuss these matters. This, too, represents "a case of socioeconomic reality shaping (partly at least) socio-economic understanding" (Ng, 1983, pp. 220–221). It therefore seems to be that up to a certain extent the development of economic notions can be accelerated through experimental and educational factors, an issue that merits further study.

Studies from Political Science

How much do young people know about the political system and the sort of government they live under? What stages or phases do they go through in acquisition of this knowledge? What experience or factors are the best determinants of this knowledge? How much do first-time voters understand the workings of the political system? How can we best educate children about politics and government in order in make them responsible, effective and participating citizens? Whereas the early work in this field had mainly to do with political knowledge, more recent research has focused on political consciousness and understanding (Haste & Torney-Purta, 1992). Adelson and O'Neil (1966) noted:

> During adolescence the youngster gropes, stumbles and leaps towards political understanding. Prior to these years the child's sense of the political order is erratic and incomplete — a curious array of sentiment and dogmas, personalized ideas, randomly remembered names and party labels, half-understood platitudes. By the time adolescence has come to an end, the child's mind much of the time, moves easily within and among the categories of political discourse. (Adelson & O'Neil, 1966, p. 295)

However, Jackson (1972) noted that children develop concepts of political symbols, like the flag, or political figures as early as childhood. A great deal more research has been done on young people's political attitudes and beliefs than on their political knowledge and on their understanding of the political process at all levels (Jaros & Grant, 1979).

Compared to research on political attitudes, there have been comparatively few studies that have looked at adolescents' knowledge of how the political system works. Dennis and McCrone (1970) found in several countries that by the age of 10 years, primary school children could accurately name the country's main political parties and express a preference for one. This was reported for 80% of British school children (Himmelweit, Humphreyes, Jaeger, & Katz, 1981). But knowing the names of politicians is quite different from knowing how parliamentary democracy or local government works.

An exception to this paucity of system research was provided by Stradling (1977). He was commissioned by the Hansard Society, first, to produce a reliable estimate of the extent of political knowledge and ignorance in a sample of 4,027 British 15- to 16-year-olds, which he believed could act as a yardstick of political literacy against which to measure the effects of future developments, and, second, to examine the sources of political information for the mid-teens in our own society. He distinguished between propositional or factual knowledge and procedural or know-how knowledge of politics. He aimed specifically to have a multidimensional approach that lessened the risk of understanding the political awareness of young people. The study attempted to discover the determinants of political awareness and found some evidence of sex differences: boys are more politically knowledgeable than girls, particularly on political officeholders and internal affairs; he found no evidence of systematic class differences, although it is uncertain if the very top and bottom of the class structure were well sampled. Stradling also found fairly strong evidence of schooling effects, with grammar or selective school boys being more knowledgeable than their comprehensive nonselective cousins. No evidence of a political education effect was obtained, but some evidence of an educational aspiration effect was found, that is, adolescents who leave school once they have attained the legal minimum age are less likely to fare well on this test. Stradling concluded that:

> The general lack of political awareness revealed in this report must make depressing reading for anyone who is concerned about the future of our representative democracy and the prospects for greater participation by the public. There is something essentially paradoxical about a democracy in which some eighty to ninety per cent of the future citizens (and the present citizenry) are insufficiently well-informed about local, national and international politics to know not only what is happening but also how they are affected by it and what they can do about it. Most of the political knowledge which they do have is of a rather inert and voyeuristic kind and of little use to them either as political consumers or as political actors. (p. 57)

Furnham and Gunter (1983, 1987, 1989) repeated Stradling's study on a smaller population and also attempted to specify various determinants (demographic, media usage, interest) of adolescent political awareness. They found that the level of adolescent knowledge about politics was similar. The best predictor of political knowledge was not media usage, but expressed interest in political affairs. There was, however, some indication that those who watched more television news tended to have greater political knowledge than those who said they watched less.

Furnham and Gunter (1987, 1989) looked at knowledge of the different political parties, knowledge of political leaders, knowledge of parliamentary and local politics, and knowledge about the public services. Between one-fifth and one-half of the adolescent respondents were able to identify a political policy with a specific party, such as "Taxes on both people and industries should be cut as soon as possible," or "The government should take over and run more industries." The more popular the party, in terms of votes and members in parliament, the more the young people were able to recognize its political creed.

It seemed that potential voters are better able to spot their chosen party's politics than those of any other party. Further, respondents overall were better at identifying the policies of the two main British political parties than those of the more minor or middle-grouped parties. Finally, the three questions, in which over 50% of the sample were correct in their answers, concerned not so much industrial or macroeconomic politics as public spending and the issues of privatization and nationalization.

Despite the fact that various researchers in psychology, education, and political science have expressed considerable interest in the growth of political knowledge in young people and the determinants of the transition from one stage or phase to another, comparatively little work has been done in this field. An exception is the research of Adelson and O'Neil (1966) who studied 11-, 13-, 15-, and 18-year-old Americans in an attempt to see how their sense of community related to their political ideas. They found that before the age of 13, young people use personalized modes of discourse and find it difficult to imagine the social consequences of political action. Most people younger than 25 years find it difficult to conceive of the community as a whole and tend to conceptualize government in terms of specific and tangible services. They are also pretty insensitive to individual liberties, preferring authoritarian options, and cannot grasp the legitimate claims of the community on the citizen. It is only near the end of adolescence that young people take into account the long-range effects of political action and use philosophic principles for making political judgments. They argue that there are five developmental factors or parameters that together bring about growth in political understanding: (a) the decline of authoritarianism and the realization that authorities may be irrational, presumptuous, whimsical, or corrupt; (b) an increasing grasp of the nature and needs of the community and the understanding of the functions of social institutions; (c) the absorption of political knowledge and feeling for the community and the understanding of the functions of social institutions; (d) the growth of cognitive capacities such as the ability to weigh the relative consequences of action and the attainment of deductive reasoning; and (e) the birth of orderly and internally consistent political ideology.

They noted that the 11-year-old is concrete, egocentric, and tied to the present in his or her political thinking, whereas 15-year-olds can deal with abstract ideas but have a lack of political information. On the other hand, 18-year-olds are more fluent, knowledgeable, philosophical, and ideological; "Taking our data as a whole, we usually find only moderate differences between 15 and 18. We do find concepts that appear suddenly between 11 and 13 and between 13 and 15, but only rarely do we find an idea substantially represented at 18 which is not also available to a fair number of 15-year-olds" (Adelson & O'Neil, 1966, pp. 305–306).

Using teenagers aged 14–19, Furth and McConville (1981) examined adolescent understanding of compromise in political and social awareness. Four aspects of political understanding were examined: the recognition of individual rights, articulation of other viewpoints, the need for reasonable compromise, and the separation of legal from conventional-moral regulations. A clear progression in mature understanding of the conflictual issues was demonstrated with the 18- to 19-year-old group quite distinct from the 16–17 group, who were closer to the youngest age group. The authors singled out a number of specific aspects of political understanding that develop over this age range. The first is the adolescent's growing recognition of individual rights vis-à-vis those of society, and that awareness of the infringement of rights increased with age. Second, older teenagers are able to articulate the viewpoint of other interested groups in society and to recognize and expect organized action or specific issues. Third, teenagers seem to acquire a much greater understanding of the concept of compromise over this period, the idea that to live in society the individual has to relinquish certain rights and that others are legally protected by the government. Fourth, older teenagers are able to distinguish between conventions and legal sanctions.

Based on his extensive interviews with 119 Australian youngsters from 5 to 16, Connell (1971, see especially Table 2.1) devised four stages in the development of political beliefs. He noted:

> Up to about the age of 9, politics is not seen by children as a problematic sphere of life in which sets of choices must be made between possible alternatives. Most of their statements of preference are ad hoc, unqualified, probably highly unstable and not necessarily consistent with each other. This situation is transformed when the children begin to recognize political alternatives and notice opposing policy positions. They are then enabled to, and do, take positions on issues and develop consistent preferences of their own. At first . . . these preferences are specific to their subject-matter and isolated from each other. Later they are linked together into coherent sets of opinions. From the combination of such inter-correlated stances with abstract and holistic interpretations, ideology may form. The expression of preferences does not necessarily involve action to realize them. There is further development when the child recognizes himself as a political actor, potential or actual and recognizes his own action as problematic, involving choice among possibilities. This development may follow rapidly on the formation of opinion, or it may be long delayed: we are here dealing with a moveable sequence rather than strict chronological stages, though there is a sense in which we can regard this development as characteristic of late adolescence. (Connell, 1971, pp. 231–232)

Young people become voters at 18 in some countries and 21 in others. Given the age distribution of some national populations, particularly of developing countries, the young are a very important numerical political force. It therefore becomes of some considerable applied interest to find out what political attitudes and knowledge young people have; how they are acquired and changed; and most importantly, how political beliefs translate into political action, whether it be through the ballot box, demonstration, or even violence. Most recent research concentrates on the way political, economic, social, and moral issues are understood by young people and interwoven with everyday private thinking. In this sense studies on economic, political and historical understanding are merging (see Berti, this volume).

Cross-cultural, Social, and Gender Differences

Various studies in different (mainly Western) countries have been undertaken, but few have investigated specifically cross-cultural differences. Furby (1978, 1980a, 1980b) compared American and Israeli (kibbutz and city) children's attitudes toward possessions and found more differences between American and Israeli subjects than between kibbutz and all others.

The most comprehensive and extensive study in a recent cross-cultural project, initiated by Leiser, Sevon, and Levy (1990), was the "Naive Economics Project." It includes samples from 10 countries—Algeria, Australia, Denmark, Finland, France, Israel (town and kibbutz), Norway, Poland, West Germany, and Yugoslavia—and was administered to 900 children aged 8, 11, and 14. Topics covered included: (a) understanding, that is, who decides what, how, and why with respect to prices, salary, savings, investment, and the mint; (b) reasoning, how well do children appreciate the consequences of economic events; and (c) attitudes, how do they account for the economic fate of individuals? In accordance with previous investigations in various countries, there was an obvious progression with age. However, there were some differences in answers between the participating countries. These could be due to the different political and economical systems and the prosperity of the respective country.

The dominance of the government as a visible economic factor was reflected by the frequency with which it appeared in children's answers. The differences in each society's values and attitudes (such as more individualistic attitudes in Western democracies, religion, the work ethic, different moral standards in Christian than in Atheist or Moslem countries) and slight differences in the conditions of the interview are all possible reasons for the disparity in country responses. Furthermore, size of the sample (90 subjects from each country) may not have been large enough to provide for representative cross-cultural comparisons. The differences, however, show that the child's understanding of how economic systems work is influenced by various factors in the child's environment as suggested by the social learning model.

Class differences were very inconsistently reported by the various researchers. Although in some cases there was some indication of class differences, on the whole they were not as significant as were the reported age differences. There is a certain difficulty in finding comparable subjects in each country, as *middle class* probably has a different meaning in Germany than in Algeria.

In a smaller study, Burgard, Cheyne, and Jahoda (1989) replicated a Scottish study by Emler and Dickinson (1985) in West Germany that asked 140 children of 8, 10, and 12 years from middle- and working-class backgrounds and 67 parents to estimate occupational incomes of a doctor, a teacher, a bus driver, and a road sweeper. They also were asked to estimate the cost of some consumer goods. Emler and Dickinson (1985) found substantial social class differences, but no age differences in their Scottish sample. In West Germany, however, significant age but virtually no social class differences were found among both parents and children. One explanation might be that socioeconomic differences in West German society are less pronounced than in the United Kingdom. Furthermore there was no relationship between parents' and childrens' income estimates. This, according to the authors, throws considerable doubt on Emler and Dickinson's (1985) contention that "class-tied social representations outweigh developmental changes" (p. 285).

Similarly, gender differences have been reported throughout several studies. Although some authors have set out quite specifically to measure these phenomena, Kourilsky and Campbell (1984) set up a study "(1) to measure sex differences in children's perceptions of entrepreneurship and occupational sex-stereotyping and (2) to assess differences in children's risk taking, persistence, and economic success" (p. 53). Nine-hundred and thirty-eight subjects aged 8–12 took part in an economics education instructional program during 10 weeks. Before the "Mini-Society" program, entrepreneurship was perceived as a predominately male domain. Of five vacant entrepreneurial positions in the class, 1 out of 6 boys and 2 out of 22 girls posted female peers as owners of a company. After the program, these numbers rose to 1.84 for boys and 2.48 for girls; boys supposedly more than girls still possess a somewhat stereotyped picture of the entrepreneur. This trend was also observable at occupational sex stereotyping. In the Mini-Society program, girls were more likely to increase the number of occupations they thought appropriate for women. As to ratings in success, profit made in a mini-business, persistence (sticking to a task until completed), and risk taking (exposure to loss and disadvantages), boys and girls achieved similar results, with girls being even slightly ahead in the first two categories. Thus no sex differences are apparent in the major characteristics associated with successful entrepreneurship in this study.

Gender differences most probably may be attributed to children's different upbringing and the role women play in society. If one parent stays at home or works only part time, it is mostly the mother. The father is seen as a source of money by young children ("brings it home from work"). All persons that are thought of as important by the child are almost entirely men (presidents), "bosses," headmasters, and priests. Children, therefore, already perceive men and women in different roles while growing up. This may again be more or less obvious in different countries. Wosinski and Pietras (1990), for instance, clearly attribute the gender differences they found in their study to traditional sex socialization, because in Poland economic problems are traditionally left to males rather than females.

As Kourilsky and Campbell's (1984) study showed, instruction can help change children's perceptions of "realities" as gender roles, as well as increase their economic knowledge.

Economic Values

The determinants and structure of adolescents' beliefs about the economy were the subject of two studies by Furnham (1987). The first examined the determinants of economic values of 86 adolescents aged 16–17 and the second looked at the economic preferences and knowledge of 150 subjects aged 18–19. Based on a questionnaire (Economics Values Inventory) by O'Brien and Ingels (1985), the determinants of economic values turned out to be most likely the subject's political belief rather than gender, religion, or personal economic experience. Those subjects that stated they would not vote believed more in economic alienation and powerlessness than the others. Potential Labour (Socialist) supporters believed more than potential Conservative (Capitalist) voters, who also were against powerful unions, that the government was responsible for social welfare. In the second study subjects were asked to state how they thought Conservatives, Labour, and Liberals distributed the budget (public expenditures) as well as their own personal preference for the distribution. On the whole, the estimates acknowledged that left-wing governments spend less on defense and more on social matters than right-wing governments. Conservative subjects' estimates tended to be more accurate than Labour subjects' estimates. Personal choices aligned most closely to what was estimated to be a Liberal government budget.

O'Brien and Ingels (1987) previously conducted the first study in the United States. Their findings, and that of Furnham, suggested socioeconomic status as the strongest predictor of economic values. Possible reasons for this could be a much weaker political interest in the United States (a far lower percentage of American citizens votes), different political traditions (there are strong trade unions in Britain), or less pronounced economical differences between socioeconomic status and political belief. Therefore, if examined, it might be the case that subjects who had a "conservative" political opinion are predominantly from a middle-class background, which would then be in accordance with the American study.

Furnham's studies showed a close affinity between political and economic beliefs and found that the latter is governed by the former. The way political parties publicly compare their agendas and families possibly discuss their present and future situation (such as jobs, education, health, and finances) at home may arouse political awareness. Being in favor of certain political ideas implies having economic priorities, because the differences between political parties are in their respective budgets. Also, the economic topics covered on the political parties' agenda were all macroeconomic and of popular debate. This suggests that there may also be "less political" topics. As only beliefs were tested (and not knowledge), the subjects only needed to "have an opinion." Opinions are shaped through debate, which again is a political process.

So far the majority of studies have concentrated on children's understanding of certain economic concepts, mainly in industrial societies. The reason for neglecting other concepts might be that children are not expected to understand them, perhaps even because not many adults are expected to understand them, topics such as exchange rates between currencies and macroeconomic situations. Studies, such as those by Wosinski and Pietras (1990), Ng (1983), and Kourilsky and Campbell (1984), have shown that children sometimes were underestimated and that they were able to understand concepts that they were not expected to understand at that age, due to being exposed to certain external stimuli (instruction, experience, economic crisis, etc.) that helped speed up their understanding.

More studies examining Third World countries would help to find out how entirely different external stimuli contribute to cross-national differences. However, although fascinating to investigate cross-national differences, one always has to bear in mind the difficulties associated with obtaining equivalent samples and asking equivalent questions.

ECONOMIC EDUCATION

Formal instruction is one means by which young people acquire an understanding of the economic and political world. However, much more research has investigated economic rather than political education.

The Effect of Economic Instruction

Whitehead (1986) investigated the eventual change in students' attitudes to economic issues as a result of exposure to a 2-year "A"-level economic course. The 16- to 18-year-old subjects were divided into a test group of 523 and a control group of 483. The questionnaires did not test economic knowledge but economic attitudes; for example, capitalism is immoral because it exploits the worker by failing to give him full value for his productive labor. In absolute terms, considerable correspondence existed between the responses of experimental and control groups with respect to those items in which a large majority expressed either conservative or radical attitudes. On the whole, experimental and control groups held completely differing views only on three items. For 6 out of the 18 items on the scale, students who had studied for 'A' level economics showed a significant shift in their economic attitudes.

In a similar study, O'Brien and Ingels (1987), who developed the economics values inventory (EVI), an instrument aimed at measuring young people's values and attitudes regarding economic matter, also confirmed the hypothesis that formal education in economics influences students' economic attitudes. The teaching of economics therefore not only increases children's understanding of certain economics contexts but also may help them review their values and attitudes that are mostly influenced by or even taken over from their parents. Understanding societal independencies better may help students learn to question prejudices, thereby contributing to an increase in maturation.

Economics Instruction in Primary Grades

Economics as a subject is mostly not taught in countries before the university level or in some cases at the secondary level. The majority of adolescents who drop out of school after 9 or 10 years of education, therefore, never receive economics instruction. As macroeconomic knowledge obviously cannot be learned by observation, such as the working of banks, there obviously is a need for the teaching of economics.

Kourilsky (1977) proved, however, that even kindergarten is not too soon to start educating economically literate citizens. In the "Kinder-Economy," an education program, children became acquainted with the concepts of scarcity, decision making, production, specialization, consumption, distribution, demand/supply, business, money, and bartering. Her study, examining 96 subjects of children aged 5 to 6 years old, was supposed to answer four questions: (a) Is the child's success in economic decision making and analysis related to instructional intervention or to increased maturity inherent in the passage of time? (b) To what extent and degree, through intervention, are children able to master concepts that psychologically they are considered too young to learn? (c) What type of school, home, and personality variables are predictors of success in economic decision making and analysis? and (d) What are the parents' attitudes toward the teaching of economic decision making and analytical principles as a part of early childhood education?

The examination of the first question showed a significant difference between the scores of the subjects in the Kinder-Economy and in the control group, which indicated that significant progress was induced by instruction. Four out of the nine topics covered yielded mastery levels of more than 70%, the total average being 72.5%. The mastery level was set at 70%, as a previous testing of 40 elementary school teachers yielded an average of 68.5% on the same test. This shows that children are in fact able to learn concepts that developmentally they are considered to be too young to learn. To answer the third question, six predictor variables were examined: parental report, verbal ability, maturation level, general ability, social ability, and initiative. The first three proved to be the best predictors of success in economic decision making; the strongest—parent report—accounted for 62% of the total variance.

Parents' attitudes toward the teaching of economics in kindergarten turned out to be rather positive: 96.7% of the parents were in favor of it, and 91.3% thought that an economics program should be continued throughout the rest of the grades. Some even mentioned that they were embarrassed to find out that their children knew more about economics than they did, encouraging them to increase their own knowledge. These findings and the general ignorance of children and adults concerning economic interdependencies and contexts seem to give clear evidence for the importance of economic education as early as possible.

Fox (1978), however, challenged the view that "any topic can be taught effectively in some intellectually honest form at any stage of development" (p. 478). She cited three things that children already possess (knapsack) when going to school: economic attitudes ("parent tapes" and pro-verbs), unprocessed direct experience (e.g., shopping trips), and cognitive capacities (level of cognitive development). Considering that children on the preoperational level are not able to think very abstractly (centered, static and irreversible), Fox saw difficulties in formal teaching of economic concepts to children who are, for instance, unable to understand the transaction of economic exchange in a shop. She warned that "the fact that kinder-garden children can learn economic terms is not compelling evidence that the concepts underlying those terms are in fact understood" (p. 480). Instead she pleaded for using direct experience as a basis for economic education in primary school and suggested that teachers use everyday situations of economic behavior in the classroom to help children make sense of what they already know, always considering the level of the child's cognitive abilities. This contradicts Kourilsky's findings that children are to some extent able to master concepts that psychologically they are considered too young to learn. This contradiction might be an indication that Piaget's stages of general cognitive development, originally explaining how the individual represents physical reality, can simply be transferred into economics without any alteration.

In the *Journal of Economic Education,* solely dedicated to research into the teaching of economics, Davidson and Kilgore (1971) presented a model for evaluating the effectiveness of economic education in primary grades. Five-hundred and four second-grade pupils in 24 classes from different socioeconomic background were subjects in one control group and two different experimental groups. Pupils in the control group were taught their regular social studies curriculum: the first experimental group was taught with The Child's World of Choices materials, and the teachers in the second experimental group also received in-service training. Analysis showed that both experimental groups scored significantly higher results on the post Primary Test of Economic Understanding (PD) than the control group, but no experimental method proved to be superior to the other. Pupils from lower socioeconomic backgrounds (target schools) scored significantly lower on both PD pre- and posttests than pupils from nontarget schools.

It could thus be concluded that elementary-grade children can be taught basic economic concepts, and growth in understanding them can be measured. Specially designed material prompted the pupils' growth in understanding but additional full-scale programs in economic education for teachers did not have any significant effects on pupils' advancement. As to the "how" of teaching economics concepts to children, Waite (1988) suggested that the child must be the center of activity, as case studies have shown that the acceleration of children's conceptual understanding, can be achieved using a number of different strategies. Because the child's economic awareness is acquired through information channels outside the classroom, case studies seem to be a good way of teaching children about the economy. Ramsett (1972) also suggested to shy always from the traditional lecture approach and use daily life classroom events that are either directly or indirectly relevant to economics as a basis for further discussion and explanation (e.g., if a pupil's family has to move away because his or her mother or father accepted a new job, the teacher could take this opportunity to discuss employment, incomes, dependencies, etc.).

More recently Chizmar and Halinski (1983) described the impact of Tradeoffs, a special series of television/film programs designed to teach economics in elementary school, on students' performance on the Basic Economic Test (BET). The results indicated that: (a) as the number of weeks of instruction increased, the rate of increase in students' scores was significantly greater for students using Trade-offs; (b) there were no sex differences in scores for students using Trade-offs, whereas for those being instructed traditionally, gender was a statistically significant predictor of students' score (girls outperforming boys). Furthermore the grade-level and teacher training (see also McKenzie, 1971; Walstad, 1979; Walstad & Watts, 1985) in economics were significant positive determinants of BET performance. These findings may indicate that gender differences here could possibly be attributed to the way instruction was given, as boys performed better under Trade-offs than under traditional instruction. Under this premise it would be interesting to examine how sex differences found in other studies possibly could have been caused.

Hansen (1985), acknowledging that the teaching of economics to elementary school children has proved effective, demanded a firm installation of this subject into the curriculum of the primary grades. He briefly summa-rized the basic knowledge about children and economic education as follows: (a) what happens in a child's early years—before the end of the primary years—has lasting effects into adulthood; (b) children enter kindergarten possessing an experience-based economic literacy; (c) children can acquire economic concepts and can do so earlier than previously thought; (d) a variety of economic materials and teaching approaches are both available and effective; (e) evaluation procedures are available, and new ones are being established, even though they need continued refine-ment; and (f) economic education programs show greater student gains when teachers are well versed in economics.

As long as economics instruction is not part of the curriculum, including goals, materials, and schedules, it will not reach the classroom. At present, the apparent cost of economics instruction (reading and mathematics still have top priority before any other subjects in today's primary schools) is still deemed too high to introduce it into primary schools. If economics is not considered as a subject to be studied on its own, competing with other subjects in the curriculum, but rather is experienced in connection with already existing subjects such as mathematics (case studies), this problem can be avoided.

Reasons for Goals and Economic Education

In order to decide what should be taught in a economics course and how such economics instruction should take place, an explicit goal needs to be defined.

Horton and Weidenaar (1975) tried to do this and interviewed more than 200 economic educators, economists, other social scientists, trainers of social studies teachers, businessmen, and others. Three goals were singled out: (a) to help us to be more capable as direct participants in the economy—that is, as consumers, workers, businessmen, or investors; (b) to "improve" decisions when we act in our society as citizens; and (c) to improve our understanding of the world in which we live.

All three goals appear to be of equal importance and probably cannot be separated completely from one another anyway. Still, depending on the emphasis that is placed on each goal, an economics course would probably touch slightly different topics. The authors suggest that for the third goal an economics course might cover such concrete questions "as why automobile mechanics often earn more than English teachers; why teenagers, females and nonwhites are disproportionately unemployed; and why more money for each of us would do so little to meet our fundamental economic problem of relative scarcity" (p. 43).

Possessing a better knowledge of the economic aspects of our environment makes us better prepared to analyze and interpret the situations and problems we face. As with any knowledge, this gives us a more vast and better choice of possible solutions, and considering the widespread ignorance about economic topics of both children and adults, economics instruction seems necessary.

A MODEL AND A CONCLUSION

This chapter reviews research on the sociopolitical and economic thinking of children and adolescents. It appears that at a preschool age (i.e., before 6 years old) children begin to gain a rudimentary economic understanding, even though most economic events are still simply observed and accepted as a mere ritual, through shopping trips with their parents, school games, and television advertisements With increasing age, a growing experience with money, exposure to television, and interaction with their peers, children gradually begin to understand more of the economic life they encounter and start to become consumers themselves. Most of the studies examined dealt with children's understanding of economic concepts; very few considered their actual economic behavior, and less still their reasoning about the economic world. The same applies to political knowledge and awareness.

Although researchers do not agree on the number of stages, points of transition, and exact nature of the understanding at each stage, there seems to be basic agreement that children do advance through stages or phases in their understanding. However, there is also evidence that there are certain factors that have great influence on the speed with which the transition from one stage to the next takes place. These factors (e.g., experience with the use of money and exposure to the economic world), in particular, parental practice, social class, economics instruction in school, and so in, need further examination in order to find out—although difficult to separate—which factor influences which concept, how and at what stage, so that it might be possible to discover how economic and political ideas and behaviors are established. In addition, children's attitudes and understanding of yet more economic, political, and historical concepts (e.g., debt, betting, exchange rates, interest rates, etc.) merit examination to gain a full understanding of the child's economic socialization. Table 2.2 presents three sets of factors from which path models may be derived and tested.

Four things need to be said about this model or, more correctly, flow chart showing the interrelationship among key variables found to be related to economic and political knowledge and understanding. First, it is unfinished in the sense that there may well be other crucial variables in any of the three sections. Second, the classification of the variables in the three

TABLE 2.2
Types of Variables and Factors Involved in Each Variable in
General Structure

Independent Variables (Psychological)	Moderator Variable (Sociological)	Dependent Variables (Economic) (Political) (Historical)
Demographic factors	Sociopolitical factors of country	Attitudes & beliefs
Age, sex, class	Type of economy	
Child rearing	GNP	Knowledge & understanding
Belief factors	Educational factors	Economic & behavior
Parental, religion politics	Type of schooling	Ability to reason with this information
Individual differences	Economic cycle	
Intelligence		
Personality		

columns is debatable. Third, the model does not have any "feedback" loops, suggesting all relationships are unidirectional, which is clearly not the case. Finally, the model specifies the relationship between, not within, the particular grouping of variables which are of course related.

But a flow chart is more than a heuristic device. It allows for path analysis hypotheses to be formulated as to the major antecedents of socioeconomic understanding and reasoning.

This flow chart was derived partly from theory and partly from research. Over 90 years of research on the Protestant work ethic has led to the development of various models that attempted to explain how and why people subscribe to the tenets of that belief system (Furnham, 1990). These models have attracted critical and empirical interest. One of the problems concerning research in this whole area is that many studies have been perceived as empirical attempts to test specific hypothesis. Nearly all the "theories" or approaches were highly derivative of other research areas. The result of 30 to 40 years research is therefore not particularly inspiring, although recent research efforts are highly promising (Berti & Bombi, 1988; Haste & Turney-Purta, 1992). Clearly for a comprehensive and programmatic research endeavor, one needs some theoretical and epistemological model on how to guide the research. Although the model is far from adequate, it at least provides a framework within which to conduct research.

REFERENCES

Abramovitch, R., Freedman, J., & Pliner, P. (1991). Children and money: Getting an allowance, credit versus cash, and knowledge of pricing. *Journal of Economic Psychology*, *12*, 27–45.

Adelson, J., & O'Neil, R. (1966). Growth of political ideas in adolescence: The sense of community. *Journal of Personality and Social Psychology*, *4*, 295-306.

Berti, A., & Bombi, A. (1979). Where does money come from? *Archivio di Psicologia*, *40*, 53-77.

Berti, A., & Bombi, A. (1981). The development of the concept of money and its value: A longitudinal study. *Child Development*, *52*, 1179-1182.

Berti, A., & Bombi, A. (1988). *The child's construction of economics*. Cambridge, England: Cambridge University Press.

Berti, A., Bombi, A., & de Beni, R. (1986). Acquiring economic notions: Profit. *International Journal of Behavioural Development*, *9*, 15-29.

Berti, A., Bombio, A., & Lis, A. (1982). The child's conceptions about means of production and their owners. *European Journal of Social Psychology*, *12*, 221-239.

Burgard, P., Cheyne, W., & Jahoda, G. (1989). Children's representations of economic inequality: A replication. *British Journal of Developmental Psychology*, *7*, 275-287.

Burris, V. (1983). Stages in the development of economic concepts. *Human Relations*, *36*, 791-812.

Chizmar, J., & Halinski, R. (1983). Performance in the Basic Economic Test (BET) and "Trade-offs." *The Journal of Economic Education*, *14*, 18-29.

Connell, R. (1971). *The child's construction of politics*. Carlton, Australia: Melbourne University Press.

Cram, F., & Ng, S. (1989). Children's endorsement of ownership attributes. *Journal of Economic Psychology*, *10*, 63-75.

Cummings, S., & Taebel, D. (1978). The economic socialization of children: A neo-Marxist analysis. *Social Problems*, *26*, 198-210.

Danziger, K. (1958). Children's earliest conceptions of economic relationships. *The Journal of Social Psychology*, *47*, 231-240.

Davidson, D., & Kilgore, J. (1971). A model for evaluating the effectiveness of economic education in primary grades. *The Journal of Economic Education*, *3*, 17-25.

Dennis, J., & McCrone, D. (1970). The adult development of political partly identification in Western democracies. *Comparative Political Studies*, *14*, 243-263.

Emler, N., & Dickinson, J. (1985). Children's representations of economic inequalities: The effects of social class. *British Journal of Developmental Psychology*, *3*, 191-198.

Fox, K. (1978). What children bring to school: The beginnings of economic education. *Social Education*, *10*, 478-481.

Furby, L. (1978). Possessions in humans: An exploratory study of its meaning and innovation. *Social Behavior and Personality*, *6*, 49-65.

Furby, L. (1980a). Collective possession and ownership: A study of its judged feasibility and desirability. *Social Behaviour and Personality*, *8*, 165-184.

Furby, L. (1980b). The origins and early development of possessive behaviour. *Political Psychology*, *2*, 30-42.

Furnham, A. (1982). The perception of poverty among adolescents. *Journal of Adolescence*, *5*, 135-147.

Furnham, A. (1987). The determinants and structure of adolescents' beliefs about the economy. *Journal of Adolescence*, *10*, 353-371.

Furnham, A. (1990). *The Protestant work ethic*. London: Routledge.

Furnham, A., & Cleare, A. (1988). School children's conceptions of economics: Prices, wages, investments and strikes. *Journal of Economic Psychology*, *9*, 467-479.

Furnham, A., & Gunter, B. (1983). Political knowledge and awareness in adolescence. *Journal of Adolescence 6*, 673-685.

Furnham, A., & Gunter, B. (1987). Young people's political knowledge. *Educational Studies*, *13*, 91-104.

Furnham, A., & Gunter, B. (1989). *The anatomy of adolescence*. London: Routledge.

Furnham, A., & Jones, S. (1987). Children's views regarding possessions and their theft. *Journal of Moral Education, 16*, 18–30.

Furnham, A., & Stacey, B. (1991). *Young people's understanding of society*. London: Routledge.

Furth, H, (1980). *The world of grown-ups*. New York: Elsevier.

Furth, H., Baur, M., & Smith, J. (1976). Children's conception of social institutions: A Piagetian framework. *Human Development, 19*, 341–347.

Furth, H., & McConville, K. (1981). Adolescent understanding of compromise in political and social areas. *Merrill-Palmer Quarterly, 27*, 412–427.

Hansen, H. (1985). The economics of early childhood education in Minnesota. *The Journal of Economic Education, 16*, 219–224.

Haste, H., & Torney-Purta, J. (1992). *The development of political understanding*. San Francisco: Jossey-Bass.

Himmelweit, H., Humphreyes, P., Jaeger, M., & Katz, M. (1981). *How voters decide*. London: Academic Press.

Horton, R., & Weidenaar, D. (1975). Wherefore economic education? *The Journal of Economic Education, 7*, 40–44.

Irving, K., & Siegal, M. (1983). Mitigating circumstances in children's perceptions of criminal justice. *British Journal of Development Psychology, 1*, 179–188.

Jackson, R. (1972). The development of political concepts in young children. *Educational Research, 14*, 51–55.

Jahoda, G. (1979). The construction of economic reality by some Glaswegian children. *European Journal of Social Psychology, 9*, 115–127.

Jahoda, G. (1981). The development of thinking about economic institutions: The bank. *Cashiers de Psychologie Cognitive, 1*, 55–73.

Jaros, D., & Grant, L. (1979). *Political behaviour: Choice and perspective*. Oxford: Blackwell.

Kourilsky, M. (1977). The kinder-economy: A case study of kindergarten pupils' acquisition of economic concepts. *The Elementary School Journal, 77*, 182–191.

Kourilsky, M., & Campbell, M. (1984). Sex differences in a simulated classroom economy: Children's beliefs about entrepreneurship. *Sex Roles, 10*, 53–66.

Leahy, R. (1981). The development of the conception of economic inequality. I. Descriptions and comparisons of rich and poor people. *Child Development, 52*, 523–532.

Leiser, D. (1983). Children's conceptions of economics - the constitution of the cognitive domain. *Journal of Economic Psychology, 4*, 297–317.

Leiser, D., Sevon, G., & Levy, D. (1990). Children's economic socialization of ten countries. *Journal of Economic Psychology, 11*, 591–614.

McKenzie, R. (1971). An exploratory study of the economic understanding of elementary school teachers. *The Journal of Economic Education, 3*, 26–31.

Ng, S. (1983). Children's ideas about the bank and shop profit: Development, stages and the influence of cognitive contrasts and conflicts. *Journal of Economic Psychology, 4*, 209–221.

Ng, S. (1985). Children's ideas about the bank: A New Zealand replication. *European Journal of Social Psychology, 15*, 121–123.

O'Brien, M., & Ingels, S. (1985). The effects of economics instruction in early adolescence. *Theory and Research in Social Education, 4*, 279–294.

O'Brien, M., & Ingels, S. (1987). The economic values inventory. *Research in Economic Education, 18*, 7–18.

Pollio, H., & Gray, R. (1973). Change-making strategies in children and adults. *The Journal of Psychology, 84*, 173–179.

Ramsett, D. (1972). Toward improving economic education in the elementary grades. *The Journal of Economic Education, 4*, 30–35.

Schug, M., & Birkey, C. (1985, April). *The development of children's economic reasoning*. Paper presented at the annual meeting of the American Educational Research Association, Chicago.

Sevon, G., & Weckstrom, S. (1989). The development of reasoning about economic events: A study of Finnish children. *Journal of Economic Psychology, 10*, 495-514.

Stacey, B., & Singer, M. (1985). The perception of poverty and wealth among teenagers. *Journal of Adolescence, 8*, 231-241.

Stradling, R. (1977). *The political awareness of the school leaver.* London: Hansarch Society.

Strauss, A. (1952). The development and transformation of monetary meaning in the child. *American Sociological Review, 53*, 275-286.

Sutton, R. (1962). Behaviour in the attainment of economic concepts. *The Journal of Psychology, 53*, 37-46.

Waite, P. (1988). Economic awareness: Context, issues and concepts. *Theory and Practice, 4*, 27-39.

Walstad, W. (1979). Effectiveness of a USMES in service economic education program for elementary school teachers. *The Journal of Economic Education, 11*, 1-12.

Walstad, W., & Watts, M. (1985). Teaching economics in schools: A review of survey findings. *The Journal of Economic Education, 16*, 135-146.

Webley, P. (1983). *Growing up in the modern economy.* Paper presented at the 6th International Conference on Political Psychology.

Whitehead, D. (1986, Spring1). Student's attitudes to economic issues. *Economics*, pp. 24-32.

Winocur, S., & Siegal, M. (1982). Adolescents' judgements of economic arrangements. *International Journal of Behavioural Development, 5*, 357-365.

Wosinski, M., & Pietras, M. (1990). Economic socialization of Polish children in different macro-economic conditions. *Journal of Economic Psychology, 11*, 515-528.

Zabucovec, V., & Polic, M. (1990). Yugoslavian children in a situation of rapid economic changes. *Journal of Economic Psychology, 11*, 529-543.

Zinser, O., Perry, S., & Edgar, R. (1975). Affluence of the recipient, value of donations, and sharing behaviour in preschool children. *The Journal of Psychology, 89*, 301-305.

3 Children's Understanding of the Concept of the State

Anna Emilia Berti
University of Padova

Although the literature on children's understanding and learning of history is not so rich as that on the natural sciences, physics, and mathematics, it has nevertheless produced interesting results (Beck & McKeown, this volume; Bombi & Ajello, 1988; von Borries, this volume, Calvani, 1988; Carretero et al., this volume; Jahoda, 1963; Jurd, 1978a; McKeown & Beck, 1990; Peel, 1967). In Italy, empirical studies are rather scanty, but theoretical research has been carried out on the peculiar characteristics of history and on the problems that arise in the teaching and learning of history. The procedures and concepts of this discipline as analyzed by historians and epistemologists suggest several sources of difficulties for learners. Of considerable importance among these is the historical lexicon (Calvani, 1986; Guarracino & Ragazzini, 1980, 1991; Lastrucci, 1989; see also Halldén, this volume).

History does not have a large specialized lexicon; historians make abundant use both of everyday language and of language taken from other disciplines, such as law, economics, politics, demography, anthropology, and sociology. From a teaching and learning point of view, this poses a series of problems in comparison to natural sciences or to nomothetic human sciences such as economics.

Unlike nomothetic science textbooks, in which key terms are introduced by explicit definitions and according to a logical order that reproduces the hierarchical organization of the conceptual framework of the discipline, history textbooks follow the chronological order of the events and processes. The sociological, economic, and political concepts used are taken for granted and not explicitly treated. Learners, especially the younger ones, therefore find many words whose meaning they do not know or know only partially (Lastrucci, 1989).

Some empirical studies bear witness to the learners' poor knowledge of the terms used in history textbooks and the misunderstandings that arise from them. For example, the meanings of *coup d'etat, reform, temporary government*, and *rising* were hardly known, at least in the 1950s, to French children between the ages of 10 and 16 (Gal, 1953); *king, commerce*, and *invasion* were incorrectly defined by 10-year-old British children (Coltham, 1960). An Italian study (Genovese, 1974) based on multiple-choice questionnaires on civic terms such as *reform, civil rights*, and *social class* revealed that high school pupils often interpreted a concept through an example or on the basis of their knowledge of the present time. In the first case, there was confusion between the part and the whole; in the second, the Italian reality was generalized. Relevant data also come from other fields: Studies on children's economic reasoning have highlighted striking differences between elementary school children's and adults' concepts (Berti & Bombi, 1988; Delval, this volume; Furnham, this volume; Furth, 1980; Jahoda, 1984); research on political concepts has shown that, before the age of 10–11, children do not understand the concept of political order (Connell, 1971; see also Moore, Lare, & Wagner, 1985).

The same terms, for example, *family, work, church, commerce, democracy, government, state, empire*, and *priest*, are applied to institutions and phenomena that exist in different forms in different places and times. This creates the risk of misunderstanding through anachronism and ethnocentrism (Jurd, 1978b). The attribution of current characteristics to past events and situations is quite a general phenomenon: American fifth graders think that bombing took place in the Revolutionary War (McKeown & Beck, 1990); Italian third graders describe everyday life in Egypt by talking about children who go to school and parents who go to work (Bombi & Ajello, 1988).

Sometimes anachronism is accompanied by the attribution of extra meaning, of evaluative components, to some social terms. During a class discussion of a historical document in which knights promised, among other things, not to attack unarmed monks and priests, Italian fourth graders did not understand how monks and priests could sometimes be armed. These children had never seen anything of the kind; furthermore, arms were associated with the idea of violence, which clashes with the notion that the clergy is pacifistic and good (Girardet, 1983). More generally, many terms used in history textbooks also carry some emotional and valuational traits with their meaning. In some cases, they are everyday language terms (e.g., *massacre*); in others, they refer to ideals as well as to institutions (*democracy, freedom*). In other cases, they come from a recent past that still gives rise to strong feelings (*fascism, imperialism, racism*, *dictatorship)*. This makes the task of distinguishing between moral judgment and historical explanation even more difficult for the students (von Borries, this volume; see also Guarracino & Ragazzini, 1991).

This chapter examines the difficulties originating from the extensive use of political terms in history textbooks. I assume that political concepts form a distinct knowledge domain within which conceptual change takes place, as has been found for other domains (see Carey, 1985; Keil, 1989; Vosniadou, 1991). Political scientists are not unanimous about the core concepts of such a domain (see Easton, 1971, Schmitt, 1932, for two diverging points of view, and Poggi, 1978, for an attempt to reconcile them). My working hypothesis is that the concept of *state*, meant as a large territory with a stable population and a government (Easton, 1971), is the kernel of a naive political theory, as the state plays a key role in both historical and in current political events.

With these premises, the focus of my research is on the concept of the state as presented in history textbooks and as understood by children 8 to 14 years old, that is, from the age in which the formal study of history starts in Italy to the age at which compulsory instruction ends. First, I examine how political terms are introduced in third-grade history textbooks; then I carry out two investigations on children's knowledge of such terms; in closing, I check their understanding of the processes through which states are formed and disrupted, in the context of history and of current and imaginary events. By comparing the data from these different studies, I attempt to trace the development of a political domain in children, to check if and how children's actual political knowledge fits that attributed to them by the authors of history textbooks, and to raise some questions about the teaching of history in elementary school.

POLITICAL CONCEPTS IN THIRD-GRADE HISTORY TEXTBOOKS

There is no available source of information on sales of textbooks in Italian elementary schools: The information is confidential and publishers do not release it. The textbooks for this research were therefore chosen on the basis of available information on the most frequently used textbooks in an Italian town (Padova). Six third-grade textbooks were chosen and their history sections examined[1]. The period usually treated in third grade begins with

---

[1]The books examined were the following: Scuola Nuova (Brescia: La Scuola), Parliamo di. . . (Milano: Nicola), Ambiente, Uomini Idee (Firenze: Giunti-Marzocco), Collaboriamo per costruire (Novara: De Agostini), and Uniti in Girotondo (Bergamo: Atlas). This survey was carried out in 1986.

prehistory and includes Mediterranean river civilizations followed by Italic ones. Most textbooks include the history of Rome, but some postpone it to the fourth-grade volume. A preliminary examination of the textbooks showed that the most used political terms were: *state* (or its particular forms such as *polis*, *kingdom*, or *empire*), *government/govern*, *war*, *law*, *democracy*, *colony*, and terms connected to special political appointments (e.g., *king*, *pharaoh*, *senator*) or functions (e.g., *to command the army*, *to administer justice*). I recorded how many times these terms, or their synonyms, were used, whether they were more or less explicitly defined, and the meaning that could be inferred from the context. Because explicit definitions were never found, the results of this analysis are presented by listing each term with the mean number and range of its appearances across the six textbooks (see Table 3.1) and by describing the context in which each term appeared.

The concept of state was usually referred to without any explicit definition or contextual information, as, for example, in the sentence "Menes was the first Pharaoh and the creator of the Egyptian state." The word *state* was often used in connection with the word *city* to explain what a polis is ("each city was independent as a small state: the Polis"). These cases are particularly interesting because they highlight the fact that textbook writers take for granted children's understanding of the word *state* so much that they use it to define another word. Only once did the word *state* appear in a paragraph in which all the components of a state were mentioned (a stable population and a defined territory with a permanent government): "Along the course of the Nile there were many small villages, each with its own chief and organization. In 3000 B.C. these villages united and the first large state in history was born. According to tradition, the first king of this state was Menes."

This passage shows how information on what a state is can be given by

TABLE 3.1
Mean Number and Range of Occurrences of Terms Referring to Particular
Political Topics in the 6 Textbooks Examined

Topic	M	Range
State	9.5	4–24
Formation of states	3.3	1–6
Alliances and trade relations between states	2.8	1–6
War	6.3	3–12
Government/Govern	9.8	3–21
Governors' functions	13.5	5–38
Government offices	15.3	3–31
Forms of government	4.8	1–7
Laws	4.8	1–9

describing the way in which the first states were formed. When this point was touched on, the textbooks introduced the term *to found* without further explanations, or mentioned a union between people or villages: "Ten tribes united and formed the kingdom of Israel"; "many small villages united and thus the largest state in history was formed (Rome)." This way of explaining the origins of a state allows some inferences: If a state is formed through the union of villages or groups of people, then it is made up of people and territories. There was, however, no mention of another fundamental component: a common government. Moreover, the words used (*unire, riunire*)[2] belong to everyday language and are known to children, but their meaning in this context — to unite politically — is different from the more usual uses. Another opportunity to supply information about states was given by the topic of relations between states (or city states), which was quite frequently treated in textbooks. The relation most frequently mentioned was war, as in, "Taranto and Rome went to war with each other to rule over the seas," and almost always involved Rome. Commercial exchanges and alliances were touched on less frequently. Both war and alliances were starting points to introduce the terms *dominion, control, conquest*, and *submission*. None of these words, however, was further explained, as in the following example: "It was no easy job to keep all those people of different races subdued, but the Romans succeeded by making an alliance."

Although the words *government* and *govern* were used without any clear definition of their meanings, as in, "the cities were governed by a small number of aristocrats," often mentioned were governors' functions (e.g., "look after public services," "command," "issue laws," "administer justice," "command the army"), government offices ("king," "pharaoh," "senator"), and forms of government ("democracy," "republic," "monarchy"). Government might then be understood as a set of functions and offices. The latter, however, were mentioned but not described; therefore, it is difficult to imagine how children could get the notion of government from them.

Also, knowledge of the word *law* was often taken for granted ("Babylonian king Hammurabi was the first to give his people some written laws"). Only in six cases were there some explanations, albeit partial, of what a law is: It was defined as a "rule of conduct" without further specification.

The term *democracy* appeared in all textbooks in the chapter on Greek civilization and was unanimously defined as a form of government based on two principles: All citizens are equal and political appointments are by

---

[2]The Italian words found in the text are *unire* and *riunire*; both mean "to join together into one" and correspond with the English verb *to unite*. *Riunire* also means "to reunite" and "to call a meeting."

election only. All the books expressed positive appreciation for democracy. Only two of them stated that whole groups of people (women, slaves, and metics) were excluded from the Athenian government.

The perusal of another 10 third-grade textbooks, randomly chosen among those available for sale, confirmed the results of this examination: Hardly ever are the political terms used in covering ancient history explicitly defined, and only seldom is it possible to infer or construe their meaning from the context in which they are used. In the very few cases in which explanations are given, they contain other unexplained political terms. The textbooks differ only quantitatively, regarding the more or less frequent occurrence of the terms, not the presence of definitions or, still less, their clarity and completeness.

THIRD GRADERS' UNDERSTANDING OF TEXTBOOKS' POLITICAL CONCEPTS

In order to determine how third graders interpret terms whose comprehension is taken for granted, 50 lower middle-class children from three different schools in two villages near Brescia (Northern Italy) were examined (mean age = 8 yr, 9 mon; boys = 20, girls = 30). The children had used the same textbook (*Uniti in Girotondo*). Their teachers stated that they had used no didactic material other than the textbook, and that the only topics studied had been the ones dealt with in the book. The children were interviewed in May, at the end of school term. By that time the topics of our investigation had already been studied: what a state is, how states are formed, what a government is, what *govern* means, the functions of governors, the concept of democracy, laws, and colonies.[3]

The State

The term *state* was never explained in the text. The interviews showed that children appeared not to possess this concept: To the question—"What is the state?"—the most frequent reply was "don't know" (54%), followed by the "state is a large territory" (28%) or "a group of people" (8%). For only 10% of the children, a state involved political bodies. The following are examples of the last two types of answer: "A state is a very large piece of

---

[3]In this and in the following studies, the interviews were carried out following Piaget's clinical procedure. Categories, constructed a posteriori on the basis of the similarities between the answers, were identified in a preliminary analysis of the protocols. The protocols were always classified by two independent judges (the present writer and a student) with agreement percentages ranging between 90% and 95%. Any disagreement was resolved by discussion.

land," or "A state is a place where the king governed . . . or one king or a few people."

State Formation

Although unable to define the word *state*, all children gave answers (correct and incorrect) to the question, "Tell me the names of some states you have studied this year at school," listing names of states of the past or of geographic areas not corresponding at that time to a single political organization, for example, Rome, Mesopotamia, and Greece. These answers show that even children unable to define the word *state* gave it some kind of meaning, perhaps that of a large territory. As they had been able to list the names of states, the children were further interviewed and asked to explain how these states had been formed. The textbook had touched on this point several times, when discussing the beginning of the kingdom of Egypt (that Menes unified "by force"), the Babylonian empire, the origins of Rome, and of Sumerian and Greek city states. In some cases, the terms *founding* and *forming* were used without any further explanation; in other cases war or the union of smaller organizations was mentioned. The information supplied by the textbook was appropriated by many children: 41% of them mentioned war or the union of villages. The others either answered "Don't know" (34%) or, construing states as mere geographic entities, said that God created them, or that they were formed through natural processes (10%); lastly, some children thought that the birth of a state coincided with the building of dwellings (15%).

Government and Govern

The terms *government* and *govern* were often used in the textbook; the former sometimes in the sense of "direction and management of power" and sometimes for indicating the body taking on the management of that power. There was never any clear definition of the terms, but their meaning could sometimes be inferred from the context. For example, after saying that Egypt was governed by the Pharaoh, the text specified the Pharaoh's functions, such as he was the supreme judge, commander-in-chief of the army, and high priest. It was further specified that the Pharaoh was "helped by officers." However, the various appointments or titles were not described further. For instance, what *supreme judge* means was not explained.

The children's answers to the questions on the meaning of governing highlighted two different conceptions. In both, the idea of governing was associated with that of command; in the first, expressed by 44% of the children, governing was command devoted to obtaining personal services for oneself and one's family. For example, *to govern* means "Like a king who commands." "Who does the king command?" "The helpers." "What does he tell them to do?" "They go round the city to get what he and his family need." In the second conception, expressed by the remaining 56% of the children, the government, although direct and personal, also had public functions, such as issuing of laws and heading the army. For example, *to govern* means "To govern a state." "That is?" "To be like a king; when he speaks, everybody must obey. . . . It means the same as belonging, that the state is yours." "Only this?" "No, it is for the laws, so that nobody steals and there are no injustices."

The Pharaoh's Tasks

As the textbook had mentioned the Pharaoh's main tasks ("supreme judge," "high priest," "army commander-in-chief"), the children were asked what the Pharaoh did. The three functions, if not mentioned, were explicitly supplied to the children, asking whether they remembered that the textbook had attributed them to the Pharaoh. None of the children spontaneously attributed these three tasks to him; when the interviewer introduced each specific task, about 60% of the children did not remember reading about them. Between 28% and 20% answered yes, the remainder (between 22% and 12%) denied that the Pharaoh carried out such functions. These answers show how difficult it is for children to imagine the exercise of power in terms of specific functions rather than as a generic command or as ordering servants about.

A detailed examination of these difficulties would require further investigation about children's conceptions of judges, priests, and military commanders. The data of the present study suggest that they arise from three main sources: (a) children do not know the meanings of the expressions used in the textbook; (b) children give meanings that refer to the present time and are incompatible with their ideas of a Pharaoh; and (c) children believe that the roles represented by these expressions are incompatible, either because they can be performed only one at a time ("The army is not under the command of the Pharaoh, but of the generals") or because they are associated with features not normally co-existing in the same person ("No, he could not be the army commander. . . . He was the high priest"; "He preached good not evil"; "He was against killing"), or, lastly, because children cannot construct a representation of a complex hierarchic organization. For example, of the Supreme Judge, one child said: "He put the bad ones on one side and the good ones on the other, but if he wanted, to he took a good one and put him among the bad ones or a bad one and put him among the good ones and administered the law."

Democracy

Democracy was mentioned only once, in connection with Athens. In a democracy, the textbook stated, the government is in the hands of the people and everybody is equal in the eyes of the law in private life. What this meant was not explained at all. When interviewed about democracy, only 7% of the children said that the citizens elected their representatives. The prevalent answer was "don't know" (64%), whereas 22% of the children gave either evaluational judgments, such as "Democratic government is fair laws, non-democratic government is not-so-fair-laws," or concrete examples, such as "Democracy is a round thing, where everybody goes to discuss things." "Why round?" "Because everybody is equal."

The Law

The term *law* often occurred in the textbook. Although there was no explicit definition and no coherent or unitary treatment of the concept, each time the term was used, some information was given. The first occurrence appeared in a chapter on prehistory: "In order to secure justice and respect for each other, the village inhabitants had established some laws." In the section on Roman history, particular laws were specified and several times the approving bodies were mentioned.

Only 18% of the children answered "don't know." All the other children defined laws as rules which must be respected. Some children emphasized the repressive and coercive aspects: Laws are "rules decided by kings" and they can be unjust as, for example, those requiring "poor people to pay taxes"; "to work and obey without complaining"; and "people who, as a joke, have cut somebody's leg off, will have their own leg cut off." Less often laws were described positively: "They are things done in consideration of others."

Colonies

The term *colony* appeared in the textbook for the first time in connection with the Phoenicians: "The Phoenicians went to every corner of the Mediterranean and founded several colonies, maritime ports and commercial centers. The most famous colonies are Cagliari, Palermo, Cadiz and Carthage." Later, colonies founded by Greeks and Romans were mentioned, always without any explicit explanation of the links between colony and metropoli.

Children's answers can be grouped into three main types. In the first type, they stated that they had never heard the word (34%); in the second, different kinds of confusion were shown (16%): Some children gave a definition of homophonous terms (in Italian the same word *colonia* means colony, cologne, and summer camp), by saying that a colony "was like perfumed water," or "a large summer park with children and teachers"; others gave wrong definitions originating from some elements found in the textbook, such as "A colony was a night shelter where all travellers rested." Lastly, in the third type of answer, children repeated some of the information in the textbook (50%), describing colonies as cities, ports, or commercial centers. The relations between colonies and their homelands were presented in spatial terms (colonies were "distant cities") or, more rarely, in commercial terms (14% of children), as the book had done.

THE INFLUENCE OF DIFFERENT TEXTBOOKS

A similar investigation was carried out with third-grade children (average age of 8.8) who had studied other textbooks in order to investigate how widespread the earlier types of answers were and to examine the effects of using different textbooks. Two textbooks were chosen: the one with the highest (text A) and the one with the lowest (text B) number of political terms of all textbooks previously examined. Two groups of children, each composed of two classes having already studied these textbooks, were compared. Each group was made up of 24 children (approximately the same number of males and females) from the lower middle class, living in Adria, a small town in Northern Italy.

The data confirmed the previous results. The data also showed how children's answers were affected by the textbook used. When asked what a state is, some children said "don't know," some defined it as a large territory, and only two mentioned a government. The "don't know" answer was given by 33% of group A children, who found the word *state* in their book 22 times, compared to 75% of group B, whose book used the word only 3 times. The difference between the two groups is significant ($\chi^2 = 6.9$, $df = 1$, $p < .01$) and suggests that when children frequently come across a word, they are stimulated to give it a meaning but succeed only partially if not supplied with adequate information. Children's conceptions also differed considerably on governing, again according to the differences in the two books. Book A mentioned more often both "government/governing" (21 times vs. 6 in book B) and governors' tasks (32 times vs. 3). Correspondingly, the percentage of children mentioning some government tasks, such as commanding the army or issuing laws, was 62% in group A and 16% in group B. The remaining children stated that people who govern give orders to their personal advantage ($\chi^2 = 10.5$, $df = 1$, $p < .01$). No significant differences were found in the answers about how states begin;

however, this topic was rarely touched on in either textbook (7 times in text A, 3 times in text B).

War

In this investigation, children were also interviewed on a topic not included in the previous study: why the wars mentioned in their textbooks occurred and what were consequences suffered by the losers of the war. War was mentioned 17 times in book A and 4 times in book B; both textbooks described its causes and effects in terms of dominion and conquest (of seas, territories, peoples), but did not give further details ("The Romans won the war and conquered Sicily"). How children interpreted such expressions can be inferred from their answers. A first category comprised "don't know" and answers likening war to a quarrel caused by revenge, hate, or disagreement and bringing about the punishment of the enemy, without any gain for the winners. In the second category, underlying wars was the wish to conquer, understood as possession of a territory taken away from its inhabitants, who were either killed or made slaves. In the third category dominion was construed in political terms, consisting of the subordination of losers to conquerors' laws and authority.

Out of the total number of children, 25% gave answers of the first category, 62% of the second, and 12% of the third. There was a significant difference between the two groups: Children using book A, in which *conquest* and *dominion* occurred more often, gave answers of the second and third categories more frequently (92% vs. 58%; $\chi^2 = 7$, $df = 1$, $p < .01$).

The results of these two studies show that the political concepts taken for granted by textbook authors are not known to third graders after completing the history course at the end of the school year. Children's answers highlighted several types of gaps in knowledge as well as some confusion. Only the territorial component of the concept of state was understood, whereas government was not taken into account; public and private powers were not differentiated, and both types of power consisted of giving orders personally, although some government tasks were mentioned, such as commanding the army and issuing laws; the dominion following a war was represented only as an expropriation of territories, not as the subordination of the losers to the laws and political authority of the winners.

All this suggests that, at third grade, children do not yet possess the concept of state, understood as a territory with a stable population and a governing apparatus. What prevents children from constructing the concept of state by linking the scattered pieces of knowledge they do have? A tentative hypothesis is that they lack one notion necessary to construct such a link, that is, the notion of dominion from a distance, through intermediaries. Whereas personal and direct power can be exerted over a few individuals such as servants, or over people envisaged as living close together, a hierarchical organization is necessary when groups living at a distance from one another are to be governed. If that is so, children should also misunderstand the processes by which larger political organizations, such as states, are built and a growing number of people are brought under the power of one authority, which their textbooks label as *unite*. To check this point, two separate studies were carried out, using two different procedures. In both cases the word *state* was substituted by a more familiar one, assumed to imply the same components, *kingdom*. In one study, the children were presented with a passage similar to those found in history textbooks, describing the foundation of the kingdom of Egypt as due to the union of the Nile villages by Menes. In the second study a hypothetical situation was presented, and children were interviewed on the possibility that several small kingdoms might unite to form a single larger kingdom.

THE CENTRALIZATION OF POLITICAL POWER: HOW THE EGYPTIAN KINGDOM WAS FOUNDED

Ninety lower middle-class children from a small town (about 10,000 inhabitants) in the province of Venice were interviewed: 23 second graders (mean age = 7.9), 20 third graders (mean age = 8.8), 21 fifth graders (mean age = 10.5) and 26 eighth graders (mean age = 13.4). Each grade was made up approximately of the same number of males and females. The interviews were carried out in May and June. Children were presented with a short text, a simplified version of a passage from a third grade history textbook: "Many years ago, the Egyptians, scattered in many villages, lived along the banks of the river Nile. Every year the river burst its banks and flooded the fields and villages. The Egyptians decided to build dams and canals to collect the river water. These works were carried out over a very large territory and many inhabitants were employed in their completion. The person who succeeded in organizing such works was Menes. He united all the Egyptian villages into a large kingdom."[4] Once the reading was over, the children were asked (a) what the sentence "Menes united the Egyptian villages into a large kingdom" meant; (b) how Menes had managed to unite the Egyptian villages into a kingdom; and (c) what, if anything, had changed in Menes's and the inhabitants' lives following the union of the villages.

At the first question, a minority (19%) of the children either answered

---

[4]The Italian verb used was *riunire* (see footnote 3), which several children interpreted as "to call a meeting."

"don't know," or stated only that Menes built a kingdom, or gave nonpertinent answers, referring back to other parts of the passage: "He gathered many men together to build a river and they called this river the Nile," or "Menes built all the dams to stop the villages from being flooded and the Egyptians thanked him." These children were equally distributed among all the age groups. Another group of children (13%, mostly from second grade) said that Menes called a meeting, misunderstanding the meaning of the word *riunire* (unite): "Menes called all the inhabitants to him, Menes said some things and then they all went back to their homes." The great majority of children (68%) mentioned instead that a union was taking place; among them, 10 eighth graders and 1 fifth grader explicitly described such a union in political terms, that is, as the imposition of the same laws and political authority on all inhabitants, using words very different from those of the text: "He formed a confederation of states"; "He imposed his dominion"; "He grouped all the inhabitants of this state under a single government." The other children said that Menes united the villages, mentioning or not mentioning the resulting kingdom: "It means: Menes grouped the Egyptian villages into a . . . large place, all the Egyptian villages into a large place"; "All the villages where the Nile overflowed were united, but there were no barriers between the villages, they were all in a single kingdom, a very large single territory." This type of answer, given by 57% of the children, is an almost literal reproduction of the text and appears to be correct. Had they been given in a class test, the teacher could have assumed that the children had understood the lesson. The analysis of the answers to the question "How did Menes manage to unite all the Egyptian villages into a large kingdom?" showed that this was not so.

Three categories were identified. In categories 1 and 2 union was represented in spatial terms, achieved respectively by moving physically the inhabitants or by creating links between the villages. In category 3 the establishment of a political organization was described. The categories were labeled as the following:

1. *Moving of inhabitants:* This category includes all the answers describing the moving of the inhabitants to a single place. Some younger children thought that the move implied pulling down the old houses and building them again in a different place: "He destroyed the villages and took all the material to his kingdom and built a big kingdom using it." Most children, however, said that the people moved to Menes's village or to a place chosen by him; some of them expressed the idea that the move was necessary to avoid the floods or to work together to build dams.

2. *The villages are linked to one another:* This is done through roads, houses, bridges, walls, dams, or by means of houses built between the villages, without the inhabitants moving: "They were scattered, then he put

other houses in between and so it became one village"; or "He built walls all around, so that the existing villages remained within Menes' kingdom."

3. *Political union:* Menes gave the villages a common organization through laws and subordinate authorities (village chiefs, viceroys). According to some children, he encouraged the use of the same customs, language, and religion: "By being a good king, by keeping taxes low, by not reducing the people to poverty; by not sending people to prison . . . by means of fair laws."

Table 3.2 shows how the answers are distributed in these categories. Categories 1 and 2, involving a union in spatial terms, has 62 out of 90 answers, supplied especially by second and third graders. As age increased, however, union was understood in political terms.

The high frequency of Category 1 answers, and their use also by fifth graders, may be due to the particular characteristics of the passage. Analyzing the protocols, we noticed that some children explicitly or implicitly justified moving the villages and/or their inhabitants because they had to escape from floods or because they had to work together. Although the text had never stated such a thing, the description of the Nile and its floods encouraged this kind of inference. We therefore ran a check and found that 22 children (24%) had supplied this type of answer. They were equally distributed over the three school grades (χ^2 not significant). The percentage was quite high, and other children may have had the same idea although they did not express it explicitly.

Analysis of the subsequent questions, especially, "Did anything change in Menes's life?" or "Did anything change in the inhabitants' lives?" attempted to identify some points that involved understanding social and political aspects of union and to check on how many children had mentioned them. The results are shown in Table 3.3.

Second graders mentioned very few points, which suggests that they understood union only as a meeting or an actual movement of the villages

TABLE 3.2
Different Answers to the Question:
"How Did Menes Manage to Unite the Villages?"
(Percentage at each grade level)

	Grades			
Categories (Levels)	2nd	3rd	5th	8th
1. Moving of inhabitants	83	70	43	27
2. The villages are linked to one another	17	15	24	3
3. Political union	0	15	33	69
Total	23	20	21	26

TABLE 3.3
Frequencies in Relation to the Consequences Mentioned
of the Union of Nile Villages

Consequent Mentioned	Grade				Total
	2nd	3rd	5th	8th	
	(N=23)	(N=20)	(N=21)	(N=26)	
Friendship/collaboration	4	12	16	6	38*
Menes gives orders/is in power/is the chief	2	9	14	16	41**
Servants/slaves	1	8	1	4	14***
Laws	0	8	3	17	28****
Working for Menes	3	3	5	0	11
Menes governs	0	0	1	5	6
Taxes	0	0	1	3	4
Religion	0	2	0	4	6
Trade	0	6	2	0	8

$*\chi^2 = 22, df = 3, p < .001$
$**\chi^2 = 19, df = 3, p < .001$
$***\chi^2 = 13, df = 3, p < .01$
$****\chi^2 = 28, df = 3, p < .001$

and their inhabitants. Instead, many third graders and most fifth graders touched on friendships and collaboration among the inhabitants, as well as laws and/or a chief. For these children, the union of the villages, although described in physical terms, also involved social and political relations. Eighth graders who, from the beginning of the interview, had construed union in political terms, very often mentioned laws, and a minority of them also mentioned state, government, and taxes.

In addition, protocol analysis showed some anachronisms, that is, mention of buildings and institutions that did not exist at the time considered in the passage. This kind of answer generally occurred when children were asked whether, in order to unite the villages into a kingdom, it was sufficient to do what they had already said (generally, as seen earlier, moving the villages) or if something else had to be done. Two types of anachronism were found: the "king's castle," mentioned only by second graders ($N = 9$), and elements typical of our modern world such as skyscrapers, motorways, factories, and churches, touched on by 4 second graders and 4 third graders. The fact that only second graders mentioned castles might be due to children's lack of any historical notion and their consequent association of the word *kingdom* to fairytales. Third graders, who had been studying history for several months, were not prey to this confusion, although they kept introducing elements of contemporary life.

To conclude, the present study shows that most elementary school children decode the expression "to unite the villages into one kingdom" as mainly indicating the construction of spatial links. This meaning is predominant among second graders, interviewed at the end of the school year, a few months before beginning the third grade, with the study of history in textbooks taking for granted their knowledge of political notions. For several third and most fifth graders, spatial links combine with the development of symmetrical (friendship, collaboration) and asymmetrical (authority, power) social relationships among the inhabitants and between them and Menes. Spatial proximity, however, appears to be an essential condition.

The passage used in this study may have encouraged the spatial interpretation of the term *unite*, as about one-quarter of the children stated that people had to get together in a safe place away from the floods. This finding shows how history passages can cause unforeseen inferences not intended by the authors and suggests that precautions must be taken while treating Egyptian history so that children do not form misconceptions. However interesting from an educational point of view, this finding casts some doubt on the validity and generality of the main result of the study, that is, that children understand the expression "unite into a kingdom" in spatial terms. To verify this fact and to study the representation of union within a different context (small kingdoms instead of villages), a second investigation was carried out.

The Union of Four Small Kingdoms Into One Larger Kingdom

Sixty children (33 boys and 27 girls) took part in this research: 20 third graders (mean age = 8.11), 20 fifth graders (mean age = 10.7), and 20 eighth graders (mean age = 13.7). The children lived in central Florence and their parents were teachers and professional people. Each child was individually shown a map depicting a large island and a section of continent where four kingdoms were represented by means of small circles; three kingdoms were on the island, at various distances from each other, and one on the land, separated from the others by the sea. The interviewer said that the drawing represented a large territory where many many years ago there were some small kingdoms. She said further: "One day the king of this little kingdom thought that he would like to unite his kingdom to this one. Do you think he could do that?" The nearest kingdom was first pointed to, and then the more distant ones, one at a time. How the union could be achieved or the reasons why it could not were examined with additional questions.

Children's answers were classified into three categories. Category 1 described the creation of a single spatial entity, by moving the inhabitants to one place or building links. When the distance between two kingdoms was too great, or the sea was in between, union was impossible or could only be achieved by moving the people from one kingdom to the other, or to another specially built one. In Category 2, in addition to the construction of spatial links, a single ruling power appeared (either one king or, in a few cases, more than one king governing together), without the mediation of subordinate political authorities. Lastly, Category 3 described a power hierarchy, established through the collaboration of the previous kings, the subordination of one or more of them to another, or the nomination of subordinate authorities by the king promoting the union. The latter two cases occurred when the union was considered as the result of a war; the former when the children believed that the union could be achieved peacefully.

The results of this study, summarized in Table 3.4, agree with those on Nile villages and confirm that the words *unire* and *riunire* (to unite), when occurring in passages on political union, are interpreted by many children in spatial terms. At first, when children do not yet have any idea of political organization, this interpretation simply reflects the meaning these words, and their derivatives, have in everyday language. In the present study, this is the case for second and third graders who did not mention any social or political relations concurrent or subsequent to spatial union. *To unite* is still understood in physical terms also when political concepts first appear, as this interpretation fits well with children's early view of political organization. As has been shown in these and the previous studies, third graders imagine a direct and face-to-face relationship between those who govern and those who are governed, both when the former are viewed as landlords and the latter as servants, and when the person who governs has public functions: as army commander he or she personally leads the soldiers, as supreme judge he or she separates the good from the bad and metes out punishment. This kind of power can be exercised only when there is physical proximity between those in power and those governed.

This may be the reason why children continued to describe the union of the kingdoms and villages in terms of spatial moves or links, even when they understood that union meant that Menes became the head of all the villages and that the four kingdoms had one and the same king. Only when children can conceive political order with some authorities at the top and others

TABLE 3.4
Frequencies Obtained to the Question:
"How Could the Four Kingdoms Be United?"

Categories (Levels)	Grade			
	3rd	5th	8th	Total
1. Creation of single spatial entity	10	4	1	15
2. Spatial links plus single ruling power	9	5	2	16
3. Power hierarchy	1	11	17	29
Total	20	20	20	60

subordinate to them are spatial links no longer necessary: Rather than moving a kingdom or a village, it is enough to send some governors. The interpretation of union in spatial terms seems to be affected by context: In the case of Menes, it is made by a larger number of children.

How widespread is this misconception? Is it formed only when children read passages similar to those used in these two studies, in which they are encouraged to think about their content by a series of questions, or is it also formed when children hear about current affairs through the media, their parents, and their teachers? In recent years, some unification processes have taken place: the unification of Germany, the annexation of Kuwait to Iraq, and the union of Europe, which is still in progress. The first two have been so extensively talked about in the mass media that even children must have heard about them; the third is devoid of visible and upsetting manifestations, but certainly personally involves the children as future European citizens. We decided to interview children on these topics to see if we would find answers similar to those given in the artificial situations of the two studies just described.

CURRENT POLITICAL EVENTS AND THE UNION OF STATES

Sixty lower middle-class children, living in a small town in the province of Treviso (Northern Italy), took part in this research: 20 third graders (mean age = 8.9), 20 fifth graders (mean age = 10.8), and 20 eighth graders (mean age = 13.7). The interviews were carried out from the beginning of April through the end of May 1991.

The interview was in three parts, one for each topic: Germany, Iraq-Kuwait invasion, and European union. The presentation order was balanced. The interviewer started by saying that in recent times very important events had taken place, and then asked the children whether they heard what had happened in Germany, about the war in Iraq, or about European union. If the children had not heard about the unification of Germany, they were asked if they knew anything about the Berlin Wall and, if they had, they were asked what had happened to it, why, and what the consequences had been. As for Iraq, the interviewer checked whether the children had heard about the war, who the parties involved were, why it had started, and if they knew that Iraq had annexed Kuwait. As for Europe, what the children understood by this term was first ascertained and then if they had heard about the union.

When the children talked about the unification of Germany, European union, or the annexation of Kuwait to Iraq, the interviewer continued to find out in what terms they imagined each process. They were first asked what changes it implied for the people involved and were then presented with a list of points: money, capital city, language, religion, laws, kinds of jobs done by people, way of dressing, flag, army, and government. For each of these they were asked whether anything had changed following the union (or annexation), how and why.

The Unification of Germany

With only one exception, third graders either did not know anything about what had happened in Germany ($N = 11$), or only stated that they had heard about the fall of a wall, of which they knew neither the functions nor the consequences ($N = 8$). Starting from the fifth grade, however, everybody knew about the two Germanies uniting. The difference between ages is significant ($\chi^2 = 55$, $df = 2$, $p < .001$). In talking about what has happened in Germany, all the fifth graders and 60% of the eighth graders began by describing the leveling of the wall and continued by explaining that this has led to the unification of the two Germanies. The remaining eighth graders explicitly talked about the unification of Germany from the first question, not mentioning the fall of the Wall, or talking about it without giving it an essential role.

The question "How did they unite?" was given only to the 41 children who had mentioned unification. The question received 8 "don't' knows" and 2 other kinds of answers; in the first, union appeared to be a direct consequence of the fall of the Wall ($N = 9$); in the second, it required a series of political changes ($N = 24$). This second kind of answer was given by 10 fifth graders and 14 eighth graders (χ^2 not significant). The political processes were described with different degrees of accuracy, from generic meetings to changes in institutions: "First of all, on the political level it was necessary to have only one capital city, as there were two before, then transform the currency into a single one, the languages into a single language, and then other things . . . only one religion."

To the question on the changes following unification, only half the fifth and eighth graders answered by describing a political change. However, the percentage of children recognizing some changes among those listed by the interviewer was much greater, ranging from a minimum of 62% (army) to a maximum of 87% (law). The fact that several children recognized more changes than they could think of shows that their knowledge of political union (and therefore of the characteristic institutions of a modern state) still lacks accessibility. Some children were convinced that some institutions were already shared even before unification. This misapprehension, which was expressed by 20% of the children about currency and flag, and by 7.5% about capital city, appears to be due to the fact that the two states had the same name.

The Annexation of Kuwait by Iraq

This part of the interview aimed at checking whether the children had understood the invasion and annexation of Kuwait to Iraq, beyond the fact that there had been a war. Bearing this in mind, answers to questions on what happened in Kuwait were categorized into five types and ordered into a level sequence, as follows:

1. *The events are misunderstood.* The occupation of Kuwait was not known: Children knew that a war occurred recently, but misunderstood its actors or causes, believing, for example, that Saddam Hussein went to war with Italy or that Bush attacked him to take away his oil.
2. *Saddam attacked Kuwait for its oil or territory.* No annexation was mentioned. Children believed the war was caused by the wish to take over Kuwait territory or oil; of the situation in Kuwait, they could see only the changes directly caused by the military occupation: destruction, deaths, people running away.
3. *The annexation of Kuwait was attempted but failed.* Children said that there had been an attempt to take over Kuwait but that it never succeeded, and therefore there were never any political changes in the listed point (capital city, government, etc.).
4. *There was a temporary annexation of Kuwait to Iraq, involving some political changes.* Children stated that Kuwait was under Iraq's domination for a certain period of time and that this caused changes in some of the listed points (capital city, government, etc.).
5. *The annexation of Kuwait has caused several political changes.* The children stated that Kuwait was occupied by Iraq and that, during the occupation, it was under Iraq's laws, government, and so on.

TABLE 3.5
Frequencies Obtained to the Question:
"What Happened in Kuwait?"

Categories (Levels)	Grade			
	3rd	*5th*	*8th*	*Total*
1. Events are misunderstood	5	4	5	14
2. Kuwait attacked for its oil or territory	12	5	4	21
3. Annexation attempted but failed	0	4	4	8
4. Temporary annexation with a few political changes	2	5	6	13
5. Temporary annexation with more political changes	1	2	1	4
Total	20	20	20	20

As Table 3.5 shows, here again most third graders misinterpreted what had happened or could only see the material causes and consequences of the war. Only three of them described an attempt to conquer associated with political changes. Instead, at the fifth and eighth grades, about half the children mentioned a conquest, either attempted or short-lived, and the ensuing political changes.

European Union

The answers on the European union were divided into four levels. In the first children did not know what Europe is: When asked to explain what it is, they either answered "Don't know" or described it as a state, a nation, or even a town. In the three following levels, they defined Europe as a set of states. In the second level, they had never heard about a European union. In the third, they described the European union as the formation of a single state, requiring various political changes, including the change of language and flag for the nations concerned. Lastly, as shown in Table 3.6, children described the European union as an integration (commercial, monetary and linguistic) among states that still exists as separate entities. Again, the age differences were significant ($\chi^2 = 31.8$, $df = 4$, $p < .001$, levels 2 and 3 grouped together).

Comparing data about Germany, Kuwait, and Europe, it is clear that knowledge of union processes varies according to the topic. A sign test ($p < .001$) revealed that it is greater in the case of Germany, in which the unification was mentioned by all the children from the fifth grade up.

The data from this study show both similarities to and differences from those on the union of the four kingdoms and of the Nile villages. In both cases, third graders did not understand the concept of political union. However, whereas in the previous studies they could imagine the union, albeit in spatial terms, or in the social terms of friendship and collaboration, in the present research they did not mention union at all. What third graders said about Germany was only the fall of a wall and, in the case of

TABLE 3.6
Frequencies Obtained to the Question:
"What does European Union Mean?"

Categories (Levels)	Grade			
	3rd	5th	8th	Total
1. Incorrect definition of Europe	14	4	0	18
2. European Union Unknown	6	10	7	23
3. Formation of a single state	0	4	4	8
4. Integration among state requiring many changes	0	2	9	11
Total	20	20	20	60

the Iraq-Kuwait conflict, that there had been a war. Lacking a naive political theory accounting for these events, children seemed to select, from the information provided through mass media and adults' talk, only what best fit their conceptual structures, confining themselves to the more concrete aspects. When their attention was drawn to the term *unite* and they were asked to explain it, they supplied interpretations in spatial terms.

The interviews were about three union processes greatly differing in media coverage and emotional charge, which was reflected in children's answers. But even the case of Germany, for months the focus of television and newspaper reports, did not leave any trace in the third graders' answers. It was from the fifth through eighth graders that children talked, albeit in broad outline, of unification, thus showing that they had the concept of centralized political organization and were able to apply it when required. This concept was not detailed and fully articulated, as shown by the approximate descriptions of how union was achieved and what the ensuing changes were; the central aspects—single government, law, capital city, currency, and flag—were nevertheless widely recognized.

In view of the frequency of state disruptions in history, and of their current topicality, a research project similar to those on union was carried out on political separation, examining this concept in an imaginary context and in the real context of the Yugoslavian war.

SECESSION IN A REAL (YUGOSLAVIA) AND IN AN IMAGINARY CONTEXT

The interviews were carried out in March 1992. Students who took part in the research included 120 lower middle-class children from three different grade levels (third grade, average age = 8.5; fifth grade, average age = 10.5; and eighth grade, average age = 13.7), from a town near Ravenna (Central Italy). Forty children from each grade level with an equal number of boys and girls were used in this study.

In each grade, the children were randomly assigned to two groups, with an equal number of boys and girls in each. One group was interviewed about an imaginary situation: They were shown the map of a kingdom and told that the inhabitants of a part of it wanted "to separate from the large kingdom and make a small kingdom by themselves." The other group was interviewed on a real situation: the war between Croatia and Serbia, which was taking place at that time. The children were asked if they knew about Yugoslavia and what was happening there. If the children did not know about the war or its principal cause, they were shown a map of Yugoslavia and told that the lines inside it represented its regions. One of these regions now wanted to separate to form "a republic of its own."[5] Both groups of children were asked to say whether the separation was possible or not, what the people had to do, and what changes this secession would affect the population. When the children suggested a way of separating, they were asked twice, "Is that enough, or do the people have to do anything else?"

In the imaginary situation (separation of a part of a kingdom), three categories of answers were found, as shown in Table 3.7:

TABLE 3.7
Frequencies Obtained to the Question:
"How Do You Separate from a Large Kingdom to Form a Small One?"

| | Grade | | | |
Categories (Levels)	3rd	5th	8th	Total
1. Physical separation	13	6	1	20
2. Physical separation and political aspects mentioned	6	7	8	21
3. Political separation	1	7	11	19
Total	20	0	20	60

1. *Physical separation.* Children understood separation only in physical terms. Some denied that it was possible, because "the land cannot be taken away." Others stated that the people who wanted to separate have to go somewhere else; yet others (this was the most frequent case) maintained that people have to build barriers, or dig ditches, explaining that these serve "to separate" or "to divide." No other kind of political change, concurrent or subsequent to the separation, was mentioned.

2. *Physical separation and mention of political aspects.* Children stated that separation was achieved by means of barriers and ditches, but when describing the changes in the inhabitants' lives, they also mentioned political aspects, such as new laws or governors.

3. *Political separation.* Children said that the separation was achieved by the appointment of an independent government and the issuing of new laws. This also involved the rest of the population and the authorities, thus requiring their assent, which could be obtained peacefully or through a war. When boundaries were mentioned, their function was to prevent the populations from entering and leaving and was just one of the aspects involved in the separation.

Children's answers on the separation mirror those on the union of small kingdoms (see Table 3.4); the kinds of answers were the same, and the

[5]The term *region* rather than *state* was used, bearing in mind that the notion of federal state was probably alien to most of the children, and that hearing about a state made up of other states might cause confusion.

frequency with which they occurred in the different grades did not differ. Chi-square comparisons, carried out for each grade, were never significant. At third grade, both union and separation were construed mainly in physical terms; at fifth grade, they were construed partly in physical and partly in political terms; and at eighth grade, both union and separation were understood as political.

Regarding Yugoslavia, with the exception of three third graders, all the children interviewed had heard of it. No third grader used the word *state*, defining Yugoslavia as a "region," "country," "city," or, less often "nation." The word *state* was used by 55% of the fifth graders and 30% of the eighth graders, whereas 10% of the fifth graders and 70% of the eighth graders properly used the expressions "federal republic" or "federation of states" ($\chi^2 = 5$, $df = 4$, $p < .001$). All the children who had heard about Yugoslavia were also aware that a war was going on. All third graders said they did not know the reasons, whereas 25% of fifth graders and 80% of eighth graders said the war was due to a wish for independence by one of Yugoslavia's states ($\chi^2 = 29$, $df = 2$, $p < .001$). In the description of how the separation could take place, no child mentioned physical separation together with political aspects (Category 2). All the third graders (except 5 children who refused to talk about separation, judging it as unjust) understood separation in physical terms. All the fifth and eighth graders construed it as a political process ($\chi^2 = 49$, $df = 2$, $p < .001$). Therefore, in the case of Yugoslavia, the fifth and eighth graders gave more correct answers than the children interviewed on the kingdom separation. For eighth graders, this can be explained by the considerable knowledge of the Yugoslavian situation shown by most children, but this cannot apply to fifth graders, who knew very little. A possible interpretation is that reference to current events encourages more correct answers by facilitating access to political knowledge. The term *kingdom* may keep a fairytale aura, leading children to give answers reflecting conceptions they have already overcome.

CONCLUSIONS

The series of studies presented in this chapter originated with an examination of the political terms used in third-grade history textbooks, which showed that such terms were neither explicitly defined nor put into contexts from which their meaning could be inferred. Italian textbook authors seem to take for granted that third graders already have a naive political theory that enables them to comprehend and relate terms such as *state, democracy, law,* and *dominion,* and to understand a series of public offices and functions. The same thing has been found in geography and social studies books in other countries (Beck, McKeown, & Gromoll, 1989; Milburn,

1972, reported in Jurd, 1978b). The interviews carried out at the end of third grade, in which children had studied such textbooks for 8 months, highlighted that the meaning of these terms is usually unknown or misunderstood. In some cases, children do grasp one aspect of the meaning, for example, that a state is a large territory. Put in these terms, this concept of state appears to be an incomplete piece of knowledge rather than a misconception. But real misconceptions also occur when *state* is seen in relation to other concepts: The onset of states is made to coincide with the natural processes that gave rise to continents, or with the union of cities and villages, achieved by means of spatial links. Conversely, disruption consists of building barriers.

Third-grade children appear to be able to represent a very simple social organization, composed of a group of people living together, with their houses close to one another, as in a village or a town, having friendly mutual relations, and being under the authority of a chief. The chief personally gives order to his subjects, often for his own benefit, issues laws, and commands the army during wars caused by revenge or the wish to conquer, that is, to possess other territories. This conception is far ahead of that found in second graders, who did not mention any social relation while talking about union of the Nile villages. However, third graders did not show any understanding of current political events, nor of hierarchical organization. What they appear to possess is therefore the idea of a chief rather than that of a government or a distinct political domain. Whether to label this conception as *political* or not is a matter of choice.

At fifth grade, the kernel of a political theory, although naive and incomplete, appears to be clearly present. Most of the children interviewed spontaneously used the word *state* when talking about Yugoslavia, correctly defined Europe as a set of states, conceived a power hierarchy comprising subordinate authorities and officers, and decoded *unite* and *separate* into political terms, describing the foundation of a centralized government and an independent local one, respectively. However, fifth graders' political knowledge is not yet well organized or easily accessible; depending on the context to which the questions referred, children gave different replies, occasionally reverting to backward answers of the kind found in younger children. At the eighth grade, naive political theory appears to be rather detailed and easily accessible; children can use it in a wider range of contexts in order to interpret both historical and political events. In our studies, eighth graders knew more than fifth graders about the war in Yugoslavia and on European union.

According to these data, the major shift in children's political conceptions, within the age range examined here, appears to occur between the third and fifth grades; it corresponds to the shift found by Connell (1971) between the "task pool" stage, when children form the notion of "political role" by combining the ideas of command and an important person, and the stage of "political order," when political roles are differentiated and hierarchically ordered. From the descriptive data presented here, it is not possible to establish how this shift occurs and what the primary cause is, whether it be school teaching or cognitive changes such as the completion of concrete operational thinking as in Connell's hypothesis. Political notions are certainly poorly taught in schools, as shown by the studies of textbooks. On the other hand, the study on the union of Nile villages revealed remarkable differences between second and third graders, which would be difficult to ascribe only to age.

There is a great discrepancy between third graders' notions taken for granted by textbook authors and those that children actually possess, which can lead to serious misunderstandings. It is obvious that textbooks must be suited to learners' knowledge and abilities, but it is less obvious how this can be done in this case: Is it better to present third graders with political concepts before or during the teaching of history, or to present them only with some aspects of past everyday life and material culture, postponing political themes to the following grades (see Calvani, 1986; Girardet, 1983)? This question cannot be answered by descriptive studies such as those presented in this chapter. More exploratory research, aimed at giving a detailed picture of children's political conceptions, is needed before we can go on to training studies.

ACKNOWLEDGMENTS

The investigations presented in this chapter were carried out with the help of several students, who collected all the data and in some cases also helped to prepare the interview schemata and to identify and define the answer categories. The first two series of data were collected by Leone Pavesi and Biancarosa Bassan; the interviews on the union of the Egyptian villages were conducted by Angela Barizza, and those on the union of the small kingdoms by Elisabetta Bonalumi. Data on state disruption were collected by Donatella Mongardi and those on union in the context of current political events by Mariacristina Calogero. The whole project was funded by the Italian CNR.

REFERENCES

Beck, I. L., McKeown, M. G., & Gromoll, E. (1989). Learning from social study text. *Cognition and Instruction, 6,* 99–158.

Berti, A. E., & Bombi, A. S. (1988). *The child's construction of economics.* Cambridge, England: Cambridge University Press.

Bombi, A. S., & Ajello, A. M. (1988). La rappresentazione della storia nei bambini [Children's representation of history]. *Orientamenti Pedagogici, 35,* 17–27.

Calvani, A. (1986). *L'insegnamento della storia nella scuola elementare* [How to teach history in elementary school]. Firenze: La Nuova Italia.

Calvani, A. (1988). *Il bambino, il tempo, la storia* [The child, time, and history]. Firenze: La Nuova Italia.

Carey, S. (1985). *Conceptual change in childhood.* Cambridge, MA: MIT Press.

Coltham, J. B. (1960). *Junior school children's understanding of some terms commonly used in teaching of history.* Unpublished doctoral thesis, University of Manchester.

Connell, R. W. (1971). *The child's construction of politics.* Carlton, Australia: Melbourne University Press.

Easton, D. (1971). *The political system. An inquiry into the state of political science.* New York: Knopf.

Furth, H. (1980). *The world of grown-ups.* New York: Elsevier.

Gal, R. (1953). Quelques recherches et expérience pédagogiques concernantes l'enseignement de l'histoire [Some studies and educational experiences about the teaching of history]. *Pour l' ère Nouvelle, 14,* 22–31.

Genovese, L. (1974). Comprensione di termini e concetti storici [Understanding of historical words and concepts]. *Scuola e Città, 24,* 106–107.

Girardet, H. (1983). Un curricolo di storia come costruzione di reti concettuali [A history curriculum for constructing conceptual networks]. In C. Pontecorvo (Ed.), *Storia e processi di conoscenza* (pp. 269–312). Torino, Loescher.

Guarracino, S., & Ragazzini, D. (1980). *Storia e insegnamento della storia* [History and the teaching of history]. Milano: Feltrinelli.

Guarracino, S., & Ragazzini, D. (1991). *L'insegnamento della storia* [How to teach history]. Firenze: La Nuova Italia.

Jahoda, G. (1963). Children's concepts of time and history. *Educational Review, 15,* 87–104.

Jahoda, G. (1984). The development of thinking about socio-economic systems. In H. Tajfel (Ed.), *The social dimension* (pp. 69–88). Cambridge, England: Cambridge University Press.

Jurd, M. F. (1978a). An empirical study of operational thinking in history-type material. In J. A. Keats, K. F. Collins, & G. S. Halford (Eds.), *Cognitive development. Research based on a neo-Piagetian approach* (pp. 315–318). New York: Wiley.

Jurd, M. F. (1978b). Concrete and formal operational thinking in history. In J. A. Keats, K. F. Collins, & G. S. Halford (Eds.), *Cognitive development. Research based on a neo-Piagetian approach* (pp. 285–314). New York: Wiley.

Keil, F. (1989). *Concepts, kinds, and cognitive development.* Cambridge, MA: MIT Press.

Lastrucci, E. (1989). Leggibilità e difficoltà di comprensione lessicale dei manuali di storia per la media inferiore [Readability and difficulty in word comprehension of history textbooks for grades 6 to 8]. *Scuola e Città, 40,* 465–480.

McKeown , M. G., & Beck, I. L. (1990). The assessment and characterization of young learners' knowledge of a topic in history. *American Educational Research Journal, 27,* 688–726.

Moore, W. M., Lare, J., & Wagner, K. A. (1985). *The child's political world.* New York: Praeger.

Peel, M. (1967). Some problems of the psychology of history teaching. In W. H. Burston & D. Thompson (Eds.), *Studies on the nature and teaching of history.* London: Routledge & Kegan.

Poggi, G. (1978). *La vicenda dello stato moderno* [The origin of the modern state]. Bologna: Il Mulino.

Schmitt, C. (1932). *Der begriff des politischen.* Berlin: Duncker & Humbolt.

Vosniadou, S. (1991). Designing curricula for conceptual restructuring: Lessons from the study of knowledge acquisition in astronomy. *Journal of Curriculum Studies, 23,* 219–237.

4 Stages in the Child's Construction of Social Knowledge

Juan Delval
Autónoma Universidad of Madrid

The first time a 9-year-old child explained to me that poor people were poor because they did not have any money to buy a job with, the answer went almost unnoticed. Occasionally more subjects repeated the idea using identical words, others mentioned the idea en passé, and a few subjects were more explicit and explained that to get a job one must pay at the beginning and later one gets paid. This is not the usual practice in our societies. Generally one does not have to pay to get a job, except for a few professions. Due to this reason we were not expecting these answers, which were frequently given by children from different social classes as an explanation of why poor people were poor, and we found them very surprising.

Our surprise increased when Mexican children gave us an identical explanation, as if they had all learned the same thing. Obviously we found no evidence that this idea was taught anywhere, especially as it did not correspond to any social practices in either of the two countries (Spain and Mexico). We also noticed that Leahy (1983b) cited an answer of this type from a 6-year-old child in the United States and Berti and Bombi (1981, 1988) from Italian children. Since then, while asking children about diverse matters concerning jobs and social status, we have found numerous children who mention this idea spontaneously.

How is it possible that children aged between 6 and 10 from different countries and varying social classes give the same explanation? How is it that these explanations do not correspond to social practices and that they mysteriously disappear around the age of 11? Furthermore, this type of belief does not constitute an isolated case, but it appears in many other subject areas. For example, now it is well documented that until 10 or 11 years of age, children maintain the idea that the shopkeeper sells goods at the same or a lower price than they cost him or her. They think that the shopkeeper earns money in this way, lives on these earnings, and replaces the sold goods. This idea can be found regularly in the answers given by children from many countries and diverse social backgrounds. This idea has been found in England, Holland, Italy, Spain, Mexico, and many other countries (Berti & Bombi, 1981, 1988; Delval & Echeita, 1991; Furth, 1980; Jahoda, 1984; Jahoda & Woerdenbagch, 1982; Ng, 1982). There are small age differences between one group of subjects and another with respect to the point in time at which they could explain that the salesperson has to sell at a higher price than the purchasing price, but all of them give the same types of explanations.

This idea even appears in children who are themselves street vendors (Delval, Díaz-Barriga, Hinojosa, & Daza, 1993; Jahoda, 1983). Those subjects, who have direct selling experience, seem to acquire the notion of profit at an earlier age. However, the types of erroneous explanations given by the Mexican children who sell goods in the streets and the Spanish children who do not sell goods in the streets are curious. One feels surprised when reading transcripts of interviews carried out by other authors with children from other countries. These transcripts are identical to those from children that we have interviewed, including details that might seem purely anecdotal. Many more examples could be given, but what we are interested in at the present is in highlighting the fact that in many cases children put forward explanations that do not coincide with those of adults. The children's explanations do not even correspond to what happens in reality, and it does not appear that anyone has taught them these ideas. How have these children arrived at these explanations? The fact that the explanations given by children show similarities to those given by adults is not at all surprising, and this is the pattern that we would expect. Without a doubt these explanations are alike in many ways and even more so as the children become older.

What turns out to be much more unexpected is that these explanations are different at a certain moment in time and that they are also very similar among subjects from distinct social classes. I believe that explaining this constitutes an important task for the developmental psychologist within the field of social knowledge. It would be understandable that they differ quantitatively, that adults and adolescents have more information available and know more. The most challenging thing is that the young children give explanations that differ qualitatively from those given by adults. How then does the child form his or her ideas about society? How it is possible that children arrive at these ideas on their own? What is the influence of the social environment? Before discussing these questions, we start by describing our own research.

UNDERSTANDING SOCIAL ORGANIZATION

For many years we have been studying children's ideas about different aspects of social institutions (Delval, 1989). More recently we started to look at the ideas they have about how society is structured and how they understand social differences and social strata change, this summarizes what sociologists call social stratification and mobility.[1]

Using clinical interviews of the Piagetian type (Piaget, 1926), we asked children about the characteristics and main features of rich and poor people. We wanted also to know how the subjects place themselves within these categories, how they explain social-level change, what the reason is for social differences, and how the problem of poverty can be solved.

First, in Madrid, we examined 82 low- and upper middle-class subjects from 6- to 16-year-olds. Later, in collaboration with a research team from the Universidad Autónoma de México (directed by Professor Frida Díaz-Barriga), we studied 180 Mexican children of equivalent social groups. We were also able to start a preliminary study with children selling in the streets in Mexico City and with Indian children in the Oaxaca Sierra. We also started to study the ideas of wealthiness, poverty, and work from children aged 4 through 8. We conducted two other studies on work and money in children between the ages of 6 and 14.

Once we started elaborating on the material, we were not satisfied with the first analysis of our interviews. We began trying to establish categories of answers and to determine their frequency. What we found were interesting regularities—similar to those in other studies—such as the increase of certain answers with age and the lowering of others. However, it was clear to us that this type of analysis did not adequately reflect the changes in explanation related to age that arise in a careful reading of protocols. This was why we initiated a more qualitative analysis, which we are still carrying out. It was clear, for instance, that a 6-year-old child saying that it is possible to change one's social level through work was saying something different from a 14-year-old child using the same word. The children's ideas about work were very different. For the 6-year-old, work was a mysterious activity for which his parents were paid. On the contrary, the older ones knew more details related to work (such as

---

[1]Ileana Enesco, Alejandra Navarro, Pilar Soto, Dolores Villuendas, Purificación Sierra, and Cristina del Barrio are taking part in this study.

education, training, status, social importance) and could differentiate among professions. Similar observations can be made regarding money; younger children could not differentiate amounts of money, nor did they know how to get it.

SOCIAL STRATIFICATION

Studies on children's knowledge of stratification are numerous. Generally they emphasize that from very early the child is sensitive to social differences. Also, children soon acquire the system of prestige associated with professions (DeFleur & DeFleur, 1967; Jahoda; 1959; Leahy, 1981, 1983a 1983b; Simmons & Rosenberg, 1971). We began this part of our study by asking what a rich man and what a poor man is and how they are different. Then we asked for self-characterizations from the subjects. Later we asked them about certain characteristics of rich and poor people's jobs, their attendance to school, and so on.

One observation was that young children attribute a close relationship between money and wealthiness; they describe rich people as those who have a lot of money and poor people as absolutely lacking it. This relationship shows up clearly in 4- to 5-year-old children, although they conceive the differences between rich and poor people by means of extreme contrasts. Rich people are millionaires, whereas poor people are beggars. Such differences are visible through physical aspects and ways of dressing: "fancy clothes" versus "rags." They add to these features by referring to things that can be bought with money, such as cars, jewels, and so on. Other aspects considered as negative by children are associated with the status of poor people: Poor people are old, sick, live in garbage or are dirty, and do not have houses. Clearly, the stereotype of a poor man is a beggar.

Descriptions from 7- and 8-year-olds become comprehensive and details are added, although big contrasts remain: Rich people live in elegance and luxury, have maids, and several belongings. Thus, there are more precise references to types of cars, houses, and so on. It appears as if subjects can make more deductions concerning what money possession allows and offers. Certain features that we can qualify as "psychological" also appear, but these are mainly associated with the status of being poor or rich; for instance, poor people are sad and rich people are happy.

For the youngest children, poor people do not work because they do not know how to or because they do not have the money to get a job, which, as we previously mentioned, has to be bought. Therefore, that is precisely why they are poor. On the contrary, rich people work, but the professions they are attributed to are not those typical of rich people. It is the quantity of the work done that determines wealthiness (Hook, 1983; Hook & Cook, 1979), as well as doing things the right way. Regarding school attendance, subjects at this age tend to think that poor children also do not go to school because of their lack of money.

At a later age of 10 or 11, characterizations and explanations become much more relativistic and qualified or elaborated. This becomes apparent in that various categories of rich and poor people are accepted or conceived: There are various levels of rich and poor, and there are some in-the-middle individuals (7- to 8-year-old children tend to include themselves in this group). Moreover, external and visible features lose importance so that wealthiness and poverty might not manifest externally. Psychological features are now numerous but are still qualified; for example, some rich people can be very generous or mean, whereas poor can be equally thieves or kind-hearted and friendly. People are not completely defined by their rich or poor condition. On the other hand, they do mention ways of behaving associated with money and status, such as traveling abroad, ways of speaking and walking, manners, and so on.

Their ideas about work also change. It is thought that everyone tries to work, but the poor sometimes do not succeed. Jobs are sharply differentiated, and the rich are professionals who perform jobs directly related to money (business, bank, etc.). All children go to school, but they go to different schools, and rich people usually attend private schools.

From 13 to 14 years old, many moral judgments appear. Many subjects talk about spiritual richness or about rich people who cannot appreciate what they have. Observations about the links between money and power also appear: Rich people usually give orders and own firms. An important role is attributed to education. Educational differences (also good or bad manners) are frequently mentioned. Personal qualities are necessary to attain a good position, and by means of those qualities one can obtain a good job that will provide a high economical level. The mental model of social differences is much more precise and elaborate; it includes more and better related elements.

The explanations of these teenagers may be determined by the proximity of their insertion into the adult world, which makes them feel much more involved in their answers. References to human beings, moral aspects, and hopes in life are much more constant, especially in upper middle-class subjects. Social order, lack of justice, and the implicit criticism of inequality are frequently mentioned. However, subjects are also very self-concerned and search for their identity and improvement. Their knowledge of the working world becomes more precise, and the difference between managing and subordinate work appears more clearly. The differentiating function of education shows up more explicitly.

UNDERSTANDING SOCIAL MOBILITY

I now consider the case of social mobility. What is necessary to understand social mobility? By *social mobility*, sociologists mean the movement of individuals into different positions in a social hierarchy based on wealth, power, and status, or any other scarce social resource. All this presupposes the existence of unequal rewards. Simultaneously, this is a process that possibly lasts a long period. Moreover, there are common characteristics among the members of the same class: unity of interests, membership consciousness, and perhaps class consciousness. It is therefore clear why it is so difficult and takes so long for subjects to understand this complex system made up of different subsystems. Therefore, the explanations regarding this problem are very interesting and show the effort that must be done by the subject.

The idea expressed by the youngest age group, around 6 years old, is that there are no permanent social groups but external features manifested in physical appearance that can be easily changed. For example, one can wear rags or be dressed in furs and jewels. By modifying this appearance one can modify the social level. To understand a change in social level involves understanding a transformation in which certain things are conserved and others are modified, namely, it requires the construction of "invariants" as pointed out by Piaget in his studies on conservation (Piaget & Inhelder, 1941). There is no well-established category, or class, of poor people. Instead, there is a kind of prototypical vignette. For this reason, in the beginning the ideas about social change seem very contradictory. On the one hand, children express themselves as if they are rejecting the possibility of change. Furthermore, they think that changes are very simple. They reject the possibility of change because, from their point of view, poor people are born poor, whereas the rich are from wealthy parents and their situation remains constant:

Patricia (6;7) *How do people become rich?* Well, their parents have money and children, when they grow up, have their parents. They give them money; then when they get married they already have money and can go to the offices and they are wealthy people. *And how do people become poor?* Well, their parents do not have money and when their children grow up, well, they are poor.[2]

Moreover, social change is very easy. Because they ignore the amount of money needed for living, a small amount of money is enough to become rich; it is also possible to find money in the street and become rich overnight. The more fantastic methods to explain social change are

---

[2]Experimenters' questions are in italics.

invoked, such as exchanging small bills for big ones, buying in stores and receiving change, playing with slot machines, or winning the lottery.

Their explanations are based on apparent and easily observable aspects, and there are no references to hidden or internal processes. The main factors determining change are the subjects' free and individual actions or the modifications taken place in the surrounding environment; in no case do the subjects have to act on the reality. In addition, the obstacles to be overcome in order to produce a change are not considered, neither is the interaction between the subjects' activities and the resistance of the reality. What is needed can be obtained, and the scarcity of resources and the competence among social actors to obtain them are not well understood. Desire plays an important role in these explanations in relation to the ignorance of the resistance of reality. At the same time, changes take place suddenly and are not realistic. References to work also appear. From a very early age, an association between work and social level is established, even if work is only quantitatively considered. It is said that one works a lot, but there is no specification as to the type of job; it is also talked about working well and carefully. We think that subjects do not yet determine a clear difference between kinds of jobs; certain subjects refer to bad and good jobs, but generally with not much detail, and it appears that they do not relate them to a given professional qualification:

Naira (8;8) *How do people become rich?* Well, sometimes one gets rich working very hard, day and night, from night to day and day to night. Then, when one has collected many piggy banks or whatever, they then get to buy a house. I think the first thing they have to do . . . , well, also the house since they need a place to live; but I think the most important is to have health and food. *And how do people become poor?* Well, being lazy, not working.

Some subjects mention education and to do well at school, but references to the relationship between a profession and a qualification for it are still missing. This is probably because differences among jobs are not very precise. To study is something very general and is also quantitatively determined (i.e., to study a lot).

To become poor is considered a very simple process, and subjects mention that one can run out of money buying many things; they are not conscious of the fact that if one buys things, possessing them is also a form of wealthiness. In the same way, one can become poor because one's money is stolen, or one can loose it in a minute. Taken into consideration, there still is no such notion as a process of change, lasting relatively long in time, with different stages. Change is considered an individual process, with references to social factors missing. However, individual properties are not important, and subjects emphasize the role played by desire, by wanting something and knowing how to obtain it. Hazard can also influence changes, but references to active participation in these changes do not appear. In summary, action and will are determining factors: Things are obtained by wanting them.

It is important to notice the absence of external factors, such as a scarcity of employment and goods. Apparently people have plenty of things, without external constraints. It is still not understood that goods can be scarce and have to be distributed, and that competence to obtain them can be necessary.

The general problem of poverty is also very easy to solve: One can individually give a small amount of money to a poor person and he or she then will become rich. Other solutions are not conceived, and the only difficulty is that if people give poor people money, they will no longer have any money. This is the reason the existence of poor people is not convenient:

Javier (6;5) *Is it possible to do something to avoid the existence of poor people?* To give them money, that's why they lend their hands. *To give them money?* Yes, since otherwise they will not earn money to buy things, or if they have a baby, they will not be able to buy things. And who will give them money? People, sure. *Do you think is it good that we still have poor people?* No, I think it is not good since if we have to give them money all the time we will stay without money. *Of course, but, what can be done?* Well, that poor people invent . . . they can make, paint, the bills, using paper; so they will think that this is money.

Around 10 to 11 years of age, a series of important modifications in the explanations have been observed. In the first place, it appears that the consideration of resources can be limited, as well as the notion that competence is related to this fact. In the second place, temporal processes lasting in time and with different stages start to be understood. Third, subjects begin to conceive social relations that do not take place among individuals but that are institutionalized, such as the relation between buyer and seller or boss and employee, namely, relations between functions instead of persons. Moreover, stages are more permanent and start to be characterized by other features than the presence or absence of money.

Concerning ways of changing the status a person has in society, work becomes the most important way to bring about this change, and the main difference is that jobs start to be distinguished, with some jobs better than others. Education, professional qualification, and personal attitudes are part of the subject's considerations. In particular, school preparation is mentioned as crucial because it opens the way to higher level studies. This last observation appears especially in upper class subjects.

Subjects start to talk about business or money-related activities, such as how to buy cheap and to sell more expensively. The notion of business is still tough, and it is more like a label that applies to a set of poorly understood activities, although clearly it is related to getting important amounts of money. It can be said, then, that it is an incipient process, which has as one of its main characteristics the necessity to run smoothly, once started. If a subject does well in his or her studies, if he or she makes an effort and chooses a good career, that subject will become rich and succeed, whereas the lazy will not. But obstacles that might emerge are omitted, and it is conceived that if the right way is chosen, it necessarily will lead to the good end. The importance of will appears, which takes into account the notion that obstacles have to be overcome. Younger children mentioned desire as one of the main factors that is necessary in order to change the social status. But desire is different from will, because will takes into account the reality of resistance — the effort to fight against it and overcome it:

Gonzalo (10;1) *How do people become rich?* Well, since their parents take them to a good school and they work a lot and get good grades and then get a good job and work as hard as their parents, they could become rich. *And their parents are rich too?* No, it is because their parents have taken them to a good school and given them a good education. My mum says that since I go to a private school I have more opportunities than the poor, so I have to take advantage of all of it. *How do you think people become poor?* Well his parents cannot give him a good education, they have to go to public schools. Then, if they are very lazy and don't want to do anything, since they do not teach them much, in the end, if they are not hard workers, they become poor.

Subjects used to refer mostly to individual factors and mention psychological differences and personal characteristics. The most intelligent and motivated individuals could obtain better results. Nevertheless, as there appears some reference to scarcity and limitation of resources, one can consider that there is an incipient conception of social or external factors, given that it is admitted that there are not enough resources for everyone. It is pointed out that things are different for individuals of poor and rich origin, given that everything is more simple for the later. One can then see that subjects regard different departure situations and sometimes ask about them.

To solve the poverty problem, it is not enough to individually give money to poor people. Instead, solutions point to the idea that those who have more have to give collectively to the poor. Limitations of these simple solutions start to be seen, though, and it is pointed out that there are too many poor people. In the same way, it is proposed that there should be more employment, but it is again noted that this is not enough for everyone:

Juan Carlos (13;4) *Do you think that something can be done so that there were no poor people anymore?* I think that if we people helped each other and we all gave the ones who need more whatever is needed to be all the same, I think that we would all be the same and there would be no poor in the country . . . the economy of the country would then be enough. *That is, would it be a good thing to do or not?* I think it would. *Could somebody give a solution to it?* I think that it could be done by everybody at once, if all the people want there to be few poor, they can get it by working together, but if they do not want to, well, that's it. There is nothing to do.

From the age of 13 to 14 on, other changes manifest themselves, among which the most relevant is the ability to conceive of a world of hypothetical possibilities and to understand the existence of interests common to groups of individuals. The subjects make big progress in their ability to understand relationships among different systems. In this way, subjects could under-stand the relationships among goods manufacturing, distribution, and demand, or between a subject's qualification for a job and the creation of new employment by social instances:

Bernardo (16;3) *How do you think people become rich?* Well, I think that to become rich one has to work hard, first thing, and, I mean, always look around, look for the alternatives one has and look forward instead of sticking to the moment, that is, to look at the consequences something you do might have. *And what have rich people done to become rich, then?* I think that there are rich people who are rich because they happened to be lucky because they have invested a lot of what they had on a very risky thing and they got profit in the end, and from then on it was easy because . . . with assistants or so they might have who can help them so they grow little by little.

This subject explains very clearly that one has to consider the possibili-ties, going beyond the actual moment, and to try to choose among them, which is a characteristic of formal thought (Inhelder & Piaget, 1955). Classes are more permanent, and some subjects even talk spontaneously about social classes and that an incipient class consciousness exists. Ways of change are based mostly on personal effort and on qualification for the profession, and business, that is, money-related activities as well as professions considered as good are frequently mentioned as professions to become rich.

Individual factors still have considerable importance, and differences in capacity among individuals as well as perseverance is considered. The will that appears at this point is different from the one in the first stage, which was mostly a simple desire not concerned with obstacles to be overcome. Differences in opportunities are mentioned, which would be external and due to the social system. Interaction between those individual capacities and opportunities is considered. Change is understood as very difficult for the poor, and changes are most easily conceived not between extremes but between relatively close positions. The social aspect, that is, the general conception of the system, is still very rudimentary.

A remarkable difference that can be observed is the ease at understanding long-term processes that go even beyond the individual such as those referring to changes in social organization and in the work system. The creation of employment is considered a fundamental factor for change to be possible. This ability to conceive long-term changes is related to the ability to conceive possible worlds. The subject also considers his or her own insertion in the adult world. Poverty cannot be solved just by giving money away, and charity solutions — very well accepted in previous years — are strongly rejected. On the contrary, it is thought that education and work, as well as institutional support, have to be provided to the poor people:

> Ricardo (14;0) Well, it could be a good solution to create factories or industries specially made for them, then they start taking money and producing things at the same time. Then they would get their money and they could save it without spending, right? and when they have it one can get them houses or areas. Well, there he has a new opportunity to start. *And who would be in charge of all that*? The State, that is, the rich ones. *Do you think that the solution would be to give money to the poor*? No. *Why*? No, because a poor person can make good or bad use of it. That person might go around wasting the money in slot machines or go to the casino as we said.

One of the most surprising things is the similarity among subjects of the same age. Lower and upper middle-class subjects give explanations of the same nature, although one can observe a certain retardation in lower class ones, which is to say that the average age in which they reach a response level is higher. On the other hand, Mexican and Spanish subjects' responses are also very similar. One can obviously find different references to elements of their social environment, but these do not affect the nature of explanations. For instance, Mexican children refer less to lottery as a means to get rich than do Spanish children. In fact, people play lottery less frequently in Mexico than in Spain. On the other hand, among Spaniards there are more references to lottery among the lower class than among the upper middle-class, although they talk more about heritage, which probably corresponds to reality.

As an example, the similarity between these two initial explanations of a Mexican and a Spanish subject can be observed:

> Eduardo (14;8) *What is a rich man*? Rich in money or in what? *What do you think*? That is, moral or material rich? *Well, tell me both*. Material, a person

who has a lot of money, and morally rich is a person who lives in peace. And what about poor? A material poor is one who does not even have enough to survive, well he works but it is difficult to support the family. Morally poor is the one who, even if he has material richness he might not have much moral richness, because he is no good to his equals.

Beatriz (16;7) *What is a rich person?* A person who has money, or he might be rich in friends, I mean, spiritually. What kind of a rich person? *What do you think?* Well, I don't know, you can be spiritually rich or be rich because you have a lot of friends and you are happy, but normally a person is rich because he has money. *What is a poor person?* Well, a person who does not have money or a person who is unhappy.

STAGES

Through the type of analysis described thus far, it becomes apparent that levels or stages of the explanations given by the subjects tend to occur. The concept of stage is a controversial matter in present developmental psychology. Yet, taking it as a tool for analysis, and without trying to give it an ontological sense, I think it is a useful instrument to understand regularities in children explanations.

In a heuristic approach, we understand stages as a cutting point in development introduced by the researcher to organize the data in a meaningful way. The stages are, of course, *ideal types*, in the Max Weber sense, therefore they are hypothetical constructs; except, they also have to be supported by the data and have to reflect observable changes. Naturally, it is an empirical question whether all stages are going to be found in all types of subjects. In this framework, the psychologist has to build a rational reconstruction of the subjects' views and is then forced to continuously look at the central topics, those that define the field. This type of enterprise, using the terms of the French sociologist Lucien Goldmann (1955), can be described as one similar to that of the anthropologist or the cultural historian who tries to find a meaningful structure in the continuum of views and explanations given by the subjects.

In the problem being dealt with here, one can observe that subjects aged 6 to 10 provide explanations based on apparent aspects, and their reality is conceived as immediate and perceptible. At the same time, systems are not understood. Society is considered as a rational order made to satisfy human needs. In this system, resources are abundant and scarcity is not understood. The only type of conceivable relations are the personal ones, and desire plays an important role in reaching a favorable position.

The discussion now centers on two of the changes taking place in the next stage, namely, that starting at 10 to 11 years old. The first one consists of the understanding that personal relations are different from social ones. This is a necessary step to understand the social world. The child from 6 to 10 considers the shopkeeper as a helpful friend who provides the objects necessary for living and who, therefore, sells the goods at the price they cost. On the contrary, after 10 years, children understand the function of the seller and the necessity to earn money through this activity. This change from the personal to the institutional (pointed out by Furth, 1980) makes an important advance in the comprehension of society.

The second change is related to the child's difficulty in understanding social concepts (Friedman, 1982; Piaget, 1946). In a series of studies on the explanation of physical and biological phenomena — like the propagation of a disease in trees, or the melting of ice — Montangero (1992) found several changes starting at 10 to 11 years old that are strikingly related to those observed in our subjects in explaining social mobility. Among these characteristics are the following: (a) an increase in the time span of the transformation imagined: for small children the "forest disease" only took a few days, and for older children, dozens of years; (b) the transformations in young (7-8) children were quantitative, and in older ones they also became qualitative; (c) for older children there was continuity between transformations, with connection between states; (d) older children could describe a process, and younger children tended to describe each image; and (e) older children imagined an invisible process to take account of observed changes.

From age 14 years old and onward, subjects are able to take possible worlds into consideration. They understand also that there are social constraints for wealth and job creation, and this creation does not depend on individual will but is related to the social system as a whole, to political change, or to changes in the modes of production. The process of social-level change is seen as much more difficult. It is not sufficient just to take the right path: Risks have to be solved at any moment, and it is necessary to anticipate them and to evaluate the possibilities and consequences of actions. There is some mention of the links between money and power. Real wealth is obtained through the property of production means, whereas poor people work for the owners of such means. Strictly associated with changes in the explanations of social change, parallel changes appear in the concepts of work and money. I do not elaborate on them here, although I consider them in Tables 4.1 and 4.2.

GENERAL PROBLEMS ON ACQUIRING SOCIAL KNOWLEDGE

After considering what we know at this point, I now discuss further different general problems about the elaboration of social knowledge. First,

TABLE 4.1
Levels of Explanation of Social Mobility

Levels	General Characteristics	Mobility
I	The reality is immediate and perceptive Systems are not understood Society is a rational order made to satisfy human needs. There is abundance. Scarcity is not understood. Relations are only personal Importance of desire	No change (born) or sudden change through receiving or finding money. Procedures: chance, lottery, work (nonspecified) Unclear connection with work and money
II	Discovery of constraints or reality Social resources are scarce There is social competition for the scarce resources. Social relations (seller, customer, worker, etc.) are different from personal ones (friend) Understanding of simple systems, and relations between simple systems Understanding of diachronic processes	Gradual and subtle change Multiple and complementary procedures Once started, the process develops naturally Importance of training Individual competition Will and effort are considered
III	Consideration of possible worlds Understanding of competition putting oneself in the role of another Social constraints Long term processes, longer lived than the individual The possibility of understanding complex relations between multiple systems. Ideological bias Equity versus equality	More realistic conception of the difficulties of change. Importance of the level of departure Active role of the subject at any moment in the process Personal qualities, risk, ambition Evaluation of possibilities and consequences Social competition Will as a way of overcoming social competition

I emphasize the importance of studying the subjects' mental representations of reality. Such representations have been poorly studied, especially concerning the social world. What the authors have studied under the label of "social cognition" refers more to the others' psychological knowledge than to the knowledge of social institutions, both of which are different domains from a theoretical point of view.

Some theories explaining the acquisition of social knowledge attribute a crucial role to socialization, that is, to adult transmission of social knowledge, but they underestimate the subject's constructive activity. They usually do not take into account, though, that social representations are constructed of different types of elements. Althouth rules, values, and

TABLE 4.2
Levels of Explanation of Money and Work

Levels	Money	Work
I	Symbolic element of exchange: to give something for something	Paid activity. Usually developed outside home. Its character is unclear.
	Quantities are not understood, only qualities	Differences between jobs not well understood
	Use of different types of coins	Payment based on quantity
	Equivalence of coins	Unclear ideas about qualitative job differences
	The price is a property of goods	
II	Value of goods is determined by work and scarcity (demand)	Comprehension of scarcity. No jobs for everyone.
	Market as a price regulator	Quality differences between jobs
	Idea of profit in the shop	Importance of training and education
	Discovery of capital and the property of the means of production	Beginning of the understanding of competition between actors
	Notion of company owners appears	It is possible to create more jobs, but limitations are not well understood
III	Ideas on company owners' profit	Creation of jobs through changes in the global system
	Surplus value and exploitation	Social constraints are better understood
	Role of banks as lenders of money	
	Banks profit	
	Generalization of the idea of profit beyond the shop	

various information are directly transmitted, subjects have to elaborate their own explanations regarding the causation of social phenomena.

Mental Models

Contrary to what happened a few decades ago, nowadays it is usually accepted that subjects are provided with, what various theoretical positions have called mental models, representations, implicit theories, naive theories, systems of schemata, and so on. Using these devices, the subjects carry out their actions and their interpretations of reality. However, the elaboration of those models or representations of reality has not been studied within developmental psychology. Although in almost all the studies concerning social knowledge it is usually thought that psychology deals more with physical knowledge, the models referring to the world of nature employed by the subjects have not been studied. There are also few studies concerned with children's explanations of the world. For example, Piaget, who was guided more by epistemological rather than psychological interests (as is widely known), was above all interested in discovering the formation of large categories of thought, such as logical-mathematical and physical concepts: space, time, causality, number, classification, seriation, and so on. Only coincidentally did he dedicate himself to some aspects of the general conception of reality in his book, *The Child's Conception of the World* (1926). He also studied some of the basic functions of the human mind, such as memory, imagery, and symbols. Something similar can be said of another important branch of developmental psychology that originates with the work of Vygotsky, who was mostly interested in higher psychological functions that he related to language.

Therefore, the formations of explanations of natural and social phenomena occurring around us have been studied very little. For example, problems such as — What are things made of? Why are there living organisms? What is the life cycle? How are mountains formed? Why do plants grow, or what is the water cycle within nature? — have not been studied in any great detail. The same can be said about the social world. Where does wealth come from? Why does the family exist? What is power and why does it remain? How do goods circulate? Nevertheless, it would be very important to discover how the subject, while growing up, starts making sense of the phenomena that surround him or her and within which he or she lives. This is what can be called the contents of thought. The growing subject is a thinker about the inanimate world, about the living world, about others, and about the social world. This kind of study cannot substitute the study of categories of the mind nor of its great functions, but it complements it. The lack of knowledge in this respect constitutes an important gap in the theory that is only just starting to be filled in.

True Social Knowledge

Many years ago when the field known as *social cognition* emerged, it seemed that the gap with respect to the social world was going to be filled. However, despite its name, the task at hand was considered the study of "knowledge of self, of others, and of relationships," although other authors, such as Shantz (1975, 1983), include the knowledge of wider social systems within this field. Researchers have studied the knowledge that subjects form about others as persons or what can be referred to as *psychological knowledge*. Regarding the subjects' activities, this can be referred to as being a *spontaneous psychologist*. At the present time, the upcoming field known as theory of mind is also concerned with studying the representations of other people's minds formed by the child.

Since Comte and Durkheim — the founding fathers of Sociology — everyone accepts that sociology and the rest of the social sciences are independent disciplines that cannot be reduced to psychology. Because of this, the denomination of social cognition seems misleading because the social relations that it studies are social from the standpoint of an external observer, who examines the interactions between subjects, but not from the subject's own viewpoint. What the latter is doing is getting to know another person who constitutes a psychological organism with feelings, beliefs, attitudes, and so on. The shift from psychological to social considerations does not depend on the number of actors that participate, as seems to be implied by social cognition theorists, but on the type of relations that are established between them. As sociologists such as Berger and Luckmann (1967) have pointed out, it is the existence of institutionalized relations that transcends people and that is established between types of actors that characterizes social phenomena.

When does the child start to understand true social relations? When does the child begin to see the shopkeeper who is in front of him or her as a salesperson as well as a person or a friend? Probably this occurs at a later point in time than the appearance of psychological knowledge, and maybe it arises as a differentiation of this former knowledge. The fact that social phenomena are different from psychological phenomena comprises an important and independent aspect of the subject's understanding. We think that the study of the subject as a social thinker differs from what social cognition studies, which the former cannot be reduced to the latter and which should constitute an independent field of study.

Many years ago a few psychologists started to study children's ideas about social institutions. The pioneering research by Strauss (1952, 1954) and Danziger (1958), regarding ideas of economics, the research by Adelson (1971), Adelson, Green, and O'Neill (1969), and by Connell (1971) concerning politics, and the sharp and original studies carried out by Jahoda (1959, 1964, 1979, 1984) in many of these fields, have shown us that the child is an active social thinker. The child is not merely limited to acquiring what adults transmit to him or her. Many other studies have addressed new fields, such as religion, the nation, sex and gender, law and rights, and war and peace. The thought-provoking study by Furth (1980) and the meticulous research by Berti and Bombi (1981, 1988), which encompasses much more than the economic world, constitute two important contributions that stand out among the research.

At present, there are several studies that deal with these and other fields. The recent review by Furnham and Stacey (1991) represents a useful instrument to sail within such a vast territory, which until now has received little systematization. The only thing that many of these studies have in common is the subject area that they are concerned with, but there is a great diversity of approaches, theoretical perspectives, and interests. It is curious that many studies do not originate from developmental psychologists but from sociologists, economists, political scientists, or social psychologists.

This explains why these studies have been published in a diverse number of journals, many of which are not even psychological. This also explains why many of these studies involving children's opinions are essentially descriptive in nature. Often the only theoretical perspective is that of the child who becomes gradually socialized and acquires adult ideas as he or she grows older.

Nevertheless, I think that it is necessary to admit that there is a series of problems common to all this research when trying to comprehend the child's activity and the adolescent as a social thinker. Some of the most relevant studies within this field allow us to begin to see the resemblance of the subject's explanations when contrasted with problems from different fields. The subject does not only acquire information about the buying-selling process, the value of each coin, the differences between rich and poor people, the equality or equity of salaries, and so on, but it would appear that the subject has wider representations within which varying aspects of social phenomena can be related. Unfortunately, many studies aim at researching very specific problems, and the subjects' development is frequently not studied throughout the period of infancy and adolescence, but only during a few years when progress is being made within a concrete research problem. This type of research masks the constructive process and the way the subject elaborates models that gradually become wider, more comprehensive, and less contradictory concerning what is happening in the reality that surrounds him or her. Consequently, I think it is very necessary to pay attention to problems regarding theory, methodology, data analysis, and to the theoretical perspectives from which these studies are carried out.

Theories of the Acquisition Process

One of the great problems underlying this kind of research is how children gradually acquire their ideas about the social world. Many studies seem to implicitly assume that adults transmit these ideas and that children progressively integrate them. Due to this reason, these studies limit themselves to determining the distance between children's and adult's ideas. This is what happens, for example, in the studies regarding the knowledge of stratification and prestige among the professions. We could call this the socialization perspective.

Nevertheless, other studies adopt a more or less explicitly constructivist position inspired by Piaget's positions. According to this, child must elaborate their own representations using the elements that they receive either by direct or indirect transmission, or through their own search for materials. But in any case, children's cognitive development level is a determining factor that limits their comprehension of certain problems so that there would be things that are out of reach for his understanding at a given moment in time. Naturally, this does not mean that all subjects have the same ideas. In the last few years there has been a growing interest in the influence of social factors in development. Although Piaget always regarded social transmission as one of the factors involved in development, nevertheless, in his concrete studies he behaved as if this factor did not exist. On the other hand, Vygotsky, who started out from Marxist positions, assumed as a postulate that the individual's development occurs completely tied to the society in which the individual lives. As Wertsch and Rogoff (1984, p. 2) rightly pointed out, to say this is much more than an affirmation that an individual's mental processes develop within a social environment, which has deep implications for research.

The psychologists who are more concerned about social influences deal with the formation mechanisms of the human mind and its ideas. They consider the human mind and its context and try to form a causal theory of its development. Piaget, on the other hand, looked at things from the interior of the individual and built a descriptive theory of his or her progress. For this reason it is not unusual that he attributed so much importance to the factor of equilibration. I believe that both points of view are necessary and complementary, without being in opposition with each other.

One has to admit that although external influences are essential and without them there would not be normal development, nevertheless, each individual must carry out his or her own internal development. To connect both things is an unavoidable goal of the psychological explanation, but to show the progress made inside each individual still remains and still is an important contribution to knowledge, although it may be incomplete.

A rising position with respect to the problem being dealt with is the theory of social representations proposed by Moscovici. In this school of thought, the group members share representations that "once created, however, they lead a life of their own, circulate, merge, attract and repel each other, and give birth to new representations, while old ones die out" (Moscovici, 1984, p. 13). Unfortunately, "who produces a representation?" seems to Moscovici to be a superficial and largely resolved question (Moscovici, 1976, p. 79). Although the theory of social representations has many attractive aspects, it is quite imprecise and slippery, and the criticism that Jahoda (1988) made underlined many of these weaknesses.

However, some authors, such as Emler (Emler & Dickinson, 1985; Emler, Ohana, & Dickinson 1990), consider this approach as "an alternate view" to the constructivist position. The acceptance of this theory would have the consequence that the differences in the knowledge children display are concerned with the social groups to which they belong. Unluckily, his own evidence is not very conclusive, and the replication by Burgard, Cheyne, and Jahoda (1989) does not appear to support his data. To analyze the influence of social factors further I make some observations about social models.

What Are Social Models Made Of?

Because man is a social being that can only develop in a society and in narrow contact with others, adults try to make sure that children convert themselves into full members of that society, transmitting norms, values, attitudes, and patterns of behavior that characterize the adult members of that society. This process is usually referred to as *socialization*. One of the first things acquired by subjects is the *norms* or rules about what they can and cannot do. Adults ensure that children's behavior follows these norms, and they make a great effort to achieve this. This is what is going to guarantee that later the children's behavior can be considered social.

These norms are closely tied to social *values* that indicate what is desirable and what isn't from other people's point of view. Therefore, these elements prescribe what should be done, and they do not refer to the being of actions, but rather to the what ought to be, which are fundamental components of social knowledge and conduct.

Beyond this, the child receives *information* about many social facts, about concrete aspects of the social reality, as well as obtains information by him- or herself when interacting with the social world, recording its regularities and reflecting upon them. With this, the child elaborates *explanations* about how and why things occur in a certain way and about the functioning of social "systems." Norms, values, further information, and explanations are some elements that make up the models or representations that the child puts together regarding the social world. These elements are of two types: normative and descriptive. This distinction may seem trivial, but not to consider them can lead to many mistakes in research, especially when establishing how social knowledge is produced. I further explain why. The norms and values that prescribe what should be done starts to be acquired from an early age and adults make a great effort to make certain that the children acquire them. Because of this, they receive explicit teaching and are stimulated to imitate adults. This activity is a passive one at the beginning of norm acquisition, because the subjects obtain them, to a large extent, already made. Commonly, the child receives information directly from adults, mass media, or school, although the child also searches for information on his or her own.

In contrast to this, the explanation of why things are like this, how social systems function, and the concepts they rely on are hardly taught. Usually no explanation is given to the child about the shop system, the distribution of goods, or the relationship with the production system. The same can be said about how social mobility comes about, and what causes wars, and so on. When they are taught these things, they have already had explanations for them for a long time, explanations that the child has constructed on his or her own. These explanations are established with the intellectual instruments that he or she usually has available, and the child arrives at explanations that do not coincide with adult ones, and strangely enough they are very similar between children of different social backgrounds.

This is why the child very quickly learns rules; in order to go shopping, one must take money to the shop. This is learned at a much earlier point in time than the child could explain what money is for, in terms of what the shopkeeper does with it, how prices are decided on, and in general how economic activity takes place. Later, the explanations act on norms and values and they reorganize them, and when these explanations give rise to a high degree of comprehension, they provide the norms and values with new meaning. At this stage it is possible to reflect on these norms and values and even to question their contents.

Something similar can be said about the information children receive. When Spanish children first go to school, they are taught that "Madrid is the capital of Spain," and they all know how to repeat it without making a mistake. However, as various researchers have pointed out and as we have found in our own research, these children do not know that there are more Spanish people than there are citizens in Madrid, that not all Spanish people live in Madrid, and that all the Madrileños are Spanish. These children do not have the faintest idea of what "being the capital of a country" means, nor what a capital or a country is (Delval, 1989; Delval, del Barrio & Echeita, 1981). Hence, the information they are taught at school is not very useful to them when they first learn it, and they cannot integrate it into their explanations of a country's administrative organization.

I think it is very important to be conscious of this when studying the models of the social world because if we center on norms, values, or information, we cannot rightly appreciate the constructive work of the subject. Actually, he or she is reproducing what has been received by transmission. Therefore, what the subject says is very much dependent on the social environment and the culture in which he or she lives. On the contrary, there is less variation in the explanations of the functioning of social systems and in the concepts they are made of. Here we possibly find constructive processes that are more universal. Contents vary in relation to the environment, but the way phenomena are explained is much more similar because this way they are linked to the subject's mental abilities.

Open Systems

In the explanations of the social world given by children and adolescents, common elements can be found in different areas. It should not surprise us, because in all cases systems connected among each other are being found, reconstruction of unexplicit elements is taking place, as well as the creation of adequate concepts.

Chandler and Boutilier (1992) have recently recalled that social phenomena constitute a clear example of open dynamic systems, of a negative entropy, opposing the physical systems. The understanding of these systems of positive entropy has been studied more during the process of development. These open systems are characterized by the lowering of entropy and the increase of their organization, instead of becoming more unorganized. Chandler and Boutilier claim that the subject needs operations that are different from the formal ones to understand those dynamic systems. These operations could characterize a different period or could develop simultaneously, but in a diverse way. Even if the question of the necessity of specific operations is a controversial matter, it is important and enriching to have pointed out the specificity of open dynamic systems of which social systems are clear examples. It is possible to guess that the subject does not treat them as open systems until later stages in development. Possibly he or she does not even understand the characteristics of a system. I think then that this approach can be fruitful and can approximate an understanding of biological and social systems.

At first sight, at least, it is apparent that in other fields of social knowledge (the ideas on war and peace or on politics; Delval & del Barrio, 1992) a similar evolution is taking place to the one I have briefly sketched for social organization. In all these cases subjects started out by not understanding the relations among different systems; they even tended to understand each subsystem in a static way (selling in a shop, for instance, or how one changes from poverty to wealth). Subjects concentrate on aspects that can easily be perceived and do not elaborate very much on the phenomena they are trying to account for. They explain social actions as a result of desires and individual personal qualities (wars, for example, start because two people want to fight).

The Determinants of Social Concepts

I finish by returning to some of the questions I mentioned earlier. Children live in a social environment that they want to explain, and they continuously pay attention to more elements and new information. They discover new phenomena, and they become interested in them. It is fascinating to observe how — when the interview proceeds — they fight to find explanations for the questions asked. Sometimes they say, "I haven't thought of this before," "I can't explain how it happens," so that in the actual interview they find an explanation that is coherent with other facts they had pointed out. When interviews are reread, it can be observed that each subject shows internal coherence in his or her answers, although it is not easy to observe this at first sight. Even contradictions can be coherent, if this makes sense, because they correspond to the level of development and are characteristic of the level that the child has reached.

In the construction of social notions, the subject models the reality he or she has in front of him or her. To do this, the child uses intellectual tools. Consequently, if one concentrates on the form of the construction, it is natural that progress is independent of the contents he or she is modeling. But if one concentrates on contents, it should be expected that the influence of the environment is important. For instance, indigenous people in Oaxaca Sierra see their society as being made up of two extreme groups of poor and rich people for a longer period than similarly aged children in Mexico City or Madrid (Barroso, 1994). This is not surprising: They live in an environment in which a middle class does not exist. It is not strange either that there is lack of a reference to banks, because they are unusual in their environment. It is also to be expected to find more references to enrichment through hazard games or through lottery among Spanish children than among Mexicans. In Spain the lottery game is important, and it receives big attention in the media. However, both groups of subjects refer to fantastic or hazardous procedures to become rich that are similar in other respects.

One of the reasons used to explain the slowness in the understanding of the social world is that children do not have a direct social experience. Although they are exposed in the same way as adults are to the physical world (they fall down or burn in the same way), they do not participate as adults in the political life, nor do they work or manage money. It has also been asserted that children do not receive explanations about social phenomena and that they lack information. This is true but is an incomplete explanation.

Returning to the case of profit, our subject sellers at the traffic lights in Mexico City (Delval et al., 1993), as well as Jahoda's (1983) subjects in Zimbabwe, were directly exposed to selling because they live from it. To the extent that the results of our researches can be compared, it appears that they acquire the idea that the young street vendor has to charge more than the cost of the beverage in order to earn money at an earlier age. However, there are various surprising facts.

First of all, it is not the case that all subjects know this, some give the same price. This could be attributed to the fact that they do not buy the product and therefore do not know the original price. Nevertheless, it is striking to find this ignorance of something in which they are so directly involved. This lack of interest is quite remarkable, but it maybe because in their system of explanation it is a natural thing to sell at the same price at which they buy, and there is no other possibility.

Second, the explanations given by children who charge a higher price show that they do not understand the idea of profit. They resort to explanations based on the size of the bottles or on the selling in boxes, which are strikingly similar to those given by children from Madrid (Delval & Echeita, 1991) or to the Italian ones (Berti & Bombi, 1981, 1988).

Third, some children who have explanations for the higher price doubt, however, that the original supplier is charging more. This could indicate that children have learned an explanation, but that they cannot generalize it to the rest of the selling process; this would imply that they have not understood the social mechanisms of the exchange of goods. If they cannot extend the explanations to similar situations, they cannot be claimed to have a real comprehension of the process. It appears that there are cognitive obstacles that oppose an earlier understanding.

This leads to the conclusion that both the characteristics of what is being modeled as well as the social transmission has an important but limited role. The subjects incorporate only that part of the environmental information that they can understand. The young street vendors know more about the amount of money necessary for living. This is a matter of fact. But, on the other hand, their explanations regarding social reality are poorer compared to those children who are not street vendors, who probably have stronger intellectual resources and have had longer schooling.

ACKNOWLEDGMENTS

I thank Violeta Demonte, Ileana Enesco, Alejandra Navarro, and Pilar Soto for useful observations on the topics treated in this chapter. I am also in debt with Violeta Demonte and Juan Martínez St. John for help with the English version.

This work has been partly supported by the grants from the DGICYT to the research projects AME89-0175 and PB91-0004.

REFERENCES

Adelson, J. (1971). The political imagination of the young adolescent. *Daedalus, 100*, 1013–1050.

Adelson, J., Green, B., & O'Neill, R. (1969). Growth of the idea of law in adolescence. *Developmental Psychology, 1*, 327–332.

Barroso, R. (1994). *Comprensión de nociones sobre organización social en niños y adolescentes indígenas de la Sierra Norte de Oaxaca* [Comprehension of notions about social organization in indigenous children and adolescents of the "Sierra Norte" of Oaxaca (Mexico)]. Unpublished Bachelor of Arts thesis, School of Psychology, UNAM, México.

Berger, P. L., & Luckmann, T. (1967). *The social construction of reality*. New York: Doubleday.

Berti, A. E., & Bombi, A. S. (1981). *Il mondo economico nel bambino*. Firenze: La Nuova Italia.

Berti, A. E., & Bombi, A. S. (1988). *The child's construction of economics* (G. Duveen, trans.). Cambridge: Cambridge University Press.

Burgard, P., Cheyne, W. M., & Jahoda, G. (1989). Children's representations of economic inequality: A replication. *British Journal of Developmental Psychology, 7*, 275-287.

Chandler, M. J., & Boutilier, R. G. (1992). The development of dynamic system reasoning. *Human Development, 35*, 121-137.

Connell, R. W. (1971). *The child's construction of politics*. Carlton, Australia: Melbourne University Press.

Danziger, K. (1958). Children's earliest conceptions of economic relationships (Australia). *Journal of Social Psychology, 47*, 231-240.

DeFleur, M. L., & DeFleur, L. B. (1967). The relative contribution of television as a learning source for children's occupational knowledge. *American Sociological Review, 32*, 777-789.

Delval, J. (1989). La construcción de la representación del mundo social en el niño [Child's representation of social world]. In E. Turiel, I. Enesco, & J. Linaza (Eds.), *El mundo social en la mente de los niños* [The social world in the children's mind] (pp. 245-328). Madrid: Alianza Editorial.

Delval, J., & del Barrio, C. (1992). Las ideas de los niños acerca de la guerra y la paz [Children's ideas on war and peace]. In F. Moreno & F. Jiménez Burillo (Eds.), *La guerra: Realidad y alternativas* [War: Reality and alternatives] (pp. 165-174). Madrid: Editorial Complutense.

Delval, J., del Barrio, C., & Echeita, G. (1981). El conocimiento de los niños de su propio país [Children's knowledge about their own country]. *Cuadernos de Pedagogía, 75*, 33-36.

Delval, J., Díaz-Barriga, F., Hinojosa, M. L., & Daza, D. (1993). *Experiencia y representación social: Un estudio preliminar sobre las ideas de trabajo y ganancia en niños trabajadores mexicanos* [Experience and social representation: A preliminary study about work and profit ideas in Mexican worker children]. Unpublished manuscript.

Delval, J., & Echeita, G. (1991). La comprensión en el niño del mecanismo de intercambio económico y el problema de la ganancia [Children's understanding of the economic exchange mechanism and the problem of profit]. *Infancia y Aprendizaje, 54*, 71-108.

Emler, N., & Dickinson, J. (1985). Children's representations of economic inequalities: The effects of social class. *British Journal of Developmental Psychology, 3*, 191-198.

Emler, N., Ohana, J., & Dickinson, J. (1990). Children's representations of social relations. In G. Duveen & B. Lloyd (Eds.), *Social representations and the development of knowledge* (pp. 47-69). Cambridge: Cambridge University Press.

Friedman, W. J. (Ed.). (1982). *The developmental psychology of time*. New York: Academic Press.

Furnham, A., & Stacey, B. (1991). *Young people's understanding of society*. London: Routledge.

Furth, H. G. (1980). *The world of grown-ups. Children's conceptions of society*. New York: Elsevier North-Holland.

Goldmann, L. (1955). *Le dieu caché*. Paris: Gallimard.

Hook, J. (1983). The development of children's equity judgements. In R. L. Leahy (Ed.) *The child's construction of social inequality* (pp. 207-221). New York: Academic Press.

Hook, J., & Cook, T. D. (1979). Equity theory and the cognitive ability of children. *Psychological Bulletin, 86*, 429-445.

Inhelder, B., & Piaget, J. (1955). *De la logique de l'enfant à la logique de l'adolescent*. Paris: Presses Universitaires de France. (Published in 1972 as *The growth of logical thinking from childhood to adolescence*. London: Routledge.)

Jahoda, G. (1959). Development of the perception of social differences in children from 6 to 10. *British Journal of Psychology, 50*, 159-177.

Jahoda, G. (1964). Children's concepts of nationality: A critical study of Piaget's stages. *Child Development, 35*, 1081-1092.

Jahoda, G. (1979). The construction of economic reality by some Glaswegian children. *European Journal of Social Psychology, 9*, 115-127.

Jahoda, G. (1983). European 'lag' in the development of an economic concept: A study in Zimbabwe. *British Journal of Developmental Psychology, 1*, 113-120.

Jahoda, G. (1984). The development of thinking about socio-economic systems. In H. Tajfel (Ed.), *The social dimension* (Vol. I, pp. 69-88). Cambridge: Cambridge University Press.

Jahoda, G. (1988). Critical notes and reflections on 'social representations'. *European Journal of Social Psychology, 18*, 195-209.

Jahoda, G., & Woerdenbagch, A. (1982). The development of ideas about an economic institution: A cross-national replication. *British Journal of Social Psychology, 21*, 337-338.

Leahy, R. L. (1981). The development of the conception of economic inequality. I. Descriptions and comparisons of rich and poor people. *Child Development, 52*, 523-532.

Leahy, R. L. (1983a). The development of the conception of economic inequality. II. Explanations, justifications, and conceptions of social mobility and social change. *Developmental Psychology, 19*, 111-125.

Leahy, R. L. (1983b). The development of the conception of social class. In R. L. Leahy (Ed.) *The child's construction of social inequality* (pp. 79-107). New York: Academic Press.

Montangero, J. (1992). The development of a diachronic perspective in children. In F. Macar, V. Pouthas, & W. J. Friedman (Eds.), *Time, action and cognition* (pp. 55-65). Dordrecht, The Netherlands: Kluwer.

Moscovici, S. (1976). *La psychanalyse, son image et son public* (2nd ed.). París: Presses Universitaires de France.

Moscovici, S. (1984). The phenomenon of social representations. In R. M. Farr & S. Moscovici (Eds.), *Social representations* (pp. 3-69). Cambridge: Cambridge University Press.

Ng, S. H. (1982). Children's ideas about the bank and shop profit: Developmental stages and influences of cognitive contrast and conflict. *Journal of Economic Psychology, 4*, 209-221.

Piaget, J. (1926). *La représentation du monde chez l'enfant*. París: Alcan. (Also published in 1929 as *The child's conception of the world*. London: Kegan)

Piaget, J. (1946). *Le développement de la notion de temps chez l'enfant* [The child's conception of time]. London: Routledge. (Original work published 1969).

Piaget, J., & Inhelder, B. (1941). *Le développement des quantités chez l'enfant: Conservation et atomisme*. Neuchâtel, Paris: Delachaux et Niestlé. (Published in 1974 as *The child's construction of quantities: conservation and atomism*. London: Routledge)

Shantz, C. V. (1975). The development of social cognition. In E. M. Hetherington (Ed.), *Review of child development research* (Vol. 5, pp. 257-323). Chicago: University of Chicago Press.

Shantz, C.U. (1983). Social cognition. In P. H. Mussen (Series Ed.), J. H. Flavell & E. Markman (Eds.), *Cognitive development* (Vol. 3, pp. 495-555). New York: Wiley.

Simmons, R., & Rosenberg, M. (1971). Functions of children's perceptions of the stratification system. *American Sociological Review, 36*, 235-249.

Strauss, A. L. (1952). The development and transformation of monetary meanings in the child. *American Sociological Review, 27*, 275-284.

Strauss, A. L. (1954). The development of conceptions of rules in children. *Child Development, 25*, 192-208.

Wertsch, J. V., & Rogoff, B. (1984). Editors' notes. In B. Rogoff & J. V. Wertsch (Eds.), *Children's learning in the "zone of proximal development"* (*New Directions for Child Development*, Vol. 23, pp. 1-6). San Francisco: Jossey-Bass.

5

Dimensions of Adolescents' Reasoning about Political and Historical Issues: Ontological Switches, Developmental Processes, and Situated Learning

Judith Torney-Purta
University of Maryland

Even with the recent explosion of research on reasoning, two important questions concerning adolescents' thinking about political and social issues remain: (a) What is conceptual change in the social and political domain of knowledge dealing with contemporary political events and with historical events? and (b) What is important about developmental processes as they intersect with instructional processes to influence conceptual change in this domain?

Conceptual change is a familiar topic for research in the sciences (Vosniadou & Brewer, 1987), but much less so in the social sciences and history. Although there is research on instructional processes and speculation about developmental stages in understanding history, there is little work within this domain that attempts to differentiate conceptual change associated with instruction from conceptual change associated with development.

These questions are explored with data from think-aloud problem solving, concept mapping, and related techniques dealing with historical and contemporary political issues. The samples come from research conducted on 14- to 17-year-old participants in a computer-assisted international simulation (Project ICONS) and a study using concept mapping of topics related to the Holocaust conducted with 12- to 14-year-olds participating in an educational program in their classroom and a museum exhibit. Both are highly involving instructional experiences in which adolescents are prompted to grapple with social and historical issues in a context of peer group discussion.

CONCEPTUAL CHANGE IN THE SOCIAL AND
POLITICAL DOMAIN

The subject matter of history and social studies differs from the subject matter of science. Concrete objects are much less prominent in social studies and history; narrative is much more important in history; problems in these fields are ill structured with few clear goals or agreed on solutions. Further, a given society participates actively in delineating valued social knowledge, resulting in the availability of certain "social schemata" that serve as frames or limiting factors within which most individuals in that society construct knowledge (see more complete discussion in Haste & Torney-Purta, 1992). We need a more coherent theoretical framework for understanding conceptual change in the social and political domain, a framework that could lead to predictions about instructional processes and their effectiveness.

One approach is to begin with fundamental domains of knowledge, such as those proposed by Wellman and Gelman (1992). They argue that the child constructs a "naive theory" in each of three domains—a naive physics (in the domain of inanimate objects), a naive psychology (in the domain of human intents and actions), and a naive biology (in the domain of plants and animals). Each of these theories includes core beliefs and more peripheral ideas. These organized systems of knowledge have different prototypes, are structured in different ways, and may have different modes of change or development. This framework is incomplete, however. The psychological domain is not adequate to understand children's grasp of social or political institutions because it deals fairly narrowly with issues such as the understanding of mind, intent, belief, and other individual qualities. A fourth domain is needed to complete Wellman and Gelman's categorization, that is, the young person's naive theory in the domain of politics and society (including sociology, economics, history, and international relations).

Assuming that this fourth domain is distinct, what is the ontological character of the elements within it? Chi's recent work on conceptual change in physics as ontological change is relevant here (Chi & Slotta, 1993). Chi proposed that when we speak of conceptual change sufficient to be called radical restructuring of knowledge, we are discussing an individual's switching of a concept from one ontological category to another (as illustrated in Fig. 5.1). In science this means, for example, a shift from viewing electrical current as a property of matter to viewing it as a process. She was especially interested in what are called *events* (which have a time course and can usually be traced to a single major cause) and *acausal processes* or *interactions*, which do not have a time course (for example, a defined beginning and end) and cannot be connected to a single or small set of precursors as causes. Further, she argued that the misconceptions in science that are difficult to change are those in which the scientists' view of a phenomenon or entity is ontologically different from the view of the novice or student. The conceptual change required of students is to shift the concept of an entity (such as forces or current) from one ontological status to another (horizontally into another category in Fig. 5.1).

In addition to noting the importance of shifting one's understanding in the physical sciences from matter to processes, she also found that young children hold many biological concepts to be "mental-state based." They believe that individual animals grow or species evolve "because they want to." Chi concluded that when a misconception arises about a biological or physical concept, the difficulty may be that students are seeing it as part of a category to which it does not belong. The ontological category for an entity in an individual's cognitive structure shapes the linkages between concepts and the kind of self-elaborations or explanations in which the individual can engage when reading or thinking about them.

Chi also raised, in passing, whether people in general find it easier to think concretely (dealing with matter) or intentionally (dealing with mental states) than to think about processes (dealing with events and acausal

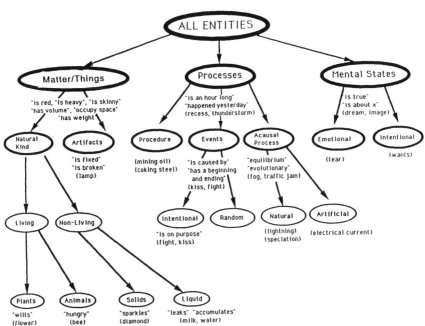

FIG. 5.1.   One possible categorization scheme. Categories that are separated horizontally on the three branches are ontologically distinct. (From "The Ontological Coherence of Intuitive Physics," by M. T. H. Chi & J. D. Slotta, 1993, *Cognition and Instruction, 10*, p. 15. Reprinted by permission of Lawrence Erlbaum Associates.)

interactions). This is an interesting way of explaining differences between young and older children. The parts of Chi's ontological tree that are especially relevant for historical and contemporary political issues and events are "social processes" and "mental states of individuals." "Matter and things" are important in other areas of social studies such as economics, geography, and environmental studies. One can use the distinctions in the top part of this Fig. 5.1 to contrast a more advanced or expert view of social/political/historical events with a novice view. The expert or more advanced view of an issue or event is: (a) more continuous in the sense that the event or issue does not have a clear beginning or end; (b) more elaborated in the sense that it is influenced but not fully explained by the emotional and cognitive states of individuals such as political leaders or in the sense that distinctions are made between political groups or institutions; (c) more complex in its causation in the sense that an event is not attributed to a single cause and in the sense that there are alternative paths conceivable between past, present, and future events or actions; (d) organized, sometimes hierarchically, in the sense that subordinate facts are understood in relation to more important ideas, conditions, or causes; and (e) contextualized in the sense that conditions associated with time and place (historical period and cultural setting) are recognized. This delineation of more advanced concepts in social sciences and history resembles the general category of acausal interactions as defined by Chi.

What is the novice's view of history or politics? First, of course, the novice has less well-organized information about these matters, perhaps knowing only that certain kinds of events and issues must be important because social studies and history teachers keep mentioning them (e.g., the existence of other countries, their locations, and differing perspectives; particular events such as wars that took place a long time ago; the existence of a distinction between important people in history and less important ones; certain important documents, such as the Constitution or Bill of Rights). Some research has indicated that these leaders or persons and their mental states are especially likely to be prominent in students' knowledge structures (Hallden, 1986, this volume), that important historical documents are not well differentiated from each other by novices but instead form a "document stew" (Beck, this volume; McKeown & Beck, 1990); that economic processes are believed to operate much like relationships between individuals (e.g., banks are not allowed to charge interest on loans because individuals lend to each other free of such charges; Berti, this volume; Berti & Bombi, 1988), and that political processes such as law enforcement and legislation are thought by young children to be subject to the whim (individual mental state) of the police or the President, respectively (Hess & Torney, 1967). This chapter further explores the extent to which conceptual change and the growth of understanding or the acquisition of expertise in

the social/political/historical knowledge domain can be viewed as a movement of concepts across ontological categories, with the most advanced type
of understanding being found in the acausal process category.

RESEARCH RELATING TO THIS CONCEPTUALIZATION

My program of research in the past 7 years has investigated the representations of and reasoning about political issues, both contemporary and of
the past, among early and middle adolescents. The findings suggest some
answers to the first question posed, about what conceptual change consists
of when dealing with contemporary and historical events. To summarize
(before detailing the research groups and methods), in the area of historical
political events such as the Holocaust or the situation in Spain in 1492,
novice-like conceptualizations are more likely to be found within the
category of mental states of leaders (particularly intentions such as Hitler's
wish to control the world or a nation's leaders "being mad" at other leaders
and thus having a war). In the area of contemporary political issues with a
strong economic cast, such as the poverty of developing countries, less
advanced conceptions are more likely to be found in the category of
materially based or time-bound and singly caused events and to be thought
of as having a single relatively simple time-bound solution (e.g., get some
more loans, pay off what the country owes, and solve the problem of debt).
Finally, in reasoning about problems of the environment, less advanced
conceptualizations are found within the category of matter and things (e.g.,
the environmental problem is one of piling up too many pollutants, and to
solve the problem one gets rid of them).[1]

The next four sections describe phases of the research program. Each of
them involves a method designed to capture students' knowledge structures;
three of them involve data collection at two or more time points with an
intervening concentrated instructional experience including peer group
interaction; all of them are interpreted in a way to shed light on the
characteristics of conceptual change in history and social studies.

Phase 1: Think-aloud Problem Solving

In the first phase of this research, begun in 1987, I used open-ended
interviews consisting of think-aloud problem solving relating to international debt and human rights violation (Apartheid). The problems were
similar to those used by Voss (Voss, Tyler, & Yengo, 1983), but related

---

[1]Note that these data were all collected before Chi's theory appeared in its current form. The
theory thus is a framework for interpreting the data and is not directly tested.

more to issues involving relations between several countries. I interviewed students about these problems and then drew graphic schema maps to represent the content of problem solutions found in the interview transcripts. This scoring system was loosely built on cognitive psychologists' notions of legitimate actors and actions in solutions to the Tower of Hanoi problem, but was modified to define actors, actions, and constraints on actions in line with current international relations theory. Interviews (and their associated maps) produced before and after experience in a highly involving computer-assisted international simulation (the ICONS project) were compared. Peer group interaction in teams in which the adolescents were role-playing diplomats from different countries pressed students toward deep processing of social, political, and economic information and toward conceptual change and elaboration.

Figures 5.2 and 5.3 show the actors, actions, and constraints mentioned by one student thinking aloud to solve a problem involving a finance minister who was unable to pay the interest on his debt (see Torney-Purta, 1990). References to mental states of actors were relatively rare, but students' representations did seem to move from singly caused events (which were seen as associated with few difficulties or constraints) to multiply caused events (acausal interactions), which had many of the links and contextualizations characteristic of the more expert views detailed earlier.

In fact, these schema maps can be arrayed along a continuum ranging from prenovice, to novice, to postnovice, to preexpert according to both the

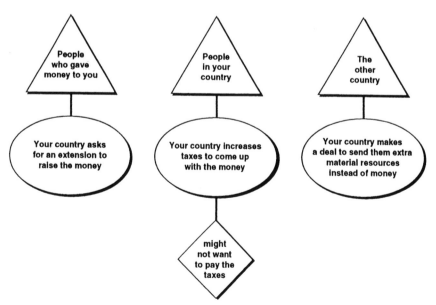

FIG. 5.2.   Schema map of respondent's presession answer to the finance minister problem (drawn based on think-aloud protocol).

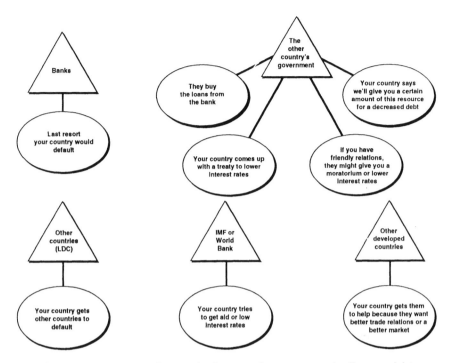

FIG. 5.3.   Schema map of respondent's postsession answer to the finance minister problem (drawn based on think-aloud protocol).

number of actors, actions, and constraints included and the way in which the respondent defined the problem and its solutions as an event or an acausal interaction (see Torney-Purta, 1992).

Phase 2: Using Concept Maps of the Holocaust

Hirsch (1992) conducted a study whose major purpose was to ascertain the impact of various levels of advance organization provided to students who were to attend a museum exhibit on the Holocaust (Remember the Children). The outcome measures were concept maps of the Holocaust that were drawn at the beginning of the history unit, after the period of advance organization (limited or intensive), and after the visit to the exhibit and a presentation by a Holocaust survivor. Following a period of cooperative group activity, students were invited to add any material they wished to the third map. Sixty-five sixth graders participated.

A coding and scoring framework for the maps' major affective and cognitive categories was designed, guided by research on schemata, the organization of knowledge representations, and on themes related to the Holocaust. The coding for the complexity of the map structure encompassed a number of elements included at different levels, the development of concept map elements in detail, and their connections to other elements. A series of analyses of covariance (covarying out prior knowledge) showed significant effects on the complexity of structure of the maps for the intensive advance organization (which took place in small groups), for the exhibit visit, and for a cooperative group experience after the visit. These students moved toward more complex, elaborated and tightly connected knowledge structures after these experiences.

Hirsch also coded the maps for content themes. There was a general movement away from attributing the Holocaust to Hitler and his personal motives (a decline from 19 Map 1s that mentioned Hitler to 10 Map 3s with this element included). In contrast, the categories that increase when Maps 1 and 3 are compared are: mistreatment (7 to 16), discrimination (9 to 15), resistance (0 to 5), and absence of concern from the rest of the world (0 to 8).

The content category of "reflective elements" showed some especially interesting differences in Hirsch's study. Reflective elements are statements that dealt with ideas, went beyond the information given, or were hypothetical or philosophical. The inclusion of these themes was more likely after the exhibit and particularly for the group with advanced organization experience. For example, there was an increase in the frequency of lessons learned from the Holocaust (e.g. "Could this happen again?" or "Happens today"), of statements expressing concern about a lack of help from the world (e.g., why did people close their eyes and not do anything?), and resistance (e.g., keeping hope and never losing faith). In the last map, which was an augmentation of Map 3 and which followed a cooperative group experience for both treatment groups, the limited advance organization group showed a surge in the inclusion of these reflective elements; for these students this was the first group discussion experienced in the study. The intensive advance organizer group experienced a group discussion task before the exhibit visit; it was after that experience that this group's surge in inclusion of reflective statements took place. It appears that, at least for early adolescents, beginning to see historical events such as the Holocaust as processes without single causes, embedded in contexts, and carrying lessons for the present requires not only a concrete presentation of information but an opportunity to interact with peers as they organize and process that information. Their understanding of what they experience and their movement toward greater reflectivity are situated within a group of peers grappling with understanding the same material.

Phase 3: Interviews About a Scenario in Spain, 1492

I conducted a set of interviews with 11 students from the same international simulation program as that in which the think-aloud problem solving and graphic schema maps (described earlier) were collected. This was a post-simulation-only interview conducted in 1992 and was intended to ascertain whether it was possible to place responses dealing with the domain of social history into ontological categories such as mental states and different types of processes. The students were presented with the following scenario:

In 1492, there was a proposal that all Jews be expelled from Spain. The two monarchs, Ferdinand and Isabella, who sent Columbus on his voyage, were very strong Catholics. Spain was very divided at the time. There were different ethnic groups, different political groups, and different religions in the country. As a way of unifying the country, it was proposed that Spain tell all the Jews they had 4 months to either convert to Catholicism or to leave Spain for good. There was a Jewish man named Abrabanel who was an advisor to the King and Queen. He was supposed to advise them on what to do about this proposal to expel the Jews from Spain. Imagine that you are Abrabanel. Think about what you would have done if you had been asked for advice.

The subjects were then presented a format for making decisions and were asked (a) to define the problem in 1492, (b) to give the causes of the problem, and (c) to offer solutions, with pros and cons for each. Finally, they were asked to think of ways in which the situation in 1492 was different from the situation for leaders today and what else they would need to know in order to understand "how it really was in 1492."

These definitions of the problem and its causes fit into two of the categories in Fig. 5.1. The first category of statements included those limited to mental states and individual actions, whereas the second included group-related and time-bound event statements. A number of respondents made statements of both types.

The best example of the representation of the problem limited to mental states and actions of individual leaders is the following: "He has to tell who has to leave the country; the King and Queen want all one kind of groups in the country." This student, when asked how things are different or the same today, had a relatively naive answer: "Now they don't kick people out of a country because they want to be a Jew or Catholic." Two of the things this student would want to know in order to understand the situation better were also personally focused: "Why they only wanted Catholics; how the government worked and how they decided who should stay or leave."

A second student's representation of the problem also focused on the King and Queen's wants as individuals: "How to get the Jews out of Spain or make them convert; Jews were a different ethnic group and the King and Queen wanted them to leave." This student also showed a tendency to believe things had changed: "Leaders today really don't have situations like this—governments don't force people out." What she wanted to know was also person focused: "What were the King and Queen really like and how did they want to handle the situation?"

There were some students whose representations of the problem referred both to the monarchs and to a process in the sense of a time-bound event involving groups and their relations: "Spain is divided and Ferdinand and Isabella want to unify it; there is a lack of understanding among religious and political groups and a lack of tolerance." This student wanted to know: "how much the educated population held these stereotypes and how strongly they believed in them." Her preferred solution was to: "educate the populations about different ethnic groups and religions so there is better tolerance and understanding." She was one of the few students whose solutions were so clearly connected to the perceived cause of the problem; however, the solution was clearly a generalization from current remedies proposed for intolerance and lacked a sense of contextualization or recognition that individuals in the past inhabited universes that differ radically from today (see Wineberg, this volume).

This case illustrates that some adolescents are capable of seeing ontological possibilities beyond the mental states of the rulers. It appears that these elaborated views were added as enrichment rather being a switch of categories, as Chi suggested for scientific concepts.

Another student also referred to a range of causes, both individual mental states as well as the processes of exercise of power and group conflict, for example, in the following problem definition: "The Jews are there and they are a threat to the King and Queen's power; there is prejudice since the Jews have wealth; there is religious conflict; Spain had earlier problems with the Muslims and feared the same again." There is reference here to mental states (fear) based on events earlier in time involving parallel groups and to processes involving conflict and power. The material this student felt he needed to know more about also included both individual and process aspects: "The exact position of the Jews in society — their social class, political power, and leadership; why Spain felt threatened; what type of man Abrabanel was"

Another student's response that stressed individuals is the following: The problem is "Abrabanel is a Jew and must decide about his loyalty to the King and Queen and to his people." The cause of the problem included processes: "religious differences increase tensions between groups." In order to understand better, she would want to know "what was happening in Spain at that time and the history of the people" (as close to a non-time-bound and contextualized process conception as any student gave).

The last student we examine defined the problem as "Spain wants to be unified; the Jews are keeping them from being unified," and the causes as "different religions; Catholic Church was very strong and intolerant of other religions; economic causes since the loss of the Jews will hurt the middle class." This focused almost entirely on social, political, and economic processes.

In summary, within this small group of students the majority gave some credence to leaders' acts and motives. There were some who gave definitions of the problem limited to the personal intents and feelings of leaders. Some of these students broadened their understanding to include both time-bounded and non-time-bounded, group-oriented notions, sometimes with considerable attention to context.

Similar to Chi's model, when the content of the issue is social history, some students defined the problem in terms of mental states of leaders and others in terms of processes of group conflict not bound to an individual or a time period. Differing from Chi's model, in this content area students with more advanced levels of reasoning appeared to add concepts of processes (both time-bound events and contextualized processes without a single cause) producing a more complex understanding, rather than replacing mental-state-based with processes-based conceptions. Wineburg (1991) also noted that expert historians give credence to leaders' motives, but go beyond them when they read historical sources. For some of these adolescents there was an elaboration and deepening in the understanding of historical situations as entities corresponding to the characteristics of expertise given earlier. However, the responses also retain a certain sense of historical narrative in which the mental states of leaders play an important role.

There is some evidence of the existence of the separate fourth domain of society and politics argued for at the beginning of the chapter. Some students conceptualized historical events in a psychological framework or theory, but others clearly used concepts within a domain of society and politics. For example, one student wanted to know "the influence of the church and power of the church over the people" as well as "the mindset of the people."

In summary, there is some indication that both for concepts of the Holocaust and concepts of events leading up to the expulsion of the Jews from Spain in 1492, conceptual change in history can be thought of as involving the addition of layers or the recognition of alternative ontological aspects of issues and problems in history. In particular, the mental states of individuals are augmented with social or political processes. For some adolescents there are singly caused events, for others multiple causes are recognized.

An interesting additional question is whether ontological augmentation with advanced process categories may take place more easily for well-known types of historical or political events. Events or topics that are in a relatively remote historical period or an unfamiliar world area may be perceived under the more primitive categories (e.g., of matter/thing, mental state of leader). An alternative is that the prototypic events of history studied repeatedly in school — for American students the men who signed the Declaration of Independence or Lincoln freeing the slaves — may be learned during elementary school under the relatively more primitive ontological categories and may remain fixed in those categories.

Phase 4: Concept Maps of the "Global Environment"

Applying this framework can also expand our understanding of conceptual change in social studies topics outside history. This section examines the concept of the global environment as a contemporary political issue and how students' concepts fit into the ontological status categories in Fig. 5.1.

Concept maps of "the global environment" were collected from 79 students in 1992 as parts of a presession and a postsession questionnaire for the Maryland Summer Center for International Studies (the ICONS project). Recall that peer group discussion within teams of 5-6 adolescents was a critical part of the program. Of special interest are the processes involved with the environment as an arena for international negotiation in which both economic and political processes are exemplified in interactions between countries. These processes include negotiation, industrialization, bringing international public pressure to bear, and standard setting.

On the whole, concept maps drawn by students before the ICONS sessions were more likely than those afterward to focus on the global environment's problems as consisting of the piling up of polluted materials (air pollution, water pollution in streams and rivers) or the loss of valuable things in the environment (natural resources, trees, the ozone layer). These are matter-based conceptions. After this experience, in which one of the major topics for between-country team negotiation was the environment, maps were more complex in their structural connections. They were also less likely to present knowledge structures for the environment that focused on the presence or absence of things; they were more likely to include issues with international connections, viewing the environment as a process-driven system, for example, foreign policies relating to treaties and standards, problems of pollution that cross national borders, and interrelations between the economy, technology and society.

Figures 5.4 and 5.5 present the pre- and postsimulation concept maps for one individual. The premap largely focused on the buildup of pollutants — chemical fertilizers, acid rain, litter — and the destruction or exploitation of valuable things in the environment — the ozone layer, natural resources, marine life, and rain forests. However, this student did have two reflective elements — "people taking time to consider the consequences of actions" and "once they're gone, they're gone." There was very little sense of international process about this map, however. This student's postsimulation map included many fewer "things" and instead focused on processes (deforestation, cross-border pollution, international pressure, standard setting). A number of economic processes were linked (industrialization, strong and weak economies), and a series of arrows and final conclusions at the bottom of the map gave a sense of the way in which these processes, many of them with multiple causes, fit together into a system and have a open-ended recursive pattern across time. It is interesting to note that this is one of the students who also took part in the interviews about 1492 (the last student quoted) and who also showed a pattern of historical understanding that focussed on groups, economic issues, and negotiation.

Another set of maps illustrates conceptual change in understanding the environment moving away from the buildup of pollutants (Fig. 5.6) and loss of valued "things" in the environment (e.g., clear water, clean air, oxygen) toward a somewhat more issue-based and quite a bit more internationalized view of an environmental system (Fig. 5.7). In the area of environmental issues, the switch or addition that took place in concepts appears to be from matter and things to process conceptions. Because the instructional experience focused on international issues, that dimension also became more clearly represented in the elements included and their interconnections.

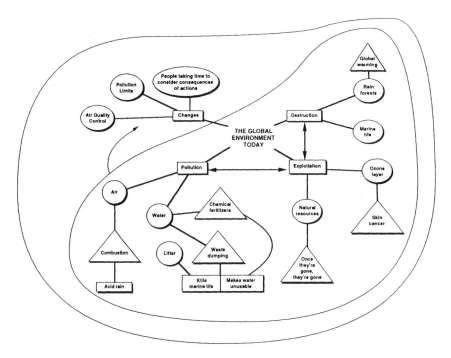

FIG. 5.4.   Concept map of "The Global Environment Today" (drawn by 16-year-old presession).

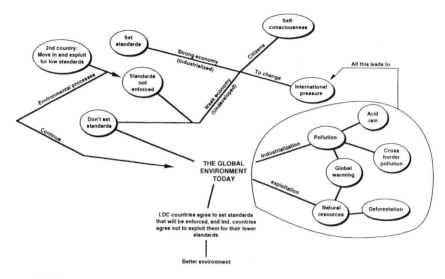

FIG.5.5. Concept map of "The Global Environment Today" (drawn by 16-year-old postsession).

CONCEPTUAL CHANGE, INSTRUCTION, AND DEVELOPMENT

Four illustrations were given of changes in the degree of focus on concepts with different ontological characteristics, all within the subject matter of social studies and history. Conceptual change seems not to consist of a switch of categories but rather an addition of process-based notions to mental state or material-based ones.

I now move to the second question posed at the beginning, concerning developmental and instructional processes. Is it possible to divide conceptual change into that resulting from development and that resulting from instruction, or do these processes overlap so completely that it is impossible to disentangle them? What are the implications of this distinction between developmental change and change resulting from instruction in the domain of social, political, and historical knowledge?

Although frameworks such as Chi's have been sophisticated in dealing with conceptual change as a product of instruction, the developmental dimension has been less convincingly drawn. Authors who write about cognitive restructuring sometimes dismiss development as "maturation" and concentrate on instruction designed to correct misconceptions, expecially in science. Those studying historical misunderstandings have largely confined themselves to using data from cross-sectional studies to describe younger children as especially likely to give personal reasons for historical events.

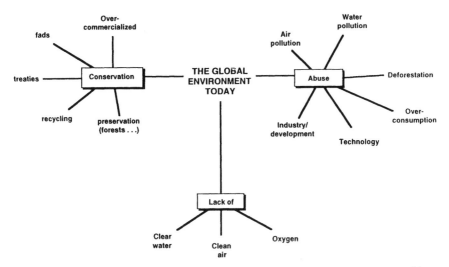

FIG. 5.6.   Concept map of "The Global Environment Today" (drawn by 14-year-old presession).

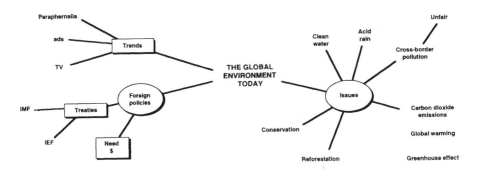

FIG. 5.7.   Concept map of "The Global Environment Today" (drawn by 14-year-old postsession).

Prescriptions such as encouraging children to reflect on their misconceptions or tailoring textbooks to match schemata for historical events have been suggested. But many writers fail to consider what it is about development that is important to know for effective instruction.

Maturation is often presented as a kind of black box. Certainly between the ages of 7 and 15 there is maturation of the nervous system (and some argue an increase in speed of processing or size of short-term memory), but there are also many things that are different about 7- and 15-year-olds that are potentially as important to consider in a discussion of developmental influences on social and political knowledge.

First is the role of generalized social experience. In the years from 7 to 15 the individual has extensive social experience, for example, meeting individuals in authority roles, observing parks becoming more polluted or recovering from pollution, hearing parents or peers talk about wealth and poverty in the community, hanging out with peers, and being a member of various organized groups. This everyday experience and cognition situated outside the classroom is widely influential in the domain of social and political knowledge. This immersion in the social and political context of society and the community is an important developmental force in constructing knowledge apart from any classroom lesson.

Instructional experience in the classroom can be contrasted with developmental experience. Developmental experience is rich in levels of meaning and social context, in redundancy as the same topics are visited and revisited, in opportunities to respond to others' ideas and to get their feedback, and in chances to construct a group identity and to experience loyalty. Instructional experience in the social studies classroom is more likely to be narrowly focused on facts, lean on context and connection, moving rapidly among topics, lacking opportunities to voice opinions without risking potential censure, and to be generalized to reach all students rather than responsive to a group identity or set of interests. Developmental experience is situated for child and adolescent in a meaningful context, often within the peer group or family or neighborhood. Instructional experience usually lacks such a context.

One result of developmental experience is the increased ability to handle complex, multicausal, multidimensional, reciprocal, and verbally mediated events in the social world. The average 15-year-old has many more of these abilities honed through experience. Reasoning about social or political matters as processes (either events or acausal processes) would certainly be more congenial to an adolescent with these kinds of abilities than to a 7-year-old who lacks many of them.

Developmental continuity is a second important dimension. This insight is sometimes reflected in prescriptions for instruction beginning with students' prior knowledge. The understanding of history at the end of the sixth grade will be built on the concepts a student had at the beginning of the sixth grade (modified by both experience and by instruction). For example, the interviews on the finance minister presented earlier when graphed into schema maps showed similarity in at least half of the actors and actions mentioned in the pre- and postinterviews, as did the concept maps of the Holocaust and the global environment.

It is not always easy to build in a continuous fashion on prior knowledge because the teacher must deliver a lesson to a group of students with very different knowledge structures. Statements of curriculum scope and sequence in social studies generally assume the average student has understood and remembered reasonably well what was taught in previous grades.

In order to build on existing knowledge to construct more complex ideas, a student is also expected, at least after about grade 4, to have developed skills of reading comprehension for written text, comprehension of oral discourse, and appropriate generalization across instances. However, more and more teachers in the United States are discovering a wide diversity of knowledge structures and skills in their classes, a variety that results from students' differential success in previous grades, their moving from school to school (often from outside the state or country), and their having very diverse kinds of out-of-school experience. Under these circumstances teaching that builds on continuity in construction of knowledge becomes even more difficult.

A third aspect of development separable from instruction is the set of expectations or schemata of the social roles and tasks of various ages that are presented by the social partners who are important for the young person outside of school—parents, peers, and media. What a 15-year-old is expected to do and be and where he or she is expected to get information are vastly different from a 7-year-old. A decline in the tendency to reference one's ideas to those of adults and an increase in referencing to one's peers is almost universally observed at around age 10 or 11 (sometimes earlier). Part of this phenomenon is linked to physical maturation. The fact that one looks more like an adult and less like a child and that both adults and peers are treating one in that way leads the young person to explore a new set of concepts for making judgments about social issues and reasoning about choices. Discussing and exploring ideas with peers becomes instrumental for conceptual change. It is probably especially important if the student is to understand processes, either events or acausal interactions. The research presented on the Holocaust and on hypothetical international problem solving showed potent effects associated with group interaction. Discussion with the peer group is an essential and developmentally appropriate context for conceptual change within the domain of politics, society, and history. The peer group "situates" this cognition in much the same way that Lave and Wenger (1991) discussed situated cognition.

Another aspect of adolescence is the fact that every part of one's identity that sets one apart from others—one's gender, race or ethnicity, or language—becomes an important potential source for a priming effect. Not only does the adolescent reference to peers in general, but differentially to those of the same and different gender, to those of the same and different race, ethnicity, or language group. A more pessimistic way of looking at this is that the student's ability to deal with past issues in a contextualized way may be problematic when current membership groups are evoked. Note the difficulty of providing a context for discussions with African-American students of why slavery existed or with female students of the difficulty of attaining women's suffrage.

In summary, these three issues are especially germane to developmental psychologists and are related to conceptual change: first, long-term social experience resulting in ability to deal with more complex and multicausal situations; second, continuity in building one knowledge structure upon another; and third, the peer group, as it situates social cognition in adolescence. These developmental dimensions, as they intersect with instructional efforts are powerful in their influence on conceptual change in the historical, social, and political domain.

How does this relate to the data described in the four phases of research? It appears that the processing of everyday experience and the contextualized application of cognitive abilities have an important role to play in the ability to understand social and historical entities as processes. The phenomena of continuity of and inertia in concepts suggests the value (but enormous difficulty) of tailoring instruction to individuals' prior knowledge. The importance of the peer group situation or context among adolescents suggests that it is not just active participation in learning in general, but participation with peers in discussions and authentic projects that is likely to be developmentally appropriate for promoting conceptual change.

CONCLUSIONS

Further research is needed on the several issues raised. What overlaps are there between the proposed fourth domain of political and societal understanding and the other domains? To what extent do other methods of eliciting responses show the same categories of political and historical concepts, and what does this mean about naive theories among adolescents as well as children? What conceptual change is seen in short-term longitudinal studies? How do young people interpret social, political, and historical information about events when the majority of their conceptions are mental-state based?

Research on situated cognition in the peer group can provide important insights into the developmental changes of adolescence and into models for developmentally appropriate and effective instruction. History and social studies instruction has a variety of aims in the United States: These include building a common body of shared factual knowledge about history, ensuring a reasonable amount of similarity in the schemata for understanding democratic institutions and principles, encouraging national identity based on shared social representations, teaching ways of reasoning about issues and political choices, and motivating students to be active political participants. Much of current instruction does not successfully relate to adolescents who are at different points on the continuum of expertise in understanding political and historical issues and who differ in their experience and developmental trajectories. It fails to present powerful lessons to help students understand processes as well as leaders' mental states or concrete manifestations of problems in the environment, and it isolates the school context too much from the contexts in which the majority of adolescents are most interested.

ACKNOWLEDGMENTS

This chapter was presented at a conference on Reasoning and Instruction in History and Social Sciences, Madrid, Spain, October 1992. I am grateful to Charles Middlestead, Susan Robertson, and Edmund Chia for assistance in data collection and coding; to James Byrnes and Joanne Hirsch for helpful discussions of the ideas underlying the paper; and to Jon Wilkenfeld, and the staff of the Maryland Summer Center for International Studies operating under the sponsorship of the Maryland State Department of Education. It is a wonderful place to observe conceptual change among adolescents.

REFERENCES

Berti, A., & Bombi, A. (1988). *The child's construction of economics.* Cambridge, England: Cambridge University Press.

Chi, M. T. H., & Slotta, J. D. (1993). The ontological coherence of intuitive physics. Cognition & Instruction, 10, 249–260.

Hallden, O. (1986). Learning history. *Oxford Review of Education, 12,* 33–66.

Haste, H., & Torney-Purta, J. (1992). Introduction. In H. Haste & J. Torney-Purta (Eds.), *The development of political understanding: A new perspective* (pp. 3–10). San Francisco: Jossey-Bass.

Hess, R., & Torney, J. (1967). *The development of political attitudes in children.* Chicago: Aldine.

Hirsch, J. (1992). *Changes in the gifted early adolescent's schemata of the Holocaust: The impact of advance organizers and a museum exhibit.* Unpublished doctoral dissertation, Department of Human Development, University of Maryland. (Available from University of Michigan Dissertation Reproduction Service, Ann Arbor, No. 9234579)

Lave, J., & Wenger, E. (1991). *Situated learning: Legitimate peripheral participation.* Cambridge, England: Cambridge University Press.

McKeown, M., & Beck, I. (1990). The assessment and characterization of young learners' knowledge of a topic in history. *American Educational Research Journal, 27,* 688–726.

Torney-Purta, J. (1990). From attitudes and knowledge to schemata: Expanding the outcomes of political socialization research. In O. Ichilov (Ed.), *Political socialization, citizenship education, and democracy* (pp. 98–115). New York: Teachers College Press.

Torney-Purta, J. (1992). Cognitive representations of the political system in adolescents: The continuum from pre-novice to expert. In H. Haste & J. Torney-Purta (Eds.), *The development of political understanding: A new perspective* (pp. 11–25). San Francisco: Jossey-Bass.

Vosniadou, S., & Brewer, W. F. (1987). Theories of knowledge restructuring in development. *Review of Educational Research, 57,* 51-67.

Voss, J., Tyler, S., & Yengo, I. (1983). Individual differences in the solving of social science problems. In R. Dillon & R. Schmeck (Eds.), *Individual differences in problem solving* (pp. 205-232). San Diego: Academic Press.

Wellman, H., & Gelman, S. (1992). Cognitive development: Foundational theories of core domains. *Annual Review of Psychology, 43,* 337-375.

Wineberg, S. (1991). On the reading of historical texts: Notes on the breach between the school and academy. *American Educational Research Journal, 28,* 495-519.

Discussion of Chapters 2–5: Cognitive Development and Representation Processes in the Understanding of Social and Historical Concepts

J. Linaza
Autónoma University of Madrid

The chapter by Furnham gives a considerable list of the different ways in which psychologists have studied human understanding of politics and economics. In this chapter he emphasizes the difficulties and frustrations one is bound to find in trying to reach conclusions from these different approaches and methodologies. One experiences the same feelings when trying to comment on papers and studies based on quite different methodologies, assumptions, and subjects. But some general points seem to come out of this section.

Furnham proposed the comparison between lay and academic theories in this field as a sensible path to follow. But the reader may not be satisfied with Furnham's claim of lay knowledge as a discipline on its own. Further, from his review of a long list of studies, he concludes that the heterogeneity of research's aims, methods, and topics makes it difficult to compare the results obtained and to draw clear conclusions.

About the more specific question of cognitive development and the understanding of social concepts, Furnham distinguishes between five types of research on children's development: (a) attitudes, values, and attributions; (b) knowledge of society (content on economic and political issues); (c) problems of reasoning and understanding in these domains; (d) questions of change and development; and (e) process of children's socialization and its relation to this type of knowledge.

From his results and some other studies it seems possible to emphasize the tendency of human beings to stress psychological factors as a cause for explanation than social or economic ones. People perform as psychologists rather than sociologists in dealing with these social and historical domains.

It looks as if jumping from social psychology with adults to the study of children's knowledge, Furnham finds plausible that early or more primitive thinking should be characterized by individualistic or psychological explanations. But one of the questions arising from several debates on this issue concerns the overgeneralization of results obtained with aduls subjects and its imposition to figure out what will be the results if the subjects interviewed were children. For example, could we assume that a "psychologist's" explanation will be more primitive than a collective or sociological one? It should be remembered that complex causal reasoning in adults does include psychological and individual factors, not only sociological ones.

But, to Furnham, even more fundamental questions have to do with the methodology used in the studies. They could be relevant for what one might consider truly developmental issues. Could these "explanations" be studied experimentally? Furthermore, is it really possible for the experimenter to get at such "explanations" when both adults or children do not offer them spontaneously? About the term *explanations*, to what extent can we really call them explanations? Are they the subject's explanations or the experimenter's interpretations? Another more intriguing developmental issue has to do with the motor for children's cognitive change. If individualistic and psychological factors are the first ones to appear, and they are reinforced by education on social and economic issues and by publicity, how do children elaborate on the structural and sociological "explanations"?

Furnham's chapter does not offer an answer to these questions. Drawing from the conclusions, he seems to see a basic agreement about children's knowledge on these topics advancing through a series of *stages* (a key word for a deep discussion in any debate on development). His conviction about the strong influence of factors such as experience, social class, instruction, and the like on the speed at which each child goes through the respective stage, brings back a recurrent debate on similar issues, when in the 1960s and the 1970s developmental psychologists had to deal with children's acquisition of knowledge in the natural sciences.

Delval's chapter pushed in exactly the opposite direction. Using careful examination of children's spontaneous representations of social reality, Delval took Piaget's ideas seriously to examine a field largely forgotten by Geneva scholars. Four "classic" but very important aspects of this approach are: (a) the clinical interview as the painful but efficient method for recollection of the data, (b) the elaboration of these data by analyzing each protocol in order to get the general pattern underlying individual differences, (c) the comparison between children's representations of different aspects of social and economic reality, and (d) the cross-cultural approach and early training (the Mexican young street vendors) to evaluate the influence of the idiosyncratic experience on these constructions.

It was mentioned that there are difficulties to generalize from studies whose methodologies were so different. In this case, the solidity of the three general stages proposed by Delval seems to develop from the procedure being used: the individual clinical interview of each child.

Berti gives an interesting example of how difficult it is for children to grasp the meaning of political terms out of their history books and lessons. Her work illustrates the naive political theories children construct and, at the same time, how their explanations work out from the most salient and external features of a concept, such as the geographical space of a state, to the less obvious of the social agreements and political structures. As in the previous studies her work also shows a stage-like process by which the subjects use to construct the very same concepts teachers take for granted in the instruction of history.

It might be worth singling out Berti's effort to approach the issues with real-life cases of today's changing picture of the world: the unification, annexation, and secession of states. The possible influence of such daily phenomena does not appear when compared with children's performance in the imaginary countries and villages made up by Berti. However, the comparison between both groups of children might not be so easy and clear. It seems that the methodology being used in this set of experiments does not allow for enough differentiation between the content of instruction (the child expects the adult to wait for the *correct* answer as being taught at the school) and the idiosyncratic "explanations" of political phenomena made up by each subject.

One should go beyond what the children said if one wants to reconstruct their plausible mental models that produce their different answers. Other disciplines are also needed for guidance about what direction the possible model can take. One suggestion along those lines is the need to amplify the notion of state and to include among the several criteria some that could deal with social agreement and consent.

Torney-Purta also designed ingenious situations to study adolescents' reasoning on political and historical issues. The Holocaust and the Spanish scenario (Phase 2 and 3) are good examples of trying to involve the subjects in a concrete task that could reveal the mental schemas with which they confront the problem. The logic of her approach seems to be that developmental change should be inferred from the comparison between young and middle adolescent children, whereas the instructional effect should show up by the influence of the intervening experience at two or more time points with the same subjects (Phases 1, 2, and 4).

Although Chi's and other approaches have been useful to guide the search for the influence of expertise on ontological dimensions, it seems important, in dealing with political and historical issues, to point out that: (a) the conceptual change is better understood as a continuum from prenovice to preexpert than as a move within clear-cut categories; and (b) although the subjects were already adolescents, there was still an attribution of individual motives and a single-cause process. More than that, as Torney-Purta speculates, concrete presentation of information and opportunity to interact with peers could play an important role for understanding historical events as the result of a multicause process.

A final consideration has to do with the comparative ages of the different groups of children involved in some of these chapters. If one remembers the age of both Furnham's and Berti's children, it is possible to interpret Torney-Purta's young adolescents as a case of slow "decentralization" or a spiral developmental process.

Although Torney-Purta addresses both instructional and developmental issues, from my point of view, her research has a slight bias toward instruction. It is not clear whether teachers and educators should be especially concerned about the distinction between developmental change and change resulting from instruction, although I am deeply convinced that psychologists and, moreover, developmental psychologists, have to tackle the developmental issue in order to explain children's spontaneous theories or "explanations." From this point of view, to identify development with "maturation" is more than a mistake: It will leave out some of the most important factors to understand children's understanding of history. Furthermore, it is important not only for psychologists to explain changes, but also for teachers to do their best with their educational practices. To reach such a goal it could be useful to concentrate scientific observations and educational activities on the following issues: (a) continuous and long-term experience that permits the child to deal with complex and multicausal situations, (b) continuity in building on prior knowledge structures and abilities, and (c) reference to peers.

One final comment refers to the sociohistorical approach in developmental psychology in Wertsch's chapter (this volume). If history is always a reconstruction of the past that plunges into the future to give a meaning to the present, for the sociohistorical approach narratives, must be a powerful cultural tool to achieve such an aim. The coherence of a narrative comes from the voice or the character to whom it belongs. However, for most historical events there are competing voices. In categorizing forms of historical representations, the focus shifted from homogeneous forms to those ("ironic" and "satiric" narratives) that try to deal with contradictions or competing voices. Although the proposal fits well with school practices to teach "stories" and to reinforce the social values with which a given society identifies, it leads to deep questions about the epistemology of history (as different from telling stories) and on the role of evidence in it.

THE ROLE OF STAGES IN EXPLAINING THE DEVELOPMENT OF UNDERSTANDING SOCIAL AND HISTORICAL CONCEPTS

Although presented only tentatively by several of the contributors to chapters of this book, the description of change in knowledge through a series of "stages" seems to be a strong argument in favor of constructivism. Social knowledge, like all knowledge, appears to be a product of a slow and nonlinear mental activity. Underneath the child's utterances this research reveals a mental model whose continuous change could be described and marked by stages. How general or domain specific they are remains an open but empirical question.

In relation to the ontological nature of these developmental milestones, it might be appropriate to compare them with the ontological nature of the historical periods established in the study of history. They stand well established as far as they help in understanding the present as a "consequence" of the past and to figure out what the future might be. When a different historical period reveals itself to be more fruitful in that task, it will soon replace the old history. Historical milestones are linked to specific cultures, and central events for one are just ignored by another.

Theories of children's development are also instruments for specific goals and stages that might be relevant in trying to measure the process, whereas for another theory this same process of change is irrelevant.

One clear implication of several studies reported in this section is that assimilation of new knowledge is limited by the underlying mental model, theory, or representation. Several authors wrote about the need to complement their studies on "knowledge" with the study of children's social and economic behaviors. For example, Delval differentiates three elements out of which the mental model developed: (a) the early acquired norms and rules (the prescriptive information), (b) the direct experience of social and economic realities, and (c) the "explanations" each child elaborates on the functioning of social systems.

If we take Piaget's own approach to children's early knowledge of social life (i.e., traditional games), norms (rules) are handed down from one generation to the next. From this point of view the "explanations" will be the spontaneous representations that each child makes out of the social system he or she interacts with, however partial that contact will be. At the same time, the cognitive apparatus must have some effect on both the possibilities and the constraints of children's social knowledge. Therefore, it is clear from several of these studies that notions such as reversibility may be of some use in explaining children's understanding of phenomena such as social mobility.

So what can be said about the direct experience that each child has of social reality? If "explanations" show such a similarity between subjects from so different milieus, this similarity must come from a deep and striking analogy between children's social practices, no matter how different they might appear on the surface. To put it another way, what looks like a very different experience, from the child's point of view, might be much more general than than the way adults can perceive it. The child's mental models reduce what he or she can assimilate from the heterogeneity of the external world. This is much the same as, when dealing with physical objects, two different toys could mean the same practical category for a baby, for example, an object to bang.

Despite so much research, as reported in this section, it seems a hard job to overcome our adult egocentrism when considering children's knowledge. It is impossible to understand other historical periods without leaving out present times. The same could be said about understanding children's representation of historical and social concepts. One must shift from the adult's point of view to reach the social reality as it is constructed by children.

II TEACHING AND INSTRUCTIONAL PROCESSES IN HISTORY

6 Learning to Reason in History: Mindlessness to Mindfulness

Gaea Leinhardt, Catherine Stainton,
Salim M. Virji, and Elizabeth Odoroff
University of Pittsburgh

Consider this list of numbers: 476; 712; 1,066; 1,215; 1,492; 1,776; 1,865; 1,936; 1,963[1]. To many people it is a meaningless string. To ask a child to memorize this list and to associate a particular list of words with it is exactly what is meant by rote memorization. But consider the last number, 1,963; add to it November 22, and delete the comma in 1963. Then this number becomes different from the rest. It becomes a date. For many Americans born before 1950, it is a date of particular significance and is immediately recognizable. This date produces a rush of memories and feelings of where we were and what we were doing when President Kennedy was assassinated. To remember *it* is not a mindless activity. It is clearly not the number or date that is mindless nor is the remembering of it. The mindlessness lies somewhere else. Indeed, for some the list of numbers at the beginning of this paragraph is a set of rich landmarks in a crowded landscape of ideas, currents, controversies, and events. Remembering them is no more effortful than remembering the route home from work. It is important to know where mindlessness lies so that we may turn to mindfulness.

Mindfulness in teaching and learning is an important goal of education in the United States. It should be the goal of history education as well. However, the movement to teach more than rote memorization to everyone,

---

[1]476, the fall of Rome to the Vandals; 712, the fall of Seville to the Moors; 1066, the Battle of Hastings; 1215, the signing of the Magna Carta; 1492, the expulsion of the Muslims and Jews from Spain, Columbus' voyage; 1776, the Declaration of Independence; 1865, the end of the Civil War in the United States; 1936, the Spanish Civil War, beginning of Franco's rule; 1963, President Kennedy's assassination.

not just the elite, is a relatively new concept (Resnick, 1987), dating from around 1900, when educators turned their attention from the goals of teaching basic facts to goals of reasoning with facts. Mindfulness suggests reasoning in a thoughtful way about something. It suggests, in the case of history, reasoning with more than an assortment of techniques or just the facts (Gagnon, 1989). For the purposes of this chapter, we focus on the particular use of facts, ideas, and issues in constructing interesting viable cases as a plausible location for reasoning to occur.

The teaching and learning of reasoning in history can be observed in three naturally occurring sites. One site is the written products of students in history classrooms. Another site is history texts, in which students often encounter comprehension problems because the texts fail to state overarching concepts (Beck & McKeown, 1988, 1989; FitzGerald, 1979). However, even a good text is not enough to ensure comprehension in history (Bean, Singer, Sorter, & Frazee, 1987). A third site is the average history classroom, in which existing surveys suggest that not much history is actually learned. However, there are glimmerings that suggest that, in some classes at least, thought-provoking ideas are exchanged, and students do have a chance to learn reasoning in the complex domain that straddles the humanities, social sciences, and history (Leinhardt, 1993; Wineburg & Wilson, 1988).

As an illustration of a distressing and unfortunately common history classroom picture, consider a scene: lights off, overhead on, students taking notes. The note taking consists of copying what is on the overhead. On the overhead is a list or diagram, often illegible, of key points—rarely are there any dates, for dates are the bad guys. In this caricature of a lesson that was observed, the topic actually was the Roman government. The textbook used the familiar version of the Roman government: It had a pair of consuls; it was a republic, not a democracy; some distinctions were made between the senate and the assemblies, and between patricians and plebeians. The content, both on the overhead and in the central classroom discussion, was inaccurate, for example, the "fact" that the Roman government was a democracy that had sprung (so the teacher indicated on the overhead) from a social reform movement against the Greeks and their dictatorial governmental approach (sic!).

Even more confusing was the discussion, which was designed to make salient to the students several admittedly abstract concepts (specifically, historical "structures"; Leinhardt, 1993): government, representation, branches of ruling bodies, and terms of office. The attempt to create salience and to clarify the topic resulted in the use of two extended analogies, both of which, in this case, did little to illuminate the subject. The first analogy tried to establish the difference between the governments of ancient Rome and the United States. The teacher introduced the analogy with a query about how (U.S.) Congressional representatives know what they should say and think. (Note that this is a rather odd conception of the job of a representative.) Congressional representatives know, the class decided, from letters of complaint and by protestors picketing. In the ensuing discussion, protestors were exemplified by those protesting abortion, such as those who supported Pennsylvania's Governor Casey (an abortion opposer), rather than Candidate Scranton (a choice supporter). There was no mention of Rome at this point, nor was any connection made to Roman government; there was no return to the notion of what it meant to be a representative; talk in the classroom drifted into a general discussion of television and protestors.

The second analogy used in the class discussion was related to the development of the self-sufficiency of Rome. This self-sufficiency was somehow connected in the teacher's mind (but never explicitly) to two high school wrestling teams, one traditionally more successful than the other. Unfortunately, the connection was never set forth clearly enough for the students to understand the link between the wrestlers and self-sufficiency.

Both of these analogical excursions took more than half of their respective class periods; both were clearly intended to make the material more relevant and real; both were highly entertaining for the teacher and for the students. Neither, however, was enlightening; neither supported the conceptual or factual material in any strong way; neither permitted the students to try out their fledgling competencies in reasoning. These analogies were merely shared stories that occurred during history time while the overhead was on. It was certainly not the use of analogies or stories per se that was mindless; it was the lack of connection to appropriate historical issues or possibly the lack of meaningful structure within them (Tierney, 1988). Further, by using such analogies the teacher modeled history as primarily an activity of free association.

Three messages emerge from this discussion: First, historical dates and facts are not the villains of history instruction (nor are they, of course, its saviors). Second, copying overheads (or looking at film strips) is probably not a thoughtful behavior designed to reinforce reasoning. Third, classroom discussions that range far afield from the core concepts, no matter how entertaining, are not thoughtful or informative.

What is it then that we want students to engage in as they learn to reason in history? Several researchers are now carefully studying just what is going on in those classrooms where mindful history *is* being taught and learned (Leinhardt, 1993, 1994; McDiarmid, 1991, this volume; Wilson, 1990; Wilson & Wineburg, 1988; Wineburg & Fournier, this volume; Wineburg & Wilson, 1988). This research, which includes research on the nature of expertise in teaching history, shows that "what expert teachers know about history, what they know about teaching, and what they know about learners are but pieces of a complex set of understandings" (Wineburg & Wilson, 1988, p. 58) that good teachers have.

AN OVERVIEW

It is assumed that teachers who have a rich understanding of subject matter can make use of their knowledge in discussions of content and in the process of modeling historical reasoning. The question remains though, "Which of the many activities that excellent teachers engage in constitute mindful activities that should and can reasonably be expected to go on in history classes?" To help answer that query, in this chapter we trace conceptions of reasoning in history through three layers: first, we consider the writings of classical historians and philosophers of historical reasoning; second, we interview currently practicing historians about case construction and explanation; and third, we analyze one excellent history teacher's construction of explanations. The teacher designed her explanations in a manner that modeled historical reasoning and gradually helped students to build their own capabilities to reason about historical phenomena.

The purpose of this excursion through three different ways of considering the problem is to construct the beginnings of a dialogue between what has been, what ought to be, and what is possible. In deciding what should go on in history classrooms we might be tempted to simply declare by fiat what is important or, more frequently, what is possible. It seems more fruitful to begin by examining the enduring features of historical recordings, then to add to these the features that more modern historians view as central to their discipline. At the same time, it is important to constantly check to determine what is sensible and possible. This last step is taken while being fully aware that what *is* possible is much more than what is already observable. But, if we can observe central elements of mindful historical reasoning in existing classes, then surely the argument that it cannot be done is laid to rest.

Before looking at actual classroom lessons, we need to lay out a framework for what is meant by reasoning in history. In terms of instructional explanations given to and by students, reasoning emerges from explanations about the metasystems of history and in explanations of the events, structures, and themes in history (Leinhardt, 1990, 1993). One component of reasoning in history is the process by which central facts (about events and structures) and concepts (themes) are arranged to build an interpretive historical case. Building a case, whether written or spoken, requires, at a minimum, analysis, synthesis, hypothesis generation, and interpretation. We return to these fundamental elements later in this discussion. First, we sketch the methodology used for all three investiga-tions and then briefly consider how classical historians enacted reasoning in the exercise of their own craft.

METHODS

We start from an admittedly Eurocentric view of historical reasoning and thinking to help enlighten the discussion of reasoning in history classrooms in the United States. We engaged in three distinct data collection efforts: examination of historical writings by Herodotus, Gibbon, Macaulay, von Ranke, Hempel, Collingwood, and von Wright; interviews with currently practicing historians; and finally, observations of a series of high school history lessons given by one history teacher.

Examination of Historical Writings

We inspected the writings of notable and colorful historians (Herodotus, Gibbon, and Macaulay) and philosophers of social science who have concerned themselves with historical explanations or reasoning (Hempel, Collingwood, von Wright, and Schwab). The inspection does not reiterate the classification of historians as having a world view, having a reform view, and so on (see Evans, 1989; Walsh, 1967). Instead, it focuses on what historians explicitly or implicitly suggest constitutes reasoning in history. We selected Herodotus because, along with Thucydides, he is usually considered the father of Western historical thought. We selected von Ranke because of his early introductions of purposive, political writing. We selected Gibbon and Macaulay because they carried on the tradition of panoramic narrative history. Gibbon, in writing about Rome connected with Herodotus in subject, but not in purpose or distance to subject. Macaulay, in writing about his own country's history, connected in purpose and relation to subject, but not in subject. Macaulay connected to Herodotus in another way as well. He was a debater and orator; his histories, like those of Herodotus, were read aloud and spoken — there is a flamboyance to the cadence. The four philosophers of social science were chosen because their dialogues seem to represent substantial departures from the concerns of earlier historians. Indeed, as the social sciences became more scientific, the dual nature of history as a member of the humanities and of the social sciences became somewhat more problematic. One aim of the analysis is to find common threads that can be knitted together so that the analysis of what is or should be mindful in history instruction might be strengthened.

Interviews with Historians

In 1991, the first author interviewed seven historians as part of a series of discussions with historians who were Fellows at the Center for Advanced Study in the Behavioral Sciences. Each interview consisted of five open-ended questions: (a) What is history? (b) Why are you a historian? (c) Why should we teach history? (d) What does it mean to or how do you establish a historical case? and (e) How do you explain something in history? The interviews were audiotaped and transcribed. Because we considered case construction to be one of the major elements in historical reasoning, we focused on historians' discussions of questions (d) and (e), synthesizing their responses from different parts of the protocol. (Since each interview was a relatively free-flowing discussion that lasted anywhere from 30 to 90 min, partial answers to the questions were often provided in different parts of the interview. When appropriate, those parts of the discussion were included.) Five constructs were consistently mentioned by the majority of the historians.

Classroom Observations

In our attempts to learn about how a teacher helps students develop thoughtful, subtle, complex knowledge of history, we observed a reputedly "good" Advanced Placement (AP) American History teacher, Ms. Sterling. She was selected based on converging nominations by the district social studies supervisor, other district administrators, her department chair, other teachers, parents, and students (current and former) in the district. She had been teaching for 34 years and had been teaching her current course for over 15 years. An avid reader of current history, she had continued to take graduate courses in her field over the years. She participated and taught in National Endowment for the Humanities (NEH) seminars and also had written and videotaped a series of history lessons for public television.

Ms. Sterling had strong views about the nature and value of history, firm ideas about the function of teaching in a democratic society, and definite opinions about which students should have access to advanced classes (anyone willing to do the work, which contrasted sharply with district and state policy). Over a 2-year period we observed a total of 88 lessons and audio- or videotaped 84 of them. Each lesson was transcribed and analyzed in several ways. Although the classroom dialogues are messy and disorderly, the language of history that emerges through types of answers to questions is the start of more formal case reasoning. In this chapter we traced the development of question formulation (hypotheses generation), analysis, and synthesis over several weeks in the beginning of the year for one of the classes so that we could see the process of constructing a case through dialogue.

HISTORICAL WRITINGS

There have been many excellent reviews of historical philosophy (e.g., Walsh, 1967). The purpose here is to give a flavor for educators and psychologists of thinking in and about history. We selected a range of historians to stress the common themes that have occurred even within a changing discipline. One of the first Western historians was Herodotus (~484–425 B.C.); his history is considered almost pure narrative. The social sciences as such had not yet come into being. However, Herodotus did at least three things that have remained central to the construction of historical cases up to the present. First, he accounted for himself and his own perspective in the narrative:

> These are the researches of Herodotus of Halicarnassus, which he publishes, in the hope of thereby preserving from decay the remembrance of what men have done, and of preventing the great and wonderful actions of the Greeks and the Barbarians from losing their due meed of glory; and withal to put on record what were their grounds of feud. (Herodotus, 1990, p. 1)

He identified who he was, where he was from, and why he was telling this tale. Two thousand years later, historians still do the same (D'Emilio, 1992; Mallon, 1983). Second, Herodotus was motivated to preserve his discussion from decay. Third, Herodotus acknowledged his sources and the existence of multiple tellings of a single tale:[2]

> Thus far I have been engaged in showing how the Lydians were brought under the Persian yoke. . . . And herein I shall follow those Persian authorities whose object it appears to be not to magnify the exploits of Cyrus, but to relate the simple truth. I know besides three ways in which the story of Cyrus is told, all differing from my own narrative. (Herodotus, 1990, p. 23)

Herodotus also assumed that there was a "truth"; therefore, his task as a historian was to find it out and tell it. In the earlier passage, Herodotus

---

[2]In the reference list three translations of Herodotus (1987, 1990) are listed (Adler, Fadiman, & Goetz's, Goold's (1920, 1921), and Grene's); Goold's contains the original Greek. They are all listed because there are, in fact, rather substantial differences among them that bear on the points being made here. The translation quoted is moderately supportive, one is stronger, and the other slightly less so.

exhibited two aspects of historical reasoning: *synthesis* of the story from multiple versions, and *analysis* of the motives of the actors as well as those of the tellers of a particular history. These features, too, will remain a part of the culture of historians, although the notion of a discoverable truth has been called into doubt. The central contents of the narrative, the enmity between Greece and Persia, appear to be about the compelling forces behind great conflicts and great people – the larger than life "events." But a closer look reveals critical, if instrumental, roles of peasant families and intensely human and personal feelings. After all, it is the poor peasant who saves the royal infant from his doom and thus aids the fulfillment of the destiny of the nation state. The inclusion of historical players other than the high and mighty was also a part of Macaulay – albeit with apologies. But neither historian took as the central story the lives of anyone other than the great heroes and the great nations. The aspects of reasoning suggested by Herodotus are a complete authentic narrative about a person or event of consequence, one that is verified and inclusive of relevant actors regardless of station.

Eighteen hundred years later, two historians – Gibbon and Macaulay – took on the same task of telling the tale of great events (the history of Rome and of England). Both did so, so that the stories would be fully appreciated ("due meed") and not be forgotten ("preserving from decay"). Both Gibbon (1776/1910) and Macaulay (1848/1879, 1897) firmly established a sense of dialogue with their present readers and with the past that they were reconstructing. Both were flamboyant storytellers, and one might assume that they too were overwhelmingly narrative in their construction of history. But there was considerable analysis of custom, economy, political science, and, in a unique sense, psychology as well. As Macaulay (1897) wrote in the beginning of his third "chapter":

> I intend, in this chapter, to give a description of the state in which England was at the time the crown passed from Charles the Second to his brother. Such a description, composed from scanty and dispersed materials, must necessarily be imperfect. Yet it may perhaps correct some false notions which would render the subsequent narrative unintelligible or uninstructive.
>
> If we would study with profit the history of our ancestors, we must be constantly on our guard against that delusion which the well-known names of families, places, and offices naturally produce, and must never forget that the country of which we read was a very different country from that in which we live. In every experimental science there is a tendency towards perfection. (p. 1)

The last sentence of this quote suggests that Macaulay considered some aspect of history to be an experimental science. In this he foreshadowed

Hempel. However, given the general broadness of Macauley's language, it may have been more gestural than substantive. Von Ranke (1830/1973, 1854/1973), while recognizing the artistic, narrative nature of history, also pressed hard for the consideration of history as a science. History was, according to von Ranke, a science in its collection and penetration of information. It was an art because of its recreation and portraiture (von Ranke, 1830/1973, p. 33). More scientific than Macauley or Gibbon, von Ranke, however, like them, took his task to be to construct realistic, relatively singular narratives that traced and explained events and people.

As we turn to the historians of the late 20th century, a greater emphasis tended to be placed on history as a social science as distinct from being solely one of the humanities. Hempel, emerging from the full flush of German scientification of the social sciences, imposed a strict set of definitions on the science of history and hence historical explanation—thus the reasoning that would lead to it. In his "covering law," Hempel imposed the requirement that history mimic the physical sciences. History, according to Hempel, should be scientific enough to interpret and predict through the use of basic laws that explain certain observed facts (see Hempel, 1962).

Although not cast in these terms, Hempel distinguished between situations with variance attached (such as probablistic situations, or situations involving personal motive) and situations that he supposed had no variance (such as laws of physics) or at least only variance that could be understood. In applying these definitions of explanation to history, Hempel asserted that many historical theses (for example, Turner's thesis) are nomological in form and function. Hempel contrasted this form and its variants with genetic explanations (events generating others) and explanation by rationale (the reasons behind) and then showed these two "exceptions," really, when properly viewed, to be cases of the nomological form (Hempel, 1965).

If Hempel's view is taken, the student of history should first be a student of the social sciences—economics, sociology, anthropology, and political science—because these fields would provide the "laws" that would undergird any reasonable historical explanation. Such a view, however, ignores the narrative, interpretive, and layered nature of history.

In contrast to Hempel, von Wright (1971) did not reject the "scientific" form of explanation or analytic history, but showed it to be only one part of the picture. Echoing Collingwood (1946), von Wright emphasized the layered nature of historical explanations and acts of reasoning. The concern was in part with the level of aggregation from the individual to groups, in which groups have collective motivations and circumstances that are different from individual motives. But von Wright also referred to the self-reflective nature of the historical enterprise, the sense that history involves interpretation.

To some extent, the spirit of von Wright is present in the earlier work of

Collingwood. Collingwood (1946) portrayed history as ever-changing interpretation and wrote:

> The evidence available for solving any given [historical] problem changes with
> every change of historical method and with every variation in the competence
> of historians. The principles by which this evidence is interpreted changes too;
> since the interpreting of evidence is a task to which a man must bring
> everything he knows: historical knowledge, knowledge of the nature of man,
> mathematical knowledge, philosophical knowledge; and not knowledge only,
> but mental habits and possessions of every kind: and none of these is
> unchanging. Because these changes, which never cease, however slow they
> may appear to observers who take a short view, every new generation must
> rewrite history in its own way; every new historian, not content with giving
> new answers to old questions must revise the questions themselves; and – since
> the historical thought is a river into which none can step twice – even a single
> historian, working at a single subject for a certain length of time, finds when
> he tries to reopen an old question that the question has changed.
>
> This is not an argument for historical skepticism. It is only the discovery of a
> second dimension of historical thought, the history of history: the discovery
> that the historian himself, together with the here-and-now which forms the
> total body of evidence available to him, is a part of the process he is studying,
> has his own place in that process, and can see it only from the point of view
> which at this present moment he occupies within it. (p. 248)

With these statements Collingwood gave voice to the suggestions present
in earlier writings of the role of the speaker in the telling of the tale. But by
giving it specific discussion, Collingwood forced the issue to be centrally
considered. The heart of this new element in historical reasoning, from the
humanistic perspective, was captured by notions of layering. Three layers
could be easily distinguished (Schwab, 1978; von Wright, 1971). The first
layer included substantive questions asked by historians, questions such as
"What are the causes of the Civil War?" The second layer included
"syntactic" questions about how to bring new knowledge into the discipline
(Schwab, 1978). For example, the debates (such as those surrounding
Hempel) about what constitutes an historical explanation raised syntactic
questions about the standards for bringing new knowledge into the discipline. Third, as von Wright (1971) as well as Collingwood pointed out,
history, like other humanities and some social sciences, asks self-reflective
questions. Thus, history, partly from the humanities and partly from the
social sciences, had, from the late 1940s, two strands of somewhat separate
growth: one leading through the modernists and postmodernists, the other
through the positivists and "postpositivists." The contribution of Hempel
with the introduction of the social sciences was the increased demand for
rigor. The sense of both what history is and what constitutes reasoning has

expanded beyond narrative accomplishment. Completeness and accuracy, coupled with motivational understanding (all requirements for the narrative portion of historical reasoning, from Herodotus, Gibbon, and Macaulay), are at this point complemented by notions of systematicity and theory (from Hempel) and notions of layering[3] and self-reflective interpretation (from von Wright, Collingwood, and Schwab).

These older disciplinary discussions of historical explanation and historical reasoning are the background that undoubtedly affects the implicit definitions of reasoning carried by modern historians. In this next section we move from the induced understandings of historical reasoning to more direct answers to questions about it.

INTERVIEWS WITH HISTORIANS

The interviews with practicing historians revealed five clusters of ideas related to the construction of a case in history. With one or two exceptions these components emerged in the context of lots of ideas and examples rather than as a step-by-step process by which one might construct a case, use it to explain data, and defend it from criticism. However, for the purpose of connecting the discussions with the historians to the writings of earlier historians and teaching practices, we discuss the components in a collapsed and more sequential fashion.

Motivational/Purposive Assumption

The doing of history implies a purpose. One of the consistent purposes mentioned was the assumption that we become and evolve, rather than that we are. This was stated humorously by one historian as "you are what you eat . . . you are what you were" (J.O., lines 280–281)[4] and more seriously by others. The motivating assumption underlying any case is that the case exists to help us understand both what was and also what is. For some historians, this was expressed as a notion of honoring the realities of what was, while for others, it was a source of liberation and fellowship. The sense of change, evolution, and unfolding is not easily detected in any direct way in the earlier writings of historians. Certainly there is a sense of lineage or

---

[3]*Layering* refers to the idea that: (a) any accounting of history is itself a part of the ever growing historical record, (b) that a particular artifact of history (poem, painting, videotape) is also a telling of history, and (c) historians themselves reflect on their role in the telling of history and are self-aware and self-questioning.

[4]These quotes are from segments of protocol from interviews with practicing historians.

connecting backward as well as a grand unfolding, but the sense of roots as a guide was not as prominent.

Compelling Narrative

All of the historians agreed that the construction of a compelling narrative with internal coherence was the major requirement for case construction. The design and development of narrative was not simply a means of conveying a case but was itself a part of the case. They all also agreed that narrative alone was not sufficient. "Historians actually write in different modes, and the simplest historians write in a narrative mode, they tell stories. And stories carry an implicit line of argumentation" (F.C., lines 111–115). Narrative was seen as considerably more than a string of interesting chronological tidbits. Narrative skill was a fundamental component in case development as it was in the historians whose writings were examined. In addition to internal coherence, narrative skill included "mystery," "discovery," evidential exhaustivity, chronology, and causality. The last three of these components helped to transform narrative into case.

Exhaustivity. Every historian mentioned evidential exhaustivity as a fundamental property of any historical narrative. Exhaustivity meant including all evidence that could be found and all evidence that might contradict the case. Evidence included written/spoken records, social/cultural artifacts, and even strong inferences about what must have been in place for the surviving piece to have been present. (For example, in order for the "humor" of 19th-century American theater to have been funny, the audience had to have been familiar with Shakespeare in a way not previously assumed [L.L., lines 421–490].) The sense of exhaustivity was present in Herodotus, not in the form of surviving records, but more in the form of differing accounts. The sense of exhaustivity and narrative together helps to form a construct of synthesis that we consider in the next section. The idea of synthesis as an exhaustive activity is one of the elements that makes history quite hard in the sense of laborious.

Chronology. Given large quantities of information, one organizing approach is the establishment of chronology. The majority of the historians mentioned the significance of establishing an accurate chronology for a case; this might or might not include subdivisions of periodicity. Chronology was always mentioned in the interviews in an off-handed, almost dismissive manner, as if, "Of course you get that right and then proceed." Achieving both exhaustivity and subtle chronology is probably beyond the abilities of most elementary and high school students. But achieving bounded exhaustivity and simplified chronology is not.

Causality. Six of the historians mentioned the establishment of "plausible" causality. Five of them contrasted this kind of causality with lawyerly causality and proof. Our interpretation of this distinction was that plausibility was closely related to narrative coherence (as several historians mentioned) and exhaustivity. For the most part, the historians' view of lawyerly causality and case proof was that it was rule-bound and perhaps game-like. (As one historian said when speaking of the overreliance on hypothesis proof, "[The proof consists of] devising tests that will confirm or falsify a hypothesis, which is the standard, and most banal, positivistic technique in the social sciences" [F.C., lines 180–183].) One historian, in contrast, held up lawyerly establishment of causality as a significant criterion for compellingness of a case. Establishing internal causal links within a narrative is one important form of analysis or pulling apart of ideas. Many of the devices that are considered to be causal relate quite directly to Hempel's notion of laws, whereas other devices reflect imposed logic or chronological adjacency.

A compelling narrative, then, is a weaving of the exhaustive evidence using time and causality as a framework for the story. The selection of the critical questions, the answer to which is the narrative, involves the use of theory or *hypothesis* development.

Theory or Hypothesis Development

The use of evidence in a case is more than a listing and yet less than a formal causal "lawyer-like" case. What is a case itself then? A case involves clustering the narrative around a central hypothesis. All of the historians developed hypotheses and supported them in their own cases, but not all of them mentioned hypotheses and theories in their interviews. Hypothesis generation is both an outcome of evidential collection and organization, as well as a guide for its collection. Hypotheses are dynamic, having the property of growth and change within a demarcated framework. Further, the theoretical frame one operates within is the filter for interpretation and the means of imposing meaning on the data. Interpretation was the fourth component in historical case development mentioned by the historians.

Contextual, Layered Interpretation. Four of the historians mentioned that any case required that the evidential list be interpreted in terms of the context of the original times, the context of the present time seeking to look at that evidence, and the implications of evidential survival. The survival record was not seen as neutral. The context of the original time was expressed as a morally honest reconnection or dialogue with the original actors. It was also seen as a way of giving voice to those who were voiceless (suppressed or ignored) in their own time. The context of the present time was portrayed as both utilitarian (an historical work might be used in Supreme Court decisions), and also as theoretically unique (Marxism vs. Foucault, for example). To some extent the contextual interpretation of events formed another basis for analysis as a particular form of historical reasoning. From the quotes given by the "written" historians, it is clear that they, too, operated with an implicit sense of context, but they did not tend to manipulate it or explicitly work with it in the way the interviewed historians seemed to. It seems to have taken nearly two decades before the words of Collingwood found form in the actions of historians.

Argue or Debate Other Historical Interpretations.   Four of the historians went into considerable depth as they discussed disciplinary debates.[5] The discussion of exactly how one made a case was extended by three of the historians into making an argument with other historians. Within that construct they identified several subconstructs:

> There were three basic elements to making an argument. . . . One involves the reconstruction of the facts . . . establishing a dialogue among all relevant documentation and trying to come up with what seems to be the best organization . . . preparing the terrain as much as possible . . . then after that is a process of interpretation, which is a relationship among facts and some sense of imputing motive to particular actors . . . and very often that's a process that involves a certain amount of counterfactual type reasoning. . . . Then, for me, the third level is the level of dialogue and debate with other historically oriented scholars . . . trying to argue . . . over the larger meaning of the interpretations . . . it also for me involves theoretical debate. (Mallon, lines 155–232)

With respect to Mallon's last point, two other historians further divided the construct of argument into three components: providing compelling logic, consistent interpretation that was deemed contextually accurate, and theoretical perspective taking. Mallon said it well when she framed case construction as a series of dialogues, one of which was with one's own current intellectual community.

TEACHING

These disciplinary issues affect secondary school teachers' interpretations of what constitutes an instructional explanation and how students should be

---

[5]Interestingly, the three historians who did not mention the alternative interpretations or debates issue were historians whose work was "original," that is, the material is unique and has not been examined before. Thus, a historian who is interpreting slavery is in a field of many other historians doing the same things with much of the same evidence, whereas an historian who is developing an analysis of labor disputes in colonial Africa is working with unique sources previously unexamined by the larger community of historians in the same field.

taught case construction. In essence, history teachers must determine a way in which to connect their teaching to the implicit and explicit discussions within the discipline itself. In this part of the study we examine one history teacher's solutions to this problem. At the beginning of this chapter we identified three locations for historical reasoning to take place within the context of schooling: students' written documents, textbooks, and class discussions. The analysis of teaching reasoning within history presented here focuses on the reasoning that emerges from discussions in class.

We examined historical writings and views of practicing historians in order to understand from the disciplinary perspective what a sensible set of requirements might be for developing a case in history. We chose case development as one fairly central and complex aspect of historical reasoning. In examining some of these elements in a classroom, we start with identifying where in the course of history instruction such a discussion might occur.

Previous research has identified four occasions for instructional explanations in history: events and people, structures and institutions, themes and trends, and metastructures of historiography (Leinhardt, 1993). These occasions were induced from observing excellent history teachers as they taught. The fourth of these occasions, metastructures, includes perspective taking and interpretation, hypothesis generation, analysis, and synthesis. Students are taught these metastructures for historical reasoning in order to reason about themes, events, and structures. We now examine the development of a class discussion of a central historical theme as a way of seeing how students learn to analyze particular events and structures and how they learn to synthesize relevant information in constructing a case. One of the themes in this particular course, the tension between agrarian and mercantile interests, served to exemplify the mindfulness and reasoning we observed in these classes.

Students need to develop a number of facilities in order to be able to think about history. The previous discussion tends to support analyses of requirements from sources such as Advanced Placement exams that require the ability to (a) analyze events and themes; (b) synthesize trends, events, or concepts; and (c) construct a case. Some of the more subtle and sophisticated capabilities include understanding the nature of historical ambiguity, following convergences and diversions, and understanding the limitations on perspective that the present imposes on us. These capabilities were also reflected in the discussion by historians. This kind of thinking requires fluid access to the content and structure of history—they eschew hand waving or simple stories. One teacher we studied, Ms. Sterling, managed to get her students to produce reasoned cases that made use of analysis and synthesis.

Analysis of an event or theme in history requires that the frame for the event be clearly established. The subject of an analysis has to be well demarcated. But the frame is amorphous in history—just when does the Revolutionary Period begin or end? What sphere of knowledge encompasses government formation and reformation in the early colonial period? Dates help with this demarcation as far as time is concerned; critical events and people also help for defining scope; and thematic regularity over time helps specify fruitful lines of inquiry into complex historical phenomena. Herodotus set off the event of the Persian war by tracing the enmity between Greeks and Persians; Gibbon demarked the start of his Rome to trace its rise and fall.

Using the demarcation of an event as a base, the analysis of key forces or moves can be sketched. A common approach easily available to younger students (junior high and high school) is to systematically inspect aspects of a particular constellation of events from the point of view of the political, social, scientific, and economic conditions prior to, during, and after their occurrence. (We pose this list of aspects tentatively as a starting place, mindful that it, like any specification, can become mechanical and vacuous.) Focusing on these aspects permits the thinker to walk around and partition the topic space. This partitioning and internal rearrangement of topic space can be considered a primitive form of analysis, a prerequisite to interpretation.

In Fig. 6.1 we present a schematized view of analyzing a particular event or constellation of events—the writing of the Constitution, or the Civil War, for example. After specifying what to include in or exclude from the scope of that particular event, that is, what might go into the inner rectangle, the event itself can be analyzed and the topic space rearranged by pulling out strands of issues that impacted on and were impacted by the event. In the context of Ms. Sterling's class, she analyzed the strands of the economic status of the writers of the Constitution, the economic conditions prior to the framing process of the Constitution, and the alteration of those conditions during the period between the Articles of Confederation and the ratification. Later, she had the students analyze the strands of economic conditions prior to the Civil War and the alteration of those conditions between the settling of Kansas and the end of Andrew Johnson's presidency. In turn, each of the political strands could be considered to elaborate a portrait of a time and of currents surrounding notable actions. Analysis, then, takes a whole and pulls apart the issue in order to illuminate it.

Synthesis, in contrast to analysis, is a process that forms an idea by weaving together strands from separate sources. This, in turn, gives form and substance to an event. For example, as shown in Fig. 6.2, in examining the Civil War, Ms. Sterling had students synthesize governmental compromises across time and events by studying the Three-fifths Compromise, the Missouri Compromise of 1820, and the Compromise of 1850. The examples of compromise could then be contrasted with examples of controversy (for

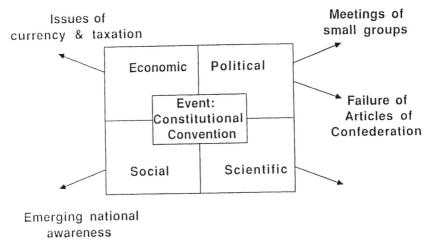

Issues of currency & taxation

Meetings of small groups

Economic   Political

Event: Constitutional Convention

Failure of Articles of Confederation

Social   Scientific

Emerging national awareness

FIG. 6.1.   Analysis

example, growing vocalizations around moral issues), which in turn were contrasted to emerging distinctions between economic bases in the North and those in the South. When each of these strands was traced along its chronological path, students came to see that many tensions gave rise to the Civil War, not just one. Firing on Fort Sumter became a moment that was indicative of rising tensions, not a cause or even a start of the Civil War.

Both analysis and synthesis were tools used by students in Sterling's class as they learned to build a case in history. In this analysis we trace some moments in the development of the students' capabilities to make a case in the context of queries set in classroom discourse. The case, as a form of classroom presentation, often has a structure that reflects hypotheses supported by specific evidence. At first, however, the evidence in the case we examined was little more than a rather compelling list. In learning how to develop a case further, students needed to be able to access the kind of detailed information given in readings and presentations. The task of the teacher was to guide the students toward facility at moving between specific evidence and general hypotheses.

Our analyses of classroom observations focused on the period from the Revolution through the Civil War (although our observations continued through the end of the Roosevelt presidency prior to U.S. entry into World War II). The task of teaching this period was especially difficult because many of the changes that occurred during these 100 years had no immediately discernible critical consequences. The lack of clearly observable consequence stemmed from the fact that regional expansion acted as a kind of social shock absorber. The emerging interests of the Western pioneers were vastly different from those of the Eastern businessmen, which were, in

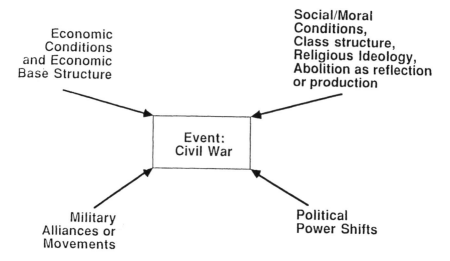

FIG. 6.2.   Synthesis

turn, different from the Southern plantation owners. The manifestations of these differences were not immediately obvious to history students, even though the differences laid seeds for problems and tensions that cropped up at later points. Until the Civil War, people with dramatically different interests were located in different and separate geographical spaces that buffered them from each other.

In teaching this segment, Sterling built up a number of themes (e.g., the role of political compromise, the changing composition of the electorate, the function and symbolism of the elastic clause in the Constitution) that started well before the Revolutionary Period and extended into the modern period. She highlighted one tension that pervaded this time period: agrarian, expansionist interests and commercial, international trade interests. This thematic tension formed a loosely connected set of ideas that were referred to within the class over several weeks as the discussion developed.

Figure 6.3 shows an elaboration of this thematic tension between agrarian and mercantile concerns. On the left, the concept node of AGRARIAN is connected to many attributes: Jefferson, the South, minimalist government or states' rights (which in turn relates to anti-federalist), Western expansionism, slave holding, and Jeffersonian/Jacksonian democracy. The concept node, MERCANTILE, is connected to commerce, international trade, federalism, Hamilton, and the North. Each of these concepts in turn had fairly elaborate minicases and narratives built up around them. Although many of these ideas were associated with each other, it is clear that some links were unusual — the link between states' rights and anti-federalist, for example. These ideas were not all directly connected during class discussion,

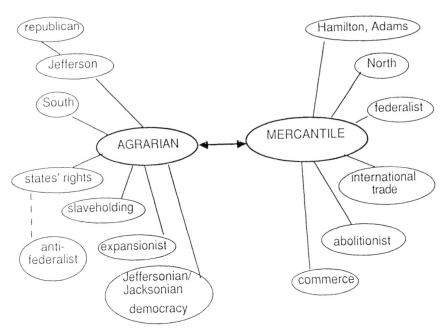

FIG. 6.3. Thematic tension

but they were often associated with other concepts in the set. These webs of ideas recurred as persistent themes throughout the 4 months of instruction that covered the 100-year span of history. They became familiar lenses for the teacher to use to bring the students to see particular positions, and they provided a frequently tagged set of concepts that empowered students with considerable reasoning capability. This power resulted from the fact that as soon as students identified one part of the net, they had very rapid access to the rest of it. The teacher was showing the students complexity while providing them with the tools to handle that complexity. She was very carefully moving them beyond historical narrative into analytic abstractions for understanding history. The theme of agrarian/mercantile tension became one of several hypotheses that would be formed around the issue of the Civil War.

To demonstrate this movement toward understanding, we examine very brief sections from three lessons. It is important to see how the recurring themes develop from early October to mid-November and to notice the teacher's modeling and students' eventual, if primitive, reproductions of reasoned cases.

Figure 6.4 shows the first of three segments from a lesson that occurred in early October on the Constitutional Convention. In the first segment (A), the teacher followed a pattern. She posed questions and sought short

A

A1 T: Can you tell me something about the way men were thinking in the post war period? Some were thinking "continentally." Have you any idea what that means?... (L. 16–20)

****

A2 T: Nationally, or thinking about a centralized government would make it a federal. You're talking about a federal system. As opposed to – what words might be used for state,instead of state? (L. 38–42)

S: Local...(L. 43)

****

A3 T: Some people were thinking about the power or sovereignty being on the local level, some were thinking it should be at least centralized, national level. Now would you have any idea of an example of a person whose view you would fit the category of being a localist or a regionalist, or one who would be a state's person that doesn't think we need to strenghen the national government? ... (L. 56–64)

S: Jefferson? ... (L. 69)

B

****

T: John Adams, Washington, Franklin, all those people on stage (referring to the picture in the text) would be the men [...] Continentalists. Who is absent from the convention? We saw the materials on the 55; that they're young, average age 42, well-educated, middle class people went to Philadelphia... (L. 135–141)

****

C

T: Was there an event that perhaps crystallized the thinking of the men like Washington, of we'd better get these Articles strengthened or this country is certainly in for big political trouble. If so, what was the event? ... (L. 173-178)

S: Shays' rebellion... (L. 179) I think the fear of anarchy. I mean, like he was probably thinking they could overthrow our government the same way everybody overthrew the English... (L. 195-198)

****

T: This could put a fear into people, and cause the leaders in various areas to want to gather, and they did, at Mt. Vernon, Annapolis, and then finally at Philadelphia. Now we are interested in the coming together of these people from various backgrounds. When they come to Philadelphia, what do they agree upon immediately? You might be able to...

(continued on next page)

FIG. 6.4.   First selection – October 10, 1988.

There are certain areas of agreement or consensus. They are not going to debate. The very first thing they are going to agree to? (L. 204–214)

S: A representative government... (L. 215)

T: What is the name of a representative government that they all agree upon? (L. 216)

S: A Republic... (L. 227)

D1

T: All agreed on popular sovereignty. Power rests with people, not with the state, in context with the states' rights. Something else they all agreed upon? (L. 246–250)

S: They believe in the power of central government to enforce laws... (L. 251–252)

D

D2

T: Okay, all agreed that the Articles of Confederation were to be strengthened, that they are too weak, and they need a more centralized federal system... (L. 253–255) [Teacher then reviews power structure within the 55 and need for secrecy and compromises.] As you look at the issues, you see the 4 issues of areas of disagreement. [1] How congress should be organized, [2] how congress ought to be regulated, and [3] how slaves are to be represented, and [4] how presidents are to be elected... (L. 417–421) What were the opposing interests? (L. 430–431)

S: Large states or small states... (L. 432)

S: State or federal tax or tariffs...

T: How about [...] group of people by occupation. Not by the interest. (L. 442–443)

S: Wealthy and wealthier... (L. 444)

T: Break it down [...] wealthy and less wealthy; anything else? (L. 445–446)

S: Vendors and merchants versus farmers... (L. 447)

T: Farmers, agrarian or farmers merchants commercial that would include your bankers... (L. 458–459) How about the third opposing interest group here at the convention. People have different opinions?... (L. 463–465)

S: North versus South... (L. 467)

T: How shall the congress be organized?... (L. 487) All right, the Great Compromise. Now sometimes you'll see this by the name of the man from Connecticut who hammered out the final compromise. It didn't come as easily as many were writing that day. Because there were two interest groups [...], the big states and the small versus... (L. 498–504) But it was a great compromise for the Connecticut compromise. And this came as the result of the two plans. Now how did it take place? ... (L. 508–511) [Answers are generated correctly. Teacher goes on to interstate commerce.]

FIG. 6.4. *(continued)*

answers to develop the agrarian/mercantile themes. The richness of this segment was in the questions asked, not in the answers sought or provided. The first question (A1) sought the distinction between regional and national; the second (A2) prompted for the distinction between local and federal. Each answer was followed by the teacher's elaboration (A3). The elaboration on the location of sovereignty extended the students' comments and modeled a more elaborate answer. As usual, the answer led into another question (B): This time the teacher asked students to elaborate by giving evidence and extending the answer. "Who thinks like this?" As soon as Jefferson was mentioned, Ms. Sterling built up the other side of the tension and simultaneously extended the set to include Adams, Washington, and Franklin. At this point a complex piece of weaving was going on, for she was both identifying and elaborating the scene at the Convention— who the players were—and building the subdivisions that she would need later in the lesson. But she backed up and asked an interesting precursor question (C): How is it that all these men with different viewpoints have agreed to come together? What galvanized them into action? The instructional move was strategic because if she had just built up the divisiveness of the Convention, the reason for the Convention's existence would be hard to fathom. What was also interesting is that we saw the first extended student answer of this segment of the lesson. The student elaborated the import of Shays' rebellion for national leadership. Again, the teacher extended and elaborated, leading to another set of questions (block D). In this next block the questions were (a) What do the 55 delegates at the Convention agree on, and (b) What do they disagree on? A workable list emerged during the ensuing discussion. We selected just a few points to show how a simple event was systematically analyzed in the discussions.

In block D, the teacher elicited from the students the ideas that the framers agreed on a republican form of government, power with the people, and the need for central government. She also took an excursion into the role and justification of secrecy of the Convention. This would eventually play into another theme of the course: the role and development of power. She then listed a set of topics around which there was some disagreement at the Convention and asked the students to provide explicit information as to the sides of the disagreement—who was against whom. The class constructed an aside together—a short essay—on the background of the Constitutional Convention. The activity was both shared and highly directed; precise terms were used, meanings were attached to them, and complex ideas were elaborated and exemplified. At this point in the lesson, students were in a position to demonstrate both the facts and spirit of the great compromises that were made.

In the second part of D (D2), Ms. Sterling drew out another element and required a more precise, less obvious answer than "wealthy and wealthier" (line 444). By the end of class, the elements of the tensions had been sketched. What was especially important about this episode is that the information established here would be the basis for extending the students' reasoning as they worked on subsequent skeins of material. The episode did not close or end; it became a basis for further work. The agrarian and mercantile themes had been developed with names, regional distinctions, and political envisioning.

The next selection to be examined occurred 2 weeks after the first and dealt with the emergence of a new political alignment and the political parties that reflected it (see Fig. 6.5). Jacksonian democracy was presented as an elaboration and realignment of Jeffersonian positions. The class was also laying further groundwork for understanding the Civil War. At the beginning of class, the teacher asked for a recounting of what happened in the 1824 election and a description of the multiple candidates. Notice in section (A) how the student provided an elaborate and backwards-referencing answer. Not only were the specifics easily available to sketch the event, but also there was a richness of detail—if somewhat clumsily stated.

In section (B), notice again the student's first and then second extended answer when the teacher was searching for the nature of the changes emerging within the executive branch at that time. In section (C) we see the student reasoning, indirectly contrasting Jackson to Adams and tying the position of the Indian negotiations back to the tensions between the agrarian Jeffersonians and the mercantile federalist position of John Adams. Here, the students cast a broad net to pull in a wide array of materials and synthesized them into a discussion, if not quite a case. It is important to remember in reading these student cases that they are spoken rapidly, not in elegant, developed ways. But the selections show, we think, the students' emerging competencies in building a coherent case.

In the third selection (see Fig. 6.6) taken from a lesson in mid-November, the class was devoted to a discussion of the underlying causes of the Civil War.[6] The students were asked to select from among six primary positions and to defend their choices in class. We examined a portion of the classroom discourse in which several students elaborated on economic sectionalism as an underlying cause of the Civil War. The statements by the students show them moving toward the complex case construction that the teacher had been modeling and helping students learn to generate. These responses began to weave a web of causes by taking economic sectionalism "back to state sovereignty" (line 1064). In other comments during this class on the causes of the Civil War, students revisited other tensions between agrarian and commercial interests, ideas that they had developed earlier.

---

[6]Note that district exams impose on the teacher incredible time pressure to be finished with the Civil War before Christmas vacation.

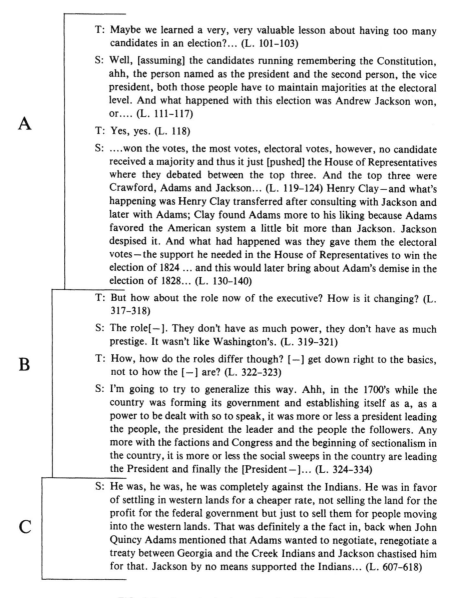

A

T: Maybe we learned a very, very valuable lesson about having too many candidates in an election?... (L. 101-103)

S: Well, [assuming] the candidates running remembering the Constitution, ahh, the person named as the president and the second person, the vice president, both those people have to maintain majorities at the electoral level. And what happened with this election was Andrew Jackson won, or.... (L. 111-117)

T: Yes, yes. (L. 118)

S: ....won the votes, the most votes, electoral votes, however, no candidate received a majority and thus it just [pushed] the House of Representatives where they debated between the top three. And the top three were Crawford, Adams and Jackson... (L. 119-124) Henry Clay—and what's happening was Henry Clay transferred after consulting with Jackson and later with Adams; Clay found Adams more to his liking because Adams favored the American system a little bit more than Jackson. Jackson despised it. And what had happened was they gave them the electoral votes—the support he needed in the House of Representatives to win the election of 1824 ... and this would later bring about Adam's demise in the election of 1828... (L. 130-140)

B

T: But how about the role now of the executive? How is it changing? (L. 317-318)

S: The role[−]. They don't have as much power, they don't have as much prestige. It wasn't like Washington's. (L. 319-321)

T: How, how do the roles differ though? [−] get down right to the basics, not to how the [−] are? (L. 322-323)

S: I'm going to try to generalize this way. Ahh, in the 1700's while the country was forming its government and establishing itself as a, as a power to be dealt with so to speak, it was more or less a president leading the people, the president the leader and the people the followers. Any more with the factions and Congress and the beginning of sectionalism in the country, it is more or less the social sweeps in the country are leading the President and finally the [President−]... (L. 324-334)

C

S: He was, he was, he was completely against the Indians. He was in favor of settling in western lands for a cheaper rate, not selling the land for the profit for the federal government but just to sell them for people moving into the western lands. That was definitely a the fact in, back when John Quincy Adams mentioned that Adams wanted to negotiate, renegotiate a treaty between Georgia and the Creek Indians and Jackson chastised him for that. Jackson by no means supported the Indians... (L. 607-618)

FIG. 6.5. Second selection—October 24, 1988.

Although oral productions of students are generally less coherent and have less evidence than written productions, it took a lot of knowledge and practice to pull together a spontaneous case in class discussion.

Each of the lessons expanded on a knowledge base that was being constructed and organized in the classroom. The knowledge base grew out

A

S: Well, I said economic sectionalism because, um, I, I feel that it was really lack of understanding by each, the different sections as to how important slaves were and weren't at the time. In the North slavery [−] wasn't morally acceptable. The South at that time couldn't survive without slaves. So I, I feel that, uh, that [−] economic sectionalism really was the dividing factor. There's sort of a lack of understanding... (L. 583–593)

S: Well I put economic sectionalism [−] Well I put it [is that] because the, uh, the Southerners depended on the slaves. And I think because they were so caught up in their slave ways that they didn't adapt to the new, the new ways of the North and the new economic will, will isolate the Industrials from the North. And in the way this causes the South to depend on the North for lots of goods... (L. 598–606)

S: Because that, because the South depended, they depended on the North because the North is growing and had all the new railroads and all the new [−]. The South depended on the North and it created lots of problems... (L. 617–622)

S: I did [−], except that, you know, [−] Civil War, it would have been avoided. But, uh, [gee, I point back]. To go a step further back in that, in the, derivation of that, I don't think that uh, there would have been that digression had there been not so much sectionalism. And that falls under the category of state sovereignty and uh, economic sectionalism. (L. 1058–1065)

FIG. 6.6. Third selection—November 15, 1988.

of the discussions as well as the very enriched and complex reading in texts and source materials that the students were doing. The students were learning to build up more elaborate and intricate explanations and supports for hypotheses formed around events and conditions. As the semester progressed the teacher turned more and more of the class time and action over to the students' control (Leinhardt, 1993).

In these lessons, there were, then, some thoughtful, reasoned discussions. But, some of the critical elements of case building that emerged from the discussions with historians were missing. The most notable was interpretive layering. Although two class days during this time period were devoted to contrasting different historians (Hofstadter, Schlesinger, and Beard) and different perspectives (those of people in western Pennsylvania, the South, and New England), these were not used as integral parts of the discussion of tensions leading up to the Civil War. Could they have been? Most probably.

ENDINGS

This research addresses three problems in the teaching and learning of history. First, it shifts the location of mindlessness (or mindfulness) from the subject matter that is learned to the minds of the students and teachers involved in the learning/teaching process. Specifically, mindlessness is located in students' and teachers' failure to reason about what is being learned and what is being taught. Second, this research differentiates between teaching content, and modeling, enacting, and demonstrating use of content. For example, there is a difference between the student's 1-word factual answer, "Jefferson," in our first lesson, and the discussion of causes of the Civil War in the third lesson (with the teacher's modeling and students' weaving together constellations of events). Finally, there is the difference between simple stories and intricate, ambiguous ones. A simple story about the Civil War might hold that differences over slavery and the firing on Fort Sumter started the Civil War; a more complex story includes social, political, and economic tensions that can be traced back to the Revolutionary Period. Students who have had opportunities to analyze, synthesize, and construct cases (at least orally) have had the opportunity to be mindful—to understand the differences between learning content and learning how to reason with content and to construct intricate and rich cases. In doing this they are learning to construct an historical stance that is evolutionary rather than absolute.

In part, mindfulness requires that we reconsider how we think students learn to think about history. As with mathematics, it appears that students at a fairly early stage in their thinking can press themselves to grapple with important ideas. They do not need to learn the facts first and then start to do the interesting "good stuff." As Mallon said when discussing these issues, "A crucial part of pedagogy is not to hide what's inside. Not to cloak it, and pretend, and give them only the outside, but to show them, allow them a view all the way in. Even if it's only partial" (lines 270–275). Students certainly can begin the process of reasoning in history from the beginning. If we admit that then we need to look hard at considering what mindfulness and reasoning are.

Reconsider the set of numbers from the beginning of this chapter. They are, of course, not mere numbers, but dates. What we would like to suggest is that students who have successfully negotiated an experience like the extended and elaborated explanation here will have a mindful response to the dates 1776 and 1865, not a mindless response based on rote memorization. The elaborated meaning of the Civil War, which included the sense of tension between agrarian and commercial interests, was used by Sterling as a cohesive glue that bound the students' understanding of the issues of Reconstruction after the Civil War to the issues that were first visible in Philadelphia during the Convention. We can expect that these students will have the intellectual power to appreciate these themes in the future when they read accounts of these times and when they themselves build cases.

History is a discipline that is framed by chronology and geography, but it is not constrained or limited by them. It is not a collection of reminiscences or anecdotal chit-chat any more than it is a list of vacuous dates. Thinking in history means being literate within these frames and being capable of analysis, synthesis, and case building. To achieve these goals, students need to have both opportunities to reason in history and guidance from history teachers who are able to think flexibly, dynamically, and powerfully within their discipline.

ACKNOWLEDGMENTS

The research reported in this chapter was supported in part by a grant from the Office of Educational Research and Improvement (OERI), United States Department of Education, to the Center for the Study of Learning, Learning Research and Development Center; in part by the Mellon Foundation; and in part by support to the first author from the Spencer Foundation. The opinions expressed do not necessarily reflect the position of the sponsoring agencies, and no endorsement should be inferred.

REFERENCES

Bean, T. W., Singer, H., Sorter, J., & Frazee, C. (1987). Acquisition of hierarchically organized knowledge and prediction of events in world history. *Reading Research and Instruction, 26*(2), 99–114.

Beck, I. L., & McKeown, M. G. (1988). Toward meaningful accounts in history texts for young learners. *Educational Researcher, 17*(6), 31–39.

Beck, I. L., & McKeown, M. G. (1989). Expository text for young readers: The issue of coherence. In L. Resnick (Ed.), *Knowing and learning: Issues for a cognitive psychology of instruction* (pp. 47–66). Hillsdale, NJ: Lawrence Erlbaum Associates.

Collingwood, R. G. (1946). *The idea of history.* London: Oxford University Press.

D'Emilio, J. (1992). *Making trouble.* New York: Routledge.

Evans, R. (1989, March). *Meaning in history: Philosophy and teaching.* Paper presented at the annual meeting of the American Educational Research Association, San Francisco.

FitzGerald, F. (1979). *America revised.* Boston: Little, Brown & Co.

Gagnon, P. (Ed.). (1989). *Historical literacy: The case for history education in America.* Boston: Houghton Mifflin.

Gibbon, E. (1910). *Decline and fall of the Roman empire.* New York: Dutton. (Original work published in 1776)

Goold, G. P. (Ed.). (1920). *Herodotus* (Vol. 1; A. D. Godley, Trans.). Cambridge, MA: Harvard University Press.

Goold, G. P. (Ed.). (1921). *Herodotus* (Vol. 2; A. D. Godley, Trans.). Cambridge, MA: Harvard University Press.

Hempel, C. G. (1962). Explanation in science and in history. In R. G. Colodny (Ed.), *Frontiers of science and philosophy* (pp. 7–33). Pittsburgh: University of Pittsburgh Press.

Hempel, C. G. (1965). *Aspects of scientific explanation.* New York: Free Press.

Herodotus. (1987). *The history* (D. Grene, Trans.). Chicago: University of Chicago Press.

Herodotus. (1990). The first book, Clio. In M. J. Adler, C. Fadiman, & P. W. Goetz (Eds.), *Great books of the Western World: Vol. 5. The history of Herodotus* (G. Rawlinson, Trans.; pp. 1-48). Chicago: Encyclopedia Britannica.

Leinhardt, G. (1990). *Towards understanding instructional explanations* (Tech. Rep. No. CLIP-90-03). Pittsburgh: University of Pittsburgh, Learning Research and Development Center.

Leinhardt, G. (1993). Weaving instructional explanations in history. *British Journal of Educational Psychology*, *63*, 46-74.

Leinhardt, G. (1994). History: A time to be mindful. In G. Leinhardt, I. L. Beck, & C. Stainton (Eds.), *Teaching and learning in history* (pp. 209-255). Hillsdale, NJ: Lawrence Erlbaum Associates.

Macauley, T.B. (1879). *The history of England from the accession of James II*. New York: Thomas Y. Crowell & Co. (Original work published in 1848)

Macauley, T.B. (1897). *England in 1685*. Boston: Ginn & Co.

Mallon, F. (1983). *The defense of community in Peru's central highlands: Peasant struggle and capitalist transition, 1860-1940*. Princeton, NJ: Princeton University Press.

McDiarmid, G. W. (1991, April). *A case of historical pedagogy*. Paper presented at the annual meeting of the American Educational Research Association, Chicago.

Resnick, L. B. (1987). *Education and learning to think*. Washington, DC: National Academy Press.

Schwab, J. J. (1978). Education and the structure of the disciplines. In I. Westbury & N. J. Wilkof (Eds.), *Science, curriculum, and liberal education* (pp. 229-272). Chicago: University of Chicago Press.

Thucydides. (1990). The history of the Peloponnesian War. In M. J. Adler, C. Fadiman, & P. W. Goetz (Eds.), *Great books of the Western world* (R. Crawley, Trans.; Vol. 5, pp. 345-593). Chicago: Encyclopedia Britannica.

Tierney, D. S. (1988, April). *How teachers explain things: Metaphoric representation of social studies concepts*. Paper presented at the annual meeting of the American Educational Research Association, New Orleans.

von Ranke, L. (1973). On the character of historical science (W. Iggers & K. von Moltke, Trans.). In G. Iggers & K. von Moltke (Eds.), *The theory and practice of history* (pp. 33-46). Indianapolis: Bobbs-Merrill. (Original work published in 1830)

von Ranke, L. (1973). On progress in history (W. Iggers & K. von Moltke, Trans.). In G. Iggers & K. von Moltke (Eds.), *The theory and practice of history* (pp. 51-56). Indianapolis: Bobbs-Merrill. (Original work published in 1854)

von Wright, G. H. (1971). *Explanation and understanding*. London: Routledge and Kegan Paul.

Walsh, W.H. (1967). *An introduction to philosophy of history*. London: Hutchinson University Library.

Wilson, S. M. (1990). *Mastodons, maps, and Michigan: Exploring uncharted territory while teaching elementary school social studies*. Unpublished manuscript, Michigan State University, East Lansing.

Wilson, S. M., & Wineburg, S. S. (1988). Peering at history through different lenses: The role of disciplinary perspectives in teaching history. *Teachers College Record*, *80*(4), 525-539.

Wineburg, S. S., & Wilson, S. M. (1988). Models of wisdom in the teaching of history. *Phi Delta Kappan*, *70*(1), 50-58.

7

Understanding History for Teaching: A Study of the Historical Understanding of Prospective Teachers

G. Williamson McDiarmid
Michigan State University

Current reform proposals and policies in teacher education are intended to increase the subject matter knowledge of prospective teachers. Reformers and policymakers assume that increasing the number of subject matter courses prospective teachers take and, concomitantly, decreasing the number of teacher education courses will result in teachers who know more about their subject matter for the purpose of teaching.

This assumption is largely unexamined. Despite years of research on student learning in college, researchers — except for a few in the sciences and mathematics (see, for example, Arons, 1990; Champagne, Gunstone, & Klopfer, 1985; Clement, 1982; Clement, Lochhead, & Monk, 1981; Maestre & Lochhead, 1983; Maestre, Gerace, & Lochhead, 1982; McDermott, 1984; Schoenfeld, 1985) — have paid little attention to the kinds of knowledge and understanding students develop in specific subject matters (Ball, 1988; Holt, 1990). Scholars in the arts and science disciplines are rewarded for furthering knowledge in their fields, not for studying their students' learning and refining their pedagogy accordingly. Undoubtedly many individual arts and science instructors gather information on their students' learning, but few write about their experiences (exceptions include Booth, 1988; Elbow, 1986; Holt, 1990; Smith, 1990).

Much of the research on college-student learning has focused on general issues of cognition rather than on the development of knowledge and understanding of specific disciplines (Pascarella & Terenzini, 1991). Recently, some psychologists have treated history as more than merely a venue for investigating cognition and have attended to issues of teaching and learning history in classrooms. This research, however, has been carried out

159

largely with precollegiate, not university, students. For instance, Beck and her colleagues (Beck, McKeown, & Gromoll, 1989; McKeown & Beck, 1990; McKeown, Beck, Sinatra, & Loxterman, 1992), in their chapter in this volume as well as elsewhere, have raised questions about the assumptions textbook writers appear to make about the knowledge students bring to texts as well as assumptions about how students learn and teachers' subject matter knowledge. The teachers they have studied appeared unprepared to supplement the accounts of history that appear in textbooks and to treat textbooks as resources rather than as gospel. Another author in this volume, Leinhardt, shows how teachers create opportunities for students to become "mindful" in addressing historical questions, engaging in some of the cognitive activities that she found characterize the work of practicing historians. A few researchers such as Wineburg (1991, this volume) have investigated the historical understanding of teachers, attending particularly to the framing assumptions—about specific events, historical actors, and their motivations—that they bring to historical texts. Wertsch's work reported in this volume focuses on college students. He attends, however, to their beliefs about the origins of their country, not to how they come to the understandings they profess.

These investigations into students' understandings and learning tend to emphasize the critical role of teachers' subject matter understandings. To address the shortcomings of history and social studies texts and the nature of the beliefs and understanding students bring with them to the classroom, teachers need opportunities to learn about the nature of historical knowledge and the construction of historical accounts. But do teachers encounter such opportunities in their university history courses? And if they do, what do they appear to learn from such opportunities?

The paucity of investigations of learning in the context of university history courses points to the importance of examining the assumption that more courses in a discipline constitute better preparation for teaching the subject. Without such investigations, teacher educators and policymakers are likely to continue promulgating reforms that do not address the problem. Given that educational credentials are widely accepted as a proxy for knowledge, attempting to improve teachers' knowledge of their subjects for teaching by requiring more arts and science courses is logically compelling.

In this chapter, I examine the knowledge and thinking of undergraduates, some of whom plan to teach, in a required historiography seminar. My purpose is to begin addressing the gap in our collective knowledge of learning in arts and science courses. After briefly describing the course I investigated as well as the instructor's goal—detailed more fully in Mc-Diarmid and Vinten-Johansen (1993)—I discuss the kinds of knowledge and understanding students seemed to develop during and after the course and speculate on the role that the experience of the course may have played in the development of these understandings. Finally, I compare students' understanding with the recommendations of reformers.

DESCRIPTION OF THE STUDY

The Undergraduate Historiography Course

In selecting a history class to study, we looked for a class: (a) likely to bring students face to face with core epistemological questions in the field; (b) whose instructor had a reputation as a successful pedagogue and, therefore, promised to be a "best case"; and (c) required of all history majors and typically taken early in students' sequence of courses in their major. The latter was important because we wanted a sample of students that we could follow over time. A section of the required undergraduate historiography course offered by the History Department at Michigan State University taught by Professor Peter Vinten-Johansen met all of these criteria. After a brief career as a high school government teacher, a stint in the Navy, and graduate work in intellectual history at Yale, he joined the faculty of Michigan State University where he has taught history for 15 years. (For an autobiographical account of his development as a teacher, see McDiarmid & Vinten-Johansen, 1993.)

The History Department limits enrollment in each section of the historiography course to 25, and senior faculty regularly teach sections of the course. This represents the history faculty's commitment to guarantee that students, early in their careers as majors, will experience relatively close interactions with senior faculty in a setting that encourages sustained discussion. Most of the other courses students take in the department enroll at least 40 students. In their senior year, they participate in a research paper seminar.

Vinten-Johansen taught the section of the course taken by students in the Honors College at Michigan State University. About half the students in the class were not in the honors program. The presence of the honors college students, for our purposes, enhanced the seminar's qualifications as a "best case" test of the idea that arts and science courses could enable students—including prospective teachers—to develop the deep and connected understandings of the subject matter some proponents argue that teachers need. According to Vinten-Johansen, in all essential respects the course was similar in organization, procedures, and pedagogy to other nonhonors courses he teaches. My subsequent observations of a senior-level, nonhonors course he taught confirmed his claim. Moreover, despite the fact that his intellectual European history sequence of courses enrolls as many as 40 to 50 students, he teaches in much the same way.

The Student Sample

Of the 20 students who started the seminar, 16 completed it. Of the 14 students for whom we have baseline data, 8 were third-year, 2 second-year, and 4 first-year students. Eight of the 14 were males. All of the students were White, all came from small towns or suburbs, and all came from middle-class families. In other words, they fit the profile of most students who enter secondary teaching. The students had taken an average of two history courses prior to the historiography seminar; 3 of the third-year students had taken as many as four courses. Although they had taken no previous college-level history courses, 2 of the first-year students had taken Advanced Placement history courses in high school. The courses students had previously taken were, by and large, survey courses taught in large lecture formats with weekly discussion sections taught by graduate students. The most common survey course taken was the 2-term sequence in American History. All but 3 of the students were history majors. Eight of the original 14 planned to teach high school history after graduation. Of the 14 students for whom we have baseline data, we have year-later data for 11, 6 of whom were prospective teachers. Of the 3 we lost from the sample, 1 was in a year-abroad program and the other 2 had left Michigan State.

Description of the Data on Student Learning

We documented the opportunities that students in the course had to learn, the instructor's rationale for the purposes and opportunities he orchestrated as well as students' understandings of critical ideas (see McDiarmid & Vinten-Johansen, 1993, for details of data collection on the course). We conducted at least two and in some cases three semi-structured interviews with each of the 11 students who remained in the sample over the first year of the study. The first section of the interview focused on students' past experience with learning social studies and history, both inside and outside of school. In the second section, we asked students about specific historical events and issues: the causes and consequences of the Civil War as well as specific events and people associated with these issues; the meaning of Reconstruction; highlights and results of the civil rights movement as well as, again, events and people from the movement; and the Tonkin Bay Resolution in relation to the war in Vietnam.

We chose these topics because they are commonly found in high school history courses and textbooks and they are topics on which historians have offered a variety of interpretations. We sought to find out not only what students knew — their recall of facts and the historical context — about these events but also how they thought historians construct accounts of these events and what historians might find problematic in writing historical accounts. We also presented students with conflicting interpretations of a historical period — Reconstruction — and asked them which account they preferred and why and how historians could produce such a range of interpretations for the same set of events.

The third section uses as a context for questions the same historical events and issues that appeared in the second, but the focus is on how the students would teach these topics to 8th and 11th graders.

Students' written work constitutes another source of data, both on the teaching of the course and on student understanding. When possible, I collected the papers the students wrote for the course. These papers included Professor Vinten-Johansen's marginal and summary comments. Consequently, the papers represent evidence of student understanding as well as the instructor's goals and purposes.

In taking field notes during the seminars, I focused on the classroom discourse, that is, the issues that were discussed and how these were related to prior and subsequent issues or questions, the roles of various participants in the discussion, the kinds of questions asked and explanations offered, and other ways in which history was represented.

Data Analysis

I entered the data from the student interviews into a database that allowed me to sort them along several dimensions and to compare their responses to each of the items at the beginning of the course and then 1 year later. For this analysis, I examined students' responses on four dimensions: knowledge of selected U.S. history topics, the nature of historical knowledge, the nature of historical inquiry, and the teaching and learning of history. Beginning with the full transcripts of the interviews, I summarized the data on each dimension for each student including illustrative quotations. Next, I wrote a brief 1- or 2-sentence summary to enable me to look for patterns across the responses of all students in the sample. This method of data reduction allowed me to trace my summaries directly and easily back to the data. Another member of the research team independently created summaries of the data to test the reliability of mine.

Problems with the Study

Obviously, case studies are not probabilistic. At the same time, the students whose knowledge and understanding we examined are representative of most students who enter teaching. They are of the same ethnicity and social class as most students who enter teaching; slightly more than half are male; and they have had experiences in school and university that seem typical of those who become teachers. We designed the study to examine prospective teachers' understandings of history and how these understandings are formed. In particular, we sought to analyze students' experiences in a course that required them to examine their beliefs about the nature of historical inquiry and knowledge and to explore the changes, if any, that seemed to occur in their knowledge and thinking about history over time. Although I cannot draw conclusions about the learning of all prospective history teachers, I believe that the thinking of these students is representative of the thinking of many, if not most, students who enter teaching. Currently, few detailed descriptions or analyses of prospective teachers' learning in history is available to historians or teacher educators. Yet, such investigations are vital if we are to examine the assumption that merely increasing the number of subject matter courses, in and of itself, will result in the kind of knowledge and understandings teachers need. I hope this chapter spurs interest in and more discussion and investigation of these issues.

THE HISTORIOGRAPHY SEMINAR: WHAT IS IT AN OPPORTUNITY TO LEARN?

By their own admission, students had never previously experienced a course quite like the historiography seminar. In the first instance, during the seminar, Professor Vinten-Johansen expected them to participate—to talk, to respond to his questions, to provide evidence for their opinions, to listen to classmates and respond, to lead discussions of the texts used in the course. At the beginning, they participated in conversations comparing two competing accounts of the Spanish Armada (Fernandez-Armesto, 1989; Mattingly, 1959). Later, as members of groups formed to research the historical question, they searched for and found information and, in discussions with their group, made sense of the information they and others uncovered. Secondly, Vinten-Johansen expected them, in their writing, to make historical arguments, both to develop a thesis and to support it. He also expected them to redraft papers on the basis of his written and oral comments. Finally, he expected the students to be resources to one another, helping each other understand particular arguments as well as providing pertinent information about the past.

Vinten-Johansen's teaching is characterized by his close attention to students' thinking as manifest in their writing and their participation in discussions in the seminar. Knowing history, in Vinten-Johansen's view, is less one's store of specific information about the past—the succession of Tudor monarchs, for instance—and more one's capacity to make reasoned arguments about the past and to evaluate the plausibility of historical accounts and explanations. This accords well with Herman's (1983) study in which university-based experts in history identified the capacity to distinguish perspectives, bias, and interpretative stance in historical accounts, to use a process of inquiry, and to analyze data as the signal attributes of history learners. As Vinten-Johansen said during an interview:

> History is a series of interpretations and viewpoints that are based in evidence but various readings of the very same evidence—issues of selectivity, the background of the historian—would eventuate in different outcomes. . . . [The students] need to see that history is not simply a series of chronological recapitulations. That it involves a process of understanding not just what happened but how and why it happened as it did.

To develop students' capacity to judge historical accounts and their understanding of the nature of historical knowledge, Professor Vinten-Johansen gave students two primary tasks. One involved comparing two accounts of the same historical events—the battle between the Spanish Armada and the English fleet in 1588. Students identified the thesis of the two accounts—Mattingly's (1959) classic narrative and Fernandez-Armesto's (1989) revisionist analysis of the event—as well as the evidence on which each was built. Then, they wrote about which account was most convincing and why.

This activity, which occupied the first third of the course, set up the central task in the experience: creating an original historical argument based on evidence students themselves gathered. Professor Vinten-Johansen designed the assignment to be manageable for undergraduates at the beginning of their history studies and within the confines of a 10-week term. The students' task was to sort out an apparently obscure dispute between two Englishmen over a seat in the House of Commons at the beginning of the 17th century. Vinten-Johansen distributed a packet of original documents and organized students into research groups. At subsequent seminars, students spent part of the time in groups, discussing the information they had uncovered and additional information they needed to find, and puzzling out together the Goodwin-Fortesque dispute. As you might expect, Vinten-Johansen chose this dispute, which he had himself had to sort out as a student of Professor Jack Hexter at Yale in the 1970s, because it reflected a larger conflict: that between James I, Stuart successor to the Tudor Elizabeth and an advocate of the divine right of kings, and Parliament, which had extracted from Elizabeth—as a quid pro quo for the wherewithal to fend off the Armada—certain rights to govern its own affairs, including elections. Students had to develop their own theses about the dispute and support them with the evidence they and their classmates had gathered. This paper constituted the final examination in the course.

From transcripts of the seminars, assignments, and interviews with Professor Vinten-Johansen, I have identified eight understandings about history that he appeared to be trying to help students develop. As I treat these fully elsewhere (McDiarmid & Vinten-Johansen, 1993), I merely list them here: (a) an accurate chronology is an essential first step in understanding the past, (b) the record of the past lends itself to multiple interpretations, (c) a given event can only be understood in the context in which it occurred, (d) part of the historian's task is to link a given event to its context in a way that produces an interpretation of the event, (e) a critical aspect of writing history consists in placing oneself in someone else's shoes and seeing the world as he or she saw it, (f) historians impose an orderliness on past events that belies both the confusion and uncertainty with which events were actually experienced as well as the essentially contingent nature of events, (g) historical accounts and interpretations should be judged on their own terms according to how well the historian substantiates his or her thesis, and (h) history is written for the present generation and, hence, the past needs to be periodically reinterpreted.

STUDENTS' KNOWLEDGE AND UNDERSTANDING OF HISTORY

We typically think that historical knowledge is, by definition, information about the past — such things as the date Columbus reached the Caribbean, the identity of the U.S. president responsible for establishing the personal income tax, and the site of the decisive battles of the U.S. Civil War. Yet, such information may not be the essence of knowledge in the discipline, particularly in the eyes of experts in the field (Herman, 1990). Information about the past does not necessarily speak for itself; the historian, in creating an account of the past, is creating a plausible explanation for why things happened as the historian believes they did. In this sense, information about the past is not history, but rather the raw material out of which historians fashion historical accounts. As Professor Vinten-Johansen told me, "The role of the historian is to impose clarity on the past for a particular purpose."

Understanding that historians impose order on the past for a particular purpose is perhaps the essential insight to understanding history as a human construct, as an imposition of our present understandings on the incomplete — and unbalanced — record of the past. And such an understanding is essential to a critical stance toward historical accounts. Such a critical stance enables teachers to evaluate the history curriculum — textbooks, tests, software, and so on. In addition, it suggests a primary objective for teaching history. As Gagnon (1988) argued, we teach history in school to help cultivate judgment in young people, judgment vital to the body politic. Information about the past, in and of itself, does not necessarily eventuate in the judgment of which Gagnon writes any more than a pile of logs eventuates in a fire.

Our interest in how prospective teachers think about history led us to gather a variety of data — on students' knowledge of information about the past, their understanding of historical knowledge and historical inquiry, and their understanding of teaching and learning history. We explored their knowledge and understanding of each of these dimensions as well as the relationships among them.

Knowledge of Information about the Past

We explored students' knowledge of four different topics: the Civil War, Reconstruction, the modern civil rights movement, and the war in Vietnam. We asked students to sort 14 cards on which we had written topics connected to the Civil War and 18 cards connected to the civil rights movement (see Tables 7.1 and 7.2). After students organized the cards, we asked them to explain their groupings and to tell us what they understood about the event, person, place, or organization written on each card.

Unlike investigations of high school students' knowledge of information

TABLE 7.1
Topics for Civil War Card Sort

Free Soilers	Know-Nothings
Popular sovereignty	Bleeding Kansas
Stephen Douglas	Dred Scott case
Fugitive Slave Law of 1850	Harper's Ferry
Harriet Beecher Stowe	Harriet Tubman
Kansas-Nebraska Act	Frederick Douglass
The Republican Party	Election of 1860

TABLE 7.2
Topics for Civil Rights Movement Card Sort

Reconstruction	Freedom Rides
Plessy v. Ferguson	Selma, Alabama
Brown v. Board of Education of Topeka	Black Power
Jim Crow laws	J. Edgar Hoover
Ku Klux Klan	Civil Rights Act of 1964
Little Rock, Arkansas	Malcolm X
Montgomery bus boycott	N.A.A.C.P.
Martin Luther King, Jr.	March on Washington, 1963
Student sit-ins	Rioting in Watts

about the past (Ravitch & Finn, 1987), we found that these students were fairly knowledgeable about the past—at least those people, events, and places from the past about which we asked. For the Civil War, 5 of the 11 students identified 70% or more of the 15 cards. Eight of the 11 students organized the cards on some conceptual basis rather than just as people, places, dates, and organizations. For the civil rights movement, 6 of the 11 identified 70% or more of the 15 cards, and all organized cards on a causal or conceptual basis. Students' knowledge seemed to change little over the year between the initial and the follow-up interviews. Given that most students had taken the required U.S. history sequence before the initial interview and few took history courses bearing on these two periods, we had no reason to believe that their knowledge of these items would change. We were interested in seeing whether changes in their ideas about history as a subject of inquiry influenced the categories they used to organize information. If such influence occurred, our methods did not pick it up.

With but one exception, we also found little change in students' responses to questions about causes of the Civil War and highlights of the civil rights movement. Most contended that economics, not slavery, was the real cause of the war. That they did not appear to consider slavery an economic as well as moral phenomenon surprised us. The implication of the way several students discussed this distinction led us to believe that they thought anyone who believes that slavery caused the war is naive:

> I don't think slavery . . . caused the Civil War. Basically, what I think it boils down to is that the Democrats had been nominating the government for a good number of years and the opposition party needed an issue to get the common people behind to defeat the Republicans. So they tried a couple things and it ended up with slavery which seemed to work pretty well. (Karen, IV#1)[1]

Most did, however, mention more than a single cause of the war. They cited cultural, ideological, and lifestyle differences; political conflict over territorial expansion, states' rights, and tariffs; differences between a burgeoning manufacturing and industrial economy and an agricultural economy. In short, their thinking, at least in the context of the Civil War, seemed to include an appreciation for the multiple influences on events.

When asked about highlights of the civil rights movement, most mentioned events in the 1960s—Martin Luther King's "I Have a Dream" speech, the March on Washington, the Detroit riots, Malcolm X, and the idea of Black power (Malcolm X is usually contrasted negatively with Martin

---

[1]The information in parentheses following quotations from student interviews include the student's pseudonym and the number of the interview (i.e., IV#1 = baseline interview and IV#2 = follow-up interview conducted 1 year later).

Luther King). The only event of the 1950s on which several remarked was the Montgomery Bus Boycott. Few mentioned the Freedom Rides, voter registration drives, Brown v. Board of Education Topeka, desegregation of schools, universities, and public facilities or any of the key civil rights organizations: SCLC, SNCC, CORE, NAACP, and so on. They seemed to view the civil rights movement as the sum of individual heroic acts like those of Rosa Parks and Martin Luther King in the face of Southern bigotry and violence. None treated the movement as the culmination of a long struggle in which people had organized themselves to challenge discrimination.

As histories of the movement such as *Simple Justice* (Kluger, 1975), Bearing the Cross (Garrow, 1988), and *Parting the Waters* (Branch, 1988) demonstrate, a key dimension of the civil rights movement, not sufficiently appreciated in popular accounts, is the thoughtfulness and strategic wisdom inherent in the series of challenges to legal and de facto discrimination. Students' discussions of the civil rights movement—its goals, its accomplishments, its long-term effects—raise several questions: Can anyone appreciate the full historical significance of the accomplishments of African Americans if they do not understand the organizational and strategic aspects of their struggle for equality? Can they appreciate the debt all U.S. citizens owe to those who fought exclusion and discrimination and, in so doing, redefined the idea of civil rights? Does the tendency to highlight the individual heroes of the movement obscure the involvement and contributions of lesser known and unknown African Americans and others to the struggle? These questions seem particularly pertinent to ask of students in our sample because most of them plan to teach. Their understanding of the civil rights movement will inform how they treat the topic when they teach.

Remember that, on the card sort, most of these students demonstrated a good recall of important information about the civil rights movement. All used some type of causal or conceptual basis to organize the cards. They recalled important historical information and used categories to group these data that indicated a conceptual organization for the information. Yet, as their responses to the question on the highlights of the civil rights movement seem to indicate, their appreciation for essential aspects of the movement— namely, its organizational character and grass-roots nature—is limited.

Ideas About Doing History

At the beginning of the historiography course, the students in our sample, although they held somewhat disparate views on doing history and the nature of historical accounts, seemed to share several conceptions. In writing history, they believed, firsthand accounts of events are more reliable than more distal accounts. In describing how they would write an historical account, they rarely mentioned the use of secondary sources. At the same time, several students also recognized that eyewitness accounts, which they regarded as highly reliable, often conflict. In such cases, the historians' task was to balance the accounts, rather like an accountant or a mathematician:

> You'd have to take everything from the South and the North like a grain of salt and then put it all together some way and see if like someone in the South said there is a 100 soldiers in this troop and then the other one said there was like 98. That's pretty close. So it must be true. Kind of like math. (Steve, IV#1)

During the interview, we gave students a copy of the text of President Johnson's speech to a joint session of Congress that eventuated in the Tonkin Bay Resolution, legitimating the military buildup in Vietnam in the mid-1960s. We asked them how they might go about writing an account of this speech for a student history journal. Nearly all the students mentioned the importance of learning more about the context in order to understand the speech and the resulting resolution. To discover more about the context and the resolution itself, nearly all said they would consult secondary sources—in contrast to their observations that historians seek out eyewitness accounts.

Most seemed to have a point of view on the issue of Vietnam and assumed that they would write the article to support that point of view. The purpose of consulting secondary sources would be to gather information to substantiate a position they had already taken, not to help them interpret the speech. None mentioned that the actual processes of researching and writing would be means to get clearer about what they thought about the issue. This assumption—that historians bring predetermined positions to the writing of historical accounts—is consistent with the view, expressed throughout the interviews, that all historical accounts are, by definition, biased. Bias can be traced to the personal circumstances—race and region of birth, for instance—of the historian.

We presented the students with brief summaries of four conflicting interpretations of Reconstruction drawn from Foner's (1988) recent reassessment (see Appendix). Most were unaware of any account of Reconstruction other than the one we christened the "Gone-with-the-Wind" view: Northern Reconstructionists—the dreaded carpetbaggers—manipulated ignorant and largely passive former slaves to their own self-aggrandizing ends. When asked which of the four versions they found most credible, not surprisingly, all but two of the students chose the one with which they were most familiar—the "Gone-with-the-Wind" version—despite the fact that historians, for several decades, have attacked and discredited this interpretation (DuBois, 1935; Foner, 1988; Stampp, 1965; Woodward, 1986). Interestingly, one student who had read Foner's account for a survey course in American history, explained Foner's differences with Donald (1965), another historian of the Reconstruction era, as a function of the fact that Donald was a Southerner and Foner a Northerner.

Virtually all of the students, asked to explain the differences among the various accounts of Reconstruction, ascribed these to the historians' personal biases: whether they were from the North or the South, whether they were Black or White, and whether or not they were prejudiced toward Blacks. As one student told us, "If Jimmy Joe Bob from the South is writing about the Civil War, I'm sure he'd be biased to reasons why the South had the right idea and the North didn't" (Jeff, IV#1). Another observed that a Southerner could not have possibly constructed the interpretation that characterized Reconstruction policies as essentially conservative because they did not entail land redistribution.

Two students, who also subscribed to the general notion that historical accounts are by nature biased, focused more on the ways that the preoccupations and concerns of a given historical moment shape historians' perspectives. Responding to a revisionist account of Reconstruction that highlighted the role of African Americans in shaping not only the agenda and policies of Reconstruction but also Southern society and institutions in the immediate postwar period (Foner, 1988), Curt said:

> I think it was written more in the time of the civil rights movement than after because I don't think that anybody would've looked at things that way before. I assume that this was written by a Black, just because I don't think that anybody before that looked to say that the Blacks were the center of everything. It just seems like something that you wouldn't think about until there was a big, Black movement again. (Curt, IV#1)

After we told her when the various interpretations of Reconstruction that we gave her to read had been published and by whom, Mary mentioned both the role of personal bias and of the historical moment when the historian wrote:

> It makes a big difference if you know where they're coming from. If you know if they're Black or White, if you know when they're writing, because you can think of what their culture is like at that time. You know what might be affecting their views. (Mary, IV#1)

Views of History

For another analytical category that we termed "views of history," we drew on several different questions in the interview as well as from students' comments in the seminar. In the interviews that we did at the beginning of the seminar, two-thirds of the students in the sample believed that historians' accounts are, to greater or lesser degrees, instruments of their personal biases—such things as their gender, race, regional origins, political commitments, and nationality. A few students do mention that historians need to be conscious of their own biases and that such awareness could help them counterbalance these biases. By and large, however, the students assumed that biases are irresistible forces against which historians are impotent. As one student commented:

> With something like the civil rights movement, our way of looking at things is not too different than it was in the 1950s, 1960s, and 1970s because it wasn't that long ago. So we would only see it from our bias. We wouldn't see it from an outside point of view. . . . Because you get emotional about something, you have strong emotions either one way or the other. It's going to blind you a little bit to the ways things really are. You may get all the facts right but it will color it a little in your mind and if you're writing about it or talking about it, it will color it in the minds of other people. . . . Like the examples I read about the four versions of Reconstruction. We had the Northerner writing that the Radical Reconstructionists were great guys because he was really caught up in that cause and he really believed in it, so he downplayed what really happened and built the Radical Reconstruction position for the Negro and doing all these wonderful things out of the goodness of their hearts. (Karen, IV#1)

Historians write accounts of the past in order to push their own political agendas. Such a belief in the dominating power of personal bias produces a fashionable cynicism, a relativism in which all accounts are equally biased. According to this view, no account is entirely wrong nor is any entirely right.

Skepticism toward historical accounts is precisely the stance most history instructors would like their students to take. Certainly, Professor Vinten-Johansen tried to help his students develop such stances. Yet, a cynicism that ignores the standards and criteria that historians have developed for judging the relative merits of various accounts is as reflexive and unthinking as a gullibility that accepts a given account as true. Having arrived at such a cynical position, students can easily mistake their stance as critical and reasoned.

This skeptical stance is, however, fertile ground for teachers bent on encouraging a critical view of history in their students. As Vinten-Johansen observed, "[h]istory is a series of interpretations and viewpoints that are based in evidence but various readings of the very same evidence—issues of selectivity, the background of the historian—would eventuate in different outcomes"—a point of view shared by numerous historians and philosophers of history (Carr, 1962; Collingwood, 1946/1956; Croce, 1941/1970; Geyl, 1955/1962; Handlin, 1979; Walsh, 1951/1984). From at least three of the students, the data we collected seemed to show an evolution of thought beyond the unreflective cynicism described earlier. In the first interview, Mary, one of the three, responded to our question of why historians' interpretations of Reconstruction differ as follows:

> I think a lot has to do with like the time they live in and their background. Like the one by W.E.B. Dubois. . . . He was Black and you can sort of tell that he's trying to make the Blacks, make it sound like they were actively involved in the Civil War and actively involved in getting themselves free. (Mary IV#1)

A year later, the focus of her remarks shifted — away from the ineluctable effects of personal bias and toward the indeterminate nature of past events. In the following, responding to a question about whether facts or concepts should be the focus of history instruction, Mary referenced her experience in Vinten-Johansen's seminar:

> When I had Peter's class, we read two different books on the Spanish Armada. One book I hated because I thought he contradicted himself the whole time and I didn't agree with what he was trying to say. But if he had made a case for it, if he'd supported himself better, I would have said, "Oh, OK, this works." But then the other book had different ideas and he supported himself well. And I don't necessarily subscribe to one or the other, but I'm like, "OK, I can see this" and "OK, I can see this." You've got to figure out what's going on from the two different ideas. But if you don't support yourself, people just aren't going to believe you. That's why I don't like textbooks because they'll say, "This happened, this happened, this happened and this is why," and that's not necessarily why. . . . You know a lot of that's up in the air. I mean you can make speculations and you know you may be right and a lot of people may think that this is why, they may think the same reasons. But you don't know, you weren't there. (Mary IV#2)

As we conducted these follow-up interviews during the Persian Gulf War, Mary used this conflict to illustrate her point in the context of a question about the war in Vietnam:

> I don't think that history is all cut and dry. . . . I mean, you can say, "Yes, this happened on this date, this happened on this date . . ." but you can't talk about motives. I don't know what I think motives for Vietnam are. Twenty years from now, me or somebody else is going to think different motives. . . . That's the kind of stuff that you can't tie down. . . . Some historian will write [about the Persian Gulf War] and say this is what happened and this is why, but then another historian's going to come out and say this is what happened and this is why and neither of those two people are going to agree. It's going to be totally different accounts. (Mary IV#2)

In this response, we can discern a focus on human motivation—that is, reconstructing what lay behind the actions of people in the past—as well as an appreciation for the fundamentally interpretative nature of all historical accounts. Evidence of similar concerns for human motivation and appreciation of the interpretative nature of historical accounts appears in the postcourse interviews of seven of the nine students for whom we have data on this dimension. In four of these cases, students' concerns and appreciation appear to have developed in the year between the first and the follow-up interviews.

In the initial interviews, three of the students expressed another view of history: history as cyclical. Again, this view appeared to be largely unreflective, perhaps a popularized version of Santayana's (1905) dictum that "Those who cannot remember the past are condemned to repeat it" (p. 284). Karen is typical of those who held this view. Asked how she would respond to a hypothetical high schooler who wondered why bother studying history, she said:

> I'd tell him, "So you don't go out and make the same mistake yourself one day and get us involved in another war." Because, like I said last time, I believe history is cyclical. Events will happen, not exactly the same over and over again, it's kind of impossible to get all the same things but same general type of things will go on again and again because history really isn't paid too much attention to by anyone. And so they'll come up to a situation . . . that had happened in the past once or several times, same basic type of situation and choices and they'll go right ahead and make the same choice that was made before when it may have had disastrous consequences. You need to have the knowledge so you can possibly avoid repeating the same mistakes and having the same problems. . . . All history is basically war, peace, war, peace, preparing for the next war. (Karen IV#1)

In the third meeting of the seminar, when Karen suggested that history was cyclical, Professor Vinten-Johansen, aware of the appeal of this view for the popular mind, spoke directly to the difference between historical parallels and the view that "history repeats itself." In the follow-up interviews we conducted a year after the seminar, Karen returned to her view that history is cyclical, but she devoted equal attention to her belief that:

> History can be interpreted in different ways. In a lot of cases, it's kind of hard to conclude that this interpretation is absolutely wrong, 100%, and this interpretation is the only right one. A lot of it is personal opinion, not fact. (Karen IV#2)

In the follow-up interviews with the other two students who had offered the view that history is cyclical in nature, both appeared less certain. Bill, for instance, who was perhaps most insistent about the cyclical nature of history, devoted, in his second interview, greater attention to the interpretative nature of history than to its putatively cyclical character.

One explanation for these apparent changes is that students learned from Vinten-Johansen's critique of this characterization that it is unfashionable among historians. This is not, however, what students communicated in the interviews. Rather, at least two of the three students who initially expressed this view seem to have moved beyond it, developing conceptions of history more textured and variegated than simplistic dicta on the character of history.

Finally, one student, particularly interested in archaeology, initially expressed a view of history as the orderly presentation of information about past political events and the people involved. Asked in her first interview about the historiography seminar, she opined:

> In this 201 class, we don't have a textbook so when we read the Armada books, they were mainly just the author's interpretation of the work. They were facts in a way but they were kind of tainted by their preferences. And I like textbooks, how they come across as straightforward and just give me the facts. . . . They don't have opinions or personal feelings in them. (Nancy IV#1)

A year later, Nancy's beliefs that the facts of history are unsullied by opinions, personal feelings, or perceptions and that textbooks are unbiased compendia of facts have not changed. In response to a question about what high school students should learn about the Civil War, she replied:

> The facts. I'd have to get my facts straight before I could teach them. I'd have to look at textbooks and make sure I was telling them the right idea. I'd just want to make sure that they knew the facts. I wouldn't want to put my opinions or perceptions over the facts. I would just want to tell them the strict facts about it. (Nancy, IV#2)

Nancy, by her own admission, went through the motions in the seminar and hoped that the instructor would pass her. Convinced that the seminar was not about what she considered history to be, she exerted a minimal, half-hearted effort. Perhaps most surprising, Nancy appeared to be alone among the students in the seminar in her beliefs about the nature of history.

In sum, most of the students in the sample believed, at the outset of the seminar, that the personal circumstances of historians — their gender, race, region — cause them to skew historical accounts. In this view, historians used historical accounts to pursue their interests and the interests of others in their group. A year later, a subtle shift seemed to have taken place in the views of about half the students: They appeared to have developed a greater appreciation for the degree to which the present moment and the preoccupations of the present moment shape how all of us, historian and nonspecialist alike, see the past. Their reflexive cynicism appears tempered by an appreciation for the constructed, tentative nature of historical knowledge. In their frequent references to the historiography seminar, moreover, we can discern influences of the course, particularly their experiences working on the Goodwin-Fortesque case and the comparison of Mattingly's and Fernandez-Armesto's treatments of the Armada. The idea that history is cyclical, a repetition of the same events in different times and places, figures less centrally in the year-later interviews of those students who argued for this view initially.

Views of Teaching and Learning History

Perhaps most striking about students' views of history and the doing of history is their relative sophistication. Most view history as interpretation of the records of the past shaped largely by the concerns and preoccupations of the present. When we look at these same students' views of teaching and learning history, however, we are struck by the extent to which they are prisoners of their own experiences as students. And, compared to the effects that the historiography seminar appears to have had on their views of history, students' beliefs about teaching and learning history seem virtually unchanged.

When asked how they would help high school students learn the knowledge of the Civil War that they believed important, most of the students said they would lecture. This reflects their own experience in secondary and university history classrooms. Outside the historiography seminar, few had experienced any approach to teaching history other than lecturing. Two of the students did mention that they might have students do projects, one touted the value of discussions, one suggested the use of primary sources, and one reported he'd tell "good stories."

To distinguish good history teachers from the bad ones, students applied two criteria: whether or not they told "good stories" and whether or not they dictated their notes or wrote them on the board. A "good story" seemed to be one that was not in the textbook and, second, one that exposed the failings and foibles of historical personages, thus making the person and the events in which he or she was involved less remote and strange, more accessible and real.

Asked how they would teach the civil rights movement, several offered lecturing as the primary approach. Most, however, also mentioned the use of documentary films. In addition, three students mentioned the use of primary sources or contemporary accounts. Four mentioned the value of discussions. Several students also suggested that they would have pupils read "real books"—that is, works of history that are not textbooks.

Although most of the students considered the historiography seminar the best history course they had taken, only one student mentioned the workshop approach in their discussion of methods they might adopt. When we asked them about using such an approach with high school students, several expressed their doubt that high school students have either the motivation or the ability to carry out work of this type. This is perhaps consistent with their belief that Professor Vinten-Johansen's seminar required them to work more than any other history class they had taken. Describing his experience in the course, one student, who liked the course in spite of receiving a failing grade, said, "Peter puts us through hell."

Most considered learning history as unproblematic, as simply a reflex of learning (Cohen, 1988). Consequently, to learn history, learners need only be told what happened and why—this despite the strong criticism most heaped on the history classes, nearly all of which were lecture courses, they had taken in high school and at university. Jeff is a notable exception. Somewhat baffled by the seminar at the outset, Jeff came to rethink not merely the nature of history but also what it means to know and learn history. Responding to a question about how he might help eighth graders learn about the Civil War, he said:

> I'd want to teach them how to learn because you can't tell someone history because then it defeats the purpose. If you learn it yourself and put your own interpretation on it, you can be guided. . . . The who, how, what, where, when, why are very important questions . . . even PhDs and doctors are still asked that when they write articles. "What do you think about this?" Or "How about this? You didn't consider this." And that's not telling someone they're wrong. It's just saying maybe you can consider this, too. . . . How to learn is important, knowing how to go to the library and look up what's interesting to you. (Jeff, IV#2)

Mark's view of learning also differed from most students in the sample:

> If you just go in and just teach out of a textbook and just have them learn things, they're going to get bored and they're not going to know why they're doing it. You have to give them a reason why they're learning and you have to give them some kind of information that they can use out of school . . . . School can't just be a place where you go and then that's the only place you use your knowledge. You should get some kind of knowledge that you can use elsewhere and I think that's what you have to try and do in teaching history.

Unlike the other students in the study, Mark took teacher education courses between the first and second interviews. He attributed his outlook on learning to a specific teacher education course:

> Before [Learning and School Subjects] I had last term I used to think more in terms of what I was going to do as a teacher instead of what they were going to do as students, and kind of a two-way thing I have to look at how I'm going to help them learn instead of just tell them I'm going to teach. (Mark, IV#2)

In sum, despite their belief that they had learned more in the historiography seminar than in any other history course, most students' views of teaching and learning changed little between the beginning of the seminar and 1 year later. Most believed learning is a reflex of teaching; most say they would lecture to students despite the fact that their own experiences of lectures are overwhelmingly negative. Several students also thought film documentaries and primary sources were appropriate for teaching about the civil rights movement. Two students offered different views of learning: one perhaps because of his own struggle to understand, and the other because of a course that focused his attention on students' experiences of learning.

DISCUSSION

Perhaps most striking about these data on the development of student thinking is that the influence of the seminar experience did not appear greater than it seems to have been. In interviews conducted a year after the seminar, students, unprompted, frequently referred to their experiences in the seminar and to the instructor. All but three identified the seminar as the best history course they had taken in either college or high school. Yet, the changes we believe we can apprehend in the data are subtle, changes in the texture of students' understanding rather than wholesale reorganizations of their understanding.

The subtlety of change over the course of a year suggests that, even under optimal conditions, the evolution of students' understanding of fundamental concepts may require time. Appreciating the constructed nature of historical accounts, the degree to which any view of the past is conditioned by the historical moment in which it is formed, the imperative to approach people and their actions in the past on their own terms rather than unreflectively imposing current moral standards, the contingent nature of past events such that small differences in circumstances could have produced quite different results — such understandings as these are considerably more complicated than recalling information. Appreciations such as these incorporate not only the ways we think about the past but also the ways we think about the present. They involve, for instance, the appreciation of the extent to which understandings of the present are directly intertwined with our pasts, with our prior experiences, and the understanding we have evolved of those experiences. Such appreciations challenge those who believe in absolutes and in a single objective truth, a Platonic "reality," or an ideal "history." Consequently, coming to understand these aspects of the nature of history may involve reconsidering not merely ideas about the past but habituated ways of thinking as well as culturally sanctioned beliefs. Such reconsiderations may require much more than 10 weeks or even the 2 years during which history majors typically take the bulk of their disciplinary courses.

Equally striking is the observation that changes in understanding of historical knowledge appear compartmentalized, cut off from students' beliefs about teaching and learning history. As noted, most students, in the interviews, attested to the power of the seminar experience, both directly and indirectly through the numerous references they made to the experience and their detailed recall of discussions and comments that Vinten-Johansen and others made. In spite of the apparently compelling nature of the seminar, students did not seem to reconsider their views of learning and teaching. They continued to believe that teaching consists principally in telling students about events in the past, explaining why events happened, and, occasionally, showing students film documentaries. Few reported considering using the history workshop or any other instructional design that paralleled their experiences in the historiography seminar.

Given that most participants found this a compelling experience, why did they not consider such an experience for high school students? One reason seems to be that the reference for most students was not their experience in the seminar but rather their experience in high school. As most experienced only lecture courses in high school, they had no vision of what it would be like to teach history differently at that level. One student reported that she would want her pupils to read "real" history books rather than textbooks, but that this would never be allowed. She and a few others seemed to believe that schooling as they had experienced it was immutable, beyond the control of human beings like certain natural phenomena. That teaching and learning in high school might occur differently appeared beyond their imaginations. Other students in the sample seemed to believe that secondary pupils would not be capable of anything beyond passively listening to lectures or watching video documentaries.

One proposal for improving teacher preparation is that, if teachers are to create opportunities that enable learners to develop connected, meaningful knowledge, teachers need to experience learning in similar ways. My findings suggest merely having such experiences may not be enough. Prospective teachers may need to examine the relationship between the opportunity to learn and the kinds of understandings of the subject matter the opportunity seems to enable. The student who had thought most about the pedagogical implications of his own understanding of history had taken a course that had focused his attention precisely on this issue.

This also raises questions about the assumption, common among some policymakers, that merely increasing prospective teachers' exposure to subject matter will produce greater knowledge for teaching the subject matter. Without an opportunity to consider what knowledge is most critical in a given field and the pedagogical implications of learning such knowledge, prospective teachers seem unlikely to figure this out on their own. If teachers, in order to teach their subject matter better, only needed more courses in their subject, would not university instructors be the best teachers? As the students in our study readily attested, this is not the case.

CONCLUSION

Current trends toward decreasing the number of teacher education courses or bypassing university teacher education altogether are posited on the assumption that more subject matter courses constitutes better preparation for teaching. Data on the historical knowledge and understandings of students in a historiography seminar raise questions about this trend. Although most of the students seemed to develop a greater understanding of the nature of historical knowledge and inquiry, and although they could recall considerable information about particular events in the past, their views of teaching and learning reflected the experiences they had as high school students. The apparent evolution of their understanding of the subject was not reflected in their understanding of teaching and learning. Most continued to view learning as a simple reflex of teaching (Cohen, 1988).

Moreover, despite direct challenges to students' accustomed ways of thinking about history, students were slow to change their beliefs. This may be due in part to the fundamental character of some of these beliefs. Reconsidering these beliefs involves rethinking basic assumptions that are fundamental to students' understanding of the nature of reality. The time required for such reconsiderations and for comprehending the implications of such reconsiderations is probably considerable. Attempts to measure such changes in the short run may well miss them.

The apparent lack of connections between students' understanding of history and their understanding of teaching and learning history suggests that the organization of teacher education makes little sense. Currently, prospective teachers consider subject matter issues in their arts and science courses and issues of teaching and learning in their professional courses. Limiting, bypassing, or eliminating access to professional courses does not address the problem. The data would suggest that prospective teachers need opportunities to consider the pedagogical and cognitive implications of the subject matter they are learning.

Some institutions have created such opportunities (for recent examples, see Project 30, 1991). Yet, these are rare and, frequently, short lived. Formidable institutional and cultural obstacles stand in the way of widespread development of such opportunities. Organized along feudal lines, with departments and colleges — not to mention individual faculty — enjoying and exercising considerable autonomy, most universities are inhospitable to courses that require cooperation between departments or colleges. In this age of tight budgets, arts and science departments are hard pressed to offer the range of courses they feel their undergraduates need. Pulling scarce faculty away to co-teach courses with teacher education faculty is simply not a priority for arts and science deans. This situation is compounded by the low status of teacher education departments and colleges on many campuses. Arts and science deans and faculty often feel teacher education courses are not intellectually rigorous. The rewards for arts and science faculty to cooperate with teacher education faculty are not immediately apparent.

The fiscal crisis facing higher education further undermines opportunities for learning about teaching history in the context of actually doing history. The push at most institutions is toward larger classes that limit faculty's pedagogical options. In short, the prospects are bleak for the kinds of experiences that the data suggest prospective history teachers may need.

ACKNOWLEDGMENTS

The author thanks Peter Vinten-Johansen and his students who all gave generously of their time and ideas. Lamar Fertig, Nancy Jennings, and Steve Smith helped collect the data on which this chapter is based and generously shared their ideas. Although their help has been instrumental, they are not responsible for any mistakes.

This work has been supported by the Spencer Foundation and the National Center for Research on Teacher Learning, College of Education, Michigan State University. NCRTL is partially funded by the Office of Educational Research & Improvement, U.S. Department of Education. The views and opinions expressed herein are those of the authors and do not necessarily reflect the position of the Spencer Foundation, the College of Education at MSU, nor OERI/ED.

REFERENCES

Arons, A. B. (1990). *A guide to introductory physics teaching*. New York: Wiley.
Ball, D. L. (1988). SummerMath for teachers program and educational leaders in mathematics

project. In NCRTE (Eds.), *Dialogues in teacher education* (Issue Paper 88-4, pp. 119-131). East Lansing, MI: Michigan State University, National Center for Research on Teacher Education.

Beck, I. L., McKeown, M. G., & Gromoll, E. W. (1989). Learning from social studies texts. *Cognition and Instruction, 6*(2), 99-158.

Booth, W. C. (1988). The vocation of a teacher: Rhetorical occasions, 1967-1988. Chicago: University of Chicago Press.

Branch, T. (1988). Parting the waters. New York: Simon & Schuster.

Carr, E. H. (1962). What is history? New York: Penguin.

Champagne, A. B., Gunstone, R. F., & Klopfer, L. E. (1985). Effecting changes in cognitive structures among physics students. In L. H. T. West & A. L. Pines (Eds.), Cognitive structure and conceptual change (pp. 163-187). New York: Academic Press.

Clement, J. (1982). Students' preconceptions in introductory mechanics. American Journal of Physics, 50, 66-71.

Clement, J., Lochhead, J., & Monk, G.S. (1981). Translation difficulties in learning mathematics. American Mathematical Monthly, 8, 286-290.

Cohen, D. K. (1988). *Teaching practice: Plus ça change . . .* (Issue paper No. 88-3). East Lansing, MI: Michigan State University, National Center for Research on Teacher Education.

Collingwood, R. G. (1956). *The idea of history*. London: Oxford University Press. (Original work published in 1946)

Croce, B. (1970). *History as the story of liberty*. Lanham, MD: University Press of America. (Original work published in 1941)

Donald, D. (1965). *The politics of reconstruction 1863-1867*. Baton Rouge: Louisiana State University Press.

DuBois, W. E. B. (1935). Black Reconstruction in America. New York: Harcourt, Brace.

Dunkin, M. J., & Barnes, J. (1986). Research on teaching in higher education. In M. C. Wittrock (Eds.), *Handbook of research on teaching* (3rd ed., pp. 754-777). New York: Macmillan.

Elbow, P. (1986). *Embracing contraries: Explorations in learning and teaching*. New York: Oxford University Press.

Fernandez-Armesto, F. (1989). *The Spanish Armada: The experience of war in 1588*. Oxford: Oxford University Press.

Foner, E. (1988). *Reconstruction: America's unfinished revolution*, 1863-1877. New York: Harper & Row.

Gagnon, P. (1988, November). Why study history? *Atlantic Monthly*, pp. 43-66.

Garrow, D. (1988). *Bearing the cross*. New York: Vintage.

Geyl, P. (1962). *Debates with historians*. London: Collins. (Original work published in 1955)

Handlin, O. (1979). *Truth in history*. Cambridge, MA: Harvard University Press.

Herman, W. L., Jr. (1983). What should be taught where. *Social Education, 47*, 94-100.

Herman, W. L., Jr. (1990). Development in scope and sequence: A survey of school districts. *Social Education, 52*, 385-388.

Holt, T. (1990). *Thinking historically*. New York: College Entrance Examination Board.

Kluger, R. (1975). *Simple justice*. New York: Random House.

Maestre, J. P., Gerace, W.J., & Lochhead, J. (1982). The interdependence of language and translational math skills among bilingual Hispanic engineering students. *Journal of Research in Science Teaching, 19*, 339-410.

Maestre, J. P., & Lochhead, J. (1983). The variable-reversal error among five culture groups. In J.C. Bergeron & N. Herscovics (Eds.), *Proceedings of the Fifth Annual Meeting* (pp. 180-189). Montreal: North American Chapter of the International Group for the Psychology of Mathematics Education.

Mattingly, G. (1959). *The Armada*. Boston: Houghton Mifflin.

McDermott, L. C. (1984, July). Research on conceptual understanding in mechanics. *Physics Today*, pp. 24–32.

McDiarmid, G. W., & Vinten-Johansen, P. (1993). *Teaching and learning history—from the inside out* (Special Rep.). East Lansing, MI: Michigan State University, National Center for Research on Teacher Learning.

McKeown, M. G., & Beck, I. L. (1990). The assessment and characterization of young learners' knowledge of a topic in history. *American Educational Research Journal, 27*, 688–736.

McKeown, M. G., Beck, I. L., Sinatra, G. M., & Loxterman, J. A. (1992). The contribution of prior knowledge and coherent text to comprehension. *Reading Research Quarterly, 27*(1), 78–93.

Novick, P. (1988). *That noble dream: The "objectivity question" and the American historical profession*. Cambridge, England: Cambridge University Press.

Pascarella, E. T., & Terenzini, P. (1991). *How college affects students*. San Francisco: Jossey-Bass.

Project 30. (1991). *Year two report: Institutional accomplishments*. Newark, DE: University of Delaware.

Ravitch, D., & Finn, C. E., Jr. (1987). *What do our 17-year-olds know? A report on the first national assessment of history and literature*. New York: Harper & Row.

Santayana, G. (1905). *The life of reason: Reason in common sense*. New York.

Schoenfeld, A. (1985). Metacognitive and epistemological issues in mathematical understanding. In E. A. Silver (Ed.), *Teaching and learning mathematical problem-solving: Multiple research perspectives* (pp. 361–379). Hillsdale, NJ: Lawrence Erlbaum Associates.

Smith, P. (1990). *Killing the spirit: Higher education in America*. New York: Viking Penguin.

Stampp, K. (1965). *The era of Reconstruction, 1865-1877*. New York: Vintage.

Stewart, D. (1989). What is an English major, and what should it be? *College Composition and Communication, 40*(2), 188–202.

Walsh, W.H. (1984). *An introduction to the philosophy of history*. Westport, CT: Greenwood Press. (Original work published in 1951)

Wineburg, S. S. (1991). Historical problem solving: A study of the cognitive processes used in the evaluation of documentary and pictorial evidence. *Journal of Educational Psychology, 83*(1), 73–87.

Woodward, C. V. (1986). *Thinking back*. Baton Rouge: Louisiana State University Press.

APPENDIX: FOUR VIEWS OF RECONSTRUCTION

[Note: These descriptions are adapted from those in Foner (1988, pp. xix-xxvi).]

Version #1

According to one version, the South, at the end of the War accepted defeat, wanted to find a solution to the problems created by emancipation, and, above all, desired to be reincorporated into the Union as quickly as possible. Andrew Johnson adopted Lincoln's policy of national reconciliation but was opposed by fanatic Radical Republicans in Congress. The

Radicals overrode Johnson to enact policy to punish the South and ensure Republican political dominance by disenfranchising ex-Confederates and bestowing the vote on newly freed blacks. Greedy and self-serving carpet-baggers from the North joined forces with corrupt scalawags—Unionists in the South—to dupe and manipulate ignorant blacks. These freedmen were unprepared to vote much less to hold the political offices to which some of them were elected. As a result, corruption and gross mismanagement of government were the order of the day. Only after Southerners managed to regain control of their region was honest government restored and genuine reconstruction begun. In short, Radical Reconstruction was an unmitigated disaster for the people of the South, both black and white.

Version #2

According to another version, Johnson was a stubborn racist whose sympathies lay wholly with poor Southern whites. The Radical Republicans, on the other hand, were idealistic reformers who were supported widely in Congress and in the North. Far from being a period of chaos and corruption, Radical Reconstruction saw a number of reforms intended to correct social, economic, and political injustice—such as equal citizenship for blacks and free public schools for all. Compared to the Tweed Ring, the Credit Mobilier scandal, and the Whiskey Rings in the North, corruption in the Republican administrations of Southern states was relatively limited. In this version, Radical Republicans and freedmen in the South tried to achieve moral and political justice, Johnson and the Democrats strove to maintain the economic and political dominance of whites, and Radical Reconstruction was not a disaster but a period of progress and hope for blacks.

Version #3

Yet another version holds that, given the depth and persistence of racism in the South, Radical Republicanism was actually quite conservative. A radicalism genuinely committed to justice for blacks would have entailed, at the least, redistribution of land. Rather than instruments of Radical Reconstruction, the army and the Freedmen's Bureau served the interests of the ruling class of white supremacists in ensuring blacks would remain economically subservient. By not redistributing land, as was done when the serfs in Russia were freed, the whites in power prevented blacks from developing an independent economic base—a requirement for genuine political equality. Rather than an abrupt change from the past, Reconstruction represents a continuation of politics as usual in the South.

Version #4

In the fourth version of Reconstruction, the experience of Southern blacks is situated at the center of the story. Rather than passive dupes and victims, blacks are portrayed as actively involved in pressuring the Lincoln administration, during the war, to make the Emancipation Proclamation and, subsequently, to pursue radical reconstruction. The political and economic agenda of Reconstruction represents their drive for economic and social independence and self-sufficiency as individuals and as communities. Emancipation and reconstruction represented an opportunity for blacks to organize, mobilize, and lead an attack on the racial caste system of the U.S. By challenging and changing their relationships with other groups in Southern society, blacks also forced a social realignment that produced new political alliances, a new class structure and new ways of organizing labor. The idea that the government could create policy with the express purpose of establishing equal rights for all citizen, rather than merely remaining passive and reactive in the face of racial injustice, originated with the changes wrought by blacks in alliance with whites during Reconstruction.

8 Constructing the Learning Task in History Instruction

Ola Halldén
Stockholm University

The following exchange of views between teacher and students took place during a history lesson in a Swedish Upper Secondary school (the Swedish *Gymnasium*). The teacher had asked the students which historical period came after the Renaissance and got the following replies:

S(tudent): The Baroque Period.
T(eacher): In the fine arts, yes.
S: The Age of Greatness.
T: Yes, but that was in Sweden.
S: The Age of Freedom.
T: That came a bit later.
S: The Age of Monarchic Absolutism.
T: Yes, or the Age of Autocracy. What's the period called that we're reading about now?
S: The Age of Freedom.
T: In Sweden, yes.
S: The Age of Enlightenment.
T: Yes.

It is tragi-comical that, in this particular case, the concepts that are supposed to help the students grasp the continuity of history become a problem in themselves. It is highly probable that this is not an exceptional case, but rather a general problem in learning history: The concepts that are used to describe the course of history are *inter alia* a part of history itself.

This state of affairs makes it difficult for the teacher to formulate the learning tasks in history and for the students to understand what it is they are supposed to learn. The aim of this chapter is to discuss these matters.

TEACHERS' ASSIGNMENTS AND LEARNERS' PROBLEMS

Learning, as opposed to cognitive development, can be described as an intentional process: There is *someone*, the learner, who is trying to learn *something*. The crucial thing about learning in educational settings, however, is that it cannot be assumed that this something is the same thing as the something that the teacher is trying to teach the students.

In the educational setting, the students are given tasks by the teacher. From the teacher's point of view, the intention behind the task is that the students are to do something, for example, to arrive at an explanation of the state of things or a description of a course of events, to memorize the meaning of a set of terms, and so on. From the students' point of view, however (and assuming that they accept becoming involved in the learning process), they must first arrive at an interpretation of what constitutes the task itself in order to understand what it is they are expected to do. Thus, the nature of the task that the teacher presents to the students as an assignment must first be interpreted by the students before they can begin to solve it. The interesting thing here is that there is a good deal of evidence to substantiate the view that the students' interpretations often differ from the nature of the task as envisioned by the teacher. Having accepted to participate in the learning process, students interpret the task as a problem that they are under obligation to solve or as a project that they are under obligation to involve themselves in. It was shown in a series of studies that the problems and projects of the students often differ in important respects from the nature of the assignments as intended by the teacher (Halldén, 1988).

Now, a crucial point in history teaching is that, in contrast to, for example, science teaching, the task refers to a state of things or a course of events that has to be established within the educational setting itself. There is no natural world or things in themselves to explain and no events that have to be accounted for before they are presented in the instruction. For the learner, there is no obvious experiential referent for the concepts treated in the instruction in the same sense as is often the case in science.

Even if the concepts in the natural sciences do not always have a direct referent in the experiential world, there is a closer relation between them than is the case with the concepts studied in history. Many of the concepts presented in science teaching do have a direct experiential referent, and they are expressed in everyday language (e.g., in physics, concepts such as heat and force). In cases in which the concepts have no direct experiential referent, there is often a range of phenomena in our experience that can be related to the concepts (e.g., in physics, concepts such as gravity and magnetic flow). In still other cases in science, the concepts are purely scientific constructs or models, and there are no corresponding labels in everyday language (e.g., the atom and the molecule). Even here, however, it is possible to infer the scientific phenomenon from the observational world (Caravita & Halldén, 1994).

Of course, this does not mean that students are always aware of what the concepts in science are actually referring to. Törnkvist, Pettersson, and Tranströmer (1993) showed how university students tend to lose their way when trying to solve problems concerning the force vectors and trajectories of particles in an electromagnetic field, and that this is probably due to difficulties in differentiating between "reality," models of reality, and different representations of the models. In another study (Halldén, 1990), students at the upper secondary level had great difficulty in understanding the relationship between the inheritance of traits like blue eyes and the genetic mechanism explaining the transmission of the trait. That is to say, they could not figure out the different denotations of the concepts describing the phenotype, in this case "blue eyes," and the concepts describing the genotype, that is, biochemical properties of the cell. But still, there is a denotation for the scientific concept, or the scientific model, that can be related to the observational world.

In history we deal with phenomena that are cultural artifacts, but in a way that differs from the kind of phenomena under study in the sciences. For the student, the historical event exists first and foremost in the historical narration of the event and it is the historical narration that brings the event to existence. This holds true even if we can point at historical buildings and other remains of the past. These first become historical when incorporated into a historical narration. One of the reasons for this can be found in the historian's interest in combining the actions of the individual with the effects of impersonal structures with the aim of describing changes in society, an endeavor that entails attributing cultural meanings to the events and situations that are being described. Furthermore, this is done *ex post facto*. Not until a chain of events has occurred do we decide what there is to be explained; history is lived forward and described backward, it has been said. These comments should not, of course, be taken as a philosophical standpoint on the existence or nonexistence of the past (see, e.g., the discussion in Atkinson, 1986). My intention here is to clarify what constitutes the basis for the students' confrontation with a historical event.

So, in teaching history, the event under study must be established within the confines of the discipline itself, without direct reference to the surrounding physical world, as it is often possible to do when teaching the natural sciences. In history instruction, the event to be studied is established through narration, especially through the classroom conversation; that is, the students are presented bits of information from which they are expected to draw conclusions as to what were the circumstances in the case in question and what was likely to occur next. (At least this is how history is taught in Sweden; Johansson, 1981; but see also Edwards, 1986, with references.) In such manner a *shared line of reasoning* is established between teacher and students that constitutes both the description and the explanation of the historical event in question. It is not shared in the sense that every single student actually adopts it, but rather in the sense that it is supported by those answers students give to the teacher's questions that fit in with the line of reasoning the teacher is trying to establish. In such a way the historical narrative becomes a joint construction by the students and the teacher. It is a shared line of reasoning also in the sense that it reflects the teacher's intention; it is how the teacher wants the students to reason. The historical narrative, so established, is then what actually constitutes the learning task.

In the following, the concept of a shared line of reasoning is explicated by drawing on some examples taken from observational studies carried out in the Swedish Upper Secondary school. I also discuss some of the educational implications. The observations were carried out continuously while students were working with specific periods in history, such as the French Revolution. The data were collected by means of audiotape and field notes, and the tapes were subsequently transcribed.

SHARED LINES OF REASONING

In one of the classes observed by my colleagues and I, the teacher gave considerable attention to the Consolidation of Farms Reform, which took place in Sweden during the 18th and 19th centuries. Toward the end of the 18th century and in the beginning of the 19th, the rulers of Sweden sought to reorganize agriculture throughout most of the country by means of what is called the Consolidation of Farms Reform. Prior to this reform, farmers lived in villages and their holdings were scattered across the surrounding countryside. In time, the process of inheritance had resulted in more and more complicated divisions of land and smaller and smaller strips for the individual farmer to till. As a result of the reform, according to the teacher's instruction, the land strips were consolidated into a single plot of land per farm and the farmers were moved out of the villages to live on the plots. In fact, the reform may not have been as successful as the teacher's narration would lead one to think, and some historians would even consider the teacher's version of history on this point to be quite incorrect. But the teacher had his own rationale for relating the story in this way. When interviewed, he emphasized that his intention was to get the students to "think as historians," and he took great pains to make the historical narrative intelligible. In this case, his intention was to describe how the feudal society in Sweden developed into a class society, that is, how a society in which the rights and duties of the community had been regulated by ancestry became a society in which they were determined by occupation and social role. One of the steps in arriving at this description was to show how new social groups developed. The following excerpts give an illustration of the classroom conversation.

The classroom conversation concerned the pros and cons of life in Sweden before the land holdings reform, particularly how agriculture was carried out in small villages:

T: What is needed in harvesting?

S: That everyone /in the village/ does it at the same time.

T: And that wasn't always so easy to do.

S: You can harvest your own fields by yourself, but it's more rational if . . . but you *can* do the harvesting on your own because they used a lie.

T: Sure, so why did they have to do the harvesting all together and at the same time? You were on to it yourself.

S: Yeah, well it's more rational, you know, if everyone . . .

T: Sure. So there's a lot to support what you said about it being easier if they all did the harvesting together. So, you see, the arguments support the view that it was irrational.

The students devoted a good deal of time to the question of how agricultural work was carried out in the villages before the strip holdings were consolidated, and they were very imaginative. They talked about how it was possible to lead the horse to the different allotments, to move the plow to the different strips, and so on. Questions of this kind were of only marginal importance to the teacher's line of reasoning. The teacher aimed at a description of how land consolidation brought about an increase in efficiency which, in turn, led to a labor surplus; thus, a new social group entered the historical scene — unemployed agricultural laborers and crafters.

It is doubtful, however, if the students realized that this was the central point. Later, when the class was discussing life in consolidated farming districts, a student raised the question of labor power, which, however, was a deviation from the main line of reasoning that the class was exploring at the time:

S: They needed manpower. If you were all alone, you could hire help.

T: Stop and think about it a minute. Before, they had a strip of land here and another strip of land there. And remember, we said that it took a long time to go from one plot of land to another. So, how had that changed?

S: Now you were all alone with your own piece of land.

T: What did that mean?

S: That you were your own boss.

T: Right, and so now, when it no longer took up a lot of your time to move your horse and tools around to the different strips of land, what could you spend the time on?

S: Doing more work.

T: Yes, so now you can draw the right conclusion yourself. If you can work more—did they need more or less people then?

S: Less.

T: Right, there you have it. What do you call it when production increases while using less labor power? What is that called in business administration?

S: Rationalization.

Here, the teacher prevented the student from straying too far from the main line of reasoning, which was to establish the fact that a new social group had emerged consisting of the unemployed. Having steered the student in the intended direction at this point in the discussion did not prevent the teacher from later reverting to the question of the increasing need for seasonal workers, but it was in a different context.

By means of classroom conversations, as in these excerpts, a narrative is constructed. It is formed by the teacher's questions and by the students' answers. The teacher's questions often have the form of an invitation to the students to interpret a set of facts or to speculate about what might happen next under a given set of circumstances. A schematic illustration of the shared line of reasoning, which was established in the instruction concerning the consolidation of land holdings reform in Sweden, is shown in Fig. 8.1.

FIG. 8.1.   The shared line of reasoning as intended by the teacher.

The diagram shows what facts were emphasized by the teacher in his causal explanation of the events that took place during the period under study. Naturally, the figure does not illustrate true causal relationships. The arrows indicate that some factor was said to lead up to or, more strongly in some cases, to cause a particular event or effect.

One reason commonly mentioned by teachers for using the method of instruction described previously is to get the students to take an active part in the instruction. In the lessons referred to earlier, it seems reasonable to conclude that the teacher did succeed in this endeavor. Out of 27 students in the class, 25 made some kind of contribution to the shared line of reasoning. In all, the students made 177 utterances, distributed as shown in Table 8.1.

The number of utterances were calculated as follows. Each time a student made a comment without being interrupted, it was counted as one utterance. If a student began to make an utterance, hesitated and fell silent, and then resumed speaking after being prompted by the teacher, it was counted as two utterances. The table does not include 19 utterances that could not be related to an identified student.

When the teacher asked what a particular set of facts mean, the students were expected to draw conclusions. Some of their conclusions were in accord with the teacher's line of reasoning, but many others were reasonable only if considered in light of a different context or narrative than the one the teacher was trying to establish at that particular moment. When the students hit upon the difference between individual and collective labor, this could have been a perfectly reasonable approach to interpreting the data, but then the discussion would have belonged to a quite different narrative.

Figure 8.2 details a condensed and schematic illustration of attempts made by the students to interpret a set of given facts, and of the interpretations accepted by the teacher as correct steps in an explanation of the decline of the feudal society in Sweden and the emergence of a class society.

The problem for the learner is to know what narrative is being constructed. It is a problem because any interpretation of a given set of facts depends on what the facts are leading up to. And, as I have argued here, the student will not know what the facts are leading up to until the narrative has been completed.

The problem being discussed here can also be illustrated, in a somewhat different way, in the following excerpt from a classroom conversation

TABLE 8.1
Number of Utterances Per Student

utterances	0	1–5	6–10	11–15	16–20	21–25
students	2	12	9	5	1	1

What is meant

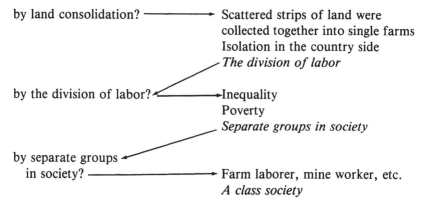

by land consolidation? ⎯⎯⎯⎯→ Scattered strips of land were
collected together into single farms
Isolation in the country side
The division of labor

by the division of labor? ⎯⎯⎯→Inequality
Poverty
Separate groups in society

by separate groups
    in society? ⎯⎯⎯⎯⎯⎯→ Farm laborer, mine worker, etc.
A class society

FIG. 8.2.   Suggestions from the students for interpreting a given set of facts and the interpretation accepted by the teacher as leading to the desired conclusion. (The interpretation accepted by the teacher in italics.)

about the French Revolution. The class was talking about the events of 1789 and the situation that gave rise to the revolution. The students were listing different factors that sparked the revolution, and the question of land distribution came up. The following is a marginally edited version of part of the classroom conversation:

S: Yeah, the priests owned a lot of land.
T: Yes, they did. And the rest of the land?
S: Yeah, and then there was the nobility.
T: OK, so what conclusion can you draw from what you're saying?
S: There was a lot of discontent, among . . .
T: Yes, so now we can go into what happens next. What do you think we should write down here?
S: Unequal distribution.

The teacher and students arrived at the fact that the Church owned three quarters of the land and the nobility owned the rest. Furthermore, they noted that more than 95% of the people of France were peasants. The teacher raised the question of how the peasants could make their livelihood:

S: They were sharecroppers and things like that.
T: Yes, they must have been. They must have tilled the land, don't you think?
S: Leased it.

T: Yes, leased it. This means that they leased land from the Church and from the nobility, and paid rent for it. So listen now, think about it! When did the situation look like this in Europe? During what period were most of the peasants tenant farmers to the manor lords and such? When did such conditions exist in Europe?

S: During the Middle Ages.

T: And that was called . . . ?

S: The feudal society.

The classroom conversation then proceeded to pick out other factors contributing to the revolution and to describe the chain of events leading up to it, particularly the summoning of Parliament, the storming of the Bastille, and the uprisings in the countryside.

Even in this case the shared line of reasoning can be diagrammed (Fig. 8.3). In the figure, the shared line of reasoning is illustrated by the arrows on the left side of the diagram; the arrow on the right side illustrates the argument of the student who wanted to go directly from the unequal distribution of land to the conclusion that there was "discontent" among the peasants.

The problem for the students was, as before, to know toward what conclusion the line of reasoning was headed. This time, however, their mistake was not about what historical event was to be explained, but about how detailed the teacher expected the explanation to be. The teacher wanted to establish the arguments that France was a feudal society, which in turn formed the basis for establishing that the peasants were "discontented," which in turn led to the uprisings in the countryside. Thus, for the students to know what was supposed to be explained required not only that they know about specific historical conditions, but also that they recognize

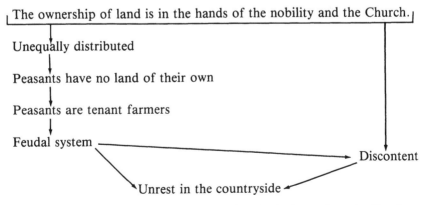

FIG. 8.3. Classroom conversation dealing with the background to the French Revolution.

which steps in the explanation require an explanation in themselves. Moreover, this latter requirement turned out to be a rather capricious one; here, it was the teacher who decided that the line of reasoning should take the route over a definition of "feudal society" (for a discussion of the arbitrariness of "causes" and "effects" in such situations, cf. Halldén, 1986; cf. also Voss, Carretero, Kennet, and Silfies, this volume).

So far I discussed the problem students encounter when trying to ascertain toward what end the teacher's questions are aiming. But the same kind of problem may arise when students study source material, as in the following example taken from the same history class.

The teacher had given the students a set of tables showing the Swedish export of bar iron during the 18th century and the countries of destination. His intention was to provide background information for the incipient process of industrialization in Sweden, as well as the growing integration of Sweden into the European economy. The table of exports showed that there were fluctuations in the amount of iron export seen in absolute numbers, with a general increase for the period as a whole. The table for the countries of destination showed the relative distribution for a number of countries, one of which was Great Britain. After establishing that the export volume fluctuated, the teacher asked questions about the export destinations. One girl stated that Great Britain was the main addressee, receiving just over 50% of the total exported volume. When asked by the teacher if there were any changes during the period, the student replied: "There was a decline." The teacher was satisfied with this answer, but several of the other students objected: "It's almost the same but when expressed as a percentage . . . " They argued that the export to Great Britain decreased in relation to the other countries but, because the total amount of exported iron increased, the export to Great Britain remained almost the same in absolute figures.

The students were quite correct in their objection, and we could stop here, noting only that the teacher had posed an impossibly imprecise question. But in one context the export to Great Britain had definitely declined, whereas in another it had remained the same. The Swedish export of iron can be discussed in several contexts. If, for example, one is talking about the international marketing potential for Swedish iron, it can be concluded that the British market had remained the same; there was no decline in the export to Great Britain. On the other hand, if one is talking about Sweden as being dependent on its exports to Great Britain, the extent of this export had definitely declined; at the end of the century a greater proportion of the total export was destined for other countries. Obviously, this was also the point the teacher was trying to make here. When commenting on the answer that export to Great Britain had declined, he said that "from now on, Sweden definitely was becoming a part of Europe." Again, which of the two interpretations of the figures one is to choose depends on which narrative one wants to tell. In this case, there is no reason to assume that the students had protested with an alternative narrative in mind; perhaps they objected only for the sake of it. Still, the example illustrates the equivocal meaning of "facts" presented to the uninformed person.

DISCUSSION

Through the use of two examples, I have tried to show how the classroom conversation, as it is commonly utilized in teaching history, establishes the learning task by building up a shared line of reasoning. As pointed out at the outset of this chapter, the line of reasoning is not shared in the sense that every single student adopts it. Rather, it is shared in the sense that it is the result of a joint exchange of views, and that it is the teacher's intention that every student will adopt this particular line of reasoning and no other. Teaching history in this manner entails some difficulties.

As shown here, the students are expected to make interpretations and draw conclusions from the sets of facts presented in the instruction. These facts can be presented orally by the teacher or they can consist of source material presented to the students. However, "the explanatory power of a statement of the form x caused y depends on the extent to which the specifications of x and y describe them under *causally relevant aspects*" (Searle, 1983, p. 117; emphasis in original). The problem for the learner, then, is to discover the meaning of the presented facts without knowing what they are leading up to. At the same time, the aim of the instruction is to get the students to arrive at this conclusion. In order to understand the explanatory value of a particular set of facts, the student has to hit on an interpretation of the facts in the context of what is to be explained.

At this point, it would seem reasonable to claim that the method of classroom conversation described here causes undue difficulties for students and therefore should be avoided. In some instances, this is probably true. There are, however, also some good reasons for utilizing this method of classroom conversation. One such reason, mentioned earlier, is that teachers see this method as a way to get the students to take an active part in what is taking place in the classroom. Furthermore, the problems do not pertain exclusively to this method of teaching. As shown here, similar problems may arise when students work with source material. The problem, then, is how to handle the concepts pertaining to history that have descriptive value as well as explanatory value. Such concepts have been called *colligatory concepts* (see, e.g., Thompson, 1967; Walsh, 1967).

Colligatory concepts, or colligating phrases, were characterized by Walsh (1967) as "complex states of affairs which are systematically changing as a result of human efforts or lack of effort" (p. 81). By the term *colligation*, Walsh intended the activity "by which the historian groups different events together '*under appropriate conceptions*'" (p. 72; emphasis added). Broadly speaking, to colligate is to organize, according to Walsh.

The problem for the learner, then, is that if a colligatory concept is lacking, there is no principle that can bring order to the disparate facts, and it seems reasonable to argue that without facts it is difficult to arrive at an understanding of a colligatory concept. In order to correctly interpret the many bits and pieces of information that surfaced during the teaching, such as those pertaining to the consolidation of land holdings in Sweden, the student has to already know that this occurred during a period that marked the decline of the feudal society and the emergence of the class society. On the other hand, understanding the meaning of the class society entails, at least in part, the recognition of the existence of separate groups in the society. Being able to arrive at a particular interpretation is both a precondition for learning and the aim of the instruction.

It would appear that we have backed ourselves into a logical paradox: in order to know A, you have to know B, but the prerequisite for knowing B is that you already know A. Related to the problem here, this means that in order to understand the historical facts and events (A), it is necessary to have some sort of colligatory concept (B) at hand. Now, one hopes that one can have at least a rough idea of the necessary colligatory concept or concepts before knowing all of A; or, one can have at least a nodding acquaintance with the speech genre appropriate to the narrative structure in question (cf. Wertsch & O'Connor, this volume; cf. also Halldén, 1994). Now, if this is the case, a reasonable conclusion would be that historical understanding is built through an oscillation between *explanans* and *explanandum*, that is, evidence and narrative structure are construed simultaneously and continuously, thereby forming a growing understanding of the historical event in question.

In spite of what was said previously regarding the differences between teaching history and teaching the natural sciences, there seems to be a similarity between understanding history and developing an understanding of a subject in science and mathematics. In the sciences the theoretical model plays almost the same role that the narrative structure plays in history. The scientific model determines which entities in a situation are to be counted as data in the model, and it gives the data their explanatory value (cf. Halldén, 1991). Wistedt (in press) showed how pupils in primary school, when presented real-world problems in mathematics, tended to take into account factors that were irrelevant to the idealized situation that was presupposed in the intended mathematical calculation. In a study by Solomon (1983) on students' understanding of energy and the transformations of energy, it was shown how the students' common-sense reasoning abounds with data and transformations compared with the more stringent physical explanation. Thus, we seem to be facing the same sort of paradox even here; in order to understand the facts constituting the explanation of an event, one has to understand the explanation that was supposed to be constituted by these same facts.

At the outset of this chapter, it was said that it is difficult for a teacher to formulate the learning task in history and for the students to understand what they are supposed to learn. The examples then discussed can be characterized as linear and piecemeal constructions of historical courses of events. It seems reasonable to claim that the difficulties encountered by the students in these examples are due to this linearity in the construction of the learning task. If the discussion here is correct, learning history is the construction of a learning task through the building up of a specific narrative out of evidence interpreted in the context of this narrative. A reasonable conclusion is that this cannot be done by means of a piecemeal, linear construction, but rather has to be done at different levels. The purpose of instruction, then, would be to highlight different interpretations of evidence as well as different types of narratives, but first and foremost, to retain and emphasize the characteristics of the specific narrative that is under construction and to continuously relate this narrative to the facts brought to the forefront.

REFERENCES

Atkinson, R. F. (1986). *Knowledge and explanation in history*. London: Macmillan.

Caravita, S., & Halldén, O. (1994). Re-framing the problem of conceptual change. *Learning and Instruction, 4*, 89-111.

Edwards, A. D. (1986). The 'language of history' and the communication of historical knowledge. In A. K. Dickinson & P. J. Lee (Eds.), *History teaching and historical understanding* (pp. 54-71). London: Heineman.

Halldén, O. (1986). Learning history. *Oxford Review of Education, 12*, 53-66.

Halldén, O. (1988). Alternative frameworks and the concept of task. Cognitive constraints in pupils' interpretations of teachers' assignments. *Scandinavian Journal of Educational Research, 32*, 123-140.

Halldén, O. (1990). Questions asked in common sense contexts and in scientific contexts. In P. L. Lijnse, P. Licht, W. de Vos, & A. J. Waarlo (Eds.), *Relating macroscopic phenomena to microscopic particles* (pp. 119-130). Utrecht: CD-B Press.

Halldén, O. (1991, August). *Conceptual change, conceptual rigidity or different domains of understanding*. Paper presented at the 4th Conference of the European Association for Research on Learning and Instruction, Turku.

Halldén, O. (1994). On the paradox of understanding history in an educational setting. In G.Leinhardt & I.Beck (Eds.), *Learning and teaching history* (pp. 27-46). Hillsdale, NJ: Lawrence Erlbaum Associates.

Johansson, M. (1981). Ämnesanalyser i historia och samhällskunskap för gymnasieutred-ningen [Subject analysis of history and social science undertaken for the survey of the

Swedish Upper Secondary School]. *Ämnesanalyser för gymnasieutredningen* [Subject analyses for the survey of the Swedish Upper Secondary School], *16*(4), 65-149.

Searle, J. (1983). *Intentionality*. Cambridge, England: Cambridge University Press.

Solomon, J. (1983). Learning about energy: How pupils think in two domains. *European Journal of Science Education, 5*, 49-59.

Thompson, D. (1967). Colligation and history teaching. In W. H. Burston & D. Thompson (Eds.), *Studies in the nature and teaching of history* (pp. 85-106). London: Routledge & Kegan Paul.

Törnkvist, S., Pettersson, K. A., & Tranströmer, G. (1993). Confusion by representation. On students' comprehension of the Electric Field Concept. *American Journal of Physics, 61*, 335-338.

Walsh, W. H. (1967). Colligatory concepts in history. In W. H. Burston & D. Thompson (Eds.), *Studies in the nature and teaching of history* (pp. 65-84). London: Routledge & Kegan Paul.

Wistedt, I. (in press). Everyday common sense and school mathematics. *European Journal of Psychology of Education*.

9 Controversial Issues in History Instruction

Carole L. Hahn
Emory University

My interest in the role of controversial issues in the teaching of history in particular and social studies in general grows out of my experiences as a student in social studies classes, as a teacher of junior and senior high school social studies, and as a professor of social studies instruction. I regularly begin my social studies instruction courses for university students who are preparing to teach either elementary or secondary school students by asking the adult students to recall their earlier experiences as pupils in elementary and secondary social studies classes. Their recollections tend to be very similar. With regard to their elementary school experiences, some have no memories at all of social studies instruction. Some recall memorizing states and capitals and have a vague sense of having read textbooks. On the other hand, with a sense of enjoyment, a few students remember projects and active learning. I myself remember constructing models of Native American villages and Spanish missions when studying early California history in the third grade.

Memories of high school social studies classes are of reading textbooks, listening to lectures about events in the past, and studying for tests. Not surprisingly, the students recall such classes with displeasure. The few students who want to teach social studies usually had one experience in which they were exposed to an alternative model: Either they had a teacher for one course who engaged them in controversial issues, or they had such an experience in extracurricular activities such as the Model United Nations, the debate club, or Close Up (a program that takes high school students to Washington, DC to see public policymaking "close up").

My own experiences of secondary school parallel those of my students. I recall in 10th-grade world history class copying from the chalkboard the outline of the teacher's lecture that followed the textbook's narrative of chronological history (mostly political and diplomatic). My interest in history and the social sciences would probably have died there had it not been followed by a positive experience in 11th-grade United States history class. The focus of instruction for that class was the exploration of complex issues primarily associated with civil liberties and landmark Supreme Court cases. To this day, I can see Mr. Curtin's handwriting on the chalkboard where he drew a continuum from liberty to security as he asked us where we would fall in resolving a particular issue. He encouraged us to express our views and to elaborate on our reasoning, citing evidence and supporting values.

Over the years since then, I have learned that my experience in Mr. Curtin's class was rare. Numerous reports have consistently documented that the dominant pattern of instruction in high school social studies classes in the United States is teacher lecture and student recitation of unproblematic "right answers" (Cuban, 1991; Goodlad, 1984; Mc Neil, 1986; Shaver, Davis, & Helburn, 1979). Studies also have documented that students do not like social studies (Shaver et al., 1979), and there are frequent laments that students do not recall what they have studied, particularly with regard to history (Ravitch & Finn, 1987). Yet, in the midst of this gloomy picture, we find examples of the exceptions, such as Mr. Curtin, who successfully engage students in history and other social studies classes by deliberately planning instruction around controversial issues with positive results. In this chapter I explore the reasons that I believe such an emphasis should be reflected in more history and other social studies instruction in schools. Before beginning that argument, however, some comments on the relationship between history and social studies instruction in the United States today may be helpful to readers who are not familiar with social studies instruction in that contemporary national context.

In the United States, history is considered one of several scholarly disciplines that contribute to the elementary and secondary school subject of social studies. The relative emphasis given to history within the social studies curriculum varies from one year to another in a student's career, from one locality to another across the country, and from one cohort of students to another because of the complex process of policymaking and the fact that professional social studies educators have long engaged in a debate about the position of history within social studies. Local school systems are responsible for the curriculum, yet often they must act within parameters set by state requirements such as those for high school graduation or in some states those requirements related to textbook adoption policies. That could lead to great variety in the nation's classrooms, but the power of tradition and the availability of a limited number of textbooks from commercial publishers result in a de facto national curriculum. For example, most students in the United States study local, state, and regional history as part of interdisciplinary studies of communities, states, and regions in grades 1 through 6. Further, most students study United States history in the 5th, 8th, and 11th grades, and world history in the 7th and 10th grades—with the remaining years devoted to economics, civics, geography, global studies, and a variety of electives (Morrisett, 1986). In the 1990s, some states modified this sequence to reflect an increased emphasis on history that grew out of a national debate over the place of history in the schools.

The debate about the relationship between history and social studies has periodically recurred ever since the 1916 report of the National Commission on the Social Studies was published. In recent years, such discussions have been particularly lively, as evidenced by the varying arguments put forth in the Bradley Commission on History in Schools report (1988), the California Framework for History and the Social Sciences, the five alternative models for social studies scope and sequence that were published in *Social Education*, the report of the Task Force on Curriculum of the National Commission on the Social Studies (1990), and the critiques of all of those models that appeared in *Social Education* and *Theory and Research in Social Education*. Downey and Levstik (1988, 1991) argued that recent debate, like those in earlier periods, unfortunately has not been informed by research on history teaching and learning. This chapter draws on the research on controversial issues teaching in history and other social studies classes. It also draws on insights gained by experienced teachers of history who like most of the secondary social studies teachers in the United States are members of social studies departments and thus responsible for a variety of courses in social studies—not only history.

CITIZENSHIP OUTCOMES

Regardless of the course title, grade level, or state or locality in which the instruction occurs, the justification given for the particular study of history usually rests on the assumption that an understanding of history is important preparation for citizenship in a democracy. Indeed, since the publication of the influential report of the Commission on the Social Studies in 1916, the primary rationale given for social studies in the United States has been citizenship education (Hertzberg, 1981). Because the essence of democracy is decision making "of the people by the people," the goal of citizenship preparation is the development of informed, reflective citizens who have the will to participate as well as the skills of analysis and decision making and values respecting human dignity and rationality. The notion that citizenship education in a democracy must be consistent with human dignity and rationality has been elaborated on by numerous social studies educators most notably, Engle and Ochoa (1988), Griffin (1942/1992), Hunt and Metcalf (1968), Newmann and Oliver (1970), and Oliver and Shaver (1966). The emphasis that those writers gave to the instructional processes appropriate to teaching for democratic goals, however, has not been appreciated by those who mandate curriculum.

Rather, state and local curricular requirements rest on the assumption that merely exposing students to more history and other social studies content will result in a more informed active citizenry. That narrow logic, however, has not been supported by empirical evidence. To the contrary, several studies found no correlation between numbers of social studies courses taken (many of which emphasize history) and students' orientation toward democratic participation (Langton & Jennings, 1968; Litt, 1963). It is likely that the predominate instructional patterns in those classes with little or no effect on participatory attitudes were lecture and recitation. The few studies that exist of what actually occurs in most social studies classes in the United States are consistent in finding there is a predominance of textbook assignments, followed by recitation, led by a teacher who likes students and tries to "pitch" the class at the students' level, while avoiding any controversial issues that might disrupt the routine (Goodlad, 1984; McNeil, 1986; Shaver et al., 1979; Stake & Easley, 1978; Weiss, 1978; Wiley, 1977). In the United States and in many other countries where the intent is to prepare youth for democratic citizenship, the dominant instructional practices in history and other social studies classes run counter to the ideals of participatory decision making and freedom of inquiry that are at the heart of democracy.

On the other hand, there is reason to believe that students' exploration of controversial issues might have a positive impact on citizenship outcomes. That is, when students are taught in an environment, or "classroom climate," that reflects the ideal of democratic discourse and open inquiry, they are more likely to develop attitudes that will incline them toward active citizenship. When students themselves engage in the process by which public issues are resolved in a democracy, they seem to develop the will to participate in civic life in ways that do not occur when they passively hear about the history of democratic ideals and institutions.

In a series of studies over the past 25 years, researchers have found positive correlations between students' civic attitudes and their reporting that they had discussed controversial issues in their social studies classes in open, supportive environments. Ehman's (1969) study of a randomly stratified sample of 10th- to 12th-grade students in a Detroit high school began the series of studies linking discussions of controversial issues in social studies classes and supportive classroom climates with civic attitudes.

Ehman found that students who reported higher degrees of controversial issues exposure, in which several sides of issues were discussed, and in which students felt free to express their opinions, exhibited lower levels of political cynicism, higher levels of citizen duty, increased participation, and increased levels of political efficacy (the belief that citizens can influence governmental decisions). Moreover, in classes in which controversial issues were presented but in a closed climate, in which only one side was presented and students were not encouraged to express diverse opinions, there were negative effects on political attitudes. The inclusion of controversial issues alone was not sufficient to produce positive attitudes. Rather, an open supportive climate for such discussions was the decisive factor.

In a longitudinal study of students from nine midwestern high schools, Ehman (1977) once again found a positive correlation between open-climate classrooms and student attitudes. After 3 years of social studies instruction, students who felt the most free to express their opinions during controversial issues discussions and who reported a wider range of views having been considered in their courses showed the most positive attitudinal changes. That was true in terms of both societal and school-level attitudes (increased levels of political interest, political confidence, and social integration—the reverse of alienation—and school-level trust in other students, trust in school adults, integration in school culture, school political confidence, and school political interest).

In a study of 9th-grade civics classes in three communities, Baughman (1975) found that students in open-climate classes—what he called "participatory classrooms"—reported higher levels of political efficacy and interest than did students in low-participatory (closed-climate) classrooms. They also exhibited higher levels of support for rights guaranteed by the Bill of Rights of the United States Constitution. Further support for this line of research came from Zevin's (1983) observational study of high school United States history classes in New York. Zevin found a positive relationship between feelings of political efficacy and higher levels of student-initiated discourse. Zevin concluded that internalizing a belief that citizens can successfully influence their political system is correlated with classroom discussions in social studies, particularly when students feel comfortable initiating the discussion.

The apparent benefits of students discussing controversial issues in open supportive classroom climates are not restricted to the United States. In Almond and Verba's (1963) cross-national study of democratic cultures, adults with the highest levels of political efficacy were those who remembered discussing and debating political and social issues in school. Similar results were obtained in a more recent study of nonrepresentative samples in Western democracies (Hahn & Tocci, 1990). Using a classroom climate scale that included items about frequency of controversial issues discussions and perceptions of the teacher's encouragement of student expression of opinions, positive correlations were obtained between an open-climate cllassroom and measures of adolescent political efficacy, political trust, political confidence, and political interest.

The major cross-national study to shed light on this theme is the International Association for the Evaluation of Educational Achievement's (IEA) research conducted in 1971 using carefully selected random samples in nine nations (Torney, Oppenheim, & Farnen, 1975). The IEA researchers concluded that students who said they had the opportunity to participate regularly in classroom discussions in which they were encouraged to express their opinions were more politically knowledgeable, more politically interested, and less authoritarian than students who did not recall such discussions.

Whereas most of the research linking controversial issues to citizenship outcomes has relied on surveys in which students agree or disagree with statements such as "in our classes we discuss controversial issues" or "teachers encourage us to express our opinions on issues," recent studies have used ethnographic techniques (Hahn, 1991; Harwood, 1991; Torney-Purta & Lansdale, 1986). Observations of classrooms and interviews with pupils and teachers reveal how open-and closed-climate classrooms differ and what effect those differences have on student perceptions. For example, in two contrasting classes, students described the more closed class as "boring" and noted, "you can't get a word in. The teacher is always talking." Observations in that class revealed that each time a student's question could have potentially opened up an issue, the teacher closed it with a statement bringing closure to a point and then moving on. In the more open climate classroom, students seemed to enjoy the class more and to see a connection between instruction and the wider world:

> She makes it fun because she keeps relating it to things now, and then she lets us get involved in everything. . . . We get in conversations . . . you get in groups together and communicate, like give your own opinions and she lets the whole class discuss their opinions out loud . . . she likes to get to everybody . . . it's my favorite class. I think it's fun because she relates it to things now . . . its one of my favorites because she lets us get involved and have our opinion . . . you've got to talk about it. (Hahn, 1991, p. 13)

A difficult challenge for history teachers is to motivate their students and to help them to see a relevance of the subject to their lives. By encouraging controversial issues discussions in an open environment, teachers may be able to meet that challenge as they help students to understand historical issues.

Because most chapters in this book focus on the teaching and learning of history, it should be noted that much of the research cited here was conducted in classes in which history was the content being taught (Hahn & Avery, 1985; Zevin, 1983) or in which students reported on their experiences across several years of social studies classes, which included some history instruction (Ehman, 1969, 1977). Because some chapters in this book deal with students' political and economic learning, it should be noted that similar results were obtained in economics (Landress, 1989), civics (Baughman, 1975; Hahn, 1991; Harwood, 1991), and international relations or global studies classes (Blankenship, 1990; Torney-Purta & Lansdale, 1986). This would suggest that if one goal of history—or other social studies—instruction in the schools is the preparation of citizens for participation in a democracy, then teachers need to be prepared to design and execute instruction that fosters the exploration of controversial issues in supportive classroom settings.

EXPERT VIEWS

Rationales for history instruction other than citizenship education reinforce the importance of teaching controversial issues. The views of expert historians and of expert secondary school history teachers complement one another around this theme, and they demonstrate that controversial issues are relevant to history in at least four distinct ways. First, controversies that existed among participants in history as their varying values and perspectives came into conflict can be explored, such as the controversies between Republicans and Royalists in both the English and French Civil Wars, or between the Unionists and Secessionists in the United States Civil War. Second, controversies that arise over interpretations of the past can be examined, such as when historians disagree over whether economic, political, or social factors are more powerful in explaining the causes and consequences of any war. The third application of controversial issues to history is by seeking insights into contemporary controversies, such as those in Northern Ireland, in the Middle East, and in South Africa by examining their roots in the past. The fourth application of controversial issues to history instruction is by making analogies between contemporary controversies and historic events, such that by examining similarities and differences students perceive the enduring nature of many issues that face human societies. From such historical study students are better able to understand the complexities in dilemmas of the present and future. These diverse uses of controversy can be seen in the ways both expert teachers and scholars work with their subject.

Historians

Expert historians are continually engaged in scholarly debates to resolve controversies in their field. The essence of their work is a constant process of resolving dilemmas by way of reinterpretation of data in light of new data or new ways of viewing the past. If one purpose for teaching history is to help young people to understand the discipline in ways that are compatible with expert historians' views of the field, then students must become comfortable with the ambiguities of scholarly controversies. Further, if we want students to develop skills of reflective judgment, then they must struggle with multiple interpretations of events and issues.

Unfortunately, many teachers in the United States did not themselves experience history as a process of interpretation, debate, and scholarly inquiry. Most elementary teachers have had no more than a year's college survey course in United States history or Western civilization. Even many secondary teachers have had no courses in historiography or seminars in which diverse interpretations were examined. Indeed, some university students with majors and minors in history have had no experiences examining primary source documents. Rather, most of their university experiences were spent conscientiously trying to acquire large amounts of information from professors' lectures that convey a unitary view of history. To overcome that socialization, Giesse (in press) recommended that teachers deliberately plan instruction with attention to three Ds:

> History is a discipline rife with *debate, disagreement,* and *discourse.* Even the facts of history are problematic and debatable, as are the interpretations and explanations historians offer. Furthermore, any given situation is interpreted by contemporaries in a multiplicity of ways because they saw a situation from varying perspectives, had different biases, and had various interests in the outcome. It is incumbent on history teachers to organize instruction so that this debate, this multiplicity of perspectives can be brought to bear on any topic of study. Perhaps most important, students must be led or allowed to participate in this discourse and debate. (p. 12; emphasis added)

History is not only a process of interpretation; it is also an account of the past, however tentative that account may be. Whether one's rationale for teaching history is to prepare citizens, to teach a scholarly discipline, to develop an appreciation for the cultural heritage, to foster an understanding of the roots of current global issues, or to develop empathy and critical thinking skills, the inclusion of past controversies is essential. Students need to understand that the lived experiences of people of the past were as filled with controversy as are the lives of people today. Debates raged in ancient Athens, in revolutionary France, and in colonial India that were as divisive of society in their day as is the debate in the United States over abortion rights today. Moreover, contemporary conflicts are often deeply rooted in the past.

Yet, in practice, school history tends to gloss over or avoid controversial material. My own observations of classrooms recently confirmed McNeil's (1986) finding that secondary teachers often take the controversy out of a topic by reducing the information to lists of causes or consequences to be memorized (Hahn, 1991). McNeil believes that instructional strategy is used to facilitate efficiency, to permit teachers to cover vast amounts of material in little time without having to slow down for explanation, much less student exploration. It may be further exacerbated by teachers feeling inadequately prepared to go beyond the simple explanations given in many textbooks. In a chapter on the history of social studies teaching, Cuban (1991) asserted that the reason we have so many studies documenting that teachers do not teach as professors recommend is because we have given insufficient attention to understanding why they teach as they do.

Teachers

The recent research on the "wisdom of practice" of "expert history teachers" offers a first step in that understanding (Mason, 1990; Wilson & Wineburg, 1988). Distinguishing features of expert history teachers are their deep understanding of the field and their wisdom about how to transform historical knowledge in meaningful ways for students. I believe that closely associated with those two dimensions is an appreciation for the role of controversy in history and an ability to present controversial topics to students in ways that are meaningful to them and that encourage them to weigh evidence and value claims, to make judgments, and to feel comfortable expressing their own views in class. To explore that notion I invited four teachers who have reputations in their school systems for being expert history teachers to a group "conversation" around questions dealing with the role of controversy in teaching secondary school history.

The four teachers – Nancy Harper, Mary Mason, Carol McCullough, and Louisa Moffitt – are all quite experienced, each having taught between 15 and 25 years. Three of the teachers had undergraduate majors in history (the fourth majored in sociology, but has had numerous graduate as well as undergraduate courses in history), and all have completed graduate programs in social studies education, during which they conducted original research. The four teachers regularly participate in state social studies conferences, and they are the school advisers for programs such as the Model United Nations. Their expertise is recognized in the local area, as evidenced by the facts that two were called on to present staff development programs on teaching about the Middle East and Latin America (history, geography, and contemporary issues), two recently taught social studies methods courses for universities nearby, and all four were selected by universities and their school systems to be mentor teachers for beginning teachers. These particular expert teachers are not "typical" of the secondary social studies teaching force in the United States in terms of gender. Most descriptive studies of social studies teachers conclude that about 70% of the secondary social studies teachers are male (Cuban, 1991; Hahn, 1978; Leming, 1991).

Interestingly, none of the four teachers thought that she consciously set about to teach controversial issues, but each was intuitively aware that she used student interest in current controversies to stimulate their interest in studying the past. Harper said that because her students were interested in the debates that arose about the celebration of the quincentennial of Columbus' voyage to the "new" world, she was able to interest them in the unit on the Age of Exploration more than she had been able to do with students in the past. She also used the interest generated by the contemporary controversy to demonstrate early in her course how historical interpretation changes as a result of controversies over evidence and points of view. Several of the other teachers also had given students statements from differing positions on the meaning of Columbus' voyage to examine and discuss.

The teachers all used student interest in particular current events to draw parallels to historical analogies. For example, some of Harper's United States history students were troubled by warring parties in Yugoslavia and Ethiopia using food as a weapon. She reminded her students that was similar to the blockade of Vicksburg in the American Civil War, and she asked them to consider whether they thought the use of starvation was ever justifiable and, if so, under what conditions. McCullough related the use of "ethnic cleansing" policies in what had previously been Yugoslavia to analogies from world history, raising questions about the differences as well as similarities between the historic and contemporary examples.

McCullough used enduring debates over the role of women, of religion, and of the military to provide a framework for students to raise questions, to organize information, and to recall it. She thus used her students' interest in contemporary issues as the basis for helping them form a meaningful schema for organizing their accumulating historical knowledge. All four of the teachers noted that in their world history courses, they capitalized on students' interest by drawing attention to the differing roles of women in ancient Egypt, Etrusca, and Greece. When teaching the French Revolution, McCullough had her students consider the differing positions of the monarchists and the radical republicans with regard to women's suffrage. Similarly, in a United States history course, Moffitt gave her students excerpts from speeches and other documents from the 1840s in which Americans debated about the rights and roles of women; she anticipated that in the year ahead she would draw attention to the contemporary analogy in Kuwait where women's suffrage is a controversial issue.

A second intuitive theme that ran through these four history teachers' practice was a sensitivity to how particular issues could make some students uncomfortable or defensive if the discussion was not handled carefully. Mason was acutely aware that the community in which she teaches has members of the Ku Klux Klan, fundamentalist Christians, and liberal whites and blacks. She does not avoid locally controversial topics, but she is careful in how she presents them. For example, when talking about Cro-Magnon and other early humans, she was careful not to offend her fundamentalist students; she acknowledged there were differing views on creation, and she sensitively chose the words she used. Mason carefully used an ancient Chinese statement describing civilized societies as those who had abolished capital punishment, realizing that her students supported capital punishment. Harper's school population contained many new immigrants from Latin America, Asia, and Africa, and she was aware that some topics could be delicate ones for them. Like Mason, she did not avoid topics, but she was careful as she approached topics such as immigration policies and human rights issues. Both of those two teachers thought that their students would be interested in the contemporary debates over an Afrocentric curriculum, but they felt that they needed to understand the differing positions better themselves before introducing the topic in class. The tendency of exemplary teachers like these to plan instruction to fit the interests and perspectives of their students was found also by Merryfield (1992) in her study of effective global teachers.

All four of the history teachers said that they felt an obligation to get students to try to understand views with which they did not agree, frequently using questions to stimulate alternative reasoning. McCullough and Moffitt taught in schools — one public and one private with a religious affiliation — with fairly homogeneous white middle-class populations. Consequently, they felt that they often needed to bring out views in class that would not have been expressed by students. McCullough emphasized that the use of questions was "a critical part of teaching controversy" because it "helped students to connect ideas" as well as to see diverse perspectives. The goals of all four teachers were to get students to listen to and understand diverse views, to make personal judgments, and to feel comfortable expressing them. This was to be done without the teachers influencing the students by stating their own opinions on contentious issues. That is, they would deliberately try to get students to see why people might take different views on many issues, moving back and forth between contemporary and historic analogies. These teachers would not state their own views on highly charged emotional issues, nor would they press their students to give their opinions on issues such as abortion, religion, or political candidates if they were not comfortable doing so. The complementary rights to expression and to privacy of both the teacher and the students were respected in classroom practices.

Creating a climate for open discourse is a major instructional consideration for these teachers of history. Each deliberately attends to it on the first day of a new class, and each gives ongoing attention to foster it on a daily basis in her class. Mason begins each term by explaining that the main rule in her class is respect — respect for oneself, for others, and for differing opinions. McCullough explains that the class will talk about some sensitive topics, and she does not want anyone to feel uncomfortable or to get his or her feelings hurt. All of the teachers intervene when they feel it is necessary to ensure a fair hearing for diverse opinions, to dispel intolerance, and to promote civility and openness. They also say that initially students would rather be told a "right answer" than to have to confront opposing viewpoints; they emphasize that it takes persistence, patience, and hard work on the teacher's part to press the students to reflect on reasons for alternative positions, possible consequences, and implications for value commitments. The teachers speak with pride in students when they challenge one another's ideas with rational arguments and mutual respect. They also recognize that personality conflicts and negative social interactions can become barriers to the open exchange of ideas and thus to students' learning of history. Consequently, for these teachers, effective history instruction requires that they be sensitive to interpersonal relations, as well as be able to relate topics to students' interests, to recognize the potential for issue analysis in a unit of content, and to be able to locate primary source materials that present differing positions from a particular time period and secondary sources that present differing historical interpretations.

These four "expert" teachers acknowledged that it took years for them to develop confidence in their ability to manage conflict positively in the classroom. It also took years for them to build a reservoir of materials that they could use to stimulate reflection about controversies. Because most school history textbooks used in the United States gloss over both historic and contemporary controversies and contain few primary sources, teachers use supplementary materials. These four teachers are alert to pro/con arguments or opposing viewpoints that appear on the opinion pages of the newspapers. They use selections from books such as *Taking Sides: Clashing Views on Controversial Issues in American History* (Madaras & SoRelle, 1989). Collections of primary sources such as *SIRS: National Archives Supplementary Teaching Units* (Boca Raton, FL: Social Issues Resources Series, 1985) and *Teaching with Documents: Using Primary Sources from the National Archives* (Washington, DC: National Archives and Records Administration and National Council for the Social Studies, 1989) are available, but their existence is not widely known. Some of the "new social studies" projects of the 1960s, such as *From Subject to Citizen* (Education Development Center, 1970) contained primary source documents that challenged students to examine conflicting evidence, multiple perspectives, and differing interpretations. Two sets of curricular materials written for high school students that focus on controversies in United States history are the reissued Harvard Public Issues series (Social Science Education Consortium, 1988–1992) and *Reasoning with Values* (Lockwood & Harris, 1985). It takes a persistent and committed teacher to find enough materials to make controversial issues investigation a major emphasis of a course. The four teachers speculated that only about one-third of the teachers in their social studies departments encouraged the investigation of controversial issues because as Louisa Moffitt said, "it's hard work, risky, and it takes time."

The four teachers thought that controversial issues teaching was not more prevalent because some teachers in their departments were teaching history without sufficient content knowledge (one art teacher was teaching world history, one American literature teacher was teaching United States history, and a physical education teacher and a band director were also teaching history classes in the teachers' schools at the time of our conversation). Additionally, some history teachers were coaches whose primary time, energy, and personal commitments were elsewhere, and others were uncomfortable with open-ended discussions in which there was not a clear right answer. Further, the four teachers observed that "for some reason the more politically liberal teachers seem to be the ones" who are more likely to encourage the investigation of issues. Interestingly, the impression these teachers have that political ideology is correlated with issues teaching is reinforced by some recent research. In a study comparing the political attitudes and orientations of social studies methods professors, teachers who belonged to the National Council for the Social Studies, and a representative sample of secondary social studies teachers, Leming (1992) found that the professors were considerably more politically liberal than were the teachers. He hypothesized that the discrepancy in values might be related to the fact that methods professors often exhort teachers to engage their students in issues investigation, but in the nation's social studies classes one finds little of such investigation. Additionally, Evans's (1990) interviews of history teachers revealed that ideology is related to how teachers view their subject, but we do not yet have either survey or observational studies that confirm a connection between issues teaching and teachers' political orientations. It is a matter that warrants further study.

Finally, a major constraint identified by the four teachers I interviewed was the pressure to cover vast amounts of material in a limited amount of time. Although they teach in different school systems, all said there were expectations that courses would cover particular time periods, and they worried that if they spent too much time on some topics they would never get "past World War II." The pressures for coverage were identified by both McNeil (1986) and Onosko (1991) as primary barriers preventing social studies teachers from teaching for understanding or what Newmann (1991) called "thoughtfulness." These latter points are noteworthy if we take Cuban's (1991) advice to heart and try to learn more about why teachers teach as they do, rather than continually berating them for not teaching as professors say they should teach.

THE FUTURE

Practice

Several of the barriers to controversial issues teaching practice are unique to a particular national context; others transcend national boundaries. I am cautiously optimistic that there are a number of signs on the horizon that could improve the environment for controversial issues teaching in the United States. For example, one of the principles that schools must support in joining Sizer's reform network is that "less is more." Giving more time to fewer topics, that is, teaching for depth rather than coverage, is essential not only for teaching critical thinking, but also for enabling students to adequately examine the dilemmas that faced people of the past, that challenge historians over time, and that make issues today controversial. Indeed, acceptance of that principle is far more important than simply extending United States and world history courses from 1 to 2 years each as some schools are beginning to do. Practice will change only when school policymakers convey that critical thinking, thoughtfulness, and respect for diverse opinions is valued more than the simple recall of facts.

A barrier to teaching issues exploration in the United States has been the widespread use of multiple-choice tests to measure student learning at the classroom, school, state, and national levels. Recent efforts toward the greater use of alternative, authentic, or performance-based assessment may help to reduce that obstacle. So far we have few models for the wide-scale evaluation of students' understanding of differing views on historic issues. The document analysis section of the Advanced Placement examination in the United States and similar sections from the General Certificate in Seconday Education (GCSE) and Advanced or "A-level" history exams in the United Kingdom might serve as starting points.

Unique perhaps also to the United States has been the dominance of the encyclopedic-type history book that presents a noncontroversial narrative history. At present, it is up to the individual teacher to supplement the textbook. This is particularly problematic when many teachers lack the knowledge to recognize the controversial nature of many historical topics, are unable to obtain appropriate supplementary materials, and are not skilled in teaching with primary sources. The practice of hiring unqualified individuals to teach history may also be a problem that is unique to some school systems in the United States. As long as this practice exists, initial teacher training in universities and staff development courses for experienced teachers will need to address it directly by giving teachers experience in exploring and discussing controversial issues in history and seeing models of teachers (on videotapes, in class observations) teaching in such a manner.

Research

More cross-national research is needed on the extent to which controversial issues are examined in history and other social studies classes. There is some indication that teachers in the western part of Germany and those in the United Kingdom may be more likely to present history as a process of interpretation than do teachers in the United States, but there is no evidence that they are any more likely to encourage students to debate, discuss, and resolve contentious dilemmas. Indeed, writers in the United Kingdom and Germany, like many in the United States, deplore the emphasis on lecture and recitation (Downey & Levstik, 1991; Wilson, 1989). In the United States, case studies of elementary history teaching have shown that some teachers effectively use narratives (Levstik, 1986) and a variety of other techniques (Brophy, 1992) to make history come alive for their students, but attention has not focused on how such teachers do or do not deal with controversy. Observational studies need to be complemented with interviews that focus on teachers' and students' perceptions of facilitating and inhibiting forces to instruction with an issues emphasis.

A number of lines of research being pursued by North American scholars complement themes in this chapter and hold potential for further understanding of the role of controversial issues in history instruction. Those studies that linked controversial issues to civic attitudes emphasized the importance of students saying that in their classes they discussed issues in an atmosphere in which they felt comfortable expressing their opinions. In teaching controversial issues, teachers might use simulations, case studies, mock trials, or writing assignments, but any of those techniques must be used with classroom discussion to have the effects that have been noted. From Dewey (Robertson, 1992) to contemporary scholars such as Barber (1989), "public talk" or discourse that explores diverse ideas in a community has been considered to be at the heart of the democratic ideal. From Vygotsky to Bruner and Resnick, cognitive psychologists have noted that individual meaning making occurs within the context of a community of learners, and recently, Seixas (1992) suggested that we pay particular attention to the classroom communities in which students learn history. There is some research to support Dewey's idea that by experiencing the process of building a democratic community in their classroom, students of history might achieve affective goals of social studies (Angell, 1991; Scott, 1991).

Cooperatively resolving conflicts—as when controversial issues are discussed in small groups—were found by Johnson and Johnson (1979) to yield both cognitive and affective benefits. Furthermore, because controversial issues discussions require students to resolve ethical dilemmas, they may work like "moral dilemma" discussions to facilitate moral reasoning. Indeed, some of the research that was conducted on the curricular implications of Kohlberg's research used adaptations of Fenton's new social studies materials in history classes. The work of researchers such as Gilligan (1982) and Noddings (1984), who explored an ethic of caring, is also applicable to adolescents' discussing and resolving dilemmas in their history classes.

Following the model of Newmann's (1991) research on thoughtfulness in social studies instruction, studies are needed of classrooms in which controversial issues are regularly explored in history classes. Such research could help identify conditions in schools, classrooms, and individuals that support such instruction. Leming (1991) called for research to answer the question: Are there certain characteristics, such as tolerance for ambiguity, open mindedness, intellectual flexibility, risk taking, and a provisional view of truth possessed by some teachers that permit them to comfortably incorporate controversial issues and democratic climates into their teaching? Finally, we need to know much more about the effects of controversial issues instruction on student learning.

CONCLUSIONS

There is a long tradition in social studies education in the United States that says that citizenship education for democratic participation ought to reflect the values of democratic dialogue. It follows that in their classrooms, students ought to experience an atmosphere in which no topics are taboo and in which all are open to reflective, rational inquiry (Griffin, 1942/1992; Hunt & Metcalf, 1968; National Council for the Social Studies, 1977). There is also empirical research indicating that when students do have regular opportunities to investigate controversial issues in their history and other social studies classes, they are more likely to develop attitudes supportive of their later civic participation. Yet, in most history classrooms in the United States, there is little discourse of this nature (McNeil, 1986; Shaver et al., 1979). To teach controversial issues in an open classroom climate, teachers must be able to sensitively lead discussions. They must have sufficient knowledge and adequate teaching materials, and they must be able to wisely select topics that join student interest with important issues in an intellectually defensible manner. Clearly, research on learning history must ultimately be complemented by changes in school policies that determine who teaches, with what resources, and in what conditions.

ACKNOWLEDGMENTS

I thank Patricia Avery, Margot Finn, Nancy Harper, Mary Mason, Carol McCullough, and Louisa Moffitt for their suggestions upon reading earlier drafts of this chapter, and special thanks to the four history teachers for sharing their insights on the teaching of controversial issues.

REFERENCES

Almond, G., & Verba, S. (1963). *The civic culture*. Princeton, NJ: Princeton University Press.

Angell, A. (1991). Democratic climates in elementary classrooms: A review of theory and research. *Theory and Research in Social Education, 19*, 241–266.

Barber, B. R. (1989). Public talk and civic action: Education for participation in a strong democracy. *Social Education, 53*, 355–356.

Baughman, J. E. (1975). *An investigation of the impact of civics on political attitudes of adolescents*. Unpublished doctoral dissertation, University of Maryland, College Park, MD.

Blankenship, G. (1990). Classroom climate, global knowledge, global attitudes, political attitudes. *Theory and Research in Social Education, 28*, 363–386.

Bradley Commission on History in Schools. (1988). *Building a history curriculum*. Washington, DC: Education Excellence Network.

Brophy, J. (1992). Fifth grade U.S. history: How one teacher arranged to focus on key ideas in depth. *Theory and Research in Social Education, 20*, 141–155.

Cuban, L. (1991). History of teaching in social studies. In J. Shaver (Ed.), *Handbook of research on social studies teaching and learning* (pp. 197–209). New York: Macmillan.

Downey, M., & Levstik, L. (1988). Teaching and learning history: The research base. *Social Education, 52*, 336–342.

Downey, M., & Levstik, L. (1991). Teaching and learning history. In J. Shaver (Ed.), *Handbook of research on social studies teaching and learning* (pp. 400–410). New York: Macmillan.

Education Development Center. (1970). *From subject to citizen*. Chicago: Denoyer-Geppert.

Ehman, L. H. (1969). An analysis of the relationships of selected educational variables with the political socialization of high school students. *American Educational Research Journal, 6*, 559–580.

Ehman, L. H. (1977, April). *Social studies instructional factors causing change in high school students' socio-political attitudes over a two-year period*. Paper presented at the annual meeting of the American Educational Research Association, New York.

Engle, S. H., & Ochoa, A. S. (1988). *Education for democratic citizenship: Decision-making in the social studies*. New York: Teachers College Press.

Evans, R. W. (1990). Teacher conceptions of history revisited: Ideology, curriculum, and student belief. *Theory and Research in Social Education, 18*(2), 101–138.

Giesse, J. R. (in press). Studying and teaching history. In *Teaching the social sciences and history in secondary schools: A methods book*. Belmont, CA: Wadsworth Publishing.

Gilligan, C. (1982). *In a different voice: Psychological theory and women's development*. Cambridge, MA: Harvard University Press.

Goodlad, J. I. (1984). *A place called school: Prospects for the future*. New York: McGraw-Hill.

Griffin, A. F. (1992). *A philosophic approach to the subject matter preparation of teachers of history*. Unpublished doctoral dissertation, Ohio State University, Columbus, OH. (Reprinted by the National Council for the Social Studies, Washington, DC.) (Original work published in 1942)

Hahn, C. L. (1978). Review of research on sex roles: Implications for social studies research. *Theory and Research in Social Education, 6,* 73–99.

Hahn, C. L. (1991, November). *Social studies classroom climate, the media, and adolescent political attitudes: A case of the complementary roles of qualitative and quantitative methodologies in political socialization research.* Paper presented to the National Council for the Social Studies, Washington, DC.

Hahn, C. L., & Avery, P. G. (1985). Effect of value analysis discussions on students' political attitudes and reading comprehension. *Theory and Research in Social Education, 13,* 47–60.

Hahn, C. L., & Tocci, C. (1990). Classroom climate and controversial issues discussions: A five nation study. *Theory and Research in Social Education, 18,* 344–362.

Harwood, A. M. (1991, April). *The difference between "democracy sucks" and "I may become a politician."* Paper presented at the meeting of the American Educational Research Association, Boston. (ED 320 846).

Hertzberg, H. W. (1981). *Social studies reform: 1880–1980.* Boulder, CO: Social Science Education Consortium.

Hunt, M. P., & Metcalf, L. E. (1968). *Teaching high school social studies: Problems in reflective thinking and social understanding* (2nd ed.). New York: Harper & Brothers.

Johnson, D. W., & Johnson, R. T. (1979). Conflict in the classroom: Controversy and learning. *Review of Educational Research, 49,* 51–70.

Landress, C. (1989). *The effect of value analysis discussions of controversial issues on secondary students' attitudes toward economics.* Unpublished Diploma in Advanced Studies in Teaching thesis, Emory University, Atlanta, GA.

Langton, K. P., & Jennings, M. K. (1968). Political socialization and the high school civics curriculum in the United States. *American Political Science Review, 62,* 852–869.

Leming, J. S. (1991). Teacher characteristics and social studies education. In J. Shaver (Ed.), *Handbook of research on social studies teaching and learning* (pp. 222–236). New York: Macmillan.

Leming, J. S. (1992). Ideological perspectives within the social studies profession: An empirical examination of the two cultures thesis. *Theory and Research in Social Education, 20*(3), 293–312.

Levstik, L. S. (1986). The relationship between historical response and narrative in a sixth-grade classroom. *Theory and Research in Social Education, 14,* 1–19.

Litt, E. (1963). Civic education, community norms, and political indoctrination. *American Sociological Review, 28,* 69–75.

Lockwood, A. L., & Harris, D. E. (1985). *Reasoning with democratic values: Ethical problems in United States history.* New York: Teachers College Press.

Madaras, L., & SoRelle, J.M. (Eds.). (1989). *Taking sides: Clashing views on controversial issues in American history* (Vols. I & II). Guilford, CT: The Dushkin Publishing Group.

Mason, M. (1990). *Pedagogical content knowledge: Case studies of expert world history teachers.* Unpublished Diploma in Advanced Studies in Teaching thesis, Emory University, Atlanta, GA.

McNeil, L. M. (1986). *Contradictions of control: School structure and school knowledge.* New York: Routledge and Kegan Paul.

Merryfield, M. M. (1992, June). *Shaping the curriculum in global education: The influence of student characteristics on teacher decision-making.* Paper presented at the Social Science Education Consortium Meeting, Puerto Rico.

Morrisett, I. (1986). Status of social studies: The mid-1980s. *Social Education, 50,* 303–310.

National Archives and Records Administration. (1989). *Teaching with documents: Using primary sources from the national archives.* Washington, DC: Author.

National Council for the Social Studies. (1977). The treatment of controversial issues in the schools. In B. Cox (Ed.), *The censorship game and how to play it* (pp. 26–30). Washington, DC: The National Council for the Social Studies.

National Council for the Social Studies. (1989). *Teaching with documents: Using primary sources from the national archives.* Washington, DC: National Council for the Social Studies.

Newmann, F. M., & Oliver, D. W. (1970). *Clarifying public controversy: An approach to teaching social studies.* Boston: Little, Brown and Company.

Newmann, F. M. (1991). Promoting higher order thinking in social studies. *Theory and Research in Social Education, 19,* 324–340.

Noddings, N. (1984). *Caring.* Berkeley: University of California Press.

Oliver, D. W., & Shaver, J. P. (1966). *Teaching public issues in the high school.* Boston: Houghton Mifflin Company.

Onosko, J. J. (1991). Barriers to the promotion of higher order thinking. *Theory and Research in Social Education, 19,* 341–366.

Public issues series. (1988–92). Boulder, CO: Social Science Education Consortium.

Ravitch, D., & Finn, C. E. (1987). *What do our 17-year-olds know? A report on the first national assessment of history and literature.* New York: Harper and Row.

Robertson, E. (1992). Is Dewey's educational vision still viable? *Review of Research in Education, 18,* 335–381.

Scott, K. P. (1991). Achieving social studies affective aims: Values, empathy, and moral development. In J. Shaver (Ed.), *Handbook of research on social studies learning and instruction* (pp. 357–369). New York: Macmillan.

Seixas, P. (1992, April). *The community of inquiry as a basis for knowledge and learning: The case of history.* Paper presented at the American Educational Research Association, San Francisco.

Shaver, J. P., Davis, O. L., Jr., & Helburn, S. W. (1979). The status of social studies education: Impressions from three NSF studies. *Social Education, 43,* 150–153.

Social Issues Resources Series. (1985). *National Archives Supplementary Teaching Units.* Boca Raton, FL: Author.

Social Science Education Consortium. (1988). *Public issues series.* Boulder, CO: Author.

Stake, R. E., & Easley, J. A., Jr. (1978). *Case studies in science education.* Urbana, IL: University of Illinois, Center for Instructional Research and Curriculum Evaluation.

Task Force on Curriculum of the National Commission on the Social Studies. (1990). *Charting a course.* Washington, DC: National Council for the Social Studies.

Torney, J. V., Oppenheim, A. N., & Farnen, R. F. (1975). *Civic education in ten countries: An empirical study.* New York: Wiley.

Torney-Purta, J., & Lansdale, D. (1986, April). *Classroom climate and process in international studies: Qualitative and quantitative evidence from the American schools and the world project, Stanford and the schools study.* Paper presented at the American Educational Research Association, New Orleans.

Weiss, I. R. (1978). *Report of the 1977 National Survey of Science, Mathematics, and Social Studies Education.* Washington, DC: National Science Foundation.

Wiley, K. B. (1977). *The status of pre-collegiate science, math, and social science education 1955–75. Vol. III: Social science education.* Boulder, CO: Social Science Education Consortium.

Wilson, M. (1989). *Girls and young women in education: A European perspective.* Oxford: Pergamon.

Wilson, S. M., & Wineburg, S. S. (1988). Peering at history from different lenses: The role of disciplinary perspectives in the teaching of American history. *Teachers College Record, 89,* 525–539.

Zevin, J. (1983). Future citizens: Children and politics. *Teaching Political Science, 10,* 119–126.

Discussion of Chapters 6–9: What Do People Consume History For? (If They Do): Learning History as a Process of Knowledge Consumption and Construction of Meaning

Alberto Rosa
Autónoma University of Madrid

This chapter is concerned with the use of history. Hahn's statement that the claim that instruction in history results in a more informed and active citizenry has not been demonstrated, and it seems to me that it is a core issue that needs to be explored. The aim in this chapter is to discuss some assumptions that underlie the teaching of history, also to offer some pragmatic suggestions concerning the way historical knowledge may be of use to the citizen (the holder of so-called "lay theories").

When listening to the voices that refer to the use of historical knowledge, the dissonance of opinions is striking. From the classic statement, "people who are not aware of their past are condemned to repeat their mistakes," to Skinner's view about the uselessness of history for future life, there is a whole range of contradictory views on this issue. The cover story of the April 19, 1993 issue of *Newsweek* magazine is a revealing example. The headlines to an article on Serbia were as follows: "Serbia's Ghosts. Why Serbs See Themselves as Victims, Not Aggressors." The story offers a Serbian view of the current war in the former Yugoslavia, framing it within a narrative that presents a history of grievances suffered by the Serbs from their Croat and Muslim neighbors.

After the caption entitled "Six Centuries of Tears," an article by Peter McGrath followed bearing the title "The Curse of the Past. An Indifference to History can be a Blessing." This latter article in particular struck me as being both a European and a teacher of history. McGrath showed approval for what he saw as the Americans' lack of concern for the past. In his view, collective memory is (using a quotation by D.H. Lawrence) "thinking with the blood" and "history, in this sense, is the enemy of civil politics" (p. 15), because it defines (borrowing a term from Geertz) "primordial attach-ments," which he paraphrased as identity, and therefore causes one group to oppose another. However, McGrath continued, "Americans are notable among the world's people for their virtual lack of primordial attachments" (p. 15), which he blamed on the fact that "America is at the bottom a nation of immigrants . . . who moved to the U.S. precisely because they wanted to escape their histories" (p. 15). That is the reason why "few events in American history are capable of arousing zeal, to say nothing of hatred" (p. 15). The article finished with a statement that I think is worth reproducing: "At the end of the day, Americans respond more to the homely claims of daily life than to bygone passions. This is in fact America's great cultural strength: its ability to plow the past under, and to start history over again at the next growing season" (p. 15).

I chose to start with these excerpts because I think they offer a good case in point to comment on some of the issues that concern the aim of this chapter. On the one hand, the idea of forgetting the past and considering this moment "the beginning of the rest of your life" is not an American monopoly, but a universal desire. What may be different is the use of history as a way of creating political identity. As a Spaniard who spent his childhood and a good portion of his youth under Franco's regime, I remember one of the mottos of the day, "forgive but not forget" (in reference to "exclusively" the atrocities of the Republican militias) and the consequences it had in the teaching of history. Moreover, perhaps to be able "to plow the past under" may not be a matter of being a young country (to my knowledge Argentina, Bolivia, Cuba, Mexico, or Panama are also countries of immigrants and younger, as independent states, than the United States, and show plenty of historical grievances toward their neighbors), but a question of the political decision to stir public emotions toward a feeling of threat, something that is not foreign either to American discourse (e.g., the association in the media of Japanese commercial strategies with Pearl Harbor during the 50th anniversary of the attack). The fact that history may not be used as much in the United States for creating a "primordial attachment" may be a consequence of the fact that a country that is now the finest in power and strength does not have a past better than the present to look at or emotional grievances easily stirred in order to create a sense of identity. However, where does this argument lead?

What has been said thus far seems to reduce the teaching of history to political indoctrination, to the transmission of a narrative tailored to convey values, emotions, "primordial attachments," and identity. However, no historian would agree that this is the purpose of making history. On the contrary, most will agree with Collingwood (1972, p. 10) that "the value of history is to teach us what mankind has done, and so what mankind is." In other words, history is a type of epistemic practice that addresses human affairs, something that it shares with the humanities and the social sciences, including psychology. What is specific to history is that it concerns human actions in the past. The question is, why is the knowledge of the past useful? Were we to follow McGrath's argument, we would feel happy being "lotus-eaters" and lose our memory, if that were not inconsistent with the ability to conserve an identity and benefit from the accumulation of knowledge that culture provides. It seems then that history is collective memory—the interpretation of the past through the use of the records received and conceptual devices we have available.

This makes history look like a type of technical memory, a reservoir of experiences, the key to which lies in the hands of professional historians who have the expertise to retrieve that knowledge and to offer it to laypeople. What is it that has to be transmitted to students of history—"the ready-made" products offered by the professional historians for the consumption of lay intellectual commoners, or the very expertise the historians master? In order to answer these questions, we have to proceed further in our exploration of what history is and its relation to its intrapersonal forebear: memory.

MEMORY AND HISTORY

The connection between history and memory may very well go beyond metaphor. In order to further our understanding of this similarity, it is necessary to explore different types of memory. The distinction between episodic and semantic memory (Tulving, 1985) echoes a former distinction made years ago by Vygotsky (1931) and Leontiev (1931/1981). These latter authors considered the existence of two types of memory, one type that is a natural function that allowed the conservation of incidents of life, and another type of memory necessarily mediated with a cultural origin that permitted the intentional recall of past events and knowledge. Middleton and Edwards (1990) offered a reading of Bartlett (1932) that views recollection not as a retrieval of information from a stockpile of previous experiences, but as a constructive process in the course of an action. In other words, a remembrance is an elaboration upon some traces of the past that is carried out to fit to the discourse at hand. These traces may be either internal or external, may be in the brain, or may be objects in the environment that act as signifiers with some meaning attached to them.

Zinchenko (1939/1983), elaborating on Vygotsky and Leontiev, put memory in a wider context, connecting it with the individual's ongoing activities. According to Zinchenko, involuntary memory produces recollections in the course of an action that is not oriented toward the goal of remembering, whereas voluntary memory is characterized by the fact that recollection itself is the object of the action.

Therefore, there are actions in which recollections appear involuntarily, and there are other actions whose goal is a recollection. In both cases, many of these recollections are mediated, have a meaning attached to them, and are not an immediate revival of previous experiences. Many objects serve as mediational tools for memory (Leontiev, 1931/1981), and some objects are produced for that purpose (souvenirs, photographs, memorials, etc.; e.g., Radley, 1990). Together with this there are "practices of remembering" in which collective activities are designed with the purpose of evoking the memory of a past event (visiting a burial place, the Fourth of July, Bastille Day, Martin Luther King's birthday, etc.). If intentional memory is a reconstruction of personal life events mediated by internal or external "records," then history is a form of discourse whose purpose is precisely the preservation of past events considered relevant for the group. There are two ways of fixing relevant events, one contemporary to the happening that then has to be significant enough to be recorded, and a later one that elaborates on that record to produce an event considered significant enough to be plotted into a narrative that serves a moral (or/and pragmatic) purpose (Mathien, 1991).

Engeström, Brown, Engeström, and Koistinen (1990), in their study of the conservation of the past in an institution (a clinic), distinguished between *primary recall* and *secondary recall*. The first refers to the memory of individual actions (what one has to do when performing the practice), whereas the second is concerned with the memory of activities of the past (the different ways in which individual actions are organized as activities at different times). This is a crucial distinction for the purposes of this chapter because this secondary memory concerns actions of recollection that have as objects the systems of activities. It is this type of memory that allows the conservation of a memory of how practices were performed, why they had the structure they had, why they were changed, and so on. In sum, secondary memory permits one to connect individual actions with a flow of practices within which that action gains its significance and makes it possible to learn from the collective experience of the past. A secondary memory, which has no salience when one has to deal with daily practice, comes to the fore when the practice itself is challenged. It is in these cases when amnesic collectivities are at a disadvantage. Then, the role of the historian is not just that of curator of these memories but also that of updating them to be ready for use.

It seems, then, that this secondary memory is a matter for historians, and laypeople only have to care about performing actions within the already stable framework of social practices, or what McGrath called "the homely claims of daily life" (i.e., primary memory). In other words, laypeople are to be consumers of ready-made products offered by the "experts" (the holders of reason and wisdom, as Plato put it). This view seems to contradict the ideal of an "informed active citizenry . . . [with] higher levels of citizen duties, increased participation, and increased level of political efficacy," as Hahn (this volume) stated. What then has to be taught in history courses? The ready-made products of "experts," or the skills needed to be "experts"? To offer "students to have a chance to learn *reasoning*," or to help them in "a movement toward *understanding*" (Leinhardt, this volume; emphasis added)? In order to answer these questions we have to go deeper into our discussion of history.

HISTORY, A POLISEMIC WORD

The word *history* carries with it a number of meanings that I will attempt to untangle. According to the original sense of the Greek word, history is "learning or knowing by inquiry, narrative." In contemporary English, it is also "A relation of incidents, a narrative, tale, story"; "A written narrative constituting a continuous methodical record, in order of time, of important or public events"; "the formal record of the past," among other different senses (*Oxford Universal Dictionary*, 1973, p. 968). Gardiner (1980) distinguished between "1) the events and actions that make the human past, or 2) the accounts given to that past and the modes of investigation whereby they are arrived at or constructed" (p. 961). In addition it is noteworthy to point out that in Spanish (*historia*), as well as in French (*histoire*) and German (*Geschichte*), it has the connotation of imaginary tale, empty rhetoric that diverts from core facts or plain forgery. This section attempts to play with these different senses and give a use for each of them.

To provide some order, I use different words for each of the various senses mentioned. Table 1 offers the different meanings described earlier, their referents and function. The main message this table attempts to convey is that in History (History 2, as in the table, intentionally with a capital letter) all the other meanings participate (including ideology). It refers to the past, but not as such as it has to rely on the records available to the historian. In addition, the historian has to explain what happened and why it happened; in order to do so, he or she must resort to two types of evidence (Danto, 1985): *empirical evidence*, provided by the records of the past, and *conceptual evidence*, provided by explanatory concepts borrowed from other disciplines. The final product is a narrative, not any narrative, but one that incorporates these two types of evidence in a flow of events. The resulting narrative should exhaust all the empirical evidence, but as Danto (1985) and White (1973, 1987) said, the narrative goes beyond evidence: It also offers a plot. This fact has two important consequences.

On the one hand, the interplay of the two types of evidence may force the narrative to assume the existence of events that cannot be documented. As Danto put it, the narrative acts then as a device for *abduction*, for the production of hypotheses that guide the search for more empirical evidence. On the other hand, a narrative has two referents: evidence (of the two kinds), and the plot (White, 1973, 1987), a product of fantasy, a way of creating a flow of events that have some potentials — among them to create a dramatic tension toward the future, to transmit an ideology of salvation and progress, of eternal return, or growth and decay (Pongratz, 1967; Wertheimer, 1985).

In addition, the use of a particular narrative form is chosen from among the ones available in the literary tradition within which the historian works (Gergen & Gergen, 1984) and conveys a political ideology (White, 1973) and a moral with implications for future action (Mathien, 1991). That is, History, in explaining the past, also implies a line of action for the future, offers a moral for the story, presents a utopia to be reached, a danger to be avoided, or a consolation for an unavoidable fate. Also, a historical narrative is a device for the creation of identity. It offers a text (remember that this word comes from the latin *texere*) within which each individual weaves his or her autobiography. Finally, I point out that the use of Aristotelian terminology, which echoes Aristotle's metaphysics, is only a rhetorical device for the creation of meaning in the reader.

Historical narrative does not have the monopoly on the creation of identity, for the transmission of values with a moral implication for future action. Literature, myth, and popular history are also powerful devices for these purposes. In this respect the truth value of a narrative does not need

TABLE 1
Three Meanings of the Word "History"

Term	Referent	Function
History 1 history-past	The real past; actual happenings in the past	Its traces are the "material cause"
History 2 Historiography	Historical science	To describe what happened and why: "efficient cause"
History 3 historical-fiction	A language production in narrative form	To offer a literary production that allows the production of meaning: "formal cause"
Ideology	A project of future, utopia	"final cause"; clausure of a historical narrative

to be relevant. One can weave his or her projection of the future in any narrative, either real of fictional, but what is impossible — unless there is a pathology — is to weave the personal memory of the past with a text that is recognized as a forgery. That is why historians are trusted as specialists for the conservation and elaboration of public memories, and their role is not to be confused with that of the writers of fiction. Table 2 attempts to summarize these points.

There are some points in this table that deserve further commentary. First, I made a distinction between *history-as-a-school-subject* and *History-Historiography* (History 2, in Table 1). This distinction is explored later. My second point involves *historical tales, historical stories*, and *historical narrations*, the products of the three types of history. Historical tales and historical stories do not have very demanding criteria of truth, but this depends on the immediate use of these types of products. This is not the case of historical narratives, because they require the fulfillment of the rules of the practice of History, in which authority resides (more or less) in the

TABLE 2
System of Production, Product, Truth Value and
Usefulness of Social Practices of Remembering

TYPE OF PRACTICE	RAW MATERIALS	PRODUCT	PSYCHOLOGICAL USE	CRITERIA OF TRUTH
Social memory (popular history)	Remembrances, Memorials, Tales, Novels, Heroes, Myths, etc. Contextual goals (purpose)	"historical tales"	representation of the past meaning of the present identity, group, or individual project of future	justification of the present recognized authority acceptance of the moral
History-as-a-school-subject	History-Historiography Moral, political, and ideological goals of teaching	"historical stories"		
History-Historio-graphy	Memorials Documents, "Previous historical constructions" Knowledge offered by other sciences, etc.	"Historical constructions" "Historical narratives"		Explicit requirements of the rules of historical practice.

community of historians. It is only insofar as history-as-a-school-subject is connected to the requirements of History 2 (as considered in Table 1) that it can be considered to have a value of truth despite its necessary abridgement. Finally, I want to comment on the concept of historical construction. Any product of historical practice is not a natural category nor a natural event, but the result of the historian's labor. If in the Natural Sciences, we cannot talk of natural facts, but of facts as a result of the application of theoretical devices for the interpretation of experience, in History (and in the social sciences), we cannot speak of events or causes as something experience dictates immediately, but as a construction that results from the application of the rules of the practice. Then, as Halldén (this volume) says, colligatory concepts in History are a social product that create a shared meaning through conversation. If we want students of History to be able to understand how historical constructions are the building blocks of historical stories and historical narratives, there is no option but to teach them the process of producing these building blocks and the means of binding them together. This takes us again to our recurrent questions: what to teach in History classes, and how to organize the curriculum of history-as-a-school-subject.

TEACHING OF HISTORY AND THE LEARNER OF HISTORY

From what has been said thus far, it seems clear that a conception of history-as-a-school subject relies mainly on the transmission of historical stories that limits itself to the offering of another story, which eventually combines with all the historical tales the cultural reservoir provides the individual with. This use of history does not seem to be very useful in going toward the creation of a more informed and active citizen, rather it seems to be very susceptible to political use, as a device for the stirring of emotions that McGrath pointed out. However, perhaps there is a slot in the early courses in history for this approach. If this is the case, special attention should be paid not only to the events portrayed there, but also to the way in which they are plotted together and the values they convey. Teaching history is a political enterprise, with potentially dangerous effects.

It seems then that there is an unavoidable need to teach the rules of the trade of historiography as a safeguard against the manipulation of the past, against what underlies the Russian half-joke "the past is unpredictable." But knowledge of the methodology of History is not a guarantee for reaching truth, it is just the learning of how to spin and weave the threads of the tapestries that provide our images of the past. And it should always to be taken into account that these tapestries are not the ones that dictate the furnishing, but they have to fit the goals of the inhabitant of the dwelling. Truth is relative to the purpose of the discourse and, as Hacking (1982) said, "the very candidates for truth of falsehood have no existence independent of the types of reasoning that settle what is to be true or false in their domain" (p. 49) and, as he continued, logic is a device for preserving a previously conceded truth. Therefore, even the products of an historical inquiry are relative to the interest of the present in which they are produced. But this does not negate the usefulness of historical products, it just calls attention to the fact that an historical production is tailored to the current needs for a representation of the past.

How can these rules of reasoning be taught? Obviously, they are mastered by expert historians, and it is useful to apply a task analysis to them to untangle the different steps that compose them. Also, there is no other way for a student to master these techniques other than to practice them. But is that enough to bring the student closer to the expertise in which he or she is being trained? To answer this question we have to change sides. As Halldén (this volume) said, students interpret the task they have to perform in a different way than that intended by the teacher. If we want to understand what is going on in the process under study, instead of keeping ourselves within the position of experts, of historians and teachers of history, we have to place ourselves in the position of the student, following Cole's wise advice of taking methodologically the position of the weaker (personal commmunication, 1984).

The challenge seems to be to devise methods that allow us to "transform accurate knowledge in meaningful ways for students," as Hahn (this volume) said. In her analysis of the "wisdom of practice" of four teachers, Hahn (this volume) reports on how teachers succeed in capturing students' attention by focusing on themes that concern them in such a way that these issues are controversial enough to stimulate their interest but not to the extent that it distracts them from learning. These teachers manage the situation and keep the interest of students alive through the use of the class as a ground for the creation of an open discourse. In this way history instruction is a process of interpersonal relations, a way of relating topics to the students' interest, of analyzing primary and secondary sources from different positions and contrasting historical interpretations. Halldén (this volume) refers to this exchange of ideas as a classroom conversation through which "a shared line of reasoning is established between teacher and students that constitutes both the description and the explanation of the event under question." As he said, the learning task is to learn that way of reasoning, and that is done through the process of collective reasoning.

After what has just been said, the results reported by McDiarmid (this volume) seem striking at first glance, but in my view they are not surprising. The teacher training students from which he gathered his data were profoundly affected in their understanding of History by their participation on a seminar that followed the prescriptions stated earlier, but they did not seem to have changed very much their view on how History should be taught. It looks as if they considered History and history-as-a-school-subject as two completely different types of activities. This concept of *activity* is the last station in our journey, and I think that careful consideration of it will cast some light on the reciprocal process of teaching and learning and to the goal of learning how to reason historically.

The concept of *activity* is a contribution of Leontiev (1978) that has been the subject of some controversy. I am not going to go into the different interpretations and debates about the concepts usefulness here (for a review see Cubero, in press), but offer instead my own interpretation in this context. Wertsch (1985) viewed activity as the institutionally defined context or scenario for human performance which results from a sociocultural construction. Pictured in this way, a particular job is structured in activities (e.g., examining a patient—as in the study by Engeström et al., 1990—is an activity that is structured in a set of actions, each with a particular goal and particular operations that adapt the performance to particularities of the circumstances at hand). Thus, every activity relies on a set of presuppositions that guide the selection of objectives and means. Leontiev said that activities are a social response to *motives*, which are the objectivation of a necessity, that is, a social need that has produced through time a particular way of dealing with it. At the same time, the motive is the objective that incites the individual to act. Therefore, the motive is responsible for what is relevant in a particular context of action: what orients the performance of the individual, what integrates his or her set of actions and gives sense to her or his activity. As Cubero (in press) said, the notion of activity offers a way of connecting macrosocial and institutional phenomena to individual psychological ones, because motives are individual inasmuch as they are perceived by the subject, although they are a reflection of a social goal in their origin.

These concepts may offer a key to understanding McDiarmid's results and provide some useful hints for the teaching of History. In order to further this argument, I resort again to the previously mentioned concept of voluntary and involuntary memory (Zinchenko, 1939/1983), and primary and secondary recall (Engeström et al., 1990). I already made a parallel between memory and History as two sides (individual and social) of the same function whose purpose is to profit from the experience of the past. Any memory recollection is either incidental (involuntary) in the course of an action that does not have as a goal the recollection, or it is an act of voluntary memory which, in turn, is instrumental to the performance of another action. What is unknown is an act of voluntary memory devoid of any purpose. This may very well be the situation many students of history see themselves in. It is as if the educational institution had evolved a practice, that of teaching history, that is loaded with meaning from the point of view of teachers and historians, but that has none for students. When in school, the student seems to be caught in the learning of a network of concepts that can be pictured as belonging to primary memory using Engeström et al.'s terminology. The set of concepts belonging to every other school subject has a purpose that reveals itself in actions that have some connection with everyday life, whereas history seems to have none. As Engeström et al. (1990) hinted at, secondary memory only becomes a necessity when the very practices (activities) that frame some of the everyday actions are threatened, when these actions begin to lose meaning. That is why when students (and everybody else) see a connection between their interests in changing the present and what History (as the store of experience) can offer to enlighten that issue, they become interested in their study. If they are not placed in such a situation, then history is just another obstacle in their race toward graduation.

Holt (1990), after reviewing some excerpts of students' opinions, offered a vivid picture of how they view history: History is "about something that every already knows about." "Students are simply asked to redigest someone else's thoughts." "History is about important events, important people, capital 'P' people." "It is told by the winners. No wonder it's boring" (p. 7).

Following de Certeau (1980/1984), I see students (and so-called laypeople) as consumers whose only role in the process of production is their capacity for using the products imposed on them. He went on to say:

> The presence and circulation of a representation (taught by preachers, educators, [etc.]) tell us nothing about what it is for its users. We must first analyze its manipulation by users who are not their makers. Only then can we gauge the difference and similarity between the production of the image and the secondary production hidden in the process of its utilization. (p. XIII)

A study of how students (and laypeople) consume History seems then of utmost importance, but meanwhile we have some suggestions to make History a product to be consumed by our students. However, these suggestions force us to change their status of students. As Holt (1990) said, "rather than teaching them to be consumers of stories, 'someone else's facts,' we might better develop their critical faculties by letting them create stories of their own" (p. 10), or, even further, substituting for activities and beliefs that belong to the culture of the historians activities and beliefs that are viewed as part of the school culture (Wineburg, 1991a, 1991b). This is not an easy task. I do not think it is enough to make students engage in the "pretended play" of being historians, but in the real thing, in the production of historical narratives that are of some use to them. They must have a motive for engaging in that activity.

REFERENCES

Bartlett, F. C. (1932). *Remembering: A study in experimental and social psychology.* Cambridge, England: Cambridge University Press.

Certeau, M. de. (1984). *The practice of everyday life.* Berkeley: University of California Press. (Original work published in 1980)

Collingwood, R. G. (1972). *The idea of history.* New York: Oxford University Press. (Original work published in 1961)

Cubero, M. (in press). Panorama actual de la Teoría de la Actividad: Algunas líneas de investigación teóricas y empíricas generadas en este marco [A current view on the theory of activity: Some empirical and theoretical studies developed within this framework]. *Infancia y Aprendizaje.*

Danto, A. C. (1985). *Narration and knowledge.* New York: Columbia University Press.

Engestrom, Y., Brown, K., Engestrom, R., & Koistinen, K. (1990). Organizational forgetting: An approach from the theory of activity. In D. Middleton & D. Edwards (Eds.), *Collective remembering.* London: Sage.

Gardiner, P. L. (1980). History, philosophy of. *Encyclopaedia Britannica. Macropaedia* (Vol. 8, pp. 961-965). Chicago: Encyclopaedia Britannica.

Gergen, M. M. & Gergen, K.J. (1984). The social construction of narrative accounts. In K. J. Gergeny & M. M. Gergen (Eds.), *Historical social psychology* (pp. 173-190). Hillsdale, NJ: Lawrence Erlbaum Associates.

Hacking, I. (1982). Language, truth and reason. In M. Hollis & S. Lukes (Eds.), *Rationality and relativism* (pp. 48-66). Oxford: Blackwell.

Holt, T. (1990). *Thinking historically. Narrative, imagination and understanding.* New York: College Entrance Examination Board.

Leontiev, A. N. (1978). *Activity, conciousness and personality.* Englewood Cliffs, NJ: Prentice-Hall.

Leontiev, A. N. (1981). The development of higher forms of memory. In A. N. Leontiev (Ed.), *Problems of the development of the mind* (pp. 327-365). Moscow: Progress. (Original work published in 1931)

Mathien, T. (1991). History and the moralist. *The Monist, 74* (2), 240-267.

McGrath, P. (1993, April 19). The curse of the past. An indifference to history can be a blessing. *Newsweek,* p. 15.

Middleton, D., & Edwards, D. (1990). Conversational remebering: A sociopsychological approach. In D. Middleton & D. Edwards (Eds.), *Collective remembering.* London: Sage.

The Oxford Universal Dictionary Illustrated (Vol. I). (1973). London: Caxton.

Pongratz, L. H. (1967). *Problemgeschichte der Psychologie.* Berna: Francke.

Radley, A. (1990). Artefacts, memory and sense of the past. In D. Middleton & D. Edwards (Eds.), *Collective remembering.* London: Sage.

Tulving, E. (1985). How many systems of memory are there? *American Psychologist, 40,* 385-398.

Vygotsky, L. S. (1931). Introducción [Introduction]. In A. N. Leontiev (Ed.), *Razvitie pamiati*(pp. 6-13). Moscow/Leningrad: Uchpedgiz.

Wertheimer, M. (1985). The evolution of the concept of development in the history of psychology. In G. Eckhardt, W. G. Bringmann & L. Sprung (Eds.), *Contributions to a history of developmental psychology* (pp. 13-25). Berlin: Mouton.

Wertsch, J. V. (1985). *Vygotsky and the social formation of mind.* Cambridge, MA: Harvard University Press.

White, H. (1973). *Metahistory.* Baltimore: The John Hopkins University Press.

White, H. (1987). *The content of the form.* Baltimore: The John Hopkins University Press.

Wineburg, S. (1991a). On the reading of historical texts: Notes on the breach between school and academy. *American Educational Research Journal, 28,* 495–519.

Wineburg, S. (1991b). Historical problem-solving: A study of the cognitive processes used in the evaluation of documentary and pictorial evidence. *Journal of Educational Psychology, 83*(1), 73–87.

Zinchenko, P. I. (1983). The problem of involuntary memory. *Soviet Psychology, 22,* 55–111. (Original work published in 1939)

III LEARNING FROM HISTORY AND SOCIAL SCIENCES TEXTS

10 Outcomes of History Instruction: Paste-up Accounts

Isabel L. Beck and Margaret G. McKeown
University of Pittsburgh

We are reading researchers who have spent a considerable amount of time over the last half dozen years engaged in a program of research about elementary social studies learning, with emphasis on young students' first formal encounter with American history. As reading researchers, our primary interest is the kind of learning that results from students' encounters with text. Given that text is a focal component of the instructional resources used to teach history, coming to understand what young students learn about history from text was a natural object of investigation.

Our research involved an in-depth analysis of a widely used elementary textbook series (Beck, McKeown, & Gromoll, 1989) and three studies that empirically investigated two major problematic features identified in textbook analysis (Beck, McKeown, Sinatra, & Loxterman, 1991; McKeown & Beck, 1990; McKeown, Beck, Sinatra, & Loxterman, 1992). The first feature was the texts' assumption of an unrealistic variety and depth of prior knowledge from target-age students. The second feature was presentation of text content that was not coherent. By *coherent* text we mean text in which the sequencing of ideas makes sense and the nature of the ideas and their relationships is made apparent.

In the studies that followed from the text analysis, we attempted to determine the extent to which inappropriate assumed background knowledge and lack of coherence were problems for target-age students, as well as to create and evaluate strategies to reduce the problems. In this chapter we synthesize the findings from the text analysis and subsequent empirical studies and extend issues raised in that work by considering some new, longitudinal data.

ANALYSIS OF ELEMENTARY TEXTBOOKS

We initiated our research with an analysis of textbooks because we saw them as providing a broad and general view of current practice in elementary classrooms. Indeed, the centrality of textbooks is a well-accepted starting point for discussion of social studies instruction. And the discussion in both popular and professional literature about social studies textbooks centers on strikingly similar negative observations and conclusions about the inadequate quality of textbooks across at least three decades (Alexander, 1960; FitzGerald, 1979; Palmer, 1967; White, 1988).

Our purpose was not to further evaluate textbooks. Rather, our goal was to try to understand the textual features that contribute to the negative evaluation of textbooks and the effects these features may have on student learning. To do so, our text analysis was done against a backdrop of recent cognitive reading research.

The cognitive orientation to reading research has brought much progress in understanding the ways that readers interact with texts. In investigations of the reading process, emphasis is now placed on understanding the mental activities involved in reading, that is, what the reader does while reading, rather than being confined to the products of reading, that is, what the reader remembers from reading. Insights gained from the cognitive perspective have also yielded understanding of how the reader's execution and coordination of the processes involved during reading affect the products of reading (see, e.g., Just & Carpenter, 1987; Perfetti, 1985).

We saw the understandings gained from cognitive reading research as having much to offer textbook analysis work. Particularly fruitful is the inherent focus on learning, which could open the way for understanding how characteristics of texts affect the way textbooks function in a learning environment. Two specific areas of research profoundly influenced our text analysis work: understandings about the nature of the reading process, with emphasis on the interaction of a reader's background knowledge and a text's content (see, e.g., Chiesi, Spilich, & Voss, 1979; Pearson, Hansen, & Gordon, 1979), and characteristics of texts that promote or impede comprehension (see, e.g., Black & Bern, 1981; Frederiksen, 1981; Trabasso, Secco, & van den Broek, 1984).

Against this research backdrop, we chose to analyze extensive topic sequences rather than categorize segments of text by problem type, such as ambiguous statements or confusing references, and present discrete examples of these problems isolated from the context in which they occur. Analysis of sequential text presentations allowed us to consider the learning that may develop as students move through a sequence. Just as cognitive psychology is concerned with "getting inside" the process of learning rather than observing the outward manifestations of performance, our interest was with getting inside student/text interactions so that findings could be understood in relation to the learning process.

Our work with history in textbook analysis involved examination of four fifth-grade textbook presentations of the American Revolutionary period, specifically, the time frame from colonial development through the events at Lexington and Concord (Beck et al., 1989). Using the chronology of important events, as identified by the programs, as our organizing device, we looked at how each of the four programs explicated the chain of events.

Our conclusion was that the presentation of history content in the programs was not oriented toward developing a coherent chain of events. We judged the biggest obstacles to students' comprehension to be unrealistic assumptions about what students already know that is related to the topic and problematic features of the text presentation, chiefly a lack of coherence and explanation. Toward demonstrating these issues, consider the following historical account:

> *The Langurian and Pitok War.* In 1367 Marain and the settlements ended a 7-year war with the Langurian and Pitoks. As a result of this war Languria was driven out of East Bacol. Marain would now rule Laman and other lands that had belonged to Languria. This brought peace to the Bacolian settlements. The settlers no longer had to fear attacks from Laman. The Bacolians were happy to be a part of Marain in 1367. Yet a dozen years later, these same people would be fighting the Marish for independence, or freedom from United Marain's rule. This war was called the Freedom War or the Bacolian Revolution. A revolution changes one type of government or way of thinking and replaces it with another.

As an adult reader of this chapter, if you experienced difficulty making sense of the events described, it might provide some understanding of how it feels to be a fifth grader reading a social studies text. That is because the text was developed by taking a fifth-grade passage about the French and Indian War and simply replacing the agents and locations with pseudonyms. This demonstration was created by Ely Kozminsky, a visiting Israeli scholar who worked with us at the Learning Research and Development Center. When Ely first showed us this text, even though we recognized that it was based on a textbook passage with which we were very familiar, we still had trouble holding the pieces together and had the feeling of being bombarded with meaningless labels.

The following is the fifth-grade textbook passage on which the Langurian and Pitoks was based. Adult readers with some knowledge of American history will not find it nearly so inconsiderate:

> *The French and Indian War.* In 1763 Britain and the colonies ended a 7-year war with the French and Indians. As a result of this war France was driven out of North America. Britain would now rule Canada and other lands that had

belonged to France. This brought peace to the American colonies. The colonists no longer had to fear attacks from Canada. The Americans were happy to be a part of Britain in 1763. Yet a dozen years later, these same people would be fighting the British for independence, or freedom from Great Britain's rule. This war was called the War for Independence or the American Revolution. A revolution changes one type of government or way of thinking and replaces it with another.

When the fifth graders with whom we worked encountered the original passage, many of them had enormous difficulty holding the pieces together — even though they had studied the exploration and early colonization of North America in their textbooks, and so had been introduced to the names here. But students' familiarity with them was just not enough to hold together a sparse, poorly connected historical account. So, for some students, *French, British, Canada,* and *Great Britain* were no more helpful than *Pitoks, Langurian,* and *Marain.*

EXAMINING FIFTH GRADERS' BACKGROUND KNOWLEDGE

After our text analysis, the first study examined the background knowledge of fifth graders by interviewing them about events leading to the Revolutionary War just before they studied that topic in school (McKeown & Beck, 1990). The interview was based on two broad concepts that the textbook analysis indicated were largely assumed by the textbooks: the role of England in the colonists' struggle for independence and ideas about representative government. The results showed that most students' knowledge about these issues and this period in history tended to be vague and contained many inaccuracies. What students seemed to have was a general landscape about their country's early history — that people came here from other countries and from there followed a long process of settling the land and seeking freedom.

What many students did not have in place were specifics — what kind of political entity the 13 colonies were, who fought whom in the Revolutionary War, or any details of why and how "freedom" was sought. Of course, such results should not be surprising for students who had not yet studied this material formally; what may seem surprising, however, is that the textbooks do seem to assume that this information is already under students' control.

COMPARING LEVELS OF BACKGROUND KNOWLEDGE AND TEXT COHERENCE

Two subsequent studies then investigated the impact of background knowledge and coherence on comprehension of text (Beck et al., 1991; McKeown

et al., 1992). In the first of those, we presented four textbook passages about events leading to the Revolution to one group of students and revised versions of those presentations to another group. The topics covered were (a) the French and Indian War, (b) the issue of "no taxation without representation," (c) the Boston Tea Party, and (d) the Intolerable Acts. The revisions were based on making the text more coherent by providing explicit connections and presenting motivations that explained why one event led to another or why a certain set of consequences emerged. Findings showed that the revised text resulted in significantly better comprehension.

One of the most striking problems students had was understanding the agents involved — who was doing what to whom. This result seemed directly traceable to the lack of background provided about Britain and the colonies in the texts. Although students had studied the text unit on the colonies just prior to being in our study, the role of Britain in the colonies was not made clear; rather, the text focus was on the lifestyle of the various colonies. Thus, in McKeown et al. (1992), we focused on building background knowledge that very strongly set up the notion of Britain as "owners" of the 13 colonies and of the colonies as, over time, developing a distinct identity separate from being British. After receiving the background knowledge lesson we developed, the students then read either the original or revised version of the text.

The result was that, again, the revised text resulted in better comprehension. But the background knowledge lesson also played a role, in that comprehension was heightened for both groups over that of students who had read either text without the background knowledge. Hence, having background knowledge did contribute to a more successful outcome, but background knowledge did not completely compensate for the problems of the text presentation — greater text coherence made for further comprehension enhancement. Thus, it seems that the students who read the original text were less able to bring this information to bear as they read.

STUDENTS' ATTEMPTS TO MAKE SENSE OF TEXTBOOK HISTORY

We now take a deeper look at some of the issues raised in our work. There are two ways to think about the effects of the revisions. The first is the positive spin, that is, the revisions did produce significantly better comprehension as measured by amount of recall and percentage of questions answered correctly. Even more importantly, in examining the nature of the revised group's advantage, we found that the difference in the content they recalled and the information they put forth in answers to questions tended to represent the concepts needed to explain the actions of the text and to

move the chain of events forward. Be that as it may, the worrisome issue is that the students who showed improved comprehension still did not constitute a majority of the revised text's readers.

The limitations of even a carefully crafted text need to be emphasized. The message that needs to be stressed is that learning complex content is difficult, and simply explaining issues to young students in text is not likely to accomplish the whole task. The caution here is that adults should not expect even a coherent, well-designed text to communicate to a young learner the information that they can glean from it. When learning complex content, young students typically need several reiterations of the ideas and opportunities to discuss what they have understood in order to clarify and elaborate their initial conceptions.

The message is not, however, that effort should not be given to developing more coherent texts. In fact, the less than coherent texts may be detrimental to students' development of historical understanding. This seems to be the case because in attempting to make sense of what they read, some students construct representations so vague that it is questionable whether anything will be remembered, whereas others create fabricated accounts. To illustrate some representations that students construct from text, we consider next several student recalls of the French and Indian War passage discussed earlier.

Consider Neil's recall in which he dealt with just one agent and one of the wars mentioned in the text: "Britain like, um, drove over to ah, um....They like had a war, and they called it the War for Independence. And so Britain won, and so Britain owned it." Neil appeared to gather information only about Britain, dropping out the other participants. His association to the text words "driven out" seemed to be to getting somewhere by motor vehicle, and so he connected the agent — Britain — and the action — driving — and asserted that "Britain drove over." With no place in his memory for Britain to go, he dropped that notion. The next tack he took was to make some decent inferences — that Britain won the war, and now had ownership of something — which he tied to the label "War for Independence." It seems that Neil tried to make some sense of the passage by greatly simplifying who and what was involved.

Another student, Sarah, picked up a few key labels and compiled them into the following account: "There was a war in 1763 that Britain attacked to Canada. The government explained that there won't be no more attacks. And for a dozen years there hasn't been attacks in Canada for a dozen years." Sarah's recall is a very word-based account in that she used important words from the text, but not in the roles they played in the text. She took one of the agents — Britain — the text words "attacks from Canada," and forced them together into what might be considered an

initiating event for the war, that is, "Britain attacked to Canada." From the text sentence, "A revolution changes one type of government," Sarah grabbed the word *government* and transformed it into an agent that "explained that there won't be no more attacks." She concluded, "for a dozen years there hasn't been attacks in Canada." These notions seem to come from the text sentences: "The colonists no longer had to fear attacks from Canada. . . . Yet a dozen years later." Thus, what Sarah seems to have done with text ideas that have no meaning for her was to take some agents and some actions mentioned in the text and paste them together into an account that has internal coherence, but that does not resemble the account in the text.

Finally, Jesse's way of handling the text was to take the one agent that was probably the most familiar at this point in his learning about the history of the North American continent — the Indians — and make them the focus of the actions. We got a lot of talk about the Indians from the students with whom we worked. Jesse told us:

> Well it was about the French and Indian War, and the Indians wanted to like be free from the British. And they wanted to start their own land. And there was a French and Indian War and the American Revolution. And they both fought and the Indians won it, and they got their freedom.

In creating a story about Indians gaining independence from the British, Jesse set up a different conflict from the one in the text, based on two of the four agents named there. He then went on to resolve the conflict he created, resulting in a coherent but fictional account.

Although we predicted many of the problems in understanding the textbook passages we used in our studies, such as the combatants in the French and Indian War, the issue of representative government, and the severity of the Intolerable Acts, the level of confusion that students displayed was a bit surprising. In particular, confusion about the agents was prevalent throughout the texts. Not only were agents confused in the French and Indian War, but the colonists were rarely mentioned. The lack of identification of the colonists as being involved in the period is particularly problematic because their role is critical to understanding the period. Clearly, when significant omission and confusion pervades this level of information, little is going to be learned from the text. And, as a result, the representations that students develop are often inaccurate conceptions of the events portrayed.

A question in which we became interested was the extent to which the confusions found in students' accounts of what they read was characteristic of what they generally knew about the period. In the following section we bring some longitudinal data to bear on this question.

A LONGITUDINAL LOOK AT HISTORY LEARNING

In this chapter we are able to extend the work on what students appear to learn from instruction by considering longitudinal data for 26 of the 35 fifth graders included in the McKeown and Beck (1990) study. We were able to interview these 26 students about the American Revolution before and after instruction in American history in fifth and eighth grade, the grades that represent the first two formal instructional encounters with American history. The responses of these students to the interviews before fifth-grade instruction were reported in McKeown and Beck (1990).

As noted earlier, the primary focus of McKeown and Beck was to characterize fifth-grade students' knowledge just before they studied the period in order to assess the match between what students know and what the texts assume. The conclusion was that the match was poor. A secondary focus of McKeown and Beck was on sixth-grade students who had studied the period the previous year. The data for the sixth-grade students were used to shed some light on what history is learned. Our findings from this cross-sectional comparison provided evidence that some learning does take place; students' knowledge about the Revolutionary period increases after instruction. Yet students still exhibit considerable confusion, and for some issues confusion increases after instruction. It was our judgment that the amount and quality of learning was very limited, and we faulted the instruction.

All 35 fifth graders who were part of the McKeown and Beck study were originally interviewed in an elementary school in a small middle-class school district in Pennsylvania. Thirty-one of the 35 students were located as eighth graders in the middle school of the district, and parental permission to interview them again was obtained for 26 of the 31 students. The history instruction the 26 students received in both fifth and eighth grade can be characterized as traditional, text-based instruction. Activities in class consisted of reading and discussing the text and teacher-prepared activities that reinforced the text content.

As a descriptor of students' abilities, we are able to provide their reading comprehension scores. The reading comprehension level of these students was somewhat above average. Evidence for this was the group's mean national percentile rank of 66.73 ($SD = 20.05$) for the reading comprehension subtest of the Metropolitan Achievement Test (1984).

The longitudinal data are responses to a general query that asked students to tell what they knew about the American Revolution at the four time periods. At all the interview occasions, vague responses were queried; for example, a student who said, "It was a war that was fought for our freedom," would be asked, "Can you tell me what you mean by saying that it was for freedom," and if the meaning of *our* had not been established, the examiner would try to establish the student's referent for *our*.

From analysis of these data we created two snapshots of the knowledge students acquired about the Revolutionary War period. The first is based on students' inclusion of three basic components of the event sequence of the American Revolution. The second describes some trends in the growth of students' overall knowledge. Following these snapshots, we provide examples of students' responses that provide some insight into students' development of or failure to develop understanding.

Toward devising an initial snapshot of the information students provide about the Revolution, responses were analyzed for inclusion of information that constitute, perhaps, the most basic components: who was involved; the motivation for fighting the war, which was independence from British rule; and the outcome in terms of the consequences, which was gaining independence. Figure 10.1 presents students' responses at the four time periods.

Generally the pattern is that learning occurs for all three components during initial exposure to American history in the fifth grade. By eighth grade, much of the learned information has been lost or contaminated, even information as basic as the participants of the Revolutionary War. After eighth-grade history instruction, students demonstrate a strong gain in knowledge of the participants and motivation for the conflict. Yet only a small gain is evident for the consequences of the war.

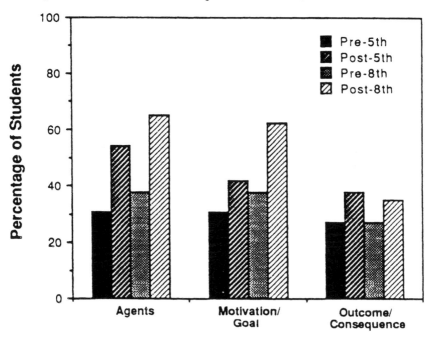

FIG. 10.1. Percentage of students exhibiting knowledge of Revolutionary War components at four time periods.

This first snapshot leaves an impression of what students accomplished through instruction and development across three years, that is, there was growth in knowledge. But we need to unpack this good news a bit and ask ourselves if the learning students demonstrate is what we would comfortably call good history education.

The second snapshot helps to dispel the foregoing general conclusion by capturing some specific trends in students' growth of knowledge. These trends suggest the path that students' understanding took from before their first encounter to after their second encounter with American history.

1. Of the 26 students interviewed, 8 had basic correct knowledge about how and why the Revolutionary War occurred before formal instruction in history. Of the 8 students with prior knowledge, 3 of them added no new ideas or elaboration of their original versions of history over the 3-year period.

2. Of the 18 students who began instruction without this knowledge, 11 made gains over the course of two rounds of instruction, whereas 7 students never exhibited an understanding of those historical events.

3. About one third of the students who did develop understanding by eighth grade exhibited substantial confusion enroute to that understanding, that is, after fifth-grade instruction and before eighth-grade instruction.

4. Although students were only called on to give a brief account of their understanding, it may be telling to note that these accounts rarely focused on the most global and historically significant outcome of the Revolutionary War, that is, the creation of the United States as a nation. Rather, the accounts frequently were sprinkled with mentions of noted events, people, or artifacts from the period—without explanation of how they fit into the historical picture: Lexington and Concord, Battle of Saratoga, George Washington, King George, Stamp Act, Declaration of Independence, Constitution, and the most prominent of all, the Boston Tea Party.

Because the language that students use to frame their knowledge gives some insight into the construction of their understanding of the historical period, we present several types of examples of students' responses. First, in order to provide a sense of the way students responded to the question and how their responses evolved across the four time periods, we present the responses of two students at each of the interview times. One is of a student who had prior knowledge and whose knowledge appeared to develop in some way over the 3 years. The other is of a student who shows what might be the more expected pattern, that is, she began with no knowledge of the Revolutionary War before instruction, but acquired a basic knowledge of the major components by the end of eighth grade. Finally, we provide specific examples of the trends noted earlier.

The first example is of Cheryl who began with a sketchy but correct account before fifth-grade instruction. This student's knowledge grew after instruction, was maintained — although in a much abbreviated form — at the beginning of eighth grade, and culminated after eighth-grade instruction in a coherent, well-expressed account with appropriate focus on the United States gaining independence.

Before fifth-grade instruction:

> It was between America and England and the French helped us, and we won, and the French gave us the Statue of Liberty.

After fifth-grade instruction:

> Whenever we came over here. . .the Pilgrims were still being ruled by England. And anything that they tried to do to help their government, England would oppose. And England would pass all these acts — the Parliament would — without even discussing it with the colonies. . . . We got mad . . . and the Boston Massacre happened and the war started.

Before eighth-grade instruction:

> We, the United States, wanted our freedom and England didn't want to give it to us so we sort of went into war to get what we thought we deserved. The French were on our side and they helped us to win the war and that's how we got our freedom.

After eighth-grade instruction:

> The United States wanted to be free from dependence on England so they started a war. . . . The war began at Lexington and Concord and the United States just wanted independence and Great Britain wouldn't give it to them, so they had to go to war to fight for their independence. In the end they won and that's why we're a free country. [Why want independence?] England was putting all kinds of taxes and all this stuff on them to pay for the French and Indian War . . . and the colonies were kind of getting sick of it.

The next example, Lisa, begins with a very general statement about war and possibly a Civil War association. After fifth grade, she exhibited correct information, albeit not well focused or complete.

Before fifth-grade instruction:

> The soldiers fighting for freedom. [Sides?] I think we wore gray, I'm not sure, and there was blue, I think. But I don't know the names of them.

After fifth-grade instruction:

> They were fighting because they wanted one part of the United States, but they wouldn't give it to them. They had the forts there, and they said, "we're not going to move." And it was us against, I think, Great Britain. They attacked and we attacked them at three different places. And then we wrote down the Dec . . . I forget what it is called. [I think you had it right.] The Declaration of Independence? Okay, and then sent it to Great Britain and Great Britain said, "no." And then they started fighting them all over again. [Why did they want their independence?] Great Britain was saying you have to pay taxes. . . . If they would have just said, "you know we need some more money to buy guns and support the soldiers and stuff," then I think we would have done it; instead of them bossing us around.

Lisa's kind of loquacious narrative response after fifth-grade instruction contrasts with a sort of bottom-line agents and motivation statement before eighth grade. After instruction in the eighth grade, Lisa returned to the more loquacious narrative style, exhibited after fifth-grade instruction, but with more sophisticated content that adds the consequences of the war.

Before eighth-grade instruction:

> The British people. . .said that they were going to rule the 13 colonies and we said no, so we fought for our freedom. [Why did we say no?] Because that's why we went away from the British in the first place, to get our freedom.

After eighth-grade instruction:

> Britain wanted to rule us, and we didn't want to go by their laws and what they had to say. . . . We wanted to be like free from Britain, but yet united over in the new world. So we asked them and they said no. So we decided. . .we got to do something about this. For freedom so we have to fight. So we fought for like a year or two, I don't know. And then [there was] like the Battle of Saratoga [and] there was like little battles [too]. And then like we finally got what we wanted. So, you know, we're free. And they made up the Constitution. . . . So we're all united.

The following examples are illustrative of three of the trends noted earlier: lack of knowledge persisting despite instruction, confusion of ideas within the development of understanding, and mentioning of associated labels within students' historical accounts.

How Students Manifested Lack of Knowledge

Jennifer is a quintessential example of no learning taking place through the two rounds of instruction. Her before fifth-grade instruction response suggests that she picked up absolutely nothing about the Revolutionary War from general experience and so handled the question by invoking what we have come to think of as components from an "empty war" schema. After fifth-grade instruction, Jennifer included some Revolutionary War labels, but with no elaboration whatsoever. At the pre-eighth-grade interview, Jennifer started with an "empty war" clause, but then admitted to the experimenter that she did not know.

Before fifth-grade instruction:

> People were fighting each other and they were bombing each other. It was a big fight. [Sides?] There was us and China. [Why war?] Because we wanted something, I guess. [End?] We won.

After fifth-grade instruction:

> They were fighting over taxes and the Stamp Act and the Sugar Act and that's how they got into the war. [What happened at the end of the war?] They made a peace treaty. [Peace treaty probe.] (No response.)

Before eighth-grade instruction:

> The American Revolution came along and people started fighting and all that stuff, and I don't really know that much about the American Revolution.

After eighth-grade instruction:

> I don't really remember this too well; I don't know why. We always learn about this and I always forget it. It's so important too. Something like, one of the colonies was too strong and something happened and they got into a war over it, and it was going on for a while and that's just one of the things. I don't know why I don't remember this. It's pretty embarrassing.

Jennifer's responses represent the three ways that students responded when they did not have the knowledge to provide an adequate response. One was to admit that they did not know; these admissions were often accompanied by metacognitive musing, such as Jennifer did after eighth grade, indicating that students felt they should have this knowledge but could not quite get a hold of it. Another way students responded when they did not have target knowledge was to access a general schema, in this case a war schema, and fill it with empty components—such as fighting over land, countries that were not getting along, and signing a peace treaty.

A third expression of low knowledge about the events of the Revolutionary War period was students' access of a label that is associated with the period, presented as an isolated token with no comment about its role in the event sequence. Jennifer used the labels "Stamp Act" and "Sugar Act" in this way. A most striking example of association to the period is one student's response after fifth grade, which came after several probes by the experimenter: "The Boston Tea Party." [What happened there?] "Somebody threw all the tea into the ocean." This was followed by more probes to which the student did not respond further.

Students' tendencies to respond with a general war schema and with isolated labels of events or artifacts suggests a mismatch between levels of information that students receive. It seems that many students accumulate some knowledge about the period, or understand that the events fit a familiar schema, but are unable to put the information together to construct a coherent sequence of the events. The general schema is too global to offer ready slots to fit the specific information that students might have gleaned, and the specific information is too sparse to be useful in connecting it to more general information.

Confusions That Students Develop
Enroute to Understanding

The single most striking pattern across all the data was the amount of confusion that was manifested in students' responses after fifth-grade instruction and before eighth-grade instruction. Typical of such responses is Eric's post-fifth-grade instruction response, which contains both of the most common confusions, confusions with the Civil War and the French and Indian War.

After fifth-grade instruction:

> I thought it was the north and the south, or is that the Civil War? [That's the Civil War. Repeats question: A long time ago there were 13 colonies . . .] The British came in and put their forts up on our land. The French were trying to get the forts out . . . [End?] We won and we wrecked [the British] forts.

Notice that the student began with a confused account, was then redirected by the experimenter, but then went off in another incorrect direction.

In his before eighth-grade response, Eric seemed unable to access any information from the period, so he resorted to notions from some then-current events — Russian/Communist enemies.

Before eighth-grade instruction:

> [Sides?] A country and us. [Can you remember what country it was?] Russia. [What were we fighting about?] Russia wanted to make our country colonist

(sic, Communist). We wanted to be free and they didn't want us to be free . . . [What do you mean by free in that case?] Well, like freedom of speech and stuff like that . . . [and Russia] wanted it run their way. [And what was their way?] It was Communist.

The invoking of communism was not unique to this student. Consider Carl's response when interviewed before eighth-grade instruction:

They wanted different rules and stuff like that. [Who wanted different rules?] The different parts of the world; they wanted different rules than other parts. [Can you tell me what you mean about they wanted different rules?] Well, like one part of the world, they wanted to be free, and other parts wanted to be like Communist and take over and tell people what to do and not let them have a choice.

Although we had found similar patterns of confusion in sixth graders we had interviewed in McKeown and Beck (1990), our hunch was that much of it was due to the intervening instruction in the year since the students had studied American history. In the present data, it was surprising to find the existence of such confusion so soon after instruction, although students were still engaged in studying the history of their country.

The pattern suggests a variation on the strongest finding in learning psychology—that forgetting begins immediately; it seems that for many of these students, under the kind of instruction they receive, confusion begins immediately. It is as if, rather than gaining a coherent sequence of motivations, events, and consequences of history, students have been set adrift in a sea of undifferentiated information.

Some students, of course, did gain relevant and coherent information from fifth-grade instruction. However, gaining this information did not necessarily mean being able to hold on to it. Indeed, some students who gave essentially accurate responses after fifth grade seemed to have become overwhelmed by confusion in grade 8, before the second round of American history. A case in point is Daniel, whose responses after fifth-grade instruction suggest some understanding. For instance, he had some sense that England was involved in the period and that there was something about "claiming" land. His understanding of the consequences of winning is clear, and he may also have had some sense that people want to have their own "government."

After fifth-grade instruction:

France, no England came and they said, "we want this government and you're not going to have it . . . we're the ones that own this country and we claimed it." So the Americans said, "no we're not going to have that." And we had a war. [What happened at the end of the war?] We won. [What does that mean?] It means that our country is free from any other countries.

But whatever understanding may have been initiated by fifth-grade instruction was not strong enough to last: Witness Daniel's Civil War confusion before eighth-grade instruction.

Before eighth-grade instruction:

> Well the president didn't; the people didn't agree that there should be slaves in the South. And the South wanted the slaves and the North didn't want the slaves. And they had a big fight over it and everyone started to rebel against the north or the south. And there were brothers and sisters fighting against each other.

Students' Historical Accounts Leave Loose Ends

The final trend we comment on is that of students who, after instruction in eighth grade, did manage to put together a decent account of Revolutionary War events. As mentioned previously, however, there was a tendency on the part of these students to underplay the most significant consequence of the war, that of the founding of their country, and to provide a number of "loose ends," associated events, artifacts, or characters of the period without tying them to the sequence of events. Note, for example, how the Boston Tea Party figured into the accounts of Eric and Daniel:

Eric — After eighth-grade instruction:

> The colonies didn't like the way they were run and so they started a rebellion. And the British didn't want them to fight. So they tried stuff like throwing the Boston Tea Party. And they decided to just start fighting. And a couple other countries joined in with them. And they fought many years and battles. . . . And the Americans finally won. [Do you know what they didn't like about the way things were run?] They didn't like all the taxes.

Daniel — After eighth-grade instruction:

> The government started taxing them. . .and the other country that the government was in, they didn't have to get taxed. . . . And people were getting upset about it. The soldiers were giving the Americans a rough time. [Tell me about that government.] It was a monarchy and the king ruled everything. [Was there a country involved?] Yeah, England . . . [Anything else?] Well, I don't know. They got upset about the taxes and they threw the tea in the river . . . and they started to fight with the soldiers. And everyone started to rebel against England.

Eric brought up the Tea Party as if it were a tantrum that the colonists threw in the midst of general anger at Great Britain; Daniel seemed at least aware that the event was associated with disputes over taxes. But neither student, as was typical of all those we interviewed, described how British and colonial interactions culminated in that event, or its role in moving the struggle toward full-blown revolution.

The concern with responses such as those Eric and Daniel gave after eighth-grade instruction is not so much that the responses are in themselves poor. Rather, given their lack of integration of ideas and lack of emphasis on the outcome, the concern is with what these students will retain of their studies in a year or two—considering the record of how fifth-grade instruction fared.

The kind of responses that are accurate but miss the mark in some way suggests that instruction is not doing well by these students. Two rounds of instruction in American history seem to leave many students with very basic facts that a dispute between Britain and the colonies led to a war that brought a successful outcome for the colonies. But instruction seems to have failed to help students construct the significance of that outcome and how the struggle with Britain laid the roots for the kind of nation the United States became.

FINAL COMMENTS

What does our longitudinal look suggest about students' history learning across 3 years' time and two rounds of instruction? The impression left from students' responses across the 3 years was that students entered their first encounter with American history with very little prior knowledge and took from their initial instruction some facts and some very general ideas about the period of the American Revolution. The information students took was often incomplete, sometimes confused. This pattern of confusion was quite evident before their next encounter with instruction in eighth grade, suggesting that what students had learned had not remained with them.

After eighth-grade instruction, much of the confusion ceased, but the same basic results seen after fifth grade—of factual details combined but not integrated with a general impression—still characterized many students' knowledge. The picture of how their country began was not complete or coherent for these students. The versions of history they had developed seemed like events pasted together, lacking connections and motivations. What had been missing from the fifth-grade accounts of history only rarely were expanded or elaborated through eighth-grade instruction. It occurred to us as we pored over the data that it was difficult to distinguish fifth-grade responses from those of students after eighth grade.

What accounts for the state of students' historical knowledge at this point in their schooling? A great portion of the responsibility rests with the textbooks. The textual materials that dominate social studies classrooms are simply not adequate to the task of presenting students with coherent, comprehensible accounts of history. A frequent response to this indictment is that the teacher should/does fill in much information, and therefore the quality of the texts is not a compelling issue. A problem with this line of thinking is that the texts do not serve as good resources from which teachers can identify and develop ways to fill in their students' knowledge. The textbooks do not offer sufficient raw material to help teachers decide what to emphasize and to generate explanations of text ideas. Many teachers need this kind of assistance because, at the elementary level, few have the background in subject matter that allows them to easily take stock of the texts and provide students with the kind of enhanced information they need.

The issue is that the distance to be covered between what textbooks offer and what comprises a coherent representation of historical events is too great for what many teachers have time or experience for. Indeed, we found in our research that even a carefully developed and crafted lesson presented before students read the text on the Revolutionary War period did not compensate for an inadequate text (McKeown et al., 1992).

How can this state of affairs in history instruction be improved? One proven ingredient is more coherent texts. Texts that exhibit more coherence have repeatedly been shown to bring about enhanced understanding of the causal sequence of events and ideas presented in textbooks (Beck et al., 1991; McKeown et al., 1992). Another ingredient in improving history learning is class discussion of the kind that prompts and allows students to reflect on what they have read and to raise issues and construct the connections that make the text content meaningful.

A third ingredient is actually a notion that is implied in both the recommendation for more coherent text and the suggestion for meaningful discussions, because they both require devoting more time to learning a topic. And that notion is captured in the phrase "coverage versus depth." What we have now in social studies books, and indeed most elementary social studies classes, are yeoman efforts at coverage — textbooks that begin with Native Americans crossing the Bering Strait and end with present day topics. And we have teachers racing to include all this material in a year's curriculum. Yet, although the material may be included in the textbook and included in the lessons, that inclusion does not carry over to students' repertoires. This kind of quick, surface coverage simply does not promote learning. It has been our experience that teachers are often reluctant to give up coverage to dwell more deeply on fewer topics, believing that their students will be missing out on something. But to the contrary, students are now getting so precious little of what is covered, it would be better to select a few topics and explore them with the kind of reflective attention that can bring about understanding and learning.

The current state of history instruction in the elementary grades represents the misuse of significant resources. A teacher's time in covering the textbook topics and drilling students on factual knowledge is not a productive use of teachers' abilities. Filling students' learning opportunities with rapid-fire presentation of inadequate text accounts is a poor use of students' time and attention. Some serious rethinking of the goals of history instruction for young students and the resources needed to achieve the goals is required. Similar thought needs to be given to the types of experiences that help students achieve those goals. In particular, some significant understandings about learning, its complexity, and its constructive nature need to come into play.

ACKNOWLEDGMENT

The research described in this chapter was supported by the Learning Research and Development Center, University of Pittsburgh, supported by funds from the Office of Educational Research and Improvement (OERI), United States Department of Education, and by a grant from the A. W. Mellon Foundation. The opinions expressed do not necessarily reflect the position or policy of OERI or the Mellon Foundation, and no official endorsement should be inferred.

REFERENCES

Alexander, A. (1960). The gray flannel cover on the American history textbook. *Social Education, 24*, 11–14.

Beck, I. L., McKeown, M. G., & Gromoll, E. W. (1989). Learning from social studies texts. *Cognition and Instruction, 6*(2), 99–158.

Beck, I. L., McKeown, M. G., Sinatra, G. M., & Loxterman, J. A. (1991). Revising social studies text from a text-processing perspective: Evidence of improved comprehensibility. *Reading Research Quarterly, 26*, 251–276.

Black, J. B., & Bern, H. (1981). Causal coherence and memory for events in narratives. *Journal of Verbal Learning and Verbal Behavior, 20*, 267–275.

Chiesi, H. L., Spilich, G. J., & Voss, J. F. (1979). Acquisition of domain-related information in relation to high and low domain knowledge. *Journal of Verbal Learning and Verbal Behavior, 18*, 275–290.

FitzGerald, F. (1979). *America revised: What history textbooks have taught our children about their country, and how and why those textbooks have changed in different decades.* New York: Vintage.

Frederiksen, J. R. (1981). Understanding anaphora: Rules used by readers in assigning pronominal referents. *Discourse Processes, 4*, 323–348.

Harcourt Brace Jovanovich, Inc. (1984). *Metropolitan Achievement Test.* Orlando, FL: Author.

Just, M. A., & Carpenter, P. A. (1987). *The psychology of reading and language comprehension.* Rockleigh, NJ: Allyn and Bacon.

McKeown, M. G., & Beck, I. L. (1990). The assessment and characterization of young learners' knowledge of a topic in history. *American Educational Research Journal, 27,* 688–726.

McKeown, M. G., Beck, I. L., Sinatra, G. M., & Loxterman, J. A. (1992). The contribution of prior knowledge and coherent text to comprehension. *Reading Research Quarterly, 27,* 79–93.

Palmer, J. R. (1967). American history. In C. B. Cox & B. G. Massialas (Eds.), *Social studies in the United States* (pp. 131–149). New York: Harcourt Brace and World.

Pearson, P. D., Hansen, J., & Gordon, C. (1979). The effect of background knowledge on young children's comprehension of explicit and implicit information. *Journal of Reading Behavior, 11,* 201–209.

Perfetti, C. A. (1985). *Reading ability.* New York: Oxford University Press.

Trabasso, T., Secco, T., & van den Broek, P. (1984). Causal cohesion and story coherence. In H. Mandl, N. L. Stein, & T. Trabasso (Eds.), *Learning and comprehension of text* (pp. 83–111). Hillsdale, NJ: Lawrence Erlbaum Associates.

White, J. J. (1988). Searching for substantial knowledge in social studies texts. *Theory and Research in Social Education, XVI* (2), 115–140.

11 How Students Use Texts to Learn and Reason About Historical Uncertainty

Charles A. Perfetti, M. Anne Britt, Jean-François Rouet,
Mara C. Georgi, and Robert A. Mason
University of Pittsburgh

To learn history is to learn a story: to come to know the major characters, events, and simple causal relations among events. Of course, an historian or history educator may reject the suggestion that story learning is the heart of history learning. Real learning in history entails going beyond simple stories to interpret, construct explanations, and generally to negotiate uncertainty surrounding the events. In effect, learning history requires at least primitive use of some of the text and interpretive skills employed in historical analysis.

The *teaching* of history, however, because of limitations in time and resources and because of traditions of testing, often emphasizes learning the story to the exclusion of introducing the student to the complexity of historical analysis. The interplay of social forces, for example, is likely to be sacrificed in the classroom for a simple story about dates and names. Carretero, Asensio, and Pozo (1991) referred to the European "Discovery" of America to make this contrast. Is it a story about Columbus and his relationship to the Spanish King and Queen? Or a story of how 15th-century social and economic forces promoted explorations with long-term consequences in Europe and America? As Carretero et al. pointed out, the concepts needed to elaborate the social forces story "pose a rather strong cognitive demand" (p. 29) and make for difficult learning. In contrast, learning history as a story takes advantage of the compatibility of story forms with the cognitive dispositions of the learner. We suggest that an educational goal that emphasizes a higher standard of learning must accommodate rather than reject the cognitive advantage of story learning.

There is nothing incompatible about a story approach and the complex explanation approach to understanding history. Stories provide the basic representations of history for the student. Knowledge of the stories of history is merely the minimum standard we would be willing to apply to answer the question of whether a student has attained competence in historical topics.

A higher standard applies to what we call "historical literacy." To engage in discourse on history goes beyond storytelling to include, as part of the analysis of the story, some implicit knowledge of the "methods" of history. Such knowledge means realizing, for example, that the received story is an interpretation, a simplification of complex events that may be distorting. It implies awareness that evidence counts, that elements of a story come from records of various kinds, and some awareness of the distinction between primary and secondary sources.

In our work we addressed both the basic cognitive representation issue – the understanding of history as a story – and the issue of the use of texts as evidence. At one level, these two issues are on either side of a boundary between basic and higher standards of historical literacy. At another level, the issues reflect complementary components of how a student uses a text in constructing an understanding of historical events. The story is the student's beliefs about the event structure. Textual evidence helps the student determine his or her belief in the story.

STORIES AND CAUSAL MODELS

In claiming that history is understood as a story, we have a specific idea in mind: Understanding history is having a mental model, a temporal-causal model, of historical events. Our assumption is that this temporal-causal model is one of the type that serves story understanding generally. Trabasso and van den Broek (1985) developed a causal analysis of narratives and argued that the comprehension of stories depends on establishing story coherence through causal relations (Trabasso, Secco, & van den Broek, 1984, Trabasso & van den Broek, 1985). Earlier work on story understanding also took note of causal structures in accounting for what readers remember from stories (Black & Bower, 1979; Omanson, 1982). Although work on story grammars, following Rumelhart (1975), emphasized story components rather than event connections in their analyses (Mandler & Johnson, 1977; Stein & Glenn, 1979; Thorndyke, 1977), even these approaches imply a role for causal connections as part of the meaning of event categories. The point of departure of more recent work has been the explicit and fine-grain analysis of causal structures.

Causal connections, which link events through causal event chains, are what make a story coherent and memorable. The "psychological reality" of these causal structures is seen when people judge the importance of story statements, recall stories, and write summaries of stories (Trabasso & van den

Broek, 1985; van den Broek & Trabasso, 1986). Although the case for causal structures as mental representations of stories appears to be quite strong, it is not completely clear how comprehension processes make use of this structure during (as opposed to after) reading. Does a search for causal structures guide comprehension, or do such structures merely reflect what comprehension brings automatically by other means? The answer to this question is not clear and probably depends on particular reader and text circumstances.[1]

In our study of history learning, we developed a system of causal analysis related to that of Trabasso and van den Broek (1985). Our use of causal structures, however, assumes not that these structures guide comprehension, merely that they represent what a person knows (or believes) about some historical topic. Additionally, we see causal structures as research tools — a means of assessing what students learn when they learn historical material. To assess what someone has learned about the Panama Canal story, we examine which parts of the causal model have been learned. To ask whether two students have the same knowledge is to ask whether their causal models are the same.

For example, we assume that to understand the Panama Canal story is to have a mental model that links a sequence of events by temporal-causal connections.[2] The Panama Canal Story relates the events leading to the

---

[1]Although we believe that *when* things occur in comprehension is a crucial question for theories of comprehension, this "online" issue is less relevant for the topic we address here. Perhaps all causal connections are established "online." Perhaps only explicitly expressed connections are established. In any case, it is sufficient to assume that causal relations have some kind of status as mental representations, regardless of whether they are established immediately as each potential causal event is encountered.

[2]There is a bit of equivocation in the idea of temporal–causal connections. First there is uncertainty about causality. Was there a causal relationship between Colombia's rejection of a canal treaty with the United States and the Panama revolution? Or just an incidental temporal relationship? Such uncertainty is abundant in history, and the goal of historical scholarship is essentially to reduce that uncertainty. For the nonexpert, however, there is either uncertainty or a belief about a causal relation. That is, someone may believe that the Colombian action was a sufficient condition for U.S. support for the revolution and that this support was necessary for the success of the revolution.

Such uncertainty is specific to a particular case. But there is a second equivocation in the basic idea of temporal–causal relations. Whether one event *causes* another in any strong sense, that is, whether one event is necessary and sufficient for the occurrence of a second event, may be unknowable in principle in history. Some events seem clearly necessary for others to have occurred — for there to be normal international negotiations with Panama, it was necessary that Panama be independent of Columbia. Most of the more interesting historical episodes, however, appear to fail this test. Was it necessary for the United States to encourage an uprising in order for the Panamanian Revolution to be successful? For it to occur? Was the Spanish-American War a necessary cause of renewed interest in the Canal Project? Finding sufficient causes is even more difficult, and finding necessary and sufficient causes seems virtually impossible in history.

U.S. acquisition of the rights to build a U.S.-owned canal on the Isthmus of Panama. Our analysis connects states (e.g., the U.S. desire for a canal) and events (e.g., the Panamanian revolution) by temporal-causal connections. Some of the links that a student must have in his or her mental model are the following: the U.S. desire to have faster commerce and military routes *motivated* the United States to begin negotiations for a canal; Panama's status as a part of Colombia *motivated* the United States to negotiate with Colombia; Colombia's rejection of the U.S.-offered treaty *motivated* Panama to revolt; and the successful Panamanian revolution *enabled* the United States to negotiate with Panama.

Figure 11.1 illustrates a causal analysis of the Panama Canal Story. It captures the essential events of the story, linking them together with temporal-causal predicates. This causal representation was also used as a reliable scoring template (95% interscorer agreement) to indicate what subjects remember from any text that tells the story. (See Britt, Rouet, Georgi, & Perfetti, 1994, and Perfetti, Britt, & Georgi, in press, for a detailed discussion of the causal analysis.)

HISTORICAL LITERACY

Historical literacy involves not only the learning of historical events, but also the use of interpretive reasoning. Reasoning about historical topics, like reasoning in other domains, requires a use of evidence, argument, and interpretive strategies. Students, like historians, can come to appreciate that history stories may reflect different lines of evidence that are illuminated through different sources. These sources can be distinguished in a number of ways — documents versus nondocuments, witness evidence versus non-witness evidence, and deliberately transmitted information versus unintentionally transmitted information (Shafer, 1974). Students can learn to evaluate uncertainties in the available evidence, not necessarily in expert fashion, but in a manner that goes beyond a naive and unanalyzed acceptance of the story as truth.

When we speak of causal relationships, therefore, we are speaking loosely, not by the rules of logical inference, but by plausible inferences. The "temporal" in "temporal–causal" suggests the sense in which this is true. When one event follows another event in time, the temporal relation is taken to be temporal–causal if the circumstances seem to support a causal inference. The first event may have been necessary for the second, it may have been sufficient, or, probably the most common case, it may have been neither. The last case can be considered a probabilistic causal relation. Event 2 was made more likely to occur because of Event 1 in the context of other factors. Temporal–causal relations include all these possibilities. When someone knows an historical topic, what he or she knows is the temporal–causal relations that are the core of the story.

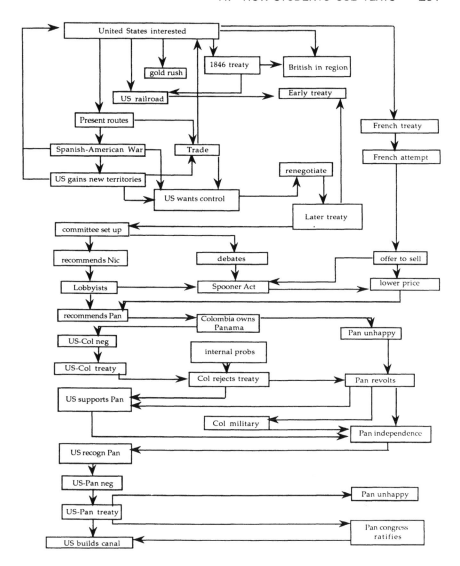

FIG. 11.1.   Streamlined representation of the history of the acquisition of the Panama Canal.

An example of what it means to expect students to have a sense of historical evidence comes from Wineburg (1991), who studied differences between historians and novices (high school students). In examining paintings depicting the Battle of Lexington, students showed little tendency to use information from written historical documents as standards against which to compare the accuracy of the pictures. Asked to choose which picture was the most accurate depiction of the battle scene, the students made limited use of historical documents that could provide critical information, even though they had just read the texts. Historians actively sought information from such documents, whereas students seemed unaware of the privileged status of the documents. As Wineburg concluded, more facts about the American revolution would not necessarily be helpful for such students

> When they remain ignorant of the basic heuristic used to create historical interpretations, when they cannot distinguish among different types of evidence, and when they look to a textbook for the "answer" to historical questions — even when that textbook contradicts primary sources from both sides. (p. 84)

Wineburg (1991) identified three heuristics used by experts in reasoning from historical evidence that could be taught to students. Experts notice and evaluate the source of the document (sourcing), check the facts mentioned in the document against those in other documents (corroboration), and set events in a larger context (contextualization).

To repeat an important caveat, we do not suggest that the goals of historical literacy correspond to the full attainment of historical research skills. However, we take the view that there is value in acquainting students with the use of evidence and argument in history learning. This implies having an appreciation of historical evidence and an awareness of the origins of the stories of history.

In the following sections, we summarize two lines of research we have carried out over the past few years. We regard the two lines of work as complementary: One focuses on learning a history story, and the other examines the use of evidence in interpreting controversial parts of the story.

THE LEARNING STUDY

The Learning Study attempted to mimic a realistic learning situation — one that approximates some of the kind of learning activities college students commonly encounter in history classes. The results of this study are reported elsewhere (Britt et al., 1994; Perfetti et al., in press) and are only summarized here.

This study had two basic parts. The first focused on the events leading up to the building of the Panama Canal (the Acquisition Story). The second part dealt with a recent historical issue related to the Acquisition Story: the 1978 negotiations between Panama and the United States over the future ownership of the Panama Canal. Here, however, we limit consideration to the first part of the study.

In this study, six paid undergraduate students (4 males, 2 females; age range 18-25) participated in an extended learning situation in which, over several weeks time, they read four different texts on the U.S. acquisition of the Panama Canal Zone. The first text was a neutral and relatively short text (about 1,700 words) written by the experimenters to provide a brief introduction to the events and characters. The second text, written by The Center for Strategic Studies (1967), was also relatively neutral. However, it was clearly authored by Americans. Texts 3 and 4 were longer texts that were mostly polemical attempts to influence public opinion in the United States. Both were published in 1978, during the debates in the United States concerning the ratification of a new U.S.-Panama treaty that returned sovereignty of the canal zone to Panama. One, by Representative Philip Crane (a republican from Illinois), strongly argued against the treaty. The other text was written by a Latin American scholar at Cornell University, Walter LaFeber. LaFeber's (1978) text argued in favor of treaty ratification.

After every text assignment, subjects were asked a series of questions about the story. Their answers provided data on the course of their learning over a period of weeks. Because the focus here is on students' use and evaluation of history texts, we do not discuss the comprehension results in detail (see Britt et al., 1994, for more details about the comprehension results). Students learned the main story rapidly. Events, as defined by our causal analysis, were largely learned by the second text assignment. Learning the supporting facts of the story was also rapid, but somewhat slower than the learning of events.

Understanding Uncertainty

Although the students learned the events quickly and gradually built up a representation of the details of the events, there was an additional question: We were also interested in whether students without much history training used some of the interpretative skills involved in reading history.

Detecting Author Bias.   One such skill is detecting the bias of the author of the text. After each text assignment we asked the subjects, "Did the author present a neutral coverage of the events? If not, what do you think the author's attitude was?" The students' first text was, in fact, as neutral as possible; there was no interpretation and no slanted or colorful wording. The second text was written for an American audience for policymaking and could be considered as taking an American perspective, but again there was very little interpretation and no biased phrasing. The final two texts were both selected because they presented a bias. The bias in text 3 was achieved by selective omission of events, including author interpretation and opinion and using slanted and colorful language. The bias in text 4 was achieved by selective omission of events and included author interpretation and opinion.

We found that all but one of the subjects could detect bias in texts; the one exception thought that all of the texts gave a neutral presentation. The five remaining subjects detected bias in at least two of the three texts with bias, while correctly judging the first text to be neutral.

Although subjects could detect bias when asked, it is not clear that they used this skill actively when reading. One subject said, "I only thought about a real bias when I was getting questioned." Although this particular comment was in response to the unbiased first text, it does illustrate the possibility that asking questions made subjects more aware of bias during later assignments.

Most responses concerning the author's attitude were simple statements that the author had an attitude about something. Occasionally, however, subjects elaborated their judgments. They suggested three factors that constituted author bias: selectively omitting events, interpreting events to persuade the reader, and using slanted or colorful language. In two cases subjects mentioned that the author skipped information. One subject mentioned, "He skips U.S. businessmen; he doesn't mention Cromwell and their involvement like LaFeber did. He was conservative, didn't say enough about the Senators." In three cases, subjects mentioned that the author was trying to support a thesis and this was why they judged it as biased. As one subject put it: "[Crane was] pretty much U.S. supportive. He wanted to make it (pause) set the record straight. Show that the U.S. was completely fair in their dealings. He was pretty much trying to show that the U.S. was the good guy."

In only one case did a subject ever specifically mention biased or slanted wording as a reason for judging a text as biased. Failure to note biased language is especially noteworthy because the author of one of the texts was quite adept at colorful prose: "Three years later, the government of Colombia (Panama was then only a geographical expression, a poverty-stricken, pestilential province of Colombia racked by chronic internal disorder)" (Crane, 1978, p. 4). It is interesting that no subject mentioned the biased language in this text.

Subjects were not uniformly quick to attribute bias, however. One subject, defending a judgment that a text was neutral, noted that "He [LaFeber] threw his opinions in but he let it be known that those were his opinions. He showed the facts then he showed how he thought. He never really took a side." One subject considered a document to be neutral if the author used distancing language: "It was pretty much neutral. He didn't even refer to Americans as Americans but always as North Americans. I found that rather odd. It was always the North Americans vs. the British or the North Americans dealing with the Panamanians." Finally, one subject seemed to think that vague writing meant that a document would be neutral: "Yes, kind of [neutral]. . . . I guess he was neutral by not giving all the facts. On the other hand, he can't sway you or give you an opinion." Interestingly, this same subject later said that text 4 was neutral because "I think he presented all the facts. I think he was pretty neutral."

Handling Inconsistencies Among Texts. A second skill needed to understand and reconstruct past events is that of reconciling inconsistencies among texts. Of special interest was a particular detail reported differently in the four texts: the time taken by the U.S.S. Oregon to get from its Pacific coast station to join battle in the Caribbean during the Spanish-American War. This long voyage around Cape Horn was mentioned to illustrate the military advantage of a shorter transoceanic route. Three of the texts gave durations of approximately 2 months (67 days in text 1, 2 months in text 2, and 68 days in text 4), but text 3 produced a much longer time (90 days).

Subjects learned this detail quickly and mentioned it quite often. The U.S.S. Oregon inconsistencies were handled in various ways, occasionally ignored, but usually assimilated either by using the most recently read text or the first-read text. One subject mentioned the Oregon only after the first text, appearing to ignore the later inconsistencies. A second subject gave the duration noted by the first text (67 days) on all but one occasion (after the second text he stated the duration, 2 months, given by second text). The other four subjects gave the duration from the most recent text. Two of these four subjects, however, also noted that there was an inconsistency in the texts about this point. One subject, after reading text 3, which gave the longest duration, said: "It took the U.S.S. Oregon 90 days or something like that — every time I read it it gets longer — to go all the way around South America."

Detecting the Incompleteness of Text. A third relevant text skill is detecting the incompleteness of the story. After each text assignment we asked the subjects, "What else would you like to know?" On only one occasion did a subject not want more information about something, and this was after having read all four texts. There were three classes of information that the subjects wanted. Some subjects wanted more information about the basic events and characters. They were still trying to be sure about details and facts of the basic story. Examples included: "They mentioned someone in Bogota and negotiations in Bogota but I don't know what Bogota is"; "I'm still hazy on how France got in there. I know we were there with Great Britain and we signed a treaty to get them out and then all of the sudden there was France." A second type of information subjects wanted was more historical context. Some examples were: "Maybe more about the Panamanian people themselves. What type of place was it to live in?"; "What happened between 1850 and 1878?"; "What was [the] political situation in Congress at the time?" Finally, subjects wanted more information on the controversial parts of the story, such as: "I'd like to probe Bunau-Varilla. Prove to me why he did the right thing for Panama even though it looks so skewed in [the] U.S.'s favor"; "More background on the treaties, what was said in the treaties — just names given"; "If Panamanians had wanted their independence, did [the] U.S. really push them? It's one thing to say Panamanians wanted to do it or they did it because if [the] U.S. was going to help [the revolution], they might as well [revolt]."

Resolving Conflicting Views. A fourth text skill is negotiating the uncertainty prompted by contradictory views given by different authors. We asked subjects four questions involving controversial issues that were covered differently by the texts: (a) "Were the United States' dealings with Colombia fair to Colombia?" (b) "Were the United States' dealings with Panama fair to Panama?" (d) "Was the United States' role in Panama's revolution justified? Why or Why not?" and (d) "Do you believe the United States should have negotiated with Bunau-Varilla or waited for the two Panamanian negotiators?" The first text, by design, was scarce in details on these controversial events. The subjects' initial response to these probes therefore provided relatively uninformed opinions. The same questions were asked again after every text. Thus, at most, subjects could change their opinion on 12 occasions (4 questions and 3 opportunities to change the response to each). We classified responses as "yes" (the United States was fair/just), "no" (the United States was not fair/just), "no answer" (no opinion or commitment on fairness/justness), or "both" (the United States was fair/just in some respect and not fair/just in other ways).

For the most part subjects did take a position in response to the opinion questions. On only 13% of the opportunities did subjects fail to draw a conclusion about the controversial issues, and most of these occasions occurred after either the first or second text, both of which were free of an opinion on the matter. Overall, subjects believed that the United States was fair in its dealings with Colombia and Panama in both the treaty negotiations and the revolution. Fifty percent of the opinions were that the United States was fair, whereas 26% of the opinions were that the United States was unfair, and 11% of the opinions were that, in part, the United States was fair and, in part, they were not fair.

We found reasoning about the uncertainties of the story to be tentative and affected by the text read most recently. There was an average of 7 opinion changes out of 12 opportunities. Five of the six subjects changed their opinion at least half the time. The opinion changes moved toward agreement with the most recently read text. The other subject was much more stable, changing his opinion on only two occasions. Additionally, this subject consistently was also very pro-American. He believed that the United States was fair on 88% of the questions, for example, "Fair is fair. If they didn't like it they didn't have to sign it"; "I think we knew we should've negotiated with Bunau-Varilla because the other guys might have gone for the other terms. I think the U.S. was just trying to get the best deal we could. Fair is fair. You signed it, that's it"; "Yes I think so. How it went for our advantage was good. If they had the advantage, they would've done it." Other than this one subject who was more driven by his prior beliefs, the subjects' opinions were rather changeable and tentative, affected by the most recent text they read.

Although subjects were swayed in their opinions, they showed little spontaneous interest in the possible role that other documents might have in helping them come to conclusions. Subjects did not mention that treaties, cables, official orders, or other types of documents might aid in their forming their own opinion or checking the validity of the author's interpretation, either in response to the fairness question, or in response to the specific question "What else would you like to know?" Only one subject read the treaties given as optional reading, and that was a subject who, after the first reading, mentioned that he would like to know more about the treaties. No other subject asked for primary documents or used the primary documents given them.

Summary

Subjects learned the basic history story rapidly, while more slowly acquiring the supporting details over successive readings. The causal model effectively captured the essentials of the story that they had learned. Subjects demonstrated mixed abilities in text-based reasoning. Although all subjects, except one, were able to detect author bias, their opinions on controversial events showed a high degree of malleability and tentativeness, using information from texts to modify judgments previously stated. When given the opportunity to ask for additional information, subjects did not request primary documents.

THE DOCUMENTS STUDY

Subjects' failure to use provided evidence (treaties) and their failure to ask for other documents (e.g., treaties, cables, letters) directed our attention toward examining their understanding of and use of documents as evidence in historical reasoning. It is not surprising that our students were not aware that they were missing evidence (i.e., primary documents) while trying to understand the story of the Panama Canal. They were satisfied learning the story as told by each author. The results are in line with those from bright high school students who rated textbooks as the most trustworthy of documents, in contrast to historians who, detecting both the text's inconsistencies with better evidence and the bias of its "subtext," rated it the least trustworthy of documents (Wineburg, 1991).

This problem leads to an examination of how students understand the relative privilege of certain types of documents when forming opinions about controversies in history. The use and interpretation of documents is of critical importance to historical researchers. Are college students aware of the privileged status documents have as evidence? How do they use texts as evidence in dealing with the uncertainties of the stories?

Twenty-four undergraduate students (17 males and 7 females) from the University of Pittsburgh participated in a 4-hour experiment. There was also one graduate student in history who served as an expert.

The undergraduate subjects were between the ages of 18 and 31, comprising 13 freshmen, 5 sophomores, 3 juniors, and 3 seniors. Reading ability, as measured by the Nelson-Denny Reading Test, ranged from the 16th percentile to the 99th percentile, with an average of the 54th percentile (based on the scale for sophomores; Brown, Bennett, & Hanna, 1981).

The subjects varied greatly in their knowledge of history, in general, and of Panama, in particular. Only 10 of the subjects had taken a college history course (one subject had taken 10, one subject had taken 3, and eight subjects had taken 1). Subjects' historical knowledge was evaluated by a three-part history knowledge test. General knowledge was assessed by subjects' answers to 15 two-part open-ended questions on general history topics (e.g., What was the Weimar Republic? When was it?). Their scores ranged from 10% to 80%, with a mean of 40% correct. The expert was able to answer every question correctly. Specific Panama history knowledge was assessed by a 21-question test covering the Panama Canal and its history (e.g., Why is the canal used?). The subjects scored between 6% and 71%, with a mean of 44% correct. The expert answered 81% correctly. Finally, geographic knowledge was assessed using a 9-question map test. Most subjects accurately located the targets relevant to the history of the Panama Canal: United States, Panama, Colombia, and the Pacific Ocean. Overall the scores ranged from 11% to 100%, with a mean of 76%. Again the expert had a perfect score.

The period of the acquisition of the Panama Canal was segmented into four controversial problems for which a large number of documents were available. For example, one controversy involved the extent to which the United States participated in the Panamanian revolution. For each of these problems, we searched the document literature and sorted documents into three very broad categories: secondary, intermediate, and primary. These categories were differentiated according to the following four features: when the document was written (before, during, slightly after, or significantly after the events), whether the author was a participant (or not), the document status (official, public, private), and the bias of the author of the document (defending own actions, commenting and interpreting events, or neutrally stating and describing events). There are, of course, additional features one can use. Our choice of these features allowed us to create a small set of documents that could be managed within the format of our study.

The features of each document for the four problems are summarized in Table 11.1. The *secondary documents* were documents written after the events, by a nonparticipant (historian or politician); they were published and were considered biased (authors supported opposing interpretations of the events). The *intermediate documents* were documents written either at the time or slightly after, by a participant in the events, with a biased perspective of either defending his or her own actions or commenting on others' actions. We considered these documents "intermediate" because each had features in common with primary documents but at least one feature that qualified it as a interpretation of the events. The *primary documents* were excerpts from letters, treaties, and official correspondences. They were written at the time of or before (e.g., 1846 Treaty) the controversy, the authors were always participants, the purpose of the document was to state rather than comment, and the document was official (except for the Roosevelt letters). These documents were unbiased (again with the exception of the Roosevelt letters) but could be interpreted to support one side or the other. All the documents were very short excerpts of between 76 and 383 words, with an average of 177 words.

In addition to these documents, we also prepared a *textbook document* and a list of facts for each problem. The facts we included represented the basic, noncontroversial version of the story and were agreed on by all the

TABLE 11.1
Features of the Documents in the Document Study

	Time written	Written by a participant	Document status	Author bias
Secondary	After	No	Public	Biased
Textbook	After	No	Public	Neutral
Intermediate	During or slightly after	Yes	Variable	Biased
Primary	Before or during	Yes	official (*)	Neutral (*)

*Except in problem 1 (Roosevelt letters).

sources. Like the secondary documents, the textbook was written after the events, by a nonparticipant. Like the primary documents, the purpose was to describe and state the events in a neutral way.

The experiment was carried out in three sessions. The first session included the history knowledge tests. Also, in order to give subjects an understanding of the basic story of the U.S. acquisition of a canal in Panama, they were given a 2,200-word text to read (a modified version of text 2 from the Learning Study). We edited the text to ensure that the material related to the four controversies was very general or vague. Afterward, subjects were given 11 comprehension questions (e.g., "Name two reasons why the French attempt to build a canal failed"; "What actions did the U.S. take during the revolution?") to ensure basic comprehension of the story. Subjects were also given each of the four controversy problem statements (e.g., "To what extent did the United States participate in the planning of the Panama revolution?"). We informed them that we merely wanted their opinion because the text was not very detailed.

Based on subjects' combined scores on the history test (general history, Panama knowledge, and geography), 12 subjects were assigned to the primary group. This group was given access to primary documents for each of the four controversy problems. The 12 other subjects were assigned to the secondary group[3]. The subjects in this group did not have access to primary documents. Instead, they received additional secondary documents. The expert was assigned to the primary group.

In the second session, subjects were given the first two controversial problems in a hypertext environment run on an Apple Macintosh IIsi. They were first given the problem statement – "To what extent did the United States participate in the planning of the Panama revolution?" Then they were given a screen that had a list of main facts presented in chronological order. When they had read these, subjects pressed a button to get a menu of the sources of the seven available documents (author name, credentials, type of document and date). Figure 11.2 shows the menu screen for problem 2. The first five documents were the same for both the primary and secondary group: two secondary documents, two intermediate documents, and the textbook passage. The final two documents were two additional secondary documents (secondary group) and two primary documents (primary group). Any selection in the menu resulted in the presentation of an extended source of the document. Subjects then could decide to read the actual documents or to go back to the menu. Previous selections were

---

[3]The groups had similar prior history knowledge as determined by the combined score on the history knowledge test. The secondary group averaged 29 correct of 60 (with a variance of 13), whereas the primary group averaged 28 correct of 60 (with a variance of 12).

marked in the menu to ease the study process. Subjects were required to select each source at least once for inspection.

For each of the four problems, subjects were given 15 min to study the list of main facts and the set of seven documents. When the subjects had studied the documents and believed they had an informed opinion on the controversy, they could exit the presentation system. Then they were to write a 1-page essay expressing their opinion. They were not able to use the documents while writing, but were given a list of the names and dates mentioned in the documents and the sources of the documents to avoid memory problems. After completing their essay, the subjects were asked to rank the seven documents according to their usefulness ("the extent it helped you build up your informed opinion") and their trustworthiness ("the extent you trust what the author says") on a 7-point scale. They were also asked to briefly justify their ranking of each document. In the third session, subjects followed the same procedure for the final two controversies.

Our focus here is restricted to the results of document evaluation. (For a

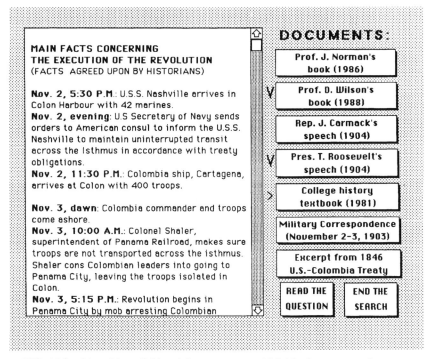

FIG. 11.2.   List of facts (left) and document menu (right) in the prototype hypertext system (the marked items have been previously selected).

more complete discussion of the results see Rouet, Britt, Mason, & Perfetti, in preparation.) First we report subjects' ranking of the various documents and their justification of those rankings. Then we examine how the results of the document study address students' ability to deal with uncertainty. In particular, we address three questions answered in the previous study: Do students detect author bias? Do they detect incompleteness of texts? Are they able to resolve conflicting views?

Evaluating Documents

We analyzed subjects' judgments of the trustworthiness and usefulness of documents. Subjects ranked the documents for each problem on a 7-point scale, with a 7 corresponding to the most trustworthy or most useful document and a 1 corresponding to the least trustworthy or least useful document. Although the results were consistent across problems, the pattern of ranking of the primary documents in problem 1 (letters) differed from the other three problems (cables and treaties). This difference may reflect the primary document features for problem 1 (type of document and the bias of the author; see Table 11.1). Because of its uncharacteristic pattern, problem 1 was excluded from any analysis about primary documents.

Ranking of Trustworthiness.   Figure 11.3 shows the average ranking of document trustworthiness collapsed across problems 2 to 4. One interesting comparison is how the textbook was judged by the two groups. The secondary subjects ranked the textbook as most trustworthy for all three problems (average ranking = 6.5). The primary group also trusted the textbook (average ranking = 5.1), but they always ranked the primary documents as more trustworthy (average ranking = 6.1). Thus, when subjects are given primary documents (e.g., treaties and cables), their trust in the textbook is reduced. It is also worth noting that the ranking pattern of the expert was similar to the pattern of the primary group: In problems 2 to 4, the expert gave the textbook an average rank of 4.7, and primary documents an average rank of 6.5.

Although there are some patterns across types of documents in their ranked trustworthiness, subjects did not make these judgments on the basis of document type alone. Their judgments showed sensitivity to the role of the document in the problem space. In each of the four problems, one of the intermediate documents was written by a participant defending his own actions (as one subject put it: "[It was] very biased, written in his best interest to cover his own ass."). Although the other intermediate document was also written by a participant, the author was commenting on the actions of another character rather than defending his own actions. As shown in Fig. 11.4, subjects in both groups were sensitive to this feature when

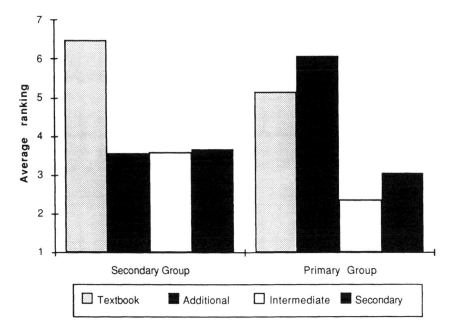

FIG. 11.3.   Average ranking of document trustworthiness (problems 2–4).

judging the trustworthiness of the document. The intermediate document written by a participant defending his own actions was clearly trusted less than the other intermediate document. Again, the expert's average rankings were similar (1.8 for defending authors; 4.8 for nondefending authors).

Ranking of Usefulness.   Figure 11.5 shows the average ranking of document usefulness collapsed across problems 2 to 4. By design, all the documents were relevant for all problem statements. Perhaps for this reason, there was less distinction among types of documents in the ranking of usefulness than in trustworthiness. The secondary group considered both the intermediate documents and textbook useful. The primary group ranked the primary documents as most useful. Thus, although the secondary group clearly trusted the textbook the most, they did not find it more useful than all other documents. Subjects given the primary documents consistently found these treaties and cables both more useful and more trustworthy than the other documents. The expert found the primary documents even more useful than the college students did (6.3 vs. 5.0).

Justification of Ranking Data.   Subjects were given the extended sources and asked to justify their trustworthiness and usefulness rankings. These revealed that subjects' answers in both groups were sensitive to

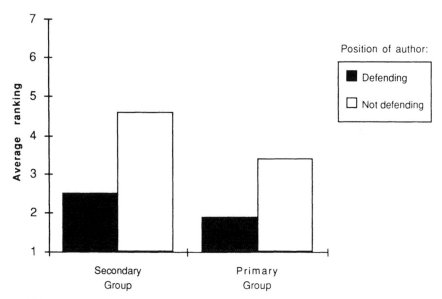

FIG. 11.4. Average ranking of trustworthiness for the intermediate documents (problems 1–4).

factors available in the extended source statement (e.g., the author or the type of document) and factors available only from their recall of the document (e.g., specific content statements). Features used by the subjects in their justifications fell into five categories. Figure 11.6 shows the proportion of judgments (collapsed over subjects and problems) in each category for both trustworthiness and usefulness justifications.

The first category concerned characteristics of the *author*; it was more frequently used in justifications of trustworthiness (33% of the responses) than in justifications of usefulness (16% of the responses). Several characteristics of the author were mentioned in these justifications, such as: author's credentials (e.g., "professor," "President"), author's motivations (e.g., "has his reputation at stake," "the President would say anything to keep from being impeached"), author's participation (e.g., "eyewitness account," "he had firsthand information"), and occasionally the subject's opinion of the author (e.g., "blind fool," "author is biased"). Characteristics of the author were mentioned equally often by both the secondary and primary subjects.

The second category was the type of *document*. Subjects mentioned both the type of text (e.g., "it's a textbook," "actual treaty") and an evaluation of the type of text (e.g., "college text would not print false facts," "as a treaty it has no bias"). Comments about the text were more frequent in justifica-

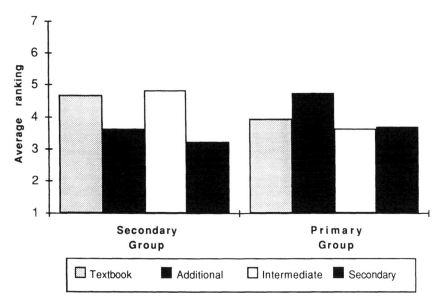

FIG. 11.5.   Average ranking of document usefulness (problems 2–4).

tions of trustworthiness (19% of the responses) than in usefulness (9% of the responses). Also the primary subjects mentioned the type of document more frequently than the secondary subjects. This increase in focus on the document type, however, occurred mainly for primary documents, rather than an overall increase across documents.

The third category of justification was a mention of the *content* of the document. Content-based justifications included: a statement of the position taken (e.g., "argued they influenced"), an evaluation of the perspective or tone (e.g., "biased," "too one-sided"), an evaluation of the argument (e.g., "nothing to support his claim," "well-supported argument"), and a statement or evaluation of the content ("mentions the New Panama Company," "denies guaranteeing intervention, but not hinting at it"). Unlike the author and document characteristics, comments about the content were more frequent in justifications of usefulness (49% of the responses) than trustworthiness (36% of the responses). Both primary and secondary subjects mentioned content characteristics equally often.

The fourth justification category was a reference to the subject's own *opinion* as part of his or her justification. A typical use of this category was the subject's explicit statement of his or her own opinion and the document's agreement with this opinion. For example, subjects made statements such as: "I don't believe it was a good deal so I don't believe him." This category of justifications was used more frequently for usefulness (10% of

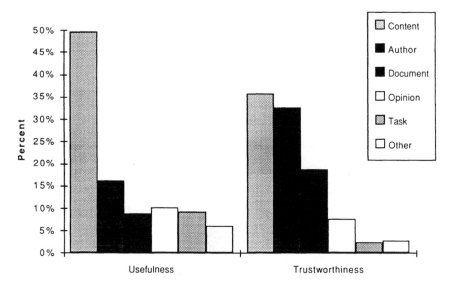

FIG. 11.6.   Percentage of each type of justification for document ranking.

the responses) than for trustworthiness justifications (8% of the responses) and was mentioned equally often by secondary and primary subjects.

The final category of justifications was *task* characteristics. Subjects occasionally justified a particular document rank by referring to another document or the document set as a whole. Examples included: "[It] did not agree with other documents he had written"; "Supplemented Stanton's arguments well"; "He informed the reader of events that the others lacked." This category was infrequent, but slightly more usefulness justifications (9% of the responses) were based on task characteristics than trustworthiness justifications (2% of the responses). Primary and secondary subjects mentioned characteristics of the task equally often.

In summary, subjects were sensitive to specific source factors in justifying both trustworthiness and usefulness of documents. Subjects judged the usefulness of a document based on its *content*, whereas they judged the trustworthiness of a document based on both its *content* and its source (i.e., *author* and *document type*).

Understanding Uncertainty

Students were sensitive to various features of documents in evaluating their trustworthiness and usefulness. They trusted primary documents more than others and mentioned many relevant aspects of the source and content in their justifications. Can we link these observations to those text-based reasoning skills we probed in the Learning Study? Although the tasks in the

Learning Study and the Documents Study were very different, we reexamine three of the skills probed in the Learning Study to see whether the Documents Study sheds any further light.

Detecting Author Bias. In the Learning Study we found that most of the students were able to detect the author's bias when reading multiple texts. Although the Document Study did not specifically ask subjects about the author's perspective, we can examine subjects' justifications to find evidence of sensitivity to author bias. Of the 169 times that subjects mentioned the perspective of the author in the justifications, 100 of these were statements that the content was biased, and 69 were statements that the content was neutral. Of the 100 cases of author bias, 99 were from either secondary or intermediate documents that were biased by design. One of the 100 cases was a judgment that one of the Roosevelt letters (considered primary here) was biased. On the other hand, the documents judged neutral were more often (90% of the time) neutral by design: the textbook and the primary documents. These were documents that did not take a stance on the controversy. In only 10% of the cases did subjects state that the author was neutral when the document was arguing for one side or the other of the controversy, that is, intermediate and secondary documents. Thus, consistent with the results of the first study, students showed a sensitivity to authors' perspectives in these texts.

Detecting Incompleteness of a Text. As in the Learning Study, we asked the subjects to indicate whether they detected incompleteness in the material given. Because the subjects' essay task went beyond merely learning the story, their responses were expected to be different from those of the Learning Study. The questions of interest concerned subjects' sensitivity to missing primary documents and missing but related parts of the story.

We asked subjects if there was anything else they would like to know about this story, if they lacked any documents, and if they would like more information on some aspect of the story. The subjects in the secondary condition were less satisfied with the documents they were given. On 60% of the occasions, the secondary subjects wanted more information, whereas on only 35% of the occasions did primary subjects state that they wanted more information. Responses of both groups of subjects included references to primary documents (e.g., treaties, orders, and correspondences). Subjects were also interested in having other points of view (e.g., the President of Panama's view and Colombia's view). Thus, subjects, even those not given any primary documents, showed an interest in having treaties and other primary documents to help them gain an informed opinion of the controversies that they addressed.

There is an interesting comparison that can be made between the two studies with respect to this question. When the task was to learn the story, as in the first study, subjects asked for information that would help fill in the gaps in their understanding of the events and relations among events. They did not ask for primary documents and, with one exception, did not read the primary documents they were given as optional reading. When the task, however, was to read multiple documents to come to an opinion about the events, as in the second study, subjects asked for both evidence and opinions.

Resolving Conflicting Views.   As in the first study, we asked subjects their opinion of controversial events for which they were provided conflicting views. Preliminary analysis of the opinion essays showed that subjects were more likely to take a stronger stance after studying the documents than before. In addition, the subjects who were given access to primary documents were more likely to change their overall opinion than secondary-documents subjects. Although both groups used facts to support their claims, the primary group was more likely to explicitly cite references. In fact, 65% of the primary group subjects made at least one reference in their essays, compared to 39% in the secondary group. Also primary group subjects referred mostly to primary documents (62%, compared to 38% in the secondary group). Interestingly, all document types (primary, secondary, intermediate) were cited, with the exception of the textbook. Thus, having access to primary documents seemed to increase the likelihood that the students would cite references for the facts that they produce in their essays.

Summary

The results of the Documents Study demonstrate that college students are able to use some relevant text-based reasoning methods. They were sensitive to bias in documents; they judged primary sources and texts as more trustworthy than sources with explicit bias (secondary and intermediate). In addition, students' understanding of and reasoning about a controversial problem in history was affected by having access to primary documents. Perhaps most interesting is the impact that such documents appeared to have on students' willingness to use documents of all types in constructing arguments. It seems clear that when several documents are simultaneously available and the nature of the historical controversy is made explicit, students understand the importance of primary documents.

GENERAL DISCUSSION

The two studies we described represent our two-dimensional approach to the question of historical literacy. On the first dimension, historical literacy was studied as the ability to understand the stories of history. On the second dimension, we approached historical literacy as a reasoning skill, a skill that involves interpreting multiple sources of historical evidence.

History As Story Understanding

History learning, at all levels, centers around the cognitive representation of events in terms of temporal-causal structures. The stories of history are learned, understood, and expressed in these terms. This is not a claim about the nature of history as a discipline, but the nature of cognitive structures. Indeed, so basic are these structures that they are accessible to young children, who show a natural grasp of stories that have the basic temporal-causal structure (Mandler & Johnson, 1977; Stein & Glenn, 1979). To put this point specifically in the context of history, we found that fifth-grade children, although they show some variability, are adept at learning the basic story of the Panama Canal (see Britt et al., 1994). (This study also found that some subjects learned an interesting tangential episode about problems with malaria encountered by the French in trying to build the canal somewhat better than the events linking the United States with Colombia and Panama. We are reluctant to overinterpret this observation, because we think it is largely a function of the text itself.)

The adult Learning Study reinforces this view of history as story learning. In addition, it provides an enriched view of the course of real learning with multiple texts. We observed the rapid learning of core events and the gradual acquisition of relevant (and even less relevant) details. But we found also that continued reading with additional assignments led to increased learning of core events. What students learned after one assignment, although quite representative of the whole story, was not in fact the whole story. Reading later assignments continued to help the student fill in the essential story. After each of the first two texts, subjects learned the early part of the story best. They focused on the U.S. motivations for building a canal and early obstacles (e.g., the Spanish-American War, the Gold Rush, the French attempt, and the British involvement). After each of the final texts, subjects began learning the end of the story much better. Here, they focused on the later obstacles and their resolution, for example, the U.S.-Colombian negotiations, the Panamanian revolution, and the U.S.-Panamanian negotiations. Although there are other possible explanations for this learning pattern, one plausible explanation is that understanding later causally related events is contingent on understanding the initial events.

An interesting question is raised by the results of the Learning Study. Is the value of multiple text assignments to increase the students' learning because of exposure to different texts or simply because of more reading? In other words, would it have mattered if our students had read the same text each time? We believe the multiple text format is uniquely responsible for effective learning on theoretical grounds. First, a new text controls students' attention in a way that a repeated text cannot. This is a simple matter of the arousal value of novel stimuli, a very general cognitive fact. More interesting is the possibility that differences in the manner of presenting information promote a more accessible cognitive representation. A representation based on a single text has a limited number of "access" points, that is, specific linguistic cues that connect to the representation. A representation based on different texts has a richer set of linguistic access points, reflecting the different ways in which the texts presented similar and identical information. Finally, there is a third level of possible advantage, related to the second. Texts with different perspectives may promote a deeper learning of the core events on which the texts agree. Having to confront contradiction may increase the stability of a representation, reinforcing the core of the story and delineating the points of contention. Our study is silent with respect to evidence on the value of multiple texts. We are pursuing the issue, however, in other work with high school students.

Reasoning with Multiple Documents

Our Learning Study tells us that college students with minimal history background are quite ready to engage history as interpretation. Our subjects were quick to engage the controversies and to detect bias in authors. Perhaps most interesting is the extent to which they showed an appropriate tentativeness in their opinions, in general. Although one student did live up to the expectation that ideologues are not about to be influenced by alternative perspectives, the majority used what they read each time to modify their understanding of the controversial issues. Between "wishy-washy" and "unalterable ideologue," our students were divided 5 and 1, respectively.

Overall, students had little trouble recognizing that history stories are interpreted events, and that controversies not only surround the interpretation but are perpetuated by historically based texts. However, they showed a dimmer awareness that additional documents might be useful to help them decide what to conclude. Part of this might be the factual and quasi-scholarly nature of the texts they read. When students have the impression that they are getting lots of real data through the author's citations, they might be less inclined to anticipate better sources. But the larger factor is probably simply the demands of the typical learning task. Although our learning study went well beyond what a typical text learning exercise might entail by forcing both multiple text reading and questioning designed to elicit awareness of controversy, it did not confront students with problems for which document use would have an obvious value. In contrast, the document study, by posing problems and presenting document choices in connection with the problems, allowed students to show their appreciation of the role of documents.

And what was the level of this appreciation? Like Wineburg (1991), we did find that students considered textbooks trustworthy. But here the question was different, because there was no built-in contradiction between the textbook and other information sources. The textbook was trustworthy, not because it was considered beyond reproach, but because it had useful information and a lack of "bias." (Students' inability to detect textbook bias is an interesting additional issue. There does seem to be a general assumption favoring the neutrality of textbooks.) More interesting, however, is the context sensitivity of students' judgments of documents. When students were given primary documents, they considered them trustworthy. When students did not have primary documents, they considered documents that have some of the features of primary documents ("intermediate" documents) as trustworthy. It is clear that college students do have a concept of document privilege that can be demonstrated in some situations.

Finally, we note the interesting value that primary documents have on how students develop arguments. We found that students provided with primary documents not only used them more in writing essays, but they made greater use of other documents. Our hypothesis was in fact that exposure to primary sources increases students' sensitivity to the possibility of citing sources in connection with arguments. The evidence supports this hypothesis.

A good deal of our work is directed to the development of accounts of causal events (Britt et al., 1994) and argument analysis (Rouet et al., in preparation). In both cases, there is a need for a clear methodological tool based on a theoretical analysis. In the first case, we linked the development of an analysis tool — the temporal-causal template — to a model of the cognitive representation of historical events. In the second case, we linked an analysis of the argument structure of an essay to assumptions (we are reluctant to term these assumptions a "theory") about the level of discourse that comprises the heart of short arguments. We believe that further progress in describing both history-as-story and history-as-interpretation depends on having such tools.

Learning to Learn History

We turn finally to the implications of our two-dimensional approach to instruction in history. If the history-as-story is justified on the grounds of cognitive compatibility, history-as-interpretation is justified by an appeal to a higher standard of historical literacy. The contrast between what is expected at the middle grades and what is expected at college is quite dramatic. Although not even college history courses typically challenge students with documents in the introductory courses, there is a clear expectation that students should gain competence in interpretation, explanation, and argument with whatever texts make up instruction. The lack of such emphasis in grade school history and even in high school history stands in contrast.

The question is whether such a division of cognitive labor is warranted by cognitive constraints, instructional resources, or both. The answer may prove to be complex. We suspect there is nothing in principle to prevent a document-based interpretation approach to history even in middle school — that is, so long as specific targets of breadth of coverage are relaxed. On the other hand, there are some constraints to deal with, including the demands that documents make on reading skill, domain knowledge, and a nondomain reasoning skill, based on something like "rules of evidence," that has quite general application in education.

Although we think there is a fairly general skill that underpins the ability to appreciate the role of evidence across domains, we suspect it is a skill fostered initially in some specific domain. Of course, domain-specificity versus generality is a complex issue, and we leave it at that — except to suggest that there is little specifically historical about realizing that evidence counts and that some kinds count more than others. How to explain such an ability short of an appeal to general scholarship-based education is a challenge. Whatever it is, there is no reason not to expect our history instruction to include it at least in secondary education. The obvious strategy is to take advantage of the superior position of story learning and to supplement it with complexity as early as possible.

ACKNOWLEDGMENTS

The research reported in this chapter was primarily supported by a grant from the Mellon Foundation. Additional funding was also provided by the Office of Educational Research and Improvement (OERI), United States Department of Education to the Center for Student Learning, Learning Research and Development Center. The opinions expressed do not necessarily reflect the position or policy of the Mellon Foundation or OERI and no official endorsement should be inferred.

REFERENCES

Black, J. B., & Bower, G. H. (1979). Episodes as chunks in narrative memory. *Journal of Verbal Learning and Verbal Behavior, 18*, 309–318.

Britt, M. A., Rouet, J.-F., Georgi, M. C., & Perfetti, C. A. (1994). Learning from history texts: From causal analysis to argument analysis. In G. Leinhardt, I. L. Beck, & C. Stainton (Eds.), *Teaching and learning in history* (pp. 47–84). Hillsdale, NJ: Lawrence Erlbaum Associates.

Brown J. I., Bennett, J. M., & Hanna, G. (1981). *The Nelson Denny Reading Test.* Chicago: The Riverside Publishing Company.

Carretero, M., Asensio, M., & Pozo, J. I. (1991). Cognitive development, historical time representation and causal explanations in adolescence. In M. Carretero, M. Pope, R. Simons, & J. I. Pozo (Eds.), *Learning and instruction: European research in an international context* (Vol. 3, pp 27-48). Oxford: Pergamon.

The Center for Strategic Studies. (1967). *Panama: Canal issues and treaty talks.* Washington, DC: Georgetown University Press.

Crane, P. M. (1978). *Surrender in Panama: The case against the treaty.* Ottawa, IL: Green Hill Publishers.

LaFeber, W. (1978). *The Panama Canal: The crisis in historical perspective.* New York: Oxford University Press.

Mandler, J. M., & Johnson, N. S. (1977). Remembrance of things parsed: Story structure and recall. *Cognitive Psychology, 9,* 111-151.

Omanson, R. C. (1982). The relation between centrality and story category variation. *Journal of Verbal Learning and Verbal Behavior, 21,* 326-337.

Perfetti, C. A., Britt, M. A., & Georgi, M. C. (in press). *Learning and reasoning from "real" texts: Case studies of history text learning.* Hillsdale, NJ: Lawrence Erlbaum Associates.

Rouet, J. F., Britt, M. A., Mason, R. A., & Perfetti, C. A. (in preparation). *Using multiple sources of evidence to study historical controversies.*

Rumelhart, D. E. (1975). Notes on a schema for stories. In D. G. Bobrow & A. Collins (Eds.), *Representation and understanding: Studies in cognitive science* (pp. 211-236). New York: Academic Press.

Shafer, R. J. (1974). *A guide to historical method.* Homewood, IL: The Dorsey Press.

Stein, N. L., & Glenn, C. G. (1979). An analysis of story comprehension in elementary school children. In R. O. Freedle (Ed.), *New directions in discourse processing* (pp. 53-120). Hillsdale, NJ: Lawrence Erlbaum Associates.

Thorndyke, P. W. (1977). Cognitive structures in comprehension and memory of narrative discourse. *Cognitive Psychology, 9,* 77-110.

Trabasso, T., Secco, T., & van den Broek, P. (1984). Causal cohesion and story coherence. In H. Mandl, N. L. Stein, & T. Trabasso (Eds.), *Learning and comprehension of text* (pp. 83-111). Hillsdale, NJ: Lawrence Erlbaum Associates.

Trabasso, T., & van den Broek, P. (1985). Causal thinking and the representation of narrative events. *Journal of Memory and Language, 24,* 612-630.

van den Broek, P., & Trabasso, T. (1986). Causal network versus goal hierarchies in summarizing text. *Discourse Processes, 9,* 1-15.

Wineburg, S. S. (1991). Historical problem solving: A study of the cognitive processes used in the evaluation of documentary and pictorial evidence. *Journal of Educational Psychology, 83,* 73-87.

12 Contextualized Thinking in History

Samuel S. Wineburg and Janice Fournier
University of Washington

Conjure up in your mind the bearded figure of Abraham Lincoln, the 16th president of the United States, "Honest Abe" from Kentucky, Commander in Chief during the Civil War and author of one of the most important documents in American history—the Emancipation Proclamation. Consider these words of the man often referred to as the "Great Emancipator" on the topic of race relations:

> I have no purpose to introduce political and social equality between the white and black races. There is a physical difference between the two, which in my judgment will probably forever forbid their living together upon the footing of perfect equality, and inasmuch as it becomes a necessity that there must be a difference, I . . . am in favor of the race to which I belong, having the superior position. I have never said anything to the contrary. (Lincoln, 1989, p. 512)

How are we to regard these words? At the very least, they complicate the image of Lincoln as enlightened benefactor of African Americans. Have we been duped? Is the image of this American "patron saint" a sham? Perhaps as one commentator claimed (Bennett, 1968), the image of Lincoln as "Great Emancipator" should be replaced by another: Abraham Lincoln as "White Supremacist."

Which image, "Great Emancipator" or "White Supremacist," is more accurate? How should we think about the past in order to come to some conclusion? What assumptions about the past enable—disable—us from understanding Lincoln well enough to render judgment?

Such questions have a longer history in research on the psychology of school subjects than many might think (cf. Wineburg, in press). They have been at the heart of discussions of "historical empathy," a fertile research area in Great Britain since the advent of the School's Council *History 13–16* project (Shemilt, 1980), and we also addressed them, however tentatively, in some of our previous writings (Wineburg, 1991a, 1991b; Wineburg & Wilson, 1988, 1991). But the first modern psychologist to devote serious thought to the psychological aspects of historical understanding was Charles Hubbard Judd, who wrote the following words in his *Psychology of High-School Subjects* (1915):

> The modern student is . . . guided in all of his judgments by an established mode of thought . . . peculiar to his own generation. We have certain notions . . . that are wholly different from the notions that obtained at the time that England was in controversy with her American colonies. When . . . [the student] is suddenly carried back in his historical studies to situations that differ altogether from the situations that now confront him, he is likely to carry back, without begin fully aware of the fallacy of his procedure, those standards of judgment and canons of ethical thought which constitute his present inheritance. (p. 379)

When we judge past actors by present standards, we wrest them from their own context and subject them to ways of thinking that we, not they, have developed. Known as *presentism*, the act of viewing the past through the lens of the present is something of a psychological default state that must be overcome before one achieves true historical understanding. The recent Bradley Commission (1989) promised that historical study sharpens the ability to "perceive past events and issues as they were experienced by people at the time . . . the develop[ment] of historical empathy as opposed to present mindedness" (p. 9). When we consider the fundamental disciplinary understandings we want students to learn, and by extension, teachers to possess, the ability to think about the past on its own terms is certainly among them. If teachers of history cannot "think in time," we can have little faith in their students' ability to learn to do so.

What does contextualized thinking look like, and how can we promote its development? Had our goal been for readers to think contextually at the beginning of this chapter, we could have committed no graver error than to display Lincoln's words shorn of any qualifying detail. For to think contextually means that words are not disembodied symbols transcending time and space. We cannot separate Lincoln's words that began this article from the occasion in which they were uttered (a debate with Stephen A. Douglas for a fiercely contested senatorial seat), the location of this debate (Ottawa, IL, a hotbed of anti-Black sentiment), the kinds of people who heard the debate (largely supportive of Douglas and suspicious of Lincoln), and the fact that both Lincoln and Douglas addressed these people not as prophets or moralists, but as candidates courting votes. Nor can we ignore what Douglas said to spark Lincoln's response, or the words Lincoln uttered immediately following the passage we quoted. And what about the other things Lincoln said in Havana, IL a week earlier or in Freeport, IL a week later? Such considerations just begin to scratch the surface when we think about what we would need to create a historical context for the brief passage heading this chapter.

Our word choice here is purposeful: A context is not "found" or "located." Words are not "situated." Rather, human beings create contexts in the full etymological sense of the word. *Context*, from the Latin *contexere*, means to weave together, to engage in an active process of forming strands into a pattern. Thus far, in trying to weave a context for Lincoln's words, we have focused mostly on piecing together the temporal and spatial context: the exigencies of the moment that might shed light on Lincoln's motivation and intention. But other forms of context—the climate of opinion, mentalité, or zeitgeist; the biography of a complex human being and his style with words and utterances; the linguistic meanings of words in the 1850s—must also be considered when thinking about the meaning of Lincoln's words.

If contexts are made not found, then the process of context creation is amenable to psychological inquiry. How do thinkers weave historical contexts? Given the fragmented and discrete nature of the documentary evidence, how are coherent understandings realized? What kinds of knowledge are needed? How do thinkers navigate between feelings of proximity and feelings of distance with the past, points of contact, and abysses of distance? What is the role of formal study in the development of contextualized thinking? And what about the inability to create a context? What does noncontextualized, or anachronistic, thinking look like? What beliefs and processes lead to and sustain anachronistic thinking?

These were some of the questions that motivated this study, an enterprise we have come to regard as a form of "applied epistemology" because it falls neither into existing categories of psychological work nor qualifies as history. Our approach highlights our own historicity and experience, especially our training as educational psychologists who design tasks for studying the nature of disciplinary thought. Indeed, it is to the design of these tasks that we now turn.

TYING KNOTS, OR, WHAT PSYCHOLOGICAL TASKS SHARE WITH DEEP SEA FISHING

Finding contextualized thinking is more complicated than it might seem. We can try to infer it from historians' written accounts, but this approach discloses few clues about the intermediate stages of contextualized thinking, the crucial decision points that allow sophisticated historical reasoning to emerge. Therefore, some means have to be found to capture people in the midst of contextualized thinking. This is the role of the psychological task, an artificial environment that brings into the laboratory something irritatingly elusive in the field.

This is not the place to defend the need for task environments, although we are not unsympathetic to the powerful critiques aimed at them (e.g., Cole & Means, 1981; Lave, 1988, especially chap. 2). Rather, our goal is to discuss briefly the criteria for building a task that would help us understand contextualized thinking, for the principles of task design within a disciplinary context are by no means self-evident.

The choices before the task maker are endless, even once a set of research questions has been specified. Which time period to study, which documents to draw on, how many genres to include, and so on open up broad vistas of possibility. One way to deal with this complexity would be to recognize that any choice is arbitrary and not to be overly concerned with decisions of topic, genre, and time period. This position would argue that one set of documents is as good as any other.

We hold the opposite position. Designing a task to capture historical reasoning can be likened to tying the knots of a fishing seine—the real work begins in dry dock. If fishermen's knots are too big for the prizes they seek, they will end up with all sorts of worthless creatures while the real beauties slip unnoticed through the net. If the knots are too small, the nets will yield so much plankton and seaweed that the larger beasts lodged in the catch will be obscured. Tying knots, then, is not just a tedious process, but one that demands tremendous clarity of purpose. So it is, we think, with task design. In putting together our task, we wanted to explore contextualized thinking by choosing a topic and time period that was at once close to us and at the same time remote from us, because contextualized thinking demands an awareness of both continuity and discontinuity with the past. This consideration eliminated topics such as Anglo-Saxon ordeals (cf. Dickinson & Lee, 1984), a topic we believed was too remote, along with topics such as the Kennedy assassination, which we believed were too close (as well as being overly popularized). We chose to explore the topic of Abraham Lincoln's views about race because race is an enduring issue in American society, but one that can only be understood historically (Takaki, 1994). Our set of documents about Lincoln began with an exchange on the campaign stump, a feature of American life that shares much similarity with modern electioneering. On the other hand, the topic under debate—the status of the slave and the justification for slavery—is an issue difficult for the modern mind to fathom.

We also wanted to build a progression in the materials we assembled.

Historical reasoning has been referred to as *adductive*, a process of "adducing answers to specific questions so that a satisfactory 'fit' is obtained" (Fischer, 1970, p. 212). We built the task in a way so that the documents we provided to subjects became increasingly complex, hoping thereby to see how historical explanations are adduced that account for this increasing complexity. Before selecting the final nine documents for this study, we reviewed well over a thousand speeches, letters, notes, and addresses given by Abraham Lincoln and his contemporaries.

Participants

The data for this chapter were drawn from a larger study on how different people (gifted high school students, beginning and experienced teachers, and historians with diverse specializations) think about historical texts. In this chapter, we focus on the contextualized thinking of two prospective public school teachers, drawn from a larger sample of preservice teachers enrolled in a fifth-year certification program at the University of Washington. Ted, a 32-year-old white male, majored in history as an undergraduate and planned to find work as a history/social studies teacher upon graduation. Ellen, a 34-year-old white female, was a physics major who had spent considerable time in the private sector prior to beginning her teacher education program. Ted's B.A. in history included coursework in ancient history, Modern Latin American history, Afro-American history, Women's History, a seminar on the history of Iran, as well as other required courses for the major. Ellen had taken two history courses as part of distribution requirements for her undergraduate major in physics. Because a number of courses is widely used as a proxy for subject matter knowledge, a comparison between a "high-knowledge" and a "low-knowledge" individual seemed like an interesting route to pursue.

Procedure

Prior to engaging in a think-aloud task using documents by and about Lincoln, all of the teachers in our study were interviewed about their prior historical study, particularly at the university level. We then taught them how to "think aloud" (see Wineburg, 1991a). They were shown a list of six rules to "keep in mind" taken from Perkins (1981). These rules included guidelines such as "say whatever's on your mind," "don't overexplain or justify," "don't worry about complete sentences," and so on.

Pilot work with these documents showed that subjects with little content knowledge quickly became confused by the sequence of events in Lincoln's life. To lessen this possibility and to help orient subjects to the task, we developed a timeline of major events in Lincoln's life, from his election to the Illinois legislature to his assassination. Subjects were given this timeline and told to refer to it at any time. A series of nine documents were presented one by one, each printed on a separate page, with source of the document appearing at the top of the page in bold, italicized print. We prominently highlighted the source of each document because previous work (Wineburg, 1991b) showed that subjects did not always focus on the source of the document, a tendency that impeded their subsequent textual processing. During participants' concurrent reporting, we kept our own comments to a minimum, only reminding teachers to verbalize their thoughts when they fell silent, or asking them to explain a nonverbal gesture or single word response. Once subjects finished commenting on each text, they were asked to report retrospectively on "anything else you remember yourself thinking as you read this document." (On "concurrent" and "retrospective" reports, see Ericsson & Simon, 1984.) If subjects did not explicitly address Lincoln's views in their comments (and had not expressed them explicitly during the course of reading), they were asked, "What light does this document shed on Lincoln's views about race?" Although retrospective reports are more susceptible to the well-known criticisms of think-alouds (Nisbett & Wilson, 1977; but see also Ericsson & Simon, 1984), they can also offer insights into cognitive processes that are not yielded by concurrent reports alone (Robertson & Ericsson, 1988; Wineburg, 1991a). For that reason they were incorporated into the protocol of this study.

Our goal in what follows is to recreate for the reader the unfolding of contextualized thinking. Our presentation is sequential in that it follows the same order of the documents presented to subjects. We invite readers to "read over the shoulders" of these two teachers, asking themselves how they would link document to document or try to weave a context for Lincoln's words. Although the full think-aloud task spans nine documents written over a 127-year period, space limitations prevent us from going beyond the fifth document in our discussion here. Joining our two readers are the voices of some of the major interpreters of Lincoln and race relations in the United States: Winthrop Jordan, George Fredrickson, Don E. Fehrenbacher, Richard Weaver, Richard Hofstadter, and others. Using these additional voices, we, as authors, try to contextualize the think-aloud voices we heard in our own study.

IMAGES OF CONTEXTUALIZED AND NONCONTEXTUALIZED THINKING

The first document presented in the task was by Stephen A. Douglas, Lincoln's opponent in the 1858 senatorial campaign. The document begins with Douglas claiming that Lincoln supported giving the franchise to slaves and supported their running for office and serving on juries. In making these claims, Douglas established his own position as one "in favor of confining citizenship to white men" and being opposed to Negro citizenship "in any and every form." He then went on to claim that Lincoln believed the "Negro was born his equal" and is "endowed with equality by the Almighty." Figure 12.1 shows the document in the same form as it was presented to subjects.

For Ted, the history major, the name Stephen A. Douglas sounded "really familiar . . . I don't remember too [many] good things about him, but nothing specific." The majority of Ted's comments during this reading were aimed at establishing textual coherence, the forming of what van Dijk and Kintsch (1983) referred to as a "textbase" model. Only when asked about what the document disclosed about Lincoln during the retrospective reporting phase did Ted venture anything that might be called an interpretation: "Well this makes it seem like Lincoln was much more . . . on the side of the Negro. But I think that there is probably another view to that."

If you desire Negro citizenship, if you desire to allow them to come into the State and settle with the white man, if you desire them to vote on an equality with yourselves, and to make them eligible to office, to serve on juries, and to adjudge your rights, then support Mr. Lincoln and the Black Republican party, who are in favor of the citizenship of the Negro. For one, I am opposed to Negro citizenship in any and every form. I believe this government was made...by white men, for the benefit of white men and their posterity forever, and I am in favor of confining citizenship to white men, men of European birth and descent, instead of conferring it upon Negroes, Indians and other inferior races.

Mr. Lincoln, following the example and lead of all the little abolition orators, who go around and lecture in the basements of schools and churches, reads from the Declaration of Independence, that all men were created equal, and then asks how can you deprive a Negro of that equality which God and the Declaration of Independence awards to him. He and they maintain that Negro equality is guaranteed by the laws of God, and that it is asserted in the Declaration of Independence. . . . I do not question Mr. Lincoln's conscientious belief that the Negro was made his equal, and hence his brother, but for my own part, I do not regard the Negro as my equal, and positively deny that he is my brother. . . . [Lincoln] holds that the Negro was born his equal and yours, and that he was endowed with equality by the Almighty, and that no human law can deprive him of these rights ... Now, I do not believe that the Almighty ever intended the Negro to be the equal of the white man. . . . For thousands of years the Negro has been a race upon the earth, and during all that time, in all latitudes and climates, wherever he has wandered or been taken, he has been inferior to the race which he has there met. He belongs to an inferior race, and must always occupy an inferior position. (cited in Lincoln, 1989, pp. 504–505)

FIG. 12.1. Document 1. In 1858, Abraham Lincoln ran against Stephen A. Douglas for a seat in the U.S. Senate. The two engaged in a series of seven public debates which attracted national attention. Although Lincoln lost the election, he became widely known for his views on slavery. The following is an excerpt from Douglas' address to Lincoln in their first debate at Ottawa, IL, August 21, 1858.

Ellen, on the other hand, although also lacking specific knowledge of Lincoln's views, was struck by the "incredibly racist language" of Douglas's speech, but noted that "it is not inflammatory" but a "matter of fact, documented belief – this is true, everybody knows it." When asked what the document told her about Lincoln, she said that it told her little. Instead she referred to a mental image that came to her during reading:

> When I was reading it I wasn't actively thinking of Lincoln. I was actively reading the words and thinking more of Stephen Douglas on the platform, orating and delivering this to a crowd. Who would be in the crowd listening and what the culture was at this time and why this was acceptable to say in 1858 but is now not acceptable to say.

There are several things worthy of note here. First, Ellen immediately began to build a social context for this utterance – political hustings, applauding crowds, and the speaker's awareness of the sensibilities of his listeners. But the second thing she did is more subtle – she recognized the discrepancy between her own beliefs and those reflected in this document. By calling attention to issues of "acceptability" and recognizing that what struck her as "incredibly racist" would have been considered "matter of fact documented belief," Ellen wove together two facets of context: issues of the social occasion and issues of mentalité, the sweeping modes of thought that formed the mental landscape of the day. She tried here to understand a world in which such views were expounded not by fringe elements or thugs, but by future senators and the voters who elected them. It is the creation of foreignness with the past, not the creation of continuity, that characterizes contexualized thinking in this instance.

The second document, shown in Fig. 12.2, is one of the most famous texts from the Lincoln–Douglas debates, the *Ur-text* of the "Lincoln as White Supremacist" school. But viewed in its entirety, this document appears hazier and less easy to classify than the shortened excerpt at the beginning of this chapter. Nonetheless, it is impossible to avoid asking whether Abraham Lincoln was a racist. In fact, to pose this question – and to formulate an answer based on evidence – thrusts us into the epicenter of historical reasoning. It is worth quoting the historian Fehrenbacher (1974):

> Anyone who sets out conscientiously to answer [whether Lincoln was a racist] will soon find himself deep in complexity and confronting some of the fundamental problems of historical investigation. In one category are various questions about the historian's relation to the past: Is his task properly one of careful reconstruction, or are there more important purposes to be served? Does his responsibility include rendering moral judgments? If so, using what standards – those of his own time or those of the period under study? Then there are all the complications encountered in any effort to read the mind of

a man, especially a politician, from the surviving record of his words and actions. For instance, what he openly affirmed as a youth may have been silently discarded in maturity; what he believed on a certain subject may be less significant than the intensity of his belief; and what he said on a certain occasion may have been largely determined by the immediate historical context, including the composition of his audience. (1974, p. 299)

As Ted read Lincoln's reply to Douglas he felt a certain familiarity. Initially he sensed that he had seen the document before, and by the sixth line of the document, this feeling grew stronger: "Yes, I have read this before." Lincoln's statement that "he was in favor of the race to which he belonged" strengthened Ted's view that Lincoln was not the "Great Emancipator" of textbooks but someone who wanted "to reunite the states not just get rid of slavery." Lincoln's words about preferring his own race made Ted more confident in his original characterization: "Yeah, see, now this makes Lincoln seem more bigoted and not so altruistic." By the end of the document, Ted's prior understanding of Lincoln was confirmed:

Lincoln was not so much in the interest — working in the interest of the Black man, for altruistic sense . . . he does say that they deserve equal treatment, in a way, but still he's not giving them equal — he's not giving them . . . equality in personhood.

For Ted, Lincoln's words stand alone. They mirror Lincoln's beliefs, unfiltered by the occasion in which these beliefs were expressed or the social ends Lincoln tried to achieve in expressing them.

I will say here ... that I have no purpose directly or indirectly to interfere with the institution of slavery in the States where it exists. I believe I have no lawful right to do so, and I have no inclination to do so. I have no purpose to introduce political and social equality between the white and black races. There is a physical difference between the two, which in my judgment will probably forever forbid their living together upon the footing of perfect equality, and inasmuch as it becomes a necessity that there must be a difference, I, as well as Judge Douglas, am in favor of the race to which I belong, having the superior position. I have never said anything to the contrary, but I hold that notwithstanding all this, there is no reason in the world why the Negro is not entitled to all the natural rights enumerated in the Declaration of Independence, the right to life, liberty and the pursuit of happiness. I hold that he is as much entitled to these as the white man. I agree with Judge Douglas [that the Negro] is not my equal in many respects — certainly not in color, perhaps not in moral or intellectual endowment. But in the right to eat the bread...which his own hand earns, he is my equal and the equal of Judge Douglas, and the equal of every living man. (cited in Lincoln, 1989, p. 512)

FIG. 12.2. Document 2. From Abraham Lincoln's reply to Stephen A. Douglas at Ottawa, IL, August 21, 1858.

Ted's reading stands in contrast to Ellen's, who devoted over one-third of her comments (107 words out of 306 spoken, or 34.9% of her verbal report on this document) to creating a social context. Lincoln's statement of equality of the Negro in the second part of the document prompted this comment from Ellen (see Table 12.1, Ted's comments are presented for comparison).

What does this document disclose about Lincoln in Ellen's view? Very

TABLE 12.1
Comparison of Ellen and Ted on Document 2

	Protocol	
Text	Ted	Ellen
But in the right to eat the bread which his own hand earns, he is my equal and the equal of Judge Douglas, and the equal of every living man.		
	He seems to be giving him equal, equal rights as far as living, but, like he says, perhaps, not morally or intellectual. He's still saying that the white man is superior, but that doesn't take away the rights of the living and life.	When I read this, and think about Lincoln, I think of him in terms of politician, a guy trying to get elected. I've kind of got this mental picture of a Roger Ailes type, you know the spin doctor who pushes his campaign director, who pushes the media director, I guess you go through Reagan's media director. Whispering in his ear, saying now this is what you got to say to this crowd. To put the right spin on this particular issue. So it, again, when I'm thinking of Lincoln, I'm viewing him as a politician, in kind of a slimy way. The kind of way I think a lot of politicians [are]. They say whatever is convenient to the crowd that's listening to them, and you never really know what they're thinking.

little, it seems. When we asked her how this document illuminated Lincoln's views, she affirmed her earlier reading: "I view [Lincoln] in the context of how I view a politician trying to get elected—that they'll say anything, do anything to get elected. And that you can't trust them." This constitutes a striking difference when compared to Ted's reading. For Ted, Lincoln's response provided evidence of Lincoln's bigotry. For Ellen, there is no mention of bigotry, no mention of what the document says about Lincoln, other than the fact that, like other politicians, Lincoln spoke out of both sides of his mouth. Instead, the document points to a social context she knows well—one in which candidates say what is needed to garner votes.

Ellen's framing of Lincoln as a disingenuous politician seeking to get elected falls within a well-established interpretative tradition. The eminent Americanist Hofstadter, who profiled Lincoln in his *American Political Tradition* (1948), characterized Lincoln's views in the earlier document as appealing at once to both abolitionists and "Negrophobes." Remarking on a speech Lincoln gave in Chicago on July 10, 1858 ("Let us discard all this quibbling about this man and the other man, this race and that race . . . and unite as one people") and comparing it to a speech Lincoln gave in Charleston on September 18, 1858 ("I as much as any other man am in favor of having the superior position assigned to the white race"), Hofstadter (1948) remarked that it was:

> not easy to decide whether the true Lincoln is the one who spoke in Chicago or the one who spoke in Charleston. Possibly the man devoutly believed each of the utterances at the time he delivered it; possibly his mind too was a house divided against itself. In any case it is easy to see in all this the behavior of a professional politician looking for votes. (p. 116)

Both Ellen and Hofstadter resolved apparent contradictions in Lincoln's words by appealing to the exigencies of a political campaign. Because Lincoln needed to woo voters from both camps, he needed to talk out of both sides of his mouth. But the "divided Lincoln" interpretation is not the only way to understand these documents.

Lincoln's statements in Document 2 thrust us into the dilemma of contextualized thinking. If we presume an essential continuity in race relations, we see inconsistencies in Lincoln's words. These inconsistencies in turn lead us to create a context to explain why, for instance, Lincoln would say different things to different people. But this is not the only way to view inconsistency. If we begin with the belief that clear language and pure logic are themselves historical, then we are given to different responses in the face of apparent inconsistencies. Inconsistencies become opportunities for exploring our discontinuity with the past, the inevitable consequence of trying to bridge spatial and temporal gaps across the ages. In this view, inconsistency is not a function of the text, but a function of a world that has been lost. The recognition of inconsistency becomes as much an opportunity to explore our own limitations in understanding Lincoln as it is an opportunity to explore Lincoln's limitations in expounding his views.

Recall that what is at issue between Douglas and Lincoln is an implied syllogism flowing from the Declaration of Independence. If, as the Declaration stated, "all men are created equal," and if, as Douglas stated, "the Negro is not my equal," then by Douglas's definition, the Negro is not to be considered a man. If this was the question Lincoln addressed, his views were unequivocal.

In his *Ethics of Rhetoric,* Weaver (1953) demonstrated how Lincoln "argued by definition," a strategy that attacked a problem by whittling away at the side issues to reveal its stark and unambiguous essence. Although other statesmen examined slavery from the perspective of past history, comparative politics, the Bible, or the exigencies of the moment, Lincoln's tack was to argue from first principles. His "Speech at Peoria," a document not included in this task but relevant to it, provides insight into this style of argument. In this case, Lincoln told his audience that he would focus on the "naked merits" of the issue of slavery. He began his speech with the question of the genus of man, precisely the issue in the exchange between Lincoln and Douglas in Documents 1 and 2:

> Equal justice to the South, it is said, requires us to consent to the extending of slavery to new countries. That is to say, inasmuch as you do not object to my taking my hog to Nebraska, therefore I must not object to your taking your slave. Now, I admit that this is perfectly logical, if there is no difference between hogs and negroes. But while you thus require me to deny the humanity of the negro, I wish to ask whether you of the south yourselves, have ever been willing to do as much? (Lincoln, 1989, pp. 325–326)

If the slave is mere chattel, like a hog or cow, then why, asked Lincoln, was the seller of slaves treated differently by Southerners from the seller of hogs:

> You despise him utterly. You do not recognize him as a friend, or even as an honest man. Your children must not play with his; they may rollick freely with the little negroes, but not with the "slave dealers" children. If you are obliged to deal with him, you try to get through the job without so much as touching him. It is common with you to join hands with men you meet; but with the slave dealer you avoid the ceremony—instinctively shrinking from the snaky contact. If he grows rich and retires from business, you still remember him, and still keep up the ban of non-intercourse upon him and his family. Now why is this? You do not so treat the man who deals in corn, cotton, or tobacco? (p. 326)

Lincoln hammered at his point with other examples as well. How, for instance, should Southerners label the 433,643 free Blacks at that time? Moreover, how did these Blacks' freedom come about, at great financial sacrifice to their owners, if these same owners did not feel that the "poor negro has some sense of natural right to himself?" It is worth quoting Weaver's (1953) summary:

> Lincoln could never be dislodged from his position that there is one genus of human beings; and early in his career as lawyer he had learned that it is better to base an argument upon one incontrovertible point than to try to make an impressive case through a whole array of points. Through the years he clung tenaciously to this concept of genus, from which he could draw the proposition that what is fundamentally true of the family will be true also of the branches of the family. Therefore since the Declaration of Independence had interdicted slavery for man, slavery was interdicted for the negro in principle. (p. 95)

If we look carefully at Lincoln's response in Document 2, we see that there are aspects of it easily overshadowed by its charged language. Notice that the only thing Lincoln was willing to concede unequivocally to Douglas is that there is a "physical difference between the two races," but from then on, Lincoln equivocated. There is only *perhaps* a difference in moral or intellectual endowment, Lincoln said. This "perhaps" goes unnoticed by most contemporary readers, but even to raise the possibility that the two races were morally and intellectually equivalent must be viewed against the backdrop of Negrophobia of the mid-19th century. Stanford historian Fredrickson has argued that Lincoln's position followed in the footsteps of his Republican mentor, Henry Clay. Clay advocated gradual emancipation of the slaves, and early in his career made this statement: "[Blacks] are rational beings, like ourselves, capable of feeling, of reflection, and of judging of what naturally belongs to them as a portion of the human race" (cited in Fredrickson, 1975, p. 42).

Fredrickson's appeal to Clay constitutes the weaving of zeitgeist with Lincoln's own personal biography. What appears as a precious distinction between moral and legal rights was a meaningful distinction in Lincoln's mind and in the minds of many of his contemporaries. Because we cannot fathom a world in which such a distinction would be viewed as "progressive," we tend to view Lincoln statements as contradictory and inconsistent, or worse—hypocritical and self-serving.

For Ted, Lincoln's words cast light on Lincoln's soul, and the image perceived is one of a bigot. For Ellen, Lincoln's words disclosed more about the social situation than the naked truth about the man in that situation. What Weaver, Fredrickson, and others suggest is that the "naked truth" is more veiled than we think.

The third document presented to teachers was drawn from a different time in Lincoln's life and exemplifies a different genre of documentary evidence. Unlike the public response to Douglas, Document 3 was a private letter written by Lincoln to Mary Speed of Kentucky, the wife of Joshua Speed, a close personal friend. In this letter, Fig. 12.3, Lincoln described a journey on a Mississippi riverboat in which a group of slaves were literally being sold down the river.

Several aspects of this document make it a provocative stimulus. First, historians consider the genre of a document when making judgments of probity (Wineburg, 1994), and, in the absence of other information, they tend to regard personal correspondence as more probative than public pronouncements (cf. Gottschalk, 1958). Second, the substance of this document presents, at first glance, a perplexing contrast. Faced with the scene of slaves chained to each other in close quarters, Lincoln felt compelled to remark, not on human misery, but on human happiness.

The first point at which an interpretation seemed to form in Ted's mind (see Table 12.2) was when Lincoln described the slave who had an "over-fondness for his wife." When Ted was asked if his image of Lincoln had changed or stayed the same, he replied:

> Well, I'm still kind of not sure. It's probably [a document] that I would have to read again, and really, I'd [like?] to know more about this. Where was he really going with this idea? What was his total summation, rather than "God renders the worst of human conditions tolerable"? He seems to be saying that it is kind of unfortunate that people, that [they] could make the best of worst conditions. . . . So it gives him a sense of being caring. Which I do believe that he was. Yet, on the other hand, like I said, that the little, seeing Blacks as just happy-go-lucky people, that kind of image. I don't know. It's offensive to me. So, I don't like to read it, I guess.

By the way, a fine example was presented on board the boat for contemplating the effect of condition upon human happiness. A gentleman had purchased twelve Negroes in different parts of Kentucky and was taking them to a farm in the South. They were chained six and six together. A small iron clevis was around the left wrist of each so that the Negroes were strung together precisely like so many fish upon a trot-line. In this condition they were being separated forever from the scenes of their childhood, their friends, their fathers and mothers, their brothers and sisters, and many of them, from their wives and children, and going into perpetual slavery. Yet amid all these distressing circumstances they were the most cheerful and apparently happy creatures on board. One, whose offense for which he had been sold was an over-fondness for his wife, played the fiddle almost continually, and the others danced, sung, cracked jokes, and played various games with cards from day to day. How true it is that God renders the worst of human conditions tolerable. (cited in Lincoln, 1989, p. 74)

FIG. 12.3.   Document 3. Letter to Mary Speed. Abraham Lincoln, writing in a letter to Mary Speed, a personal friend, September 27, 1841.

TABLE 12.2
Ted's Interpretation of Document 3

Text	Protocol
One, whose offense for which he had been sold was an overfondness for his wife, played the fiddle almost continually	
	I was having trouble with that sentence — *whose offense for which he had been sold* — okay, so that's why he was sold.
was an overfondness for his wife, played the fiddle almost continually	
	So he looks like the happy jovial little boy
and the others danced, sung, and cracked jokes, and played various games with cards from day to day.	
	They were just playing up to the image that they were happy little people in their form of life . . . He seems to be saying that they're — they're good people, but they're portraying that stereotypical image of the little happy "negro" no matter what the conditions are. They "enjoy" their circumstances.

Several aspects of this comment deserve note. First, Ted is a sufficiently self-aware reader to know that the document leaves him uncertain, and that to understand it better he should probably read it again. Second, there is an elaboration of Ted's earlier image of Lincoln as bigot, though the comment about Lincoln "being caring" hints at some vestige of the "patron saint" view of the 16th president. Finally, Ted displayed an awareness of his emotional reactions to the text, reactions to images that he perceived as deeply bigoted.

Ellen's reading was remarkably similar (see Table 12.3). Mary Speed's letter generated perplexity — How can Lincoln be so callous as to mistake human misery for cheerfulness? But is Lincoln as callous as his words suggest? What pieces of context might be missing that might lead us to view the Speed letter differently?

Was Abraham Lincoln blind to the suffering of people wrenched from their homes and families? What better evidence could there be for a gross insensitivity to the pain of slaves than those earlier words? Fredrickson (1975) had in mind how Lincoln's words would strike the modern ear when he wrote that:

Such philosophizing [in the Speed letter] was hardly indicative of antislavery zeal, and it can easily be condemned as a manifestation of complacency,

TABLE 12.3
Ted and Ellen's Interpretation of the Speed Letter

Reader	Textual Prompt	Protocol
Ted	*and all the others danced, sung, cracked jokes, and played various games with cards from day to day*	They were just playing up the image that they were all happy little people in their form of life.
Ellen	*and all the others danced, sung, cracked jokes, and played various games with cards from day to day. How true it is that God renders the worst of human conditions tolerable*	It's kind of a depressing—I'm really depressed when I read this. That there were people that were being sold into slavery, being separated, and somehow, that the people in power could justify this by saying, "Look, how happy they are. Look how beautiful they are." "They don't mind." They're just—kind of like this is their lot in life. This is what they were brought into existence to be. When I think about Lincoln, I mean, well at least he is clearly cognizant. . . that they are being separated. But how can he feel that they're happy? Doesn't—I mean those two conditions aren't—can't code this together. That you'd be separated from your family, your home, and your brothers and sisters and your children and yet be happy and cheerful. How does he know they were cheerful?

insensitivity, or lack of imagination. But it was nevertheless based on the assumption, increasingly rare in the 1840s, that blacks responded to conditions in a way that could be understood in terms of a common humanity and not as the result of peculiar racial characteristics. (p. 44)

It is difficult to imagine a world in which the human status of slaves was in question, but it precisely the kind of world into which Abraham Lincoln was born. Trying to reconstruct a world we cannot completely know may be the difference between a contextualized and an anachronistic reading of the past.

Document 4 (see Fig. 12.4) was the last of three documents by Lincoln presented to subjects. This document was accompanied by a lengthy preamble because pilot work had showed that few readers, even those with coursework in this period, were familiar with Lincoln's plans to establish colonies of freed slaves in Central America. Ted had relatively little to say about this document. He noted that he was broadly familiar with plans for colonies of freed slaves, and reading this document did little, he said, to influence his views about Lincoln. Ellen, on the other hand, used this document to flesh out her image of Lincoln. She began by noting the temporal aspects of the document, coming as it did during the middle of the Civil War. As she read the text, a different image of Lincoln came into view:

> [Lincoln] is conscientiously trying to deal with a problem that is something that apparently made sense in that time frame. And I get the feeling that he is wrestling with something that doesn't really have a good solution. This is the best you can have for now. So I kind of see him as problem solver . . . not the slimy politician trying to give (unclear). [He is a] CEO or some type of decision maker trying to deal with a problem or acute problem. He was real one dimensional in the first article [Doc. 2], kind of a slimy politician. Then he has another side with the letter to Mary Speed, kind of human. And now this is again another, it's beginning to fill out, but now I see him more as the Chief Executive and trying to deal with problems, trying to balance a war, thinking ahead, what are we going to do after the war and sort of coming up with — and this is prior to the Emancipation Proclamation. Is this prior to the Emancipation Proclamation? Yes, this is prior to the Emancipation Proclamation. So, I mean he may have had this idea in mind, so he's thinking forward, and how are we going to deal with this great, this huge number of slaves? Maybe colonizing is certainly a viable option in 1862. It kind of reminds me of what the British did with Australia. Ship all the undesirables down to Australia.

Ellen provided a deeply intertexual reading here. She made reference to two of the three previous documents, and her understanding of this document was formed with these prior documents as backdrop. What

Why . . . should the people of your race be colonized, and where? If we deal with those [Negroes] who are not free at the beginning, and whose intellects are clouded by slavery, we have very poor materials to start with. If intelligent colored men . . . would move in this matter, much might be accomplished. It is exceedingly important that we have men at the beginning capable of thinking as white men, and not those who have been systematically oppressed. . . . The place I am thinking about having for a colony is in Central America. . . . The country is a very excellent one for any people, and with great natural resources and advantages, and especially because of the similarity of climate with your native land — thus being suited to your physical condition. (Lincoln, 1989, p. 368)

FIG. 12.4.   Document 4. Colonization of freed blacks was an idea proposed early in the nineteenth century. Many whites who opposed slavery actively advocated colonization, maintaining that true freedom and equality could be realized only by relocating the black population. Abraham Lincoln had long favored the idea and, in 1862, a sum of money was appropriated by Congress to aid in a colonization program. The following is from Lincoln's "Address on Colonization" delivered to a group of free black men at the White House on August 14, 1862.

emerged in her mind was an image of a multifaceted human being, a "slimy politician" in one instance, a caring human being in another, and in this document, a CEO strategically planning for the future. There seems also to be recognition that although such a plan is outlandish today, it made more sense in the later half of the 19th century. The analogy to Australia represented a search for parallels that would further contextualize Lincoln's plan. In understanding Lincoln, she combined elements of the zeitgeist with temporal elements from the events of the Civil War, and in so doing began to form the basis for a biographical context of Lincoln's life.

John Bell Robinson begins his address (see Fig. 12.5) by advancing a religious argument for slavery: "God himself has made them for usefulness as slaves and requires us to employ them as such and if we betray our trust and throw them off on their own resources, we reconvert them into barbarians." These are powerful words that strike us as absurd, but we should recognize that Negro slavery and its religious justification had been linked from the inception of English contact with Africa (see Jordan, 1968). Throughout his reading of Robinson, Ted bristled at ideas foreign to his own views on race. When Robinson linked slavery to the Divine mission, he blurted: "My mind is going Argh! I can't describe it in words." When Robinson stated that if Negro slaves were sent back to Africa, they would fall back into "heathenism and barbarism in less than fifty years," Ted composed himself and responded: "Is that what he thinks that they were—barbarians—I mean it's putting down their own natural life style and culture as they were, which I don't think should be done." And when he was asked if reading Robinson's words shed any light on the views of Abraham Lincoln, views he had been reacquainted with in the previous three documents, Ted responded this way: "No, because it's, I don't see Lincoln being addressed in this or, rereading his name who wrote it, that name doesn't sound familiar and I can't connect it to Lincoln at all."

How should we construe Ted's reading? On one level, of course, Ted is right. John Bell Robinson is "putting down the natural life style" of the Africans he knew, and his words smack of intolerance and disrespect for people not like himself. But on another level, Ted's comments provide a glimpse into a view of the past shared by many students, a view Lowenthal (1985, 1989) called a "timeless past" in the constructs we use to make sense of our present ("racism," "bigotry," "tolerance," "multicultural understandings") stand as static categories unmoved and unchanged across time and space. In this timeless past, John Bell Robinson should have thought differently. But to be charitable to Mr. Robinson, he also should not have been born into a world that, as Jordan and Fredrickson reminded us, embraced the White European Male as the very standard by which humanity was to be judged.

We also see what contextualized thinking does *not* look like when Ted

God himself has made them for usefulness as slaves, and requires us to employ them as such, and if we betray our trust, and throw them off on their own resources, we reconvert them into barbarians. Our Heavenly Father has made us to rule, and the Negroes to serve, and if we set aside his holy arrangements for the good of mankind and his own glory, and tamper with his laws, we shall be overthrown and eternally degraded, and perhaps made subjects of some other civilized nation. Colonization in their native land of all the Negroes would be so nearly impracticable that it will never be done and no other spot on this green Earth will do for them. It would be the height of cruelty and barbarism to send them anywhere else. If they all could be colonized on the coast of Africa they would fall back into heathenism and barbarism in less than 50 years. (Robinson, 1863)

FIG. 12.5. Document 5. John Bell Robinson. *From pictures of slavery and antislavery, advantages of negro slavery and the benefits of negro freedom morally, socially, and politically,* considered by John Bell Robinson, a white pro-slavery spokesperson, Pennsylvania, 1863.

stated that Robinson tells him nothing about Lincoln. Ted is right in saying that Robinson does not mention Lincoln. But on another level, Ted is profoundly wrong, for Robinson tells us a great deal about the mental landscape that prevailed in Lincoln's day. Robinson is a marker of one end of that landscape, just as William Lloyd Garrison is a marker at the other end. In a universe of ideas of different textures, what is the texture of Lincoln's ideas? Where can he be located on the spectrum of ideas? This question provided a stumbling block for Ellen as well.

Robinson's document elicited no spontaneous comments about Lincoln. Ellen was consumed by Robinson's charged words, drawing comparisons between Robinson and Adolf Hilter's plans for the "Final Solution." Particularly difficult for her to understand was Robinson's statement that repatriated slaves would "fall back into heathenism and barbarism," a statement that elicited this comment:

I mean I can't believe that anybody thinks this. I can't believe! I mean this is awful. It really doesn't impact how I think about Lincoln. I'm really focused on this guy. I'm just outraged. The thing that is really strange is that, again, I can picture him speaking in some type of lecture hall, and again this being delivered and it not being—this is pretty inflammatory stuff, but I mean it probably wasn't all that inflammatory back in 1863. [It] kind of emphasizes how one section of the population viewed slaves as sub-humans and we're doing this for their own good and if we didn't bring them into our servitude that they would be heathens and they'd be lost.

Ideally, Ellen would have recognized that the religious justification for slavery that Robinson provides is precisely the kind of statement Lincoln eschewed. Indeed, when Lincoln did refer to God in the context of slavery, it was to comment on the common bond under God shared by peoples of different races (Document 3). Robinson and Lincoln could not have been farther apart.

CONCLUSION

These two teachers differed dramatically in their approach to these documents. For Ted, the history major, Abraham Lincoln's views corresponded directly to the words in these documents. On the other hand, Ellen, a physics major, was wary of pursuing the "real" Lincoln among these documents, trying instead to understand the different Lincolns who responded to different circumstances. Further distinguishing Ellen's reading from Ted's were the number of intertextual connections she made across documents. We view these cross-references as attempts to create a context within the confines of this task by reconstructing the climate of opinion in which Lincoln dwelled. At the end of the task, when Ellen encountered Bennett's (1968) claim that Lincoln was a "tragically flawed figure who shared the racial prejudice of most of his white contemporaries" (p. 42), Ellen was able to add texture to this statement based on what she had learned in this task. Agreeing in part with Bennett's assertion, Ellen added this qualifier: "Lincoln clearly wasn't on the same wavelength as . . . Robinson." Moreover she contextualized Bennett's article itself: "1968, let's see that was a year, this is just prior to the Bobby Kennedy and Martin Luther King assassination."

Throughout the task, Ellen gauged Lincoln's views without losing sight of her own. She was able to disapprove without being astonished. She could reject yet still understand. When reading Stephan Douglas, she called attention to the "incredibly racist language," but noted that "its not inflammatory. It's matter of fact, documented belief, this is obviously true, everyone knows it. It's what they would call conventional wisdom, common knowledge." Ellen here achieved a fundamental historical understanding. The past is not mere prologue to the present, but is discontinuous with it. The distance she created between her own views and those of the people she read about allowed her to view history, in Mink's (1987) words, as a "standing invitation to discover and enter into modes of seeing quite different from our own" (p. 103). As Mink, drawing on the work of art historian Ernst Gombrich, noted:

> The conventions of visual perception have themselves changed over time with the assimilation of different inventions of representational illusion. To put the thesis most simply, we can no longer assume that the Egyptians saw as we see, but could not draw as we can. To us, their conventions of representation

appear totally two-dimensional . . . but rather than dismissing this as technical ineptitude, we can consider that the Egyptians knew how to read these forms, as we invented and learned how to read the forms of linear perspective—and that therefore their way of seeing—not just their conventional iconography—was different from ours. (pp. 102–103)

What Ellen understood is analogous. What White society saw in 1850, what allowed this society to propagate the institution of slavery on American soil, is not what we see today.

We chose to focus on these two teachers because they present the puzzle of an inverse relationship, or so it would seem, between academic training in history and the disposition to think contextually. This pattern, however, is not entirely anomalous; our early findings, although based on a very small sample (12 teachers), showed no clear-cut relationship between undergraduate major and the ability to create a historical context.

This finding, tentative and provisional as it is, is not entirely new to researchers concerned with teachers' subject-matter knowledge (cf. National Center for Research on Teacher Learning, 1992). The undergraduate major proceeds on the assumption that students have mastered fundamental disciplinary conceptions prior to coming to the university. It is precisely these fundamental conceptions that are at the center of teaching that discipline to the young. But as is often the case, the notions presumed to exist in the minds of college freshmen, sophomores, juniors, and seniors are rarely checked, tested, or assessed. In many cases, the foundation assumed by university instructors is a figment of their imagination.

When history majors come to teacher education, we presume, especially in a fifth-year program such as ours, that they know their history. Our job is to teach them about teaching. But what happens when assessments such as these, assessments that allow us to examine fundamental disciplinary assumptions, cast doubt on our confidence about students' fundamental knowledge (cf. Wilson & Wineburg, 1988)? Our job becomes doubly complicated and politically sensitive when, in the midst of teaching people how to teach, we realize that we first must teach them how to know.

We end this preliminary report of our work with the "so what" question, for one hears a great deal nowadays about "authentic assessments" that tap students' ability to "think like historians." These pronouncements are often greeted with enthusiastic nods of assent often by people who never ask a prior—and in our eyes more basic—question: Why should we care if students, or teachers for that matter, are able to think like historians?

Historical thinking of the type described here, and in particular the disposition to think about the past by recognizing the inadequacy of one's own conceptual apparatus, is essential in teaching people how to understand others different from themselves. If we never recognize that our individual experience is limited, what hope is there of understanding people whose logic defies our own, whose choices and beliefs appear inscrutable when judged against our own self?

We decided to conduct this study after observing an 11th-grade social studies class on the civil rights movement. The class had just been shown a segment of the PBS series "Eyes on the Prize," which showed Mississippi Governor Ross Barnett physically barring James Meredith from registering at Ole Miss. In the discussion that followed, the teacher asked students why Governor Barnett objected to Meredith's enrollment at the University of Mississippi. One student raised his hand and volunteered the answer "prejudice." The teacher nodded and the discussion moved on.

Prejudice is a very dangerous answer to this question: Dangerous because it substitutes labeling for understanding; dangerous because it psychologizes and individualizes a problem that can only be understood across time; dangerous because it gives students a false sense of having understood something when, in fact, they have understood little; dangerous because in viewing the past in terms of the present, it distorts the role of culture and history and creates an undisciplined optimism in the face of complex and often intractable problems.

Many questions remain in our project. We do not know how, exactly, people learn to think contextually. We do not know where they learn it when they do. We do not even know the role of formal study in its development. We are convinced however of one thing: The ability to think contextually is not, in the words of Fischer (1970), some "pristine goal of scholarly perfection":

> If we continue to make the . . . error of conceptualizing the problems of a nuclear world in prenuclear terms, there will not be a postnuclear world. If we persist in the error of applying yesterday's programs to today's problems, we may suddenly run short of tomorrow's possibilities. If we continue to pursue the ideological objectives of the nineteenth century in the middle of the twentieth, the prospects of a twenty-first are increasingly dim. (p. 215)

Reason, as Fischer reminds us, is a pathetically frail weapon in the face of the problems that threaten to rend our society and our world. It is, however, the only weapon we possess.

REFERENCES

Bennett, L. (1968, February). Was Abe Lincoln a White Supremacist? *Ebony*, pp. 35–42.

Bradley Commission on History in Schools. (1989). *Building a history curriculum.* New York: Educational Excellence Network.

Cole, M., & Means, B. (1981). *Comparative studies of how people think.* Cambridge, MA: Harvard University Press.

Dickinson, A. K., & Lee, P. J. (1984). Making sense of history. In A. K. Dickinson, P. J. Lee, & P. J. Rogers (Eds.), *Learning history* (pp. 117–153). Liverpool, Great Britain: Heinemann.

Ericsson, K. A., & Simon, H. A. (1984). *Protocol analysis: Verbal reports as data.* Cambridge, MA: MIT Press.

Fehrenbacher, D. E. (1974). Only his stepchildren: Lincoln and the Negro. *Civil War History, 20,* 293–310.

Fischer, D. H. (1970). *Historians' fallacies: Toward a logic of historical thought.* New York: Harper & Row.

Fredrickson, G. (1975). A man but not a brother: Abraham Lincoln and racial equality. *Journal of Southern History, 41,* 39–58.

Gottschalk, L. (1958). *Understanding history: A primer of historical method.* Chicago: University of Chicago Press.

Hofstadter, R. (1948). *The American political tradition and the men who made it.* New York: Vintage.

Jordan, W. D. (1968). *White over black: American attitudes toward the Negro, 1550–1812.* New York: Norton.

Judd, C. H. (1915). *Psychology of high-school subjects.* Boston: Ginn.

Lave, J. (1988). *Cognition in practice.* New York: Cambridge University Press.

Lincoln, A. (1989). *Speeches and writings* (Vols. 1 and 2). New York: Library of America.

Lowenthal, D. (1985). *The past is a foreign country.* Cambridge, England: Cambridge University Press.

Lowenthal, D. (1989). The timeless past: Some Anglo-American historical preconceptions. *Journal of American History, 75,* 1263–1280.

Mink, L. O. (1987). *Historical understanding* (B. Fay, E. O. Golob, & R. T. Vann, Eds.). Ithaca, NY: Cornell University Press.

National Center for Research on Teacher Learning. (1992). *Findings on learning to teach.* East Lansing, MI: Author.

Nisbett, R. E., & Wilson, T. D. (1977). Telling more than we know: Verbal reports on mental process. *Psychological Review, 84,* 231–259.

Perkins, D. N. (1981). *The mind's best work.* Cambridge, MA: Harvard University Press.

Robertson, W. C., & Ericsson, K. A. (1988, April). *Methodological issues in the use of verbal reports as quantitative data.* Paper presented at the annual meeting of the American Educational Research Association, New Orleans, LA.

Robinson, J. B. (1863). *Pictures of slavery and anti-slavery and the benefits of negro freedom morally, socially, and politically considered.* Philadelphia: Horton.

Shemilt, D. J. (1980). *History 13–16: Evaluation study.* Edinburg, Great Britain: Holmes McDougall.

Takaki, R. (1994). Reflections from a different mirror. *Teaching Tolerance, 3,* 11–15.

van Dijk, T. A., & Kintsch, W. (1983). *Strategies of discourse comprehension.* New York: Academic.

Weaver, R. (1953). *The ethics of rhetoric.* South Bend, IN: Gateway.

Wilson, S. M., & Wineburg, S. S. (1988). Peering at history through different lenses: The role of disciplinary perspectives in teaching history. *Teachers College Record, 89,* 525–539.

Wineburg, S. S. (1991a). Historical problem solving: A study of the cognitive processes used in the evaluation of documentary and pictorial evidence. *Journal of Educational Psychology, 83,* 73–87.

Wineburg, S. S. (1991b). On the reading of historical texts: Notes on the breach between school and academy. *American Educational Research Journal, 28,* 495–519.

Wineburg, S. S. (1994). The cognitive representation of historical texts. In G. Leinhardt, I. L. Beck, & C. Stainton (Eds.), *Teaching and learning in history* (pp. 85–135). Hillsdale, NJ: Lawrence Erlbaum Associates.

Wineburg, S. S. (in press). The psychology of learning and teaching history. In R. C. Calfee & D. C. Berliner (Eds.), *Handbook of educational psychology*. New York: Macmillan.

Wineburg, S. S., & Wilson, S. M. (1988). Models of wisdom in the teaching of history. *Phi Delta Kappan, 70,* 50–58.

Wineburg, S. S., & Wilson, S. M. (1991). Subject matter knowledge in the teaching of history. In J. E. Brophy (Ed.), *Advances in research on teaching* (pp. 303–345). Greenwich, CT: JAI Press.

Discussion of Chapters 10–12: Promoting Narrative Literacy and Historical Literacy

María José Rodrigo
University of La Laguna (Spain)

The contributors to this section addressed the study of the students' cognitive processes in the comprehension of history. They provided relevant data that reveal how students of different educational levels, as compared with historians, understand, learn, or reason about certain passages of American history (e.g., the American Revolution, Abraham Lincoln's attitude toward African Americans, and the building of the Panama Canal). Particular attention was paid to the analysis of students' cognitive representations of such historical events. Given that texts are used to convey those contents, the contributors also devoted a great deal of effort to understanding the textual features that may affect students' learning. The analyses of texts were carried out on school textbooks, on historical documents of different sources, or on texts created by the experimenters. Overall, the contributors shared great concern in the instructional implications of their work. Their conclusions led them to call for improving both the quality of historical texts and the teaching methods.

It is not my intention to try to capture the richness of the chapters in a dense summary. Instead, I try to organize the discussion around three important themes, explicitly mentioned by the authors, that weave in and out of different parts of the chapters. These include: (a) the approaches to understanding history, (b) the educational goals for learning history, and (c) the instructional means for teaching history. Understanding, learning, and teaching history are clearly related issues. Our conception of what history is may influence the educational goals we pursue when we include it as a subject in the academic curriculum. In turn, these goals may influence the methods we develop to teach history to students.

APPROACHES TO UNDERSTANDING HISTORY

History is conceived by many authors as a scientific discipline. One way to interpret this statement is by considering that history does not depart from other disciplines except in its method (Hempel, 1962). Thus, history, as other natural sciences, should be oriented to explore general regularities or "laws" underlying particular events. The explanatory principles should rely on economical, political, cultural, geographical, or technological factors, rather than on particular human actions and motivations, attempting to avoid any personal perspective. In addition, the chronological structure of historical events should be minimized to offer a synchronic account. Finally, historical contents should be described using a network of abstract concepts to generate scientific arguments. In this sense, historical accounts should be presented with the formal appearance of expository texts.

There is, however, another way to interpret this statement. History is a scientific discipline that belongs to the branch of humanities. History diverges, but is also in the nature of the world that it tries to build (see also Carretero et al., this volume). As Bruner (1986) posited it: "[Natural] science attempts to make a world that remains invariant across human intentions and human plights . . . the humanist deals principally with the world as it changes with the position and stance of the viewer" (p. 50). Thus, history as a discipline of humanities should deal with human agents living in a particular time and space, who undertake things based on their beliefs, intentions, and goals. In this way, historical stories share with ordinary stories similar ingredients: characters performing actions with intentions and goals, living in certain settings and using particular means (mental or physical) to achieve their goals (Burke, 1945). Historical texts attempt to be true descriptions of facts, whereas stories are usually fictional descriptions, but both can be considered, in principle, as particular cases of narratives (Bruner, 1990; Gallie, 1964; Stone, 1979). Thus, although natural sciences use temporal arguments placed in an expository form, history uses stories presenting a chronological order of events in a narrative form. According to Bruner (1986):

> A good story and a well-formed argument are different natural kinds. Both can be used for convincing another. Yet what they are trying to convince us *of* is fundamentally different: Arguments convince one of their truths, stories of their lifelikeness. This one is verified by eventual appeal to procedures for establishing formal and empirical proof. The other establishes not truth but verisimilitude. (p. 11)

The view of history as a collection of stories does not go without problems (see Porter, 1981, and White, 1981, for extensive reviews about its strengths and shortcomings). For instance, one of its problems is that historical narratives would present different accounts for a given fact depending on the perspective of the author. But the proper way to handle this and other problems is to consider history as going beyond storytelling to include its own methods of dealing with historical phenomena. As Perfetti et al. state in their chapter, there is nothing incompatible between a story approach and a discipline approach to history. Each introduces a different level of complexity in the analysis of historical phenomena. Moreover, historical methods have been developed largely to overcome most of the biases produced by the narrative nature of historical accounts. Consequently, history, as a discipline of humanities, involves a selection of historical stories presented in narrative form, along with historical concepts and methods of historical analysis. Wineburg (1991) described three methods used by experts in dealing with historical evidence: sourcing (evaluating the source of the document), corroboration (checking facts presented from different accounts), and contextualization (placing facts into their historical context).

EDUCATIONAL GOALS FOR LEARNING HISTORY

The distinction made here between history as a collection of stories and history as a discipline is heuristic when designing the educational goals for learning history. In the former case, students' learning should be directed to promote narrative literacy, that is, a good level of comprehension of historical stories. In the latter case, students should reach a certain level of historical literacy, that is, they should approach the historian's scientific job. This means that students should know and use some research skills used by the historians, although a full command of them is not required. As Perfetti et al. suggest in their chapter, both goals should be accomplished by students following a hierarchical order: first narrative literacy and then historical literacy. The reason is that any practice on historical methods must use narratives as the raw materials.

Narrative Literacy

The cognitive competencies involved in the oral comprehension of narratives have an early onset in child development. One can trace back their origin to the first year of life because the most primitive forms of narrative discourse are prelinguistic. For instance, Bauer and Mandler (1989) showed that babies between 1 and 2 years of age could reproduce a sequence of causally related actions. The fact that the narrative structure is present in the praxis of human interaction from the very beginning is not alien to this early emergence (Bruner, 1990). Thus, babies are surrounded by a social context that emphasizes human agency, that is, humans performing goal-directed actions. Human actions produce consequences extended in time that give a sequential order to the occurrence of events. As language develops, the semantic relations involving agents, objects, events, and locations are the first linguistic forms found by children. Therefore, as Perfetti et al. remark, there is a compatibility of narrative forms with the cognitive dispositions of the learner.

Humans are especially skillful both in processing episodic information organized around human characters and preserving the temporal-causal structure of events. Several findings can be presented with respect to the central role played by characters in the reader's mental model of narratives. For instance, objects or landmark positions become more accessible to the readers when they are consistent with the character's motion in a scenario (Morrow, Greenspan, & Bower, 1987). The presence in the narrative of two characters with different spatial perspectives makes objects or landmark positions less accessible to the reader than when characters share the same perspective (de Vega, 1994). The shift from the protagonist's spatial perspective to the secondary character's perspective takes longer for the reader than vice versa (de Vega, 1994). The reader may model the character's emotional states, although no emotional word is explicitly mentioned in the narrative (Gernsbacher, Goldsmith, & Robertson, 1992). Beck and McKeown (this volume) report two previous studies that provide good instances of the difficulties that face students when they have to learn historical stories that do not make the role of characters and motivations clear. They show that emphasizing this sort of information improves the students' comprehension of the stories.

The mental dispositions of the characters involved in a story, along with the chronological order of events, are critical for providing causal connections between events and actions. The structure of causal relations is one of the main factors responsible for story coherence which, in turn, facilitates the comprehension of stories (Trabasso & van den Broek, 1985). Particularly, events with many causal connections to other events in a narrative are recalled better and perceived as more important than events with few causal connections. In addition, events connecting a narrative's opening to its outcome are also recalled better and judged more importantly than causal "dead ends" (Trabasso & Sperry, 1985). Perfetti et al.'s chapter illustrates the way readers progressively learn the temporal-causal structure of historical events. According to their findings, students became very sensitive to the core events (those involving crucial information to understand the story), increasing the number of core events reported after each reading. In contrast, the students' report of noncore events did not significantly increase. This means that students were progressively more aware of the causal structure of the events.

Students learn historical stories using their cognitive resources to understand narratives. In doing so, readers try to integrate their previous historical knowledge, if any, with the historical contents involved in the narrative. In order to facilitate meaningful learning, it should be a good match between what students already know and what the text assumes. This condition is rarely met according to the findings of Beck and McKeown. A first approach to their longitudinal data leaves the impression that what students accomplished, through instruction and development (from fifth grade to eighth grade), was growth in knowledge. But more qualitative analysis reveals that students' learning followed several patterns: lack of knowledge persisting, despite instruction (using general schema or empty labeling); confusion of ideas within the development of understanding; and fragmentary accounts mentioning events, artifacts, or characters of the period without tying them to the sequence of events. Is this a problem of a lack of knowledge or inaccuracy of previous knowledge? In the former case, the growth of knowledge should provide students with an enrichment of their repertoire of historical stories. The latter case is much more controversial, because students' inaccuracies may stem from alternate interpretations of facts. What is required, then, is a replacement of the "wrong" views by the "right" ones. There is no sense, however, in keeping students within one line of interpretation. As shown in the next section, what students have to learn is just the opposite. They should be ready to deal with inconsistency and uncertainty produced by the accumulation of several pieces of evidence with respect to the same historical facts.

Historical Literacy

The cognitive competencies involved in the development of historical literacy are far from being well delineated. It seems reasonable to propose that, at least, two groups of competencies should be promoted in students: to master key historical concepts and to approach the historian's job as a scientist. Concerning the learning of concepts, it is frequently observed in the students' accounts of historical facts the use of "important" words exhibited as amulets to make the teachers' opinion about them more favorable. As Berti (this volume) and Beck and McKeown (this volume), note, the students' use of concepts such as *government, nation, Constitution*, and *parliament* does not guarantee the correct understanding of their meaning. Given that meaning is context-dependent, students should have the opportunity to come across several instances of the same historical concepts during their readings. For instance, reading the episodes of the

U.S. War of Independence, students can learn that the concept of nation has different meanings when referring to the Indians, the English, or the North Americans. Eventually, the correct use and understanding of concepts would transform the students' ordinary accounts of historical events into more precise versions closer to historical stories.

The main task for students as they learn the historian's job as a scientist is to use multiple pieces of evidence coming from different sources. Perfetti et al. (this volume; see also Wineburg & Fournier, this volume) analyze the group of competencies involved in this task and their level of accomplishment in the sample of students. University students were good at evaluating primary and secondary documents, in terms of their trustworthiness and usefulness, detecting author interpretative biases (except with textbooks), or resolving tentatively conflicting views. Students found more difficulties in handling inconsistencies among documents or asking for additional information when given the opportunity. Perhaps the most difficult skill has proved to be contextualizing historical facts. This ability requires the creation of a historical context to interpret the past, that is, placing the facts into the temporal and spatial coordinate, the climate of opinion, the linguistic meanings of words at different times, and so on. The ability to think in time requires the use of intertextual links and background knowledge of the epoch to construct a proper interpretative context of past events. Neither of the novices in Wineburg and Fournier's sample (teacher education students) exhibited this ability.

Suppose that students were taught the group of abilities already mentioned. Even so, there is something left in the goal of promoting historical literacy. Students should be aware of the cultural significance of the historian's activity. Students should also learn the role of natural sciences in modern societies (Smith, 1991). But there is an important difference with respect to history. The students' introduction into the natural science culture, although it does not go without effort, is facilitated because they are more aware of new discoveries and new technological advances made by natural scientists. To understand the historian's scientific inquiry as a cultural activity requires much more teaching efforts and imagination by the teacher. Students should place their already learned abilities to deal with documents into a meaningful context of learning. What is history for in our modern societies? Does it help to understand the complex world we are living in? Does it promote cognitive abilities useful in other domains of knowledge?

These and many other questions, although controversial, would be the sort of questioning in which students of history would like to engage. Some answers have already been given in the chapters of this section. For instance, it is quite clear that the competencies involved in narrative literacy should improve students' modeling skills to be readily applicable to other domains of knowledge. But even those competencies included in historical literacy can be very useful for making students aware of the complexities of our plural societies. Wineburg and Fournier suggest that the teaching of contextualized thinking is essential in teaching people how to understand others different from themselves. In the same vein, it is also reasonable to predict that the use of multiple perspectives and the awareness of multiple interpretations should promote cognitive flexibility and a good level of metacognition. Moreover, it would contribute to the development of general thinking skills such as those involved in the ability to coordinate theory and evidence (Kuhn, Amsel, & O'Loughlin, 1988).

INSTRUCTIONAL MEANS FOR TEACHING HISTORY

Teaching is a complex task that should not be reduced to the use of instructional means. One has to consider other important aspects, such as the teacher's knowledge about the subject, the interactive climate in the classroom, or the structure of school tasks. But, nevertheless, instructional means play a central role in the organization of teaching activities. From now on, I comment on some means that should be used to promote both narrative literacy and historical literacy.

Teaching Narrative Literacy

One of the instructional means widely used is the textbook. Therefore, it is crucial to have good textual materials to provide students with coherent and comprehensible accounts of history, as Beck and McKeown suggest. In this way, historical texts must be "good stories," taking advantage of human modeling skills. This means that historical texts should be mainly narrative, rather than expository texts. The expository format does not guarantee additional objectivity to the historical facts. Any historical account might involve bias in the selection and the interpretation of facts, and the use of an expository format does not preclude the possibility of this occurring. On the contrary, expository texts are more difficult to understand and learn than narrative texts (Britton & Black, 1985). The following are some important guidelines to be considered when constructing historical texts:

1. Historical narratives should take advantage of the psychological prominence of protagonists. Characters are more accessible in the reader's working memory and regulate the activation of other pieces of the discourse linked to them. Thus, texts should make clear the characters of the story, individuals, or collectives.

2. Narrative perspective should be locally consistent. At the global level, perspective shift might be necessary for a full comprehension of historical facts. However, a continuous shift of perspective makes comprehension harder, because each shift competes for the reader's cognitive resources.

3. Actions and events should be linked by intentional and causal relations. This psychological "glue" produces a better integration of the text into fewer thematic units.

4. The events described in the historical narrative should preserve the world temporal order. Temporal isomorphism between the mental entities and world events improves comprehension.

5. Relevant descriptions of environments and artifacts can be critical for understanding some historical events. These descriptions should be embedded in the narrative plot at the "appropriate moments," when their functional relevance becomes apparent to the reader.

This list is tentative and does not aim to be exhaustive in the least. It is not speculative, however, because it is inspired by well-established findings from the literature of text comprehension and from some results presented by the contributors.

Improving historical texts, particularly those included in textbooks, would simplify the teacher's task in promoting narrative literacy. But this is only the half of it. The assessment procedures used to evaluate students' learning should also be revised. For instance, when assessing the students' level of comprehension of historical texts, one probably can distinguish between different levels of representation of the story content. Perfetti et al.'s chapter provides two examples of analysis tools that could be potentially useful to this purpose. The temporal-causal template may serve to detect to what extent students have properly identified a causally connected chain of events included in the story. In turn, the analysis of the structure of the argument provides an interesting approach to the students' level of discourse used in their historical accounts.

But there are more examples in the literature of text comprehension. For instance, the use of a multiple-choice question procedure has proven to be very useful to distinguish between levels of representation in memory for discourse in experts and novices (Tardieu, Ehrlich, & Gyselinck, 1992). The typical procedure works as follows: while reading a text, experts and novices are interrupted at different points in time, either by a question containing a paraphrase of a sentence, or by an inference that provides new information not explicitly stated in the text. Results showed that performance on paraphrase questions is usually equivalent in both groups, because it involves a surface level of representation of the discourse. Performance on inference questions is better for experts, or more knowledgeable students, than for novices. The production of elaborative inferences generated from several sentences in the text is a useful cue to the existence of higher levels of representation (e.g., propositional representation, or a situational model of the content of the story).

Of course, I am not simply suggesting that these or other experimental procedures should be directly used to evaluate students' learning. My claim is that assessment procedures should take advantage of the relevant empirical findings and theoretical proposals available, both in text comprehension and memory for discourse literatures.

Teaching Historical Literacy

The instructional means for promoting historical literacy are mainly based on the use of inductive techniques, such as case-based analysis, documenting, and hypertext environments. A common feature of these techniques is that students are exposed to multiple texts presenting several facets on the same topic, either in a fixed order or on a self-selection basis. There are several theoretical reasons for expecting effective learning with the multiple text format. First, according to Perfetti et al., the cognitive representation of historical facts generated from several documents is more accessible than the one generated from a single text. Students have to deal with multiple linguistic cues that connect to their representation, because documents present similar information, but in different ways. As the number of linguistic access points increases, the cognitive representation becomes more accessible.

A second reason for using multiple texts is that the general view presented to the reader would be contradictory. At first sight, this might be considered a serious shortcoming, but, in fact, it would increase the stability of the student's representation by reinforcing the core of the story and delineating the points of contention (see Perfetti et al., this volume). In addition, the representation generated from texts containing different points of view were also more flexible. Thus, the elaboration of inferences about others' opinions or actions (which involves a change of perspective) is facilitated when the others hold contradictory views, either among themselves or with respect to the subject's view.

Two studies recently undertaken in my own laboratory are very relevant to this respect (Correa & Rodrigo, 1992; Rodrigo & Triana, 1993). University students believing in the "sustained growth" view about ecology were exposed to the ideas sustained by two characters presented under two conditions, each holding contradictory views (the "sustained growth" and the "unlimited growth" views) and holding the same "sustained growth" view. Then, students had to verify a list of sentences describing alternately each person's opinion on ecology. The students' change of perspective between the two characters with contrasting views were performed better (sentences were verified faster and with more accuracy) than when both had the same view. In the second study, parents believing in the "environmentalist" view about child development and education were presented with a target couple under two conditions, holding the same belief as them or the opposite "constructivist" belief. This time, parents had to judge the couple's childrearing practices performed in concrete episodes. Again, when parents judge the practices performed by the couple with opposite views to them, sentences were verified faster and with more accuracy than when the couple had the same view. Therefore, it seems that the alternative foregrounding of character's opinions or actions within a context providing multiple views is performed better than within a single-view context.

Finally, a multiple text format would reinforce effective learning as it creates a learning atmosphere similar to that taking place in informal contexts of learning. In these contexts, people gather multiple pieces of episodic experiences coming from different sources (direct or vicarious observation, informal talks, readings, formal education, mass media) to construct everyday knowledge. It is frequently the case that evidence is served with multiple interpretations leaving enough space to the subject's construction of several alternative views with respect to the same phenomena. Thanks to that, we not only are equipped with our own beliefs, but also with knowledge about others' views (Rodrigo, Rodriguez, & Marrero, 1993). However, there is an important ingredient in informal contexts of learning that is frequently disregarded in multiple text learning environments. People construct their knowledge in the presence of others who are also engaged in the same task. Moreover, evidence, and its respective interpretation, is not served individually, but "traded" during social exchanges. I agree with Beck and McKeown's claim that students should be given the opportunity to discuss and contrast what they have understood during the class lessons. The use of good text materials coming from different sources and presenting different perspectives should be complimented with a naturalistic learning atmosphere. This should provide the appropriate "milieu" in which the co-construction of knowledge as a shared activity achieved through negotiations between the students and the teacher is possible.

My final commentary suggests that the time has come to make an exercise of realism. The students' accomplishment of narrative literacy and historical literacy involves a challenge to any educational system. Narrative literacy as it is based on the reader's natural dispositions to understand narratives seems to represent a low but necessary standard for learning history. In turn, historical literacy is particularly difficult to achieve, because it requires the development of complex skills that are not naturally granted by human evolution. But, in both cases, careless or unpracticed teachers using questionable methods may hinder students from learning history.

I believe that what I have distilled from the chapters of this section, and the complementary information I have added, is sufficient to illustrate the importance of the task we are facing. Changes in the curriculum should be afforded, programs of teacher training should be designed, and instructional means and resources should be mobilized to meet all these needs. But it is not only a matter of institutional change. Researchers and teachers can do something by themselves, as they would find the effort worthwhile and the potential results very rewarding. The chapters of this section are good examples of the fact that it is possible to clarify our educational goals and to improve the quality of our methods in teaching history. What is at stake is the students' learning of a subject that can be really considered as formative. A subject that helps them to make sense of their past and that, in doing so, provides a multiperspectivistic view to understand the present.

REFERENCES

Bauer, P. J., & Mandler, J. (1989). One thing follows another: Effects of temporal structure on 1- to 2-year-olds' recall of events. *Developmental Psychology, 25*, 197–206.

Britton, B. K., & Black, J. B. (1985). *Understanding expository texts*. Hillsdale, NJ: Lawrence Erlbaum Associates.

Bruner, J. (1986). *Actual minds, possible worlds*. Cambridge, MA: Harvard University Press.

Bruner, J. (1990). Acts of meaning. Cambridge, MA: Harvard University Press.

Burke, K. (1945). *A grammar of motives*. New York: Prentice-Hall.

Correa, N., & Rodrigo, M. J. (1992, September). *Beliefs about ecology and the effects of self-other perspective in a verification task*. Paper presented at the Vth European Conference on Developmental Psychology. Seville, Spain.

Gallie, W. B. (1964). *Philosophy and historical understanding*. New York: Schocken Books.

Gernsbacher, M. A., Goldsmith, H. H., & Robertson, R. R. S. (1992). Do readers mentally represent characters' emotional states? *Cognition and Emotion, 6*, 89–111.

Hempel, C. (1962). Explanation in science and in history. In R. G. Colodny (Ed.), *Frontiers of science and philosophy* (pp. 7–33). Pittsburgh: University of Pittsburgh Press.

Kuhn, D., Amsel, E., & O'Loughlin, M. (1988). *The development of scientific thinking skills*. New York: Academic Press.

Morrow, D. G., Greenspan, S. L., & Bower, G. H. (1987). Accessibility and situation models in narrative comprehension. *Journal of Memory and Language, 26*, 165–187.

Porter, D. (1981). *The emergence of the past: a theory of historical explanation*. Chicago: University of Chicago Press.

Rodrigo, M. J., Rodriguez, A., & Marrero, J, (1993). *Las teorías implícitas: Una aproximación al conocimiento cotidiano*. Madrid: Visor.

Rodrigo, M. J., & Triana, B. (1993, July). *Parental beliefs about child development and parental inferences about actions during child-rearing episodes*. Paper presented at the Symposium on Social Representations. III European Congress of Psychology. Tampere, Finland.

Smith, E. L. (1991). A conceptual change model of learning science. In S. M. Glynn, R. H. Yeany & B. K. Britton (Eds.), *The psychology of learning science* (pp. 43–63). Hillsdale, NJ: Lawrence Erlbaum Associates.

Stone, L. (1979). The revival of narrative: reflections on a new old story. *Past and Present, 85*, 3–24.

Tardieu, H., Ehrlich, M. F., & Gyselinck, V. (1992). Levels of representation and domain-specific knowledge in comprehension of scientific texts. *Language and Cognitive Processes, 7* (3/4), 335–351.

Trabasso, T., & van den Broek, P. (1985). Causal thinking and the representation of narrative events. *Journal of Memory and Language, 24*, 612–630.

Trabasso, T., & Sperry, L. (1985). Causal relatedness and importance of story events. *Journal of Memory and Language, 24,* 595–611.

de Vega, M. (1994). Characters and their perspectives in narratives describing spatial environments. *Psychological Research, 56*, 116–126.

White, H. (1981). The value of narrativity in the representation of reality. In W. J. T. Mitchell (Ed.), *On narrative* (pp. 1–24). Chicago: University of Chicago Press.

Wineburg, S. S. (1991). Historical problem solving: A study of the cognitive processes used in the evaluation of documentary and pictorial evidence. *Journal of Educational Psychology, 83*, 73–87.

IV COMPLEX PROCESSES IN HISTORY AND SOCIAL SCIENCES

13 Struggling with the Past: Some Dynamics of Historical Representation

James V. Wertsch
Clark University

The ideas that a citizenry has about its history play an essential role — for better or worse — in shaping its political discourse and action. Historical accounts may be invoked in order to remind others of shameful episodes of the past that should not be repeated or of democratic traditions that should be upheld. They may also be invoked to incite groups to deprive others of their rights, property, or lives in the name of reversing past injustices or returning to an earlier glorious (and often highly mythologized) period.

A fact that underlies all these processes is that some form of representing the past must be involved. Because the only access we have to the past is through its representation, that is, through history, it is crucial to understand the factors that shape the production and uses of these representations. Among other things, it is important to understand the historical representations that ordinary citizens hold. It is these historical representations that political discourse often draws on to mobilize action. What cultural and psychological processes are involved in the production of historical representation, and how do these processes operate in various sociocultural settings?

In what follows, I examine these issues by approaching historical representation as a form of "mediated action" (Wertsch, 1985, 1991). In this approach historical representations are viewed as deriving from the employment of "mediational means," or cultural tools (I use the two terms interchangeably here). The cultural tools involved are semiotic devices such as stories or narratives, strategies of argumentation, and mythic structures. They are provided by the cultural, historical, and institutional settings in which people live, and they play a fundamental role in shaping the form

323

that mediated action—in this case, the action of producing historical accounts—takes. As in the case of any form of mediated action, the cultural tools employed here operate both to empower and to constrain action.

Mediational means and their unique, contextualized instantiation or use are two ingredients that come together in an irreducible tension in carrying out mediated action. Thus, it is neither the case that cultural tools mechanistically determine our thinking and speaking about the past nor that we somehow produce our representations of the past de novo, "without outside interference" (Taylor, 1985), as it were. Both ingredients are inherently involved in mediated action, the interaction, or tension between them taking on a variety of forms.

As is often the case in mediated action, more than one mediational means from a "cultural tool kit" (Wertsch, 1991) may be invoked when carrying out an episode of mediated action such as producing an account of the past. Instead of organizing historical texts around a single story line, they may be shaped by more than one, creating a kind of "multivoiced" (Bakhtin, 1981) account. The different voices or perspectives involved may be woven together in a smooth and coherent way, but in many cases their simultaneous presence results in struggles, or conflicts, that reflect patterns of power and authority in the sociocultural setting.

In some cases this struggle may be quite one-sided in the sense that even though individuals using a cultural tool may try to "resist" (de Certeau, 1984) its influence, they may not be successful in finding an alternative to using it in the end, thereby succumbing to a kind of "domination by mediational means." In actuality it is perhaps more appropriate to speak of domination *through* mediational means because a key to understanding the meaning systems introduced into the process by cultural tools is that these tools always "belong" (Bakhtin, 1986; Wertsch, 1991) to some individual or group, and it is hence that individual's or group's voice that is entering the picture.

In the case of historical accounts, the struggle over which cultural tool should be used emerges on the social and overtly political level in the form of disputes such as those between proponents of social and of political history (e.g., Himmelfarb, 1987) or between proponents of Afrocentric and more traditional, Eurocentric approaches to history instruction in the United States. If one accepts Vygotsky's (1981) formulation of how social ("intermental") processes give rise to mental processes in the individual (i.e., on the "intramental" plane), one would expect some form of struggle between "conflicting narratives" (Holt, 1990) to be characteristic of individual psychological functioning as well. For example, this struggle may be between two or more conflicting accounts of an historical episode known to an individual, or it may take the form of an individual's resistance to a dominant narrative account of the past. In the case of intramental as well as intermental processes, an analysis grounded in mediated action requires one to take into account the mediational means provided by the sociocultural setting on the one hand and the dynamics of their unique use in a particular context by particular individuals or groups on the other.

In examining historical representation as mediated action, the cultural tool I focus on is narrative. The importance of narrative in historical representation has been widely discussed by historians, historiographers, and philosphers of history (e.g., Carr, 1986; Mink, 1978; Ricouer, 1984; White, 1987). Issues of narrative form have also been recognized as having major implications for how instructional texts are written (Beck & McKeown, this volume), for the cognitive processing of history texts (e.g., Perfetti, this volume; Rodrigo, this volume), and for other aspects of historical representation and the teaching of history.

Even a cursory reading of the literature on narrative reveals that it has no single, generally accepted definition. The particular understanding held by scholars concerned with narrative varies with their theoretical, methodological, and disciplinary orientation. My intention here is not to sort through this complex literature, but to focus on a few, widely accepted properties of narrative outlined by several theorists in an attempt to illuminate some fundamental aspects of historical representation as mediated action.

Perhaps most theorists agree that a defining feature of narratives is that they have a beginning, middle, and end. These components involve the kind of temporal closure that Aristotle associated with the wholeness or unity of action in a tragedy. In this view, the "sense of an ending" (Kermode, 1968), along with the beginning and middle that lead up to it, are what give narrative accounts, including historical narratives, their organization and distinguish them in essential ways from other forms of historical representation such as chronicles (White, 1987).

In general, several options exist for organizing the beginning, middle, and end of an account of the past into a coherent whole. If White (1973) is correct, the range is actually quite limited at the level of fundamental structuring, reflecting basic tropes such as tragedy, comedy, and romance that have organized Western myth and literature for millenia.

Regardless of the particular story or of the general category of story employed, authors such as Mink and Ricouer see the task of producing a narrative account of the past as sharing certain basic elements. It involves a "synthesis of the heterogeneous" in which "agents, goals, means, interactions, circumstances, unexpected results, etc." (Ricouer, 1984, p. 102) are sifted through, brought together, and organized into some kind of coherent narrative whole.

In developing his account of the narrative structuring of history, Ricouer emphasized the importance of the narrator's activities of selecting, organizing, and presenting events from the past. In his view, "The ideas of beginning, middle, and end are not taken from experience: They are not traits of real action but effects of poetic ordering" (p. 67). That is, they emerge in the process of a narrator's imposing order on information about the past. In Ricouer's account, this activity of poetic ordering is carried out through *emplotment*, a process that mediates between two basic aspects of a narrative: the chronological and the nonchronological. The events reported in a narrative occur chronologically; they succeed one another in a linear fashion and constitute an "episodic" dimension. Emplotment is a "configurational act" that transforms the chronologically organized events into a story or narrative by "grasping them together" in a particular way to form a coherent story line leading up to an ending.

In what follows, I focus primarily on one aspect of the configurational act of emplotment: the representation of the agent or subject of historical narratives. To a lesser extent, I also consider a second, inextricably related aspect of narratives: the representation of events. The agents I consider may be individuals, groups, or institutions, but in all cases they are presented as having goals and motivations and as being primarily responsible for initiating and carrying forward the events reported in the narrative. One of my underlying assumptions in carrying out this analysis is that like the beginning, middle, and end of a narrative, the agents involved are "not traits of real action but effects of poetic ordering" (Ricouer, 1984, p.67). Furthermore, I assume that the particular way that agents are represented will be heavily shaped by the mediational means invoked by individuals to produce historical accounts; they are not simply assigned or invented by individuals acting in isolation. Instead, the process occurs through invoking a particular narrative, or story line, with its unique perspective on beginning, middle, and ending events, its assignment of agents, and so forth. The resulting representation of an individual or group as the agent of an historical narrative reflects an active process involving the unique, contextualized use of cultural tools.

AN EMPIRICAL STUDY

As part of a larger study examining the historical representation of lay adults (i.e., adults who are not professional historians) in several nations, 24 students from a small New England university were asked to write an essay describing "the origins of your country." They were told that the task should take between 30 and 60 min, and that the goal of the study was to understand their account of these origins rather than to find out how much they knew about history. The students carried out this task in individual sessions and were paid 10 dollars for their participation. The texts these students produced varied widely in length ($r = 203$ to 856 words; M length $= 533.4$ words; SD

= 109.7) and in coherence and quality. At the level of certain fundamental properties of narrative structure, however, the students' texts manifested striking uniformity. This basic uniformity can be seen in: (a) the events included in the narratives, and (b) the representation of agency.

Events Mentioned in the Texts

The texts were coded for references to all events mentioned by more than 5 of the 24 students. This resulted in a list of five items: Columbus's arrival in America, the Pilgrims' arrival in America, the Declaration of Independence/ the Revolutionary War, the writing and signing of the U.S. Constitution, and the Civil War/Emancipation Proclamation (events marked by a slash indicate either/or). In some cases students mentioned a specific date for an event, and in some cases they referred to an event with a proper term such as "Declaration of Independence." However, neither of these criteria was required for a student to be given credit for mentioning the event as long as he or she provided some readily recognizable description.

There was wide variability in how frequently these events were included in the students' accounts. However, two events were mentioned by the great majority of the 24 students: the arrival of the Pilgrims (mentioned by 18 students) and the Declaration of Independence/Revolutionary War (mentioned by 19 students). The other three were mentioned by between roughly one third and one half of the students: Columbus's arrival in America (13 students), the signing of the U.S. Constitution (10 students), and the Civil War/Emancipation Proclamation (9 students). Several other events such as the expedition by Lewis and Clark were mentioned, but only sporadically.

In addition to this focus on a few events there was a high level of agreement on the motivation of the Europeans who settled America. Of the 24 students, 23 made some explicit mention of the notion that European settlers came to America because they wanted to find freedom and/or escape persecution in their native country. As O'Connor (1991, 1992) and Wertsch and O'Connor (in press) have noted, the pattern of focusing on the specific events mentioned by the students is quite consistent with the reference to the search for freedom. In particular, events such as the arrival of the Pilgrims and the writing of the Declaration of Independence and of the Constitution were almost always presented as steps in the European settlers' attempts to secure freedom from the British and to avoid other forms of oppresive government. For this reason, O'Connor has argued that the three events and the mention of a search for freedom constitute two components of a theme that could be termed the "quest for freedom."

These two components already provide some insight into the narrative structure of the students' texts. First, they provide some indication of what the students considered to be the essential points of the beginning, namely, the arrival of European settlers in America, and to some extent the middle and end of the narrative. And second, they provide information about what the students considered to be the major goal of the actors in these events.

Representation of Agency

From what has been said about the events included in these narratives, it would seem that good candidates for agents would be the European settlers. After all, it is likely that their motivations and actions would be viewed as being essential for understanding events such as the Revolutionary War and the writing of the U.S. Constitution. This does not mean that other individuals and groups were not mentioned by the students, but it does suggest that the frequency of mention and the ways in which these other individuals or groups were presented might differ from patterns associated with the European settlers. In order to examine this supposition, I first examine frequency and then turn to forms of presentation.

Using the appearance of noun phrases, including pronouns, in surface form as the criterion for mentioning an individual or group, differences in how often various groups are mentioned are quite striking. European settlers were mentioned 505 times, Native Americans were mentioned 94 times, the British were mentioned 48 times, and African Americans were mentioned 40 times (other groups such as Spanish and French colonizers were also mentioned, but at much lower frequencies). Every one of the 24 students mentioned European settlers more frequently than any other group, and in many cases they mentioned no group other than European settlers. Because some of the most interesting issues concerning agency emerge in connection with two specific groups—European settlers and Native Americans—and because the frequency of mention of other groups is quite small, I focus on only these two groups in what follows.

Frequency of mention is often highly associated with agency, but it is necessary to go beyond this simple measure to understand agency for at least two reasons. First, it is entirely possible for one individual or group to be mentioned more than any other in a narrative, yet not be the agent of the narrative. For example, it would be possible for the most frequently mentioned group in a text to be an essential component of the scene (Burke, 1969) of the actions reported rather than the source of goals and action. For this reason alone, it is important to employ additional ways of assessing agency. Second, simple frequencies provide little insight into the structure and meaning of agency in narratives. Agency is seldom simply a matter of presence or absence. Instead, it may vary along several dimensions that lend important qualities to how a narrative text is organized. In the following analyses I address two such dimensions: (a) patterns of "propositional referentiality," and (b) "presupposed presence."

Patterns of Propositional Referentiality

One of the first things needed in order to explicate the structure and meaning of agency is an analysis of the roles of individuals and groups with regard to the events and actions reported. Who initiated and carried out the actions, and who was a bystander or a victim? Who did the acting, and who was acted upon? One way of getting at these issues is by examining the structure of *propositional referentiality* (Silverstein, 1980) in a text. Propositional referentiality is an essential aspect of language as a mediational means (Wertsch, 1985). It is concerned with the roles that arguments or constituents play within propositions or their linguistic expression, sentences.

For purposes of the present analysis, it is useful to focus on two general groupings of propositional referentiality: both a *superordinate* and a *subordinate* category. Each of these categories groups together several grammatical roles that are normally distinguished in linguistic analyses. In the category superordinate I include noun phrases in the position of: (a) subject of an active transitive clause, (b) subject of an intransitive clause, (c) subject of a copula clause, and (d) noun phrase following "by" (either present in surface form or deleted) in a passive transitive clause.

Linguistic analyses concerned with propositional referentiality or grammatical roles within clause structure would typically include only items (a) and (d) under the heading of agency. In an attempt to explicate agency as a narrative property, however, I employ the more general category of superordinate. This broader notion is aimed at capturing at least most cases in which an individual or group referred to by a noun phrase is given a primary status. It may be given this status by being represented as being the initiator of action, the party that carries out action on another party, or the focus of description. Examples (1), (2), (3), and (4) from the students' texts are examples of (a), (b), (c), and (d), respectively.

1. *They* [the Indians] taught them [the Pilgrims] how to fish, grow, and fertilize crops, prepare for long hard winters, and to appreciate nature.
2. *The population of white people* grew disproportionately.
3. *The settlers* were an ambitious sort.
4. The Indians, with a different culture, dress, language, religion, etc. were feared *by the newcomers*.

Like the category superordinate, the category *subordinate* used here does not correspond to any single role of propositional referentiality. Instead, it groups together several grammatical roles, the common thread being that noun phrases in all of them indicate a secondary status of the individual or group mentioned vis-à-vis the individual or group mentioned in the position of a superordinate noun phrase. This secondary status could derive from the fact that the subordinate noun phrase refers to a group that receives the action of the actor (sometimes as a victim), or it could derive from the fact that the group is referred to in a way indicating that it is a secondary but not the main actor. The following items were coded as noun phrases in the subordinate category: (e) direct object in a transitive clause (either active or passive), (f) indirect object in a transitive clause (either active or passive), and (g) noun phrases following "with" in the sense of "in collaboration with." Examples (5), (6), and (7) from the students' texts are examples of (e), (f), and (g), respectively.

5. Within a decade or two, he [Columbus] had completely decimated *the entire Arawak Indian tribe.*
6. This enraged the colonies because England refused to give *them* representation in Parliament.
7. The settlers also exploited the Indians by trading goods with *them* that complicated the Indians' way of life.

All noun phrases referring to European settlers or to Native Americans that occurred in superordinate or subordinate positions were coded. Of the noun phrases in the students' texts that referred to the European settlers, 89.1% appeared in superordinate position. The corresponding figure for noun phrases that referred to Native Americans was 64%. Hence, whenever European settlers were mentioned, they were very likely to be given primary status in a clause. This tendency was markedly less pronounced for Native Americans. Indeed, Native Americans often were presented as recipients or victims of action. As already noted, in many cases the appearance of noun phrases in the subordinate position indicated a status of being acted on by groups mentioned in superordinate noun phrases. For example, consider the following paragraph from one student's text, coded for noun phrases in superordinate ("[sup]") and subordinate ("[sub]") positions:

> However, *the settlers*[sup] did not stay thankful for long. *The Pilgrims*[sup] felt that it was their duty as good Christians to save *these "savages"*[sub] from sin. *The settlers*[sup] also exploited *the Indians*[sub] by trading goods with *them*[sub] that complicated the Indians' way of life. *They*[sup] also took the Indians' land, and hunting grounds. *The settlers*[sup] also used the delicate situations that were between tribal enemies to set *the Indians*[sub] against each other for economic benefit.

Throughout this paragraph the pattern is for noun phrases referring to European settlers to be in a superordinate position and for noun phrases referring to Native Americans to be in a subordinate position. The resulting picture is one in which the European settlers' goals, motivations, and actions are represented as paramount and in which they are the active agents. In contrast, the goals, motivations, and actions of the Native Americans are not mentioned. Instead, Native Americans are represented as recipients or victims of the European settlers' actions. The pattern of propositional referentiality within clauses obviously is quite consistent with, and indeed may be seen as being an essential constitutive factor of, the agency assigned to the narrative as a whole.

Although the pattern of mentioning Native Americans in the subordinate role was not always as straightforward as in the preceding paragraph, it was quite strong across students. One indication of this is the relative tendency of the students to mention Native Americans and European settlers in the subordinate position. The texts of 18 of the 24 students included at least one mention of Native Americans or European settlers in the subordinate position. Of these 18 cases, 7 included more references to Native Americans than European settlers in the subordinate position, 8 included an equal number of references to Native Americans and European settlers in the subordinate position, and only 3 included more references to European settlers than Native Americans in the subordinate position. This pattern is particularly striking, given the much greater number of references overall to European settlers than to Native Americans.

The general pattern of propositional referentiality, then, is one in which the vast majority of references to European settlers were made in superordinate position, whereas this tendency was less pronounced in the case of Native Americans. Furthermore, there was a tendency for noun phrases in subordinate positions to be used to refer to Native Americans rather than to European settlers.

Presupposed Presence

A second dimension of narrative agency to be examined has to do with what I term the *presupposed presence* of various characters in the historical narratives provided by the students. The notion of presupposed presence is associated with "discourse referentiality" as opposed to "propositional referentiality" (Silverstein, 1980; Wertsch, 1985). That is, it has to do with the relationship between unique, situated utterances and the contexts in which they occur. More specifically, it has to do with how utterances function to presuppose the context of speech in which they occur, on the one hand, and to create or entail the context, on the other.

The notion of presupposed presence is concerned with the fact that individuals or groups mentioned in a text can be treated as being more or less present in the speech context and hence accessible to speaker and listener (or writer and reader). This is manifested in a speaker's tendency to refer to characters as if their presence is obvious and hence can be assumed. In such cases there is no need to identify the character by using elaborate explicit forms. Indeed, a speaker may go so far as to use no explicit surface form at all. In contrast, a speaker may assume that the character is not obvious or is not present in the attention or consciousness (Chafe, 1974) of the interlocutors involved in the speech setting. In such cases, there will be a need to introduce or reintroduce the character through the use of explicit referring expressions.

There are certain parallels between the notion of presupposed presence and the notions of "given information" (Chafe, 1974, 1976), "old information" (Halliday, 1967), or "psychological subject" (Vygotsky, 1987). In these latter three cases, the basic claim is that information is available either in the "extralinguistic" or "intralinguistic" speech event context (Wertsch, 1985), and this makes "attenuation" (Chafe, 1976; Wertsch, 1985) or "abbreviation" (Vygotsky, 1987) possible, typically in the form of pronominal referring expressions or deletions. The relationship is a "presupposing" one (Silverstein, 1976) in the sense that information is available in the context and can therefore be presupposed when producing utterances. In this sense the speech event context shapes the utterance.

In contrast to this, the relationship between utterance and context is the opposite in the case of instances of what I call presupposed presence. Instead of a genuinely presupposing relationship, it is a "creative" (Silverstein, 1985) or "performative" (Silverstein, 1976) one. In such cases producing utterances with certain forms creates and recreates a context. The specific focus in this case is on the assumed presence of certain characters in the speech event context. Instead of the context shaping the utterance, the focus is on how an utterance shapes the context.

This is not to deny that a precondition for attenuation in instances of presupposed presence is that certain information is available from the extralinguistic or intralinguistic context. If no such information is available, the utterance may be uninterpretable or may appear to be "egocentric" in the sense that Piaget (1926) proposed. However, in many cases such information is equally available for two or more protagonists in a text, yet attenuation may be much more pronounced in the case of references to one than the other. In such cases, there is a kind of "as if" effect. One protagonist is treated as if he or she is more obvious, more present in the consciousness of the speaker and listener than another, and this treatment is precisely what creates the impression of presupposed presence.

In an effort to examine the presupposed presence of various characters in the texts students produced for this study, two forms of attenuation were analyzed: (a) pronouns (in any position of propositional referentiality), and (b) agent noun phrase deletions that occurred in passive clauses. Other forms of noun phrase deletion such as gapping and dropping noun phrases from compound sentences also occurred in the texts, but in many instances it was difficult to be certain of the identity of the referent in such cases. For such reasons the analysis of noun phrase deletion was limited to the more conservative measure of agent deletion in passive clauses. An example of attenutation in the form of pronominalization from the students' texts is example (8), and an example from students' texts of agent noun phrase deletion from a passive clause is shown in (9):

8. In short, *they* [settlers from England] were beginning to feel smothered, just as *they* had in England.
9. The situation became worse and worse, and finally the Indians were driven west *[i.e., by European settlers]*.

In both the case of pronominal attenuation and the case of agent noun phrase deletion from passive clauses, there was a strong pattern of presupposed presence for European settlers, but a near absence of presupposed presence for Native Americans. There were 93 pronominal references to European settlers and only 4 such pronominal references to Native Americans in the texts. The difference was even more striking in the case of agent noun phrase deletion from passive clauses. Eighty-nine such deletions occurred when the referents were European settlers, whereas only 1 such deletion occurred in the case when the referent was a Native American.

To some extent, these differences can be attributed to differences in the frequency with which European settlers and Native Americans were mentioned in the texts. However, the difference in the use of attentuated reference is much more pronounced than differences in frequency of mention. The striking differences in both patterns of attenuation suggest a very strong presupposed presence of European settlers in contrast to that of Native Americans. The students producing these texts tended to assign European settlers the role of being much more obviously present than Native Americans in their own and their interlocutors' consciousness, or in the speech event contexts in which they were operating. Indeed, in many cases the European settlers were presupposed to be so obviously present that there was no need to mention them at all in surface form each time they came up; their presence could simply be assumed or presupposed. In contrast, when mentioning Native Americans, the students tended to use explicit forms, a practice indicating that the Native Americans were not considered to be so readily present in the speech event context (i.e., the context of writing the texts).

RESISTANCE AND COMPETING NARRATIVES

In the previous section, I outlined a few findings about how events and agency were represented in 24 students' narrative accounts of the origins of the United States. The overall picture is one that can be summarized by saying that in the students' view, the story of these origins is a story about the motivations and agency of European settlers as they carried out a basic set of events.

Additional events were mentioned, but only sporadically. Also, other characters, especially Native Americans, were mentioned, but they appeared in the texts less frequently, and when they did appear, they were less likely to be treated as the agents of the narratives. Instead, there was often a tendency for Native Americans to appear in the role of victims or recipients of the actions of the European settlers. Furthermore, the measure of "presupposed presence" indicates that the texts were organized as if the existence of European settlers, but not Native Americans, could be readily assumed, a tendency that serves to enhance the central position already given to European settlers in the texts.

The various properties of the texts I outlined may be viewed as dimensions of a single, integrated pattern of organization in the students' narratives. It is an organization based on a small set of key events with their associated motivation (the "quest for freedom") carried out by a specific set of agents who had that motivation. The resulting picture is one in which the beginning, middle, and end of the narratives were a very particular and delimited beginning, middle, and end coordinated with a particular and delimited motivation and a particular and delimited set of agents. The European settlers, with their motivations and actions, dominated center stage to such an extent that the students producing the texts seemed to find it difficult to incorporate information about other events, agents, and motivations. The type of narrative organization employed served to allow the presentatioan of only one perspective, or one voice, and made it difficult for other voices to emerge in an effective way.

Why did the students come up with such "monological" or "univocal" (Wertsch, 1991) accounts? One explanation is that they had gone through a process of considering alternative narratives of the past and had arrived at the conclusion that a story line that focuses almost exclusively on European settlers is the best one available. Research by Wineburg (1991) that indicates only minimal levels of critical reading and questioning by students when confronted with historical texts does not support such an explanation. Furthermore, the history instruction to which these students had been exposed was unlikely to present fully developed alternative narrative accounts of the origins of the United States.

Another explanation for the appearance of the students' monological accounts is that they had some motivation, political or otherwise, for focusing exclusively on European settlers. At least in a few cases, this may have been the case. For example, one student who finished his account with, "Very impressive for being only two hundred years old," focused exclusively on European settlers, never mentioning groups such as Native Americans. However, celebratory accounts such as this seem to have been the exception rather than the rule.

Indeed, several students indicated in one way or another that they did not fully accept an account of the origins of the United States that focused so exclusively on the European settlers. For example, one student finished by writing:

> So as far as the "beginnings," it is necessary to distinguish *whose* beginnings. My upbringing and historical knowledge has been grounded in the nation's "Founding Fathers" and the ideals of democracy. I am not 100% sure I agree with all the original premises, but according to the perspective I've been born into, it is these values which have influenced me. But to be objective is to say that the beginnings of this land we live on are not those of the white man, but of the Indians.

Such overt expressions of dissatisfaction with the monologic accounts they produced surfaced in several students' texts. Six of them made explicit comments critical of the single perspective of their text and/or of the single perspective they had encountered in history instruction. They spoke of the need to specify *whose* history was at issue or of the need to question and criticize what they had learned from textbooks and teachers. Furthermore, other forms of questioning or rejecting the accounts they produced emerged in many students' texts. O'Connor (1991, 1992) and Wertsch and O'Connor (in press) have outlined several ways in which students who introduced Native Americans into their accounts attempted to deal with the contradiction that many of them saw between the treatment of this population and the quest for freedom theme. In all, half of the students indicated in one way or another some recognition and criticism of the basic monologic text they produced.

If there was such widespread unease or dissatisfaction with the organization of their stories, why did the students produce the narratives that they did? It seems that an answer to this can be formulated by again focusing on the properties of mediated action when considering the production of these historical texts. This perspective asserts that the students produced their narratives by invoking a tightly organized mediational means in the form of a narrative, or story line, having to do with an integrated set of events, motivations, and agents. This cultural tool had been provided by the sociocultural setting in which these students had been socialized (e.g., schooling, official holidays, and so forth). The use of this particular cultural tool introduced a dominant focus on certain events and agents to such an extent that there seemed to be little room left for others. It is this exclusionary focus that created the univocal form of these texts, allowing the students to talk about a single set of events and a single set of agents and allowing other events and characters into the picture in a subordinate role at best.

If this is the form of the mediational means that seemed to be used by the students, what can be said about the processes and reasons for using it? The first and most obvious point is that the main reason the students used it was that they had no other mediational means available. Some students who recognized this made explicit statements about it. For example, one student stated at the outset that she considered the history of the United States to be the history of the land and its early inhabitants. After making this point, however, she went on to say, "Since . . . I know relatively little about the geological and anthropological aspects of the ancient United States, I will deal with aspects of history with which I am more familiar. Suffice it to say, however, that I do not consider the history of the 'US' to begin at this point." Following this disclaimer, she went on to write about European settlers, their relations with Native Americans, and so forth.

In general, then, even though roughly half the students expressed some form of discomfort with the story line they employed, they proceeded to use it. I argue that this tendency reflects the fact that the students invoked a single cultural tool. Many of them tried in one way or another to engage in "tactics of resistance" (de Certeau, 1984) against the power of this mediational means to shape their text, but these tactics were generally quite ineffective, both because the students had access to no well-developed alternative cultural tool and because the tool they *were* using had an integrated and exclusionary structure that made it very difficult for other voices to participate in the production of the texts in any elaborate way.

What this suggests is that in addition to examining ways in which individuals master accounts of the past, we need to learn much more about how they enter into specific kinds of "use relations" with these accounts. Do they accept them wholeheartedly, or do they question or even reject them? By viewing the production of historical narratives as a form of mediated action, it is possible to keep these questions in focus. In addition to inserting an essential dimension into our understanding of how the teaching and mastery of historical knowledge takes place, this focus will perhaps allow us to address more fully issues of what citizens' historical beliefs are and how these beliefs are used for beneficial and detrimental purposes.

ACKNOWLEDGMENTS

An earlier version of this chapter was presented at the Conference on "Cognitive and Instructional Processes in Social Sciences and History," Autonoma University, Madrid, October 23–25, 1992. The research for this chapter was assisted by a grant from the Spencer Foundation. The statements made and the views expressed are solely the responsibility of the author.

REFERENCES

Bakhtin, M. M. (1981). *The dialogic imagination: Four essays by M.M. Bakhtin* (M. Holquist, Ed.; C. Emerson & M. Holquist, Trans.). Austin: University of Texas Press.

Bakhtin, M. M. (1986). *Speech genres and other late essays* (C. Emerson & M. Holquist, Eds.; V.W. McGee, Trans.). Austin: University of Texas Press.

Burke, K. (1969). *A grammar of motives.* Berkeley: University of California Press.

Carr, D. (1986). *Time, narrative, and history.* Bloomington: Indiana University Press.

de Certeau, M. (1984). *The practice of everyday life* (S. F. Rendall, Trans.). Berkeley: University of California Press.

Chafe, W. L. (1974). Language and consciousness. *Language, 50,* 111–113.

Chafe, W. L. (1976). Givenness, contrastiveness, definiteness, subjects, topics, and point of view. In C. N. Li (Ed.), *Subject and topic* (pp. 25–56). New York: Academic Press.

Halliday, M. A. K. (1967). Notes on transitivity and theme in English, II. *Journal of Linguistics, 3,* 199–244.

Himmelfarb, G. (1987). *The new history and the old.* Cambridge, MA: Harvard University Press.

Holt, T. (1990). *Thinking historically: Narrative, imagination, and understanding.* New York: College Board Publications.

Kermode, F. (1968). *The sense of an ending.* New York: Oxford University Press.

Mink, L. O. (1978). Narrative form as a cognitive instrument. In R. H. Canary & H. Kozicki (Eds.), *The writing of history: Literary form and historical understanding* (pp. 129–149). Madison: University of Wisconsin Press.

O'Connor, K. (1991, April). *Narrative form and historical representation: A study of American college students' historical narratives.* Paper presented at the Conference for Pedagogic Text Analysis and Content Analysis, Harnosand, Sweden.

O'Connor, K. (1992). *Narrative form and historical representation.* Unpublished master's thesis, Clark University, Worcester, MA.

Piaget, J. (1926). *The language and thought of the child.* New York: Harcourt Brace.

Ricouer, P. (1984). *Time and narrative* (Vol. 1). Chicago: University of Chicago Press.

Silverstein, M. (1976). Shifters, linguistic categories, and cultural description. In K. Basso & H. Selby (Eds.), *Meaning in anthropology* (pp. 11–55). Albuquerque: University of New Mexico Press.

Silverstein, M. (1980, November). *Cognitive implications of a referential hierarchy.* Paper presented at the Max-Planck-Institut fur Psycholinguistik. Nijmegen, The Netherlands.

Silverstein, M. (1985). The functional stratification of language and ontogenesis. In J. V. Wertsch (Ed.), *Culture, communication, and cognition: Vygotskian perspectives* (pp. 205–235). New York: Cambridge University Press.

Taylor, C. (1985). *Human agency and language* (Philosophical papers 1). Cambridge, England: Cambridge University Press.

Vygotsky, L. S. (1981). The genesis of higher mental functions. In J. V. Wertsch (Ed.), *The concept of activity in Soviet psychology.* Armonk, NY: M.E. Sharpe.

Vygotsky, L. S. (1987). *The collected works of L.S. Vygotsky. Vol. 1: Problems of general psychology. Including the volume thinking and speech* (N. Minick, Ed. & Trans.). New York: Plenum.

Wertsch, J. V. (1985). *Vygotsky and the social formation of mind.* Cambridge, MA: Harvard University Press.

Wertsch, J. V. (1991). *Voices of the mind: A sociocultural approach to mediated action.* Cambridge, MA: Harvard University Press.

Wertsch, J. V., & O'Connor, K. (in press). The cognitive tools of historical representation: A sociocultural analysis. *Journal of Narrative and Life History.*

White, H. (1973). *Metahistory: The historical imagination in nineteenth-century Europe.* Baltimore: Johns Hopkins University.

White, H. (1987). *The content of the form: Narrative discourse and historical representation.* Baltimore: Johns Hopkins Press.

Wineburg, S. S. (1991). On the reading of historical texts: Notes on the breach between school and academy. *American Educational Research Journal, 28,* 495–519.

14

(Re-)Constructing History and Moral Judgment: On Relationships Between Interpretations of the Past and Perceptions of the Present

Bodo von Borries
University of Hamburg

There are comparatively few empirical studies of the processes of historical socialization in the Federal Republic of Germany. This in itself precludes an overview of the state of research. After some qualitative work using classroom protocols, autobiographies, and interviews (cf. Borries, 1988), a series of quantitative studies was conducted with four main aims: (a) to provide measures of the basic dimensions of historical consciousness (knowledge, attitudes, collective identity, etc.); (b) to trace the developmental logic of historical awareness; (c) to map the relationships among cognitive, motivational, moral, and affective constituents of historical learning; and (d) to explore correlations between interpretations of the past, perceptions of the present, and expectations of the future. The findings of a major study conducted in 1990, using closed-response questionnaires (N = 1,915 respondents from 6th-, 9th-, and 12th-grade classrooms, from both East and West Germany), is worth mentioning here (Borries, 1992). Some of the more important findings were:

1. Cognitive, motivational, moral, and affective responses can be identified as representing four distinct dimensions; these can be measured with some degree of validity as separate traits.

2. Cognitive differences among students are closely associated with age, type of school, and scholastic achievement in history. Differences in moral judgments are linked to gender, party preference, and attitudes toward present-day issues. Motivational and emotional differences are almost completely independent of social background variables. Motivation and knowledge are almost completely uncorrelated.

3. The eminent outcome of historical learning as a whole (both within and outside school) appears to be an orientation toward fundamental values, such as the internalization of human and civil rights. It is likely, however, that this orientation is not derived from historical material, but transferred from highly generalized social norms and applied to past conflicts.

4. Past constraints on action, if deviating from present-day concepts, are hardly ever reconstructed historically. Moral judgments rooted in the present are substituted for historical analysis. Empathy with the historical other does not take place.

5. The findings concerning students understanding of historical origins, transformations, and progress are particularly puzzling and inconsistent. Indeed, probably the outcomes of historical learning themselves lack clarity.

6. The differences between East and West Germany appear to be substantial, but only at the surface level. In terms of deep structure, differences are negligible or nonexistent. At least this was true in the euphoric situation during the summer of 1990; new differences since that time may have emerged.

Further results from an additional pilot study (conducted at the end of 1991) are reported next. Almost 1,000 students, again from 6th, 9th-, and 12th-grade classrooms of different school types and from three different Federal States (City of Hamburg, Northrhine-Westphalia, Saxony), were subjected to three overlapping versions of a questionnaire. Most of the items asked for responses on a 5-point Likert scale, but some also asked for multiple-choice or for response rankings. Multivariate analyses using classical item analysis, factor analysis, and path analysis were also performed. In spite of relatively small sample sizes (City of Hamburg = 423; Northrhine-Westphalia = 317; Saxony = 253) and in spite of some imperfections in the sampling, the findings may be taken as being highly plausible and as sources of additional insight. The three subsamples, where they lead to parallel conclusions, reinforce each other; from a technical standpoint, joint analyses were only partially possible so that some open questions remain.

The research questions clearly transcended those of the 1990 study in that media-related variables and socialization practices were also investigated. The following is an attempt to shed light on the relationships among historical reconstruction (i.e., a higher level cognitive operation of historical awareness), moral decision (i.e., an application of concepts of human rights to past societies), general concepts of historical progress (i.e., an eminently interpretative category for fundamental processes of change), and mental operations of historical insight (i.e., the concepts of historical methods in the students' perceptions).

CRUSADE

In 1991, the respondents from Hamburg confronted an extended text passage on the First Crusade and the conquest of Jerusalem in 1099. In a lengthy quotation from an original source, for example, the massacre of the inhabitants of that city was described rather intensely. Several groups of items were used to elicit the students' responses at different levels. First, researchers attempted to measure reading comprehension by eliciting student responses to text-related statements, responding to reject, confirm, or leave undecided. Eight (out of 10) items formed a scale — "Text comprehension of Crusade" — of rather low internal consistency (Cronbach's α = .54). Its moderate correlation with a general measure of "chronological knowledge" (r = .39) implies, however, that this scale renders some approximation for a set of elementary cognitive operations.

Questions concerning concomitant emotions turned out to be more important: "What do you feel when reading (. . .)?" The 16 responses comprise, very clearly, two groups: Emotions of sadness and guilt, made up one side, for example, "sympathy with the Muslims' grief," "shame over the atrocities of European Christians," and "being appalled by the unchristian sermon of the Pope." Eight items formed a highly reliable scale — "Offense with the Crusade" (α = .81). Comparing the scale mean values for the three age groups (see Fig. 14.1) clearly shows that these negative emotions are dominant from the very beginning and that they increase with age (and educational status).

Quite analogously, the positive emotions were also closely associated with each other: for example, "Fascination with adventurous travel and exciting battle," "pride in the valor and supremacy of the Christian knights," and "admiration for the strong faith of the pilgrims," form a scale — "Fascination with the Crusades" — which, because of the small number of constituting items, is somewhat less internally consistent (K = 4; α = .64). The low correlation with "Offense" (r = -.15) indicates that this item group does, indeed, represent a substantially independent trait of its own. "Fascination" was strongly and negatively related to age. Positive emotions related to adventure, exotic circumstance, and the use of force were rejected very early, and increasingly so with growing age. Apparently, not only was "Offense" acquired over time, but also, and independent of it, was the tendency to reject manifestations of "fascination," which were extinguished (cf. Fig. 14.1).

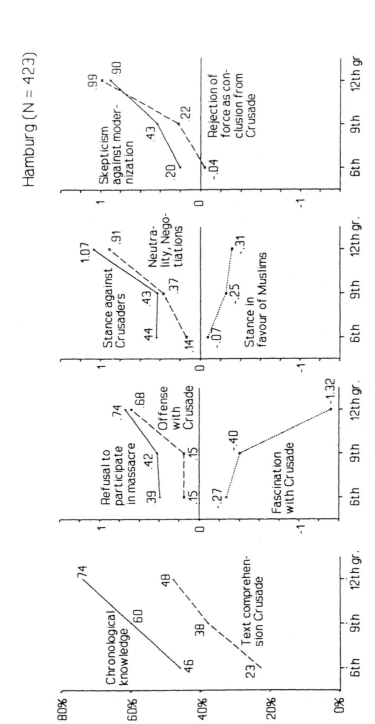

FIG. 14.1. Evaluation of crusade (mean values by grade, mostly scales ranging from −2.0 to +2.0).

As a third component, following text comprehension and the emotional items, responses were evoked that were meant to indicate the stance taken by the respondents toward the conflict: "Which side do you take in the conflict described? Whom do you favor?" The five arguments in favor of the Crusaders appear as parallel measures, constituting a fairy reliable scale — "Stance in favor of Crusaders" — ($\alpha = .78$). All age groups displayed distinctly negative mean values on this scale and all the more so during the course of historical socialization (Fig. 14.1). Therefore, this scale was recoded to form an inverted scale — "Stance against Crusaders." Appeal to one's own kin was as little appreciated as appeal to valor or to medieval moral standards. Although this renunciation of the Christians is easily understandable in the face of the described Jerusalem massacre, it would likely have been much less pronounced 30 years ago.

Similarly, the five items in favor of the Muslims form a consistent scale — "Stance in favor of the Muslims" ($\alpha = .77$). In other words, the divergent justifications (tolerance at the time, defense, right of a home, military inferiority) were used indiscriminately and conjointly. "Stance in favor of the Muslims" displays negative mean values from 6th grade onward. Reluctance to align with the Muslims increased during the course of historical socialization, albeit less than the case with the Christians. At first sight, this simultaneous detachment from both sides in the conflict may be surprising. Obviously, the sympathies were not expended in a simple symmetrical pattern.

One explanation for this remarkable observation can be found in the two items measuring the tendency to stay neutral. The respondents rejected, increasingly so with age, the assertion that they "align with neither side, because such a long-past, superfluous conflict does not really concern me." At the same time, however, they affirmed even more strongly that they "align with neither side, because negotiations could have prevented war and bloodshed" (cf. Fig. 14.1). In other words the respondents' decisions — above all that of the older ones — were unrelated to any identification with their forefathers and their own cultural traditions, nor were they influenced by nostalgic and emotional sympathies for the victims of history, and least of all by lack of interest. Rather, rational and moral reasoning lead them to withhold their solidarity with any party in the conflict. They argued in favor of reason, tolerance, and peace which — according to the students — were promoted neither by the Christians nor by the Muslims in 1099.

It is easy to substantiate this interpretation by looking at the consequences drawn from the events of the First Crusade. Almost all the generalizations and statements on historical change can be taken to form a reliable scale — "Rejection of force as conclusion from the Crusade" ($\alpha = .76$). It includes the following assertions: "Human rights are more important than Christian mission" and "Religious tolerance and freedom of faith are late products of history; they have to be maintained and reinforced." Taken together, these conclusions and value statements are surprisingly consistent and clear. Whereas the youngest students (6th grade) were undecided yet as to the use of force, the middle group (9th grade) and even more so the oldest group (12th grade) were, on the average, firmly determined to renounce the use of force (Fig. 14.1). Consequently, the neutrality item quoted earlier would fit well into this scale ($r = .35$).

These consequences, motivated by human rights considerations, are easily understandable and even desirable as judgments related to the present. From a medieval perspective, however, they could—and even should—have been quite different. Therefore, the students were asked: "Imagine yourself in the position of a Crusader during the conquest of Jerusalem after a long and trying journey as well as a bloody siege. Would you have participated in the massacre?" Following this opening prompt, 14 statements (both positive and negative) were to be responded to, for example, "The Pope as God's vicar has given his explicit permission— therefore yes, by all means!" and "Slaughtering women and children can never be justified—therefore no, guard my sword!"

The students hardly ever distinguished history-based arguments from grossly anachronistic statements. Rather, all of the 14 statements produce a highly reliable scale—"Refusal to participate in the massacre" ($\alpha = .92$); confirmatory statements, of course, were inverted. Even the younger respondents did not (in spite of the explicit instruction) follow the specific medieval options and patterns of action but, typically, they opposed the historical course of events—"contrafactually," so to speak. With increasing age and educational status, the intensity of this opposition also increased. As is shown later, this tendency does not amount to an ability to deliver professional historical judgments, but rather purely moral evaluations.

This interpretation can be grounded on a factor analysis based on all scales extracted from the Hamburg pilot study. This factor analysis produced three dimensions with quite different loadings for the Crusade-related constructs (cf. Table 14.1).

Just like "Text comprehension," "Rejection of force" appears to refer to predominantly cognitive operations with only moderate moral overtones. "Loss of fascination" and "Stance against Crusaders" are equally based on cognitive and moral determinants. In fact, both must be viewed as negative achievements, that is, the rejection of adventure and the refusal to identify with one's "own" kin. It is, therefore, hardly a coincidence that only these two scales have zero or even negative loading on the motivational dimension.

"Offense" and "Refusal to participate" are manifestations of predomi- nantly moral principles with slight cognitive and motivational influence. Likewise, "Stance in favor of the Muslims" appears to be primarily an ethical reaction, accompanied by a weak negative correlation with cogni-

TABLE 14.1
Evaluations of Crusade
(Correlations of Scales with Factor Scores)

Hamburg (N = 423)	Factor		
	Cognitive	Motivational	Universal Ethic
Text comprehension Crusade	.51	.05	−.10
Rejection of force as conclusion	.68	.17	.27
Loss of fascination with Crusade	.49	−.05	.41
Stance against Crusaders	.37	.00	.56
Offense with Crusade	.26	.21	.59
Refusal to participate in massacre	.18	.20	.67
Stance in favor of Muslims	−.15	.13	.54

tion. It is not unlikely that an addition emotional factor (adventure, projection) plays a role here.

The extracted rotated factor scores correlated with social background data. As expected, cognition was highly dependent on grade level and also to some extent on school type (educational status) and sociocultural background. There was only a weak relationship with gender (boys know a bit more), and none at all with party preference. The motivational factor showed much lower correlations with social background variables; girls and the younger students were somewhat less interested in history. The dimension referring to moral judgments was almost independent of grade tested, school type, and social class. It was, however, quite closely related to the female gender and to left-wing party preference.

AMBIGUITIES

The reported findings can be regarded as being fairly accurate, even though the convenience sample on which they are based is rather small (N = 423) and not perfectly stratified. This is because one is really dealing with replicated results:

> In 1990, 2,000 respondents produced highly comparable findings on four different historical dilemmata (Prussian occupation of Silesia in 1740; Opium War of 1840; American Civil War of 1861-65; early modern persecution of witches). In 1991, a sample from Northrhine-Westphalia (N = 317) using the US Civil War dilemma and another dilemma from Saxony (N = 253) using the witch persecution once again produced very similar results. (Borries, 992, p. 57)

Thus, all indications are that the reported findings may be generalized. Many challenging historico-politico-moral dilemmas have reproduced almost identical factor patterns that allow the separation of cognitive, moral, and emotional (nostalgic) responses and that also serve to measure cognitive-moral compounds. On the other hand, it has not been possible to operationalize historical reconstructions, interpretations of the historical other, and historical empathy. Following the example of Classical Enlightenment around 1750, the respondents appeared to judge rashly and unconsciously, simply on the basis of present-day principles. Moralizing obstructed historical explanations. More than anything, the request to deliver historical reconstructions was rejected consciously or unconsciously, for reasons of cognitive inability or moral disapproval. Instead, the respondents based their historical conclusions much more on moral decisions than they did with respect to consequences referring to present times. This phenomenon appears as paradoxical and as a most remarkable cross-over: (a) requests explicitly related to the present (i.e., conclusions) were responded to with a mixture of knowledge and human rights moral reasoning, and (b) requests explicitly related to the past (i.e., reconstructions) were dodged on the basis of purely moral decisions.

It is possible that the personal format of these items is responsible for this. Perhaps the respondents perceived more acutely that their judgment was asked for than that contemporary constraints were to be reflected. Use of the third person might have changed the response considerably ("Imagine yourself in the position of a Crusader. How might *he* have reasoned and decided?"). But the politically important objective — "understanding of the other" — includes the ability to change perspectives, and it assumes the ability to abstract from one's own person while thinking from the standpoint of the other in a first-person mode. The exercise of experimental role playing was explicitly called for. But this was not achieved by the students; quite to the contrary, they appeared to be decreasingly able or willing to perform in that way as they grew older.

It should be emphasized that historical socialization into an ethic of human rights and universalist moral principles, as well as its internalization and execution, represents high levels of development, which is, of course, outstandingly desirable. Civil wars and persecutions of present times clearly demonstrate that such behaviors are rather loosely rooted in many societies (including the German). With particular regard to history, however, this must not obscure constraints and patterns of reasoning that were different in other times. The students appeared to base their judgments on rather primitive formulae, such as "Those people were all criminals/fools," or "Those people didn't know what we know." They even dismiss such simple alternatives as "Times were different then" or "Different times — different practices."

What is lost, then, is the ability to construct adequate historical explanations and insight that involve the labor of reconstructing and perceiving differences. If history is really "a dialogue between past and present with regard to the future," if historical consciousness is defined as the "complex network of interpreted past, perceived present, and expected future" (cf. Jeismann 1985; Jeismann et al., 1987, Rüsen, 1983, 1986, 1989; Borries, Pandel, & Rüsen, 1991, pp. 221–344), then empathy, role taking, and the change of perspective within a distant time frame is essential (even if not perfectly possible!), no less essential than reference to the present and to present-day moral principles. This is not only an epistemological and normative principle of the discipline, but it fundamentally concerns the pragmatic and political justification for teaching history. Whoever is unable to reconstruct, by way of understanding the other, the logic of action of that person's "strange" forebears will also fail to recognize the different reasoning patterns among his or her contempories of the current world theater.

All indications are that German observers (not only adolescents!) have been unable to comprehend the Gulf War, the Yugoslavian massacres, the disintegration of the Soviet Union, and anti-European sentiments. The inability to penetrate into other people's logic of action entails the betrayal of reality in favor of illusionary universalist principles whose historicity and limited acceptance is not properly appreciated. Cognitive psychology and game-theoretical analyses of communications (e.g., the famous "prisoners' dilemma") have shown very clearly, however, that rational interaction presupposes an iterative regress on anticipated actions and reactions ("I think that he thinks that I think that he thinks. . . .") with the aim of a mutual balance of interests. Or, to phrase it somewhat cynically, in such situations, the person has an advantage who knows and understands the other better. Thus, understanding of the other is not *just* a give-away, but also, at least potentially, a gain in terms of one's own goals.

It should be added that a lack of understanding of the other includes inadequate definitions of oneself. One who believes that he or she could never have slaughtered like a Crusader has illusions about oneself, as to one's seducibility through noble aims, as to one's own control of instincts, and as to the precarious weaknesses of culture and civilization as guides of human behavior. This may generate unjustified self-confidence, even feelings of superiority over others. In fact, a study conducted a few years ago found that an overwhelming majority of adolescents asserted that they themselves would have joined the active resistance during the Nazi period. Although these manifestations of anti-fascist values may be laudable, the recognizably illusionary self-confidence is alarming. Only if one admits that, out of conflict or deception, one might personally serve as an instrument in mass murder, is one likely to be sensitized and rendered immune against the repetition.

As the present chauvinistic and racist excesses and the helpless reactions to them show, these relationships are complex. Whoever believes that an ethic of human rights is eternally valid and guaranteed will fail to understand, in times of conflict, both others and oneself. Whoever recognizes human rights as the recent product of long historical processes, as always endangered and never complete, will be able to master critical situations better with a mixture of patience, tolerance, and fortitude. He or she will also be better able to refute appraisals of human rights as a "European ethnocentric tribal ethic," for there is a real dilemma involved when juxtaposing cultural diversity and authenticity on the one hand and the universal claim of human rights on the other. This dilemma can only be balanced in a long historical process.

Most present-day adolescents do not define their identity in ethnocentric terms, in spite of the new wave of right-wing radicalism and violence against immigrants. German nationality, the white race, European culture, and the successful materialization of interests are, for the majority of German adolescents, far from being self-evident, quasi-natural values; they are, to the contrary, worthy of ideological critique and self-reflection. This detached attitude could, if it were reliably grounded in everyday experience and not just a "socially desirable response," form the basis of a new identity. The moral shock of National Socialism has probably provided the decisive motive. On that basis, generalizations, critique, and judgments are articulated.

MENTAL OPERATIONS

The discovery of strong moralizing elements in the students' historical reasoning leads to the question of their concepts of progress, particularly their perceptions of "moral progress." The respective analyses cannot be presented in great detail here, but the following has been found. Overtly (i.e., if explicitly asked), the students displayed strong skepticism as to historical progress that primarily referred to the future (e.g., of the Third World), as well as to important elements of the recent past. Covertly (i.e., if questioned indirectly), students showed a strong and unmitigated recognition of progress, for example, with reference to development since the Middle Ages and the time of Absolutism or the Industrial Revolution. "Skepticism of progress" and "Recognition of progress" had joint cognitive overtones, that is, the older and better informed students displayed higher mean values on these scales. However, "Recognition of progress" (since older times) was somewhat related to "egocentric" and "group-egocentric" ("ethnocentric") values, whereas "Skepticism of progress" (with respect to present and future times) showed slight correlations with "altruistic" and "group-altruistic" ("universalist") tendencies. But these moral overtones were very moderate.

This is a remarkable result for an essential dimension of historical consciousness, even if it is, obviously, not an explanation, but rather a product of the fundamental tendency to moralize. This raises the problem of what are, according to the students' opinion, typical mental operations and contributions of history to life. In Northrhine-Westphalia, the following questions, among others, were asked: "Which of the following statements do you think are more or less true for an historically conscious person? An historically conscious person (. . .)." Typical operations followed, such as "gets involved in politics" or "knows 'the basic facts' of history"; these were assessed on Likert-type scales.

Instead of longer and internally consistent scales, in this case, pairs of related items were used. "Collection of data" met with high approval, as did "Reference to the present" and "Desire to reconstruct," and much less the "Motive of excitement" (cf. Fig. 14.2). Conservativism, ethnocentrism, revolutionary attitude, and tendentiously also political involvement were rejected as typical traits of historically conscious persons. A factor analysis demonstrated that the various operations, as perceived by the students, depended on quite different underlying dimensions. The collection of data and the desire to reconstruct as a sign of historical consciousness carried slight motivational and cognitive connotations, but without an ethical component; reference to the present also had a positive correlation with the moral dimension. The motive of excitement, however, was neutral with respect to "motivation" and negative with respect to the "moral" and "cognitive" dimensions (cf. Table 14.2). Students look at history as an aesthetic-adventurous enterprise with suspicion. In other words, the less informed students and those whose judgments were less altruistic and universalist emphasized more strongly the motive of excitement.

Self-reports present a slightly different picture, however. They were elicited by the question—"Which of the following statements applies to *yourself* when you deal with history outside your class?"—followed by the same list of operations. The students viewed themselves as being clearly more directed toward excitement, less engaged politically, more reserved toward the concepts of nation, but also much less informed, less embedded in the present, less able to explain, and less curious. If the same item pairs are used as with the "historically conscious persons," a different structure emerges: Collection of data and reference to the present are, for the respondents themselves, above all a matter of motivation, not of cognition. The desire to reconstruct has high positive loadings with cognition and motivation, but not with the moral dimension. The motive of excitement is, for the students themselves, closely related to less altruism ("egocentrism") and less knowledge ("foolishness"), as is shown by the correlations with the respective factor scores (cf. Table 14.2).

Unfortunately, only a single item in each of the two lists directly probed

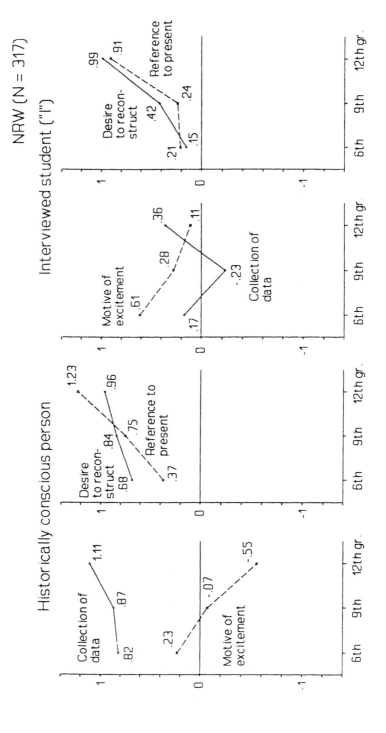

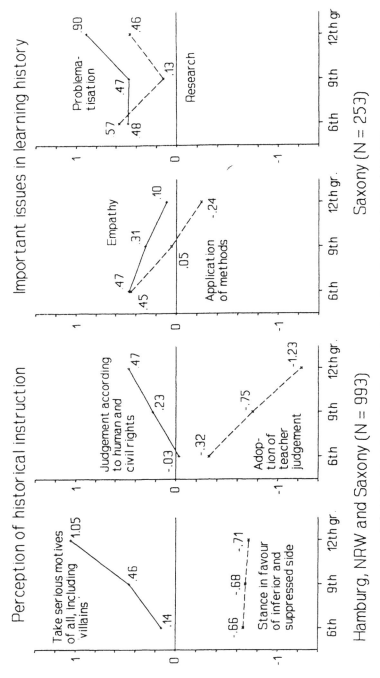

Perception of historical instruction

Important issues in learning history

Take serious motives of all, including villains
1.05
.46
.14

Judgement according to human and civil rights
.47
.23
-.03

Empathy
.47
.31
.10

Problematisation
.57
.48
.47
.90
.46
.13

Research

Stance in favour of inferior and suppressed side
-.66 -.68 -.71

Adoption of teacher judgement
-.32
-.75
-1.23

Application of methods
.45
.05
-.24

1

0

-1

6th 9th 12th gr.

6th 9th 12th gr.

6th 9th 12th gr.

6th 9th 12th gr.

Hamburg, NRW and Saxony (N = 993)

Saxony (N = 253)

FIG. 14.2. Mental operations (mean values by grade, scales ranging from −2.0 to 2.0).

TABLE 14.2
Mental Operations
(Correlations of scales with factor scores)

Northrhine-Westphalia (N = 317)	Factor		
	Cognitive	Motivational	Universal Ethic
Historically conscious person			
Collection of data	.40	.17	− .01
Reference to present	.51	.25	.24
Desire to reconstruct	.44	.22	− .06
Motive of excitement	− .32	.10	− .36
Interviewed student			
Collection of data	.14	.65	.01
Reference to present	.31	.54	.22
Desire to reconstruct	.46	.46	.02
Motive of excitement	− .16	.26	− .41

Saxony (N = 253)	Factor		
	Cognitive	Motivational	Universal Ethic
Main interest			
Power	.28	.55	− .34
Everyday life	.04	.64	.34
Activities			
Application of methods	− .62	.36	.02
Empathy	− .43	.35	.29
Research	− .30	.66	.11
Problematization	.05	.58	.14

the historical operation of "moralizing": "Above all, I want to judge whether the actions of people in history were good or bad" (and a parallel version for the "historically conscious person"). Both items (with an intercorrelation of $r = .36$) had close to neutral mean values with a slightly positive tendency for the younger students and a slightly negative one for the older students. There was a weak negative correlation with the factor "cognition," none at all with "motivation," and a very weak negative one with the "moral" factor. In other words, the outright demand for history as a moralizing enterprise was neutralized in every respect. The students moralized in practice; in theory, they did not seem to have any opinion on this subject.

The Saxonian data of 1991 ($N = 253$) allow, to a certain degree, a check on this finding. In that data set, there were two focuses in terms of content interest. "Interest in power" (clearly stronger among boys) appeared to be less associated with a universalist ethic in the above sense, but more "informed." Contrary to this, "Interest in everyday life" (more frequent among girls) was correlated with a universalist ethic, but cognitively neutral (cf. Table 14.2). Both constructs were, of course, above all measures of historical motivation.

Also, the following question in the Saxonian data set aimed at historical operations: "What is particularly important for you in learning history?" Four distinct subscales could be extracted from the respective set of items: "Application of methods," "Research," "Problematization," and "Empathy." "Application" and "Empathy" were especially popular with the younger students, "Problematization" with the older ones. All four operations were clearly indicators of "motivation," but hardly of "cognition" and the "moral" dimension (cf. Table 14.2). "Empathy," that is, an important part of the truly historical operation of reconstructing the other's inner perspective and his or her logic of action through role taking, was slightly correlated with a universalist ethic, but also with a lower level of knowledge. Likewise, "Application" and "Research" were negatively correlated with cognition; in other words, they were appreciated more by the less well-informed students.

If asked directly, the students in all three samples asserted that in their history lessons they "take seriously the motives and justifications of all persons concerned, even the 'villains,' when forming a judgment" (cf. Fig. 2). This claim to historical truth grew with age and was reinforced by rejecting the notions of teacher indoctrination ("We hear from the teacher what was good and bad and which stance we should take") and of an ethic of compassion ("In the case of conflict, we take the stance of the inferior or oppressed side"). But even at this normative level, historical reconstruction out of contemporary constraints was mitigated. With growing age, the following statement was met with increasing approval (although with somewhat less appraisal than the statement on justice for the villains): "We judge the historical conflicts analyzed according to human and civil rights."

In Hamburg, the item concerning the "villains" and the moral constructs ("Refusal to participate in a massacre," "Offense with Crusade," "Stance in favor of the Muslims") showed virtually no correlation, and very similar results were obtained for Northrhine-Westphalia. On the other hand, theoretical consideration of the "villain's motives" and support for "human and civil rights as a guideline" were cognitively positive, that is, a trait of the older, higher aspiring, and better informed students. The evidence for historicism as an inconsequential normative platform could easily be accumulated further.

Thus, we repeatedly found structurally identical contradictions. Consciously and explicitly, any concept of progress, historical moralizing, ethnocentrism, and fascination by historical adventure was strictly rejected. The fact that this tendency increased with age and educational level suggests an interpretation by which these values are learned, that is, internalized as manifest, programmatic values of society. If, however, the behaviors and response patterns under more indirect questioning techniques were analyzed, at least the concept of progress and the tendency to moralize were almost unmitigated against, albeit unconsciously and without reflection. The reasons for this gap between theory and practice, norm and implementation, illusion and reality, are in urgent need of further research.

The teacher questionnaire data of the 1991 pilot study provide an indirect clue although the sample is much too small for definite answers ($N = 60$, reduced to $N = 32$ for some items). Althought the students were unable or unwilling to distinguish systematically among "Offense with Crusade," Stance in favor of Muslims," and "Refusal to participate in the massacre," as well as among "Loss of fascination," "Stance against Crusaders," and "Rejection of force as conclusion from Crusade," there were noticeable differences between the respective concepts in the perceptions of teachers. For the latter, "stance," "conclusion," and "reconstruction" were analytically different. Where stance and conclusions were concerned, they decided — quite rightly — much more on the basis of present ethical considerations than on their reconstructions of past situations. Nevertheless, their empathy showed just as much moralization as that of the students; only their stance and consequences were even more determined and morally rigorous than those of the students. Their historical reconstructions, then, were just as moralizing as those of the students; their transfer and conclusions were much more so than those of the students.

At the same time, the interviewed teachers supported, with great emphasis, the approach of historicism in history teaching, and they strictly rejected the notion of condemning the past. It appears as if a split concept (historism as a norm, antihistorism in practice) was also a trait of the teachers, as if this incoherence were acquired and internalized during the process of historical socialization. When watching historical and political programs on television and reading respective articles in newspapers and magazines, one was forced to state: This is a general cultural trait, not a specific one confined to teachers and schools. This fundamental tendency to moralize could not be missed, for instance, during the "Columbus Year" of 1992 in the treatment of New World discoveries.

Meanwhile, at the end of 1992, a survey similar to the studies of 1990 and 1991 was conducted based on a representative sample of 6,479 students in the 6th, 9th, and 12th grades in East and West Germany (Borries, 1993a, 1993b, 1994). The analysis, although not yet complete, confirms the older findings in many respects. It will be a particularly important cross-check to investigate whether the reported findings refer to specifically German or more generally European phenomena. The 1992 comparative pilot study of nine countries ($N = 900$) did not produce short, simple, and unambiguous answers. As a general tendency, however, Germany does *not* appear to play a special role, but shows characteristics in this domain, as in many others that locate it in the middle of Europe (cf. Borries & Rüsen, 1994).

REFERENCES

Borries, B. V. (1988). *Geschichtslernen und geschichtsbewußtsein. Empirische erkundungen zu erwerb und gebrauch von historie.* Stuttgart: Klett.

Borries, B. V. (also with Mitarbeit von Dähn, S., Körber, A., & Lehmann, R. H.). (1992). *Kindlich-jugendliche geschichtsverarbeitung in west-und Ostdeutschland 1990. Ein empirischer vergleich.* Pfaffenweiler: Centaurus.

Borries, B. V. (1993a). Vorstellungen zum nationalsozialismus und einstellungen zum rechtsextremismus bei ost- und westdeutschen Jugendlichen. Einige empirische Hinweise von 1990, 1991, und 1992. *Internationale Schulbuchforschung, 15,* 139–166.

Borries, B. V. (1993b). Geschichtliche vorstellungen und politische einstellungen in ost- und westdeutschland 1992. Ein werkstattbericht über eine repräsentative schülerbefragung. In D. Klose & U. Uffelmann (Eds.), *Vergangenheit – geschichte – psyche: Ein interdisziplinäres gespräch* (pp. 125–149). Idstein: Schulz-Kirchner.

Borries, B. V. (1994). Lernergebnisse und lehrerkonzepte im fach geschiche. Einige befunde einer empirischen untersuchung 1992. *Geschichte, Politik und ihre Didaktik, 22,* 6–28.

Borries, B. V., Pandel, H. J., & Rüsen, J. (Eds.). (1991). *Geschichtsbewußtsein empirisch.* Pfaffenweiler: Centaurus.

Borries, B. V., & Rüsen, J. (1994). *Geschichtsbewußtsein im interkulturellen Vergleich. Zwei empirische Pilotstudien.* Pfaffenweiler: Centaurus.

Jeismann, K. E. (1985). *Geschichte als horizont der gegenwart.* Paderborn: Schöningh.

Jeismann, K. E., Kosthorst, E., Schäfer, B., Schlöder, B., Teppe, K., & Wasna, M. (1987). *Die teilung deutschlands als problem des geschichtsbewußtseins. Eine empirische untersuchung.* Paderborn: Schöningh.

Rüsen, J. (1983). *Historische vernvnft* (Grundzüge einer historik I). Göttingen: Vandenhoek.

Rüsen, J. (1986). *Rekonstruktion der vergangenheit* (Grundzüge einer historik II). Göttingen: Vandenhoek.

Rüsen, J. (1989). *Lebendige geschichte* (Grundzüge einer Historik III). Göttingen: Vandenhoek.

15 Historical Knowledge: Cognitive and Instructional Implications

Mario Carretero, Liliana Jacott, Margarita Limón,
Asunción López-Manjón, and Jose A. León
Autonoma University of Madrid

Early in this century two very influential authors in psychology and education were interested in how history was taught and understood in schools. They considered the topic of introducing historical content in elementary school. One of them, Dewey (1915), wrote:

> Whatever history may be for the scientific historian, for the educator it must be an indirect sociology—a study of society which lays bare its process of becoming and its modes of organization . . . history must be presented, not as an accumulation of results, a mere statement of what happened, but as a forceful, acting thing. The motives—that is, the motors—must stand out. To study history is not to amass information but to use information in constructing a vivid picture of how and why men did thus and so; achieved their successes and came to their failures. (p. 151)

Thus, it appears clear that Dewey was in favor of teaching meaningful historical content, and because of this he advocated presenting social content as an introduction to historical content. His brief but insightful paper also included some thoughts about what type of specific social and historical topics would be especially appropriate for elementary education.

For his part, Piaget (1933) also considered some children's conceptions about history using his insightful version of the clinical method. His conclusions provided empirical support for Dewey's position, showing that elementary school children have a very simple representation of basic historical notions.

More recent research into the relationship between cognitive development and the comprehension of specific school subject matter has made enormous progress. Important contributions have been made in physics, chemistry, biology, and mathematics. Nevertheless, researchers seem to have forgotten the topic of history understanding, for only a small number of contributions have been devoted to this topic. Thus, we know little regarding how students of different ages reason about social and historical problems and how they represent and solve such problems. Moreover, much of this work has been conducted within an educational perspective rather than from a psychological one. In this sense, the recent publication of the *Handbook of Research on Social Studies Teaching and Learning* (Shaver, 1991) and some other works on social sciences (Kuhn, 1991; Voss 1991) and history (Leinhardt, 1993; Wineburg, 1991) are positive signs that there is increasing interest in the topic from both a cognitive and an instructional point of view.

In recent years, there also has been an increasing trend to establish a relationship between school content and thinking abilities (Resnick & Klopfer, 1989). This means that thinking abilities should not be considered as something separate from the curriculum, but as a tool for promoting better understanding in different areas, and vice versa. But in order to achieve that goal, it is essential to be able to answer the following questions: What kind of cognitive processes are involved in historical cognition? What kind of thinking abilities could be developed by student learning of history and social sciences? Unfortunately, we cannot draw on a substantial body of research to answer these questions. It would be easier to answer them in the case of natural sciences, because it is much clearer how their content has to be presented in order to be really understood. Moreover, it is clear what kind of thinking abilities those topics could promote. In fact, an impressive amount of work has been devoted to analyzing the relationship between the structure of scientific content and either student misconceptions (Minstrell, 1989) or scientific reasoning skills (Kuhn, Amsel, & O'Loughlin, 1988). However, to consider the case of social and historical knowledge appears to be a more complex matter. Thus, the main objective of this chapter is to contribute to a clarification of reasoning skill and complex processes, in general, involving historical knowledge. For this purpose, we think it is essential to consider the nature of historical knowledge, especially as compared to natural sciences knowledge, because it may be that the two types of content require different reasoning processes in order to be properly understood. It also might be that they contribute to developing very different thinking abilities.

We first take into consideration some features of historical knowledge that we consider essential for these matters. Nevertheless, we want to make it clear that our purpose is not to present an extended view of epistemological and methodological problems related to history as a discipline, but rather to consider which features are most crucial in characterizing historical cognition, especially for their instructional implications. Meanwhile, we feel it is necessary to state that even though history and social sciences share a substantial number of epistemological and methodological characteristics, a clear distinction from both cognitive and instructional points of view has to be established, because their respective subject matters also have important differences. This chapter, in fact, is devoted only to history, even though some of our points could also be applied to social sciences in general. First, we present some general and theoretical characteristics of historical knowledge. Second, some of our empirical work about understanding historical causality is described. Finally, we offer some general conclusions, including instructional implications.

IDEOLOGY, VALUES, AND HISTORICAL KNOWLEDGE

We think that there is an enormous ideological influence on the way historical contents are selected and taught in the schools. A dramatic but literary example of this characteristic of historical knowledge is offered by Orwell's novel *1984*, a celebrated attempt to criticize authoritarian regimes. As is well known, in this work there was a "Ministry of Truth," in which the main character of the novel used to work as a bureaucrat. One of his daily tasks was to change the history according to specific orientations provided by the Party-State at different moments. Those orientations could be contradictory from one moment to another. This task included, for example, either removing or including different political figures in the pictures shown in the newspapers, encyclopedias, and other books and documents. Of course, this could be considered as a falsification of history, but as a matter of fact it is not very different from the real situation in many countries.

Ferro (1981) analyzed how history has been taught according to the textbooks used in different societies (Soviet Union, Spain, Poland, China, Japan, United States, Australia, and others), and his conclusion is straightforward. According to his exhaustive study, historical contents are modified and seriously altered depending on political interests, without any respect for objective data. Most of the cases described by Ferro (1981) corresponded to situations that occurred decades ago, but a number of examples could be considered as contemporary.

One case recently occurred in Mexico. In Mexico, textbooks, which are free, are modified under the supervision of the Ministry of Education. In September 1992, an important number of modifications were introduced. For example, some traditional and important figures of Mexican nationalism disappeared from the textbooks. The most famous case involved the so-called "Children Heroes," who fought against North American troops in the last U.S. invasion battle before Mexico lost the northern part of its territory. It is hard not to see the Ministry of the Truth back again! As can be imagined, the action produced an enormous controversy in Mexican newspapers and mass media. Interestingly, there were even teacher demonstrations against the new textbooks, with the teachers asking for the right to use the old ones. Thus, it looks like the teachers are rejecting what could be considered conceptual change imposed by the government. As a matter of fact, the issue is still open, and there will be several national conferences, historically research oriented, to deal with the problem. It is hard to think of any other school content that could experience such an intense ideological influence.

There is no reason to delve more deeply into this Mexican controversy, but there are some interesting elements of it that are applicable for the purpose of this chapter. Some of the Mexican intellectuals that participated in the public debate on the issue agree that one of the possible reasons for changing history textbooks so drastically is related to the new American Free Commerce Treaty. Some of them maintain that the underlying argument is that the Mexican government considered it more appropriate for Mexican society to take a less aggressive position with respect to the United States.

On the other hand, the present situation of history textbooks in all the former communist countries can also be considered. Most of their contents have been changed from one year to the next, especially in those countries under the control of the former Soviet Union such as East Germany. It is hard to think of any faster curriculum reform in relation to any other topic. In fact, the same has happened in countries that have had a civil war (e.g., Spain, 1936–39).

We can conclude then that historical contents always play an important role in order to both set up a national consciousness and to justify ideological beliefs. This probably means not only that political leaders are aware of this, but that any society selects its historical contents to be taught according to the most prevalent ideological values. Consequently, it is impossible to understand historical cognition without considering those values. One could not imagine something similar to the Mexican situation in the case of physics textbooks (for example, physics teachers asking for Aristotelian instead of Newtonian physics books!). However, there is the case of the debates on creationism versus Darwinian natural selection.

Considering instructional implications, we think it would be advisable to teach historical contents giving students the opportunity to consider their relationship to different values. Otherwise, it would be difficult to produce a complete understanding of historical school contents without taking into account this ideological influence that also often implies moral options (see von Borries, this volume). Indeed, it probably would be more difficult to change an ideological belief rather than a scientific one.

HISTORY AS THE STUDY OF THE PAST

History is the study of the past, and this implies that it constitutes a different discipline from sociology and other social sciences. This distinction probably seems obvious to many, but is not so obvious from either the epistemological or the instructional point of view. Thus, some authors pointed out that history is a different type of knowledge from sociology (Habermas, 1970; Marrou, 1959; Mink, 1973). The main difference is based on the idea that history is a discipline that deals with events remote in time, and such past events have a rather ambiguous epistemological status. For example, it is unclear how we can establish an understanding of 16th-century political situations using 20th-century political concepts. Berti (this volume) maintained that, properly speaking, there are no historical concepts because most of the concepts used in history come from the social sciences vocabulary, such as *state, imperialism, social class*, and so on. Of course, this is a controversial matter that cannot be fully understood independently of the complex relationship between history and social sciences.

It can also be maintained that a number historical concepts are quite specific and limited to the scenario of a given period, and for that reason they are more difficult to understand than social concepts, for example, *ancient regime, feudalism, roman aristocracy*, and so on. On the other hand, a number of historical concepts have different meaning along with different periods. For instance, the present meaning of *democracy* is different compared to that of *democratic* institutions in Athens (5th-century B.C.). There have been a number of studies about social concepts understanding, most of them limiting their efforts to children and early adolescents (see chapters by Berti, Delval, Furnham, and Torney-Purta, this volume), but unfortunately this is not the case of historical concepts.

In one of our studies (Carretero, Pozo, & Asensio, 1983), we presented a multiple-choice questionnaire with a number of historical textbook concepts to sixth, seventh, and eighth graders. For example, *imperialism, feudalism, colonialism*, and others were included. In general terms, only about one half of the answers were correct. It is interesting to note that Beck and McKeown (this volume) similarly concluded in their study about historical text comprehension that students lacked a complete representation of basic historical terms.

From an instructional point of view, the distinction between past and present is not so clear in many school activities and curricula. For example, if a teacher is explaining a lesson about the Roman Empire, is he or she teaching history? Our answer to this question is "not necessarily," for he or she may only be describing the social characteristics of that period. In this case, the teacher is explaining a sociological content of those times, but not teaching history. Thus, in our opinion, in order to teach history, it is necessary not only to consider past events, but to include some kind of causal relationships between past and present or, more generally, two different points in time. But this also implies it is important to understand the complex concept of historical time. The notion of time related to both personal experience and to physics has been investigated (Friedman, 1982; Piaget, 1946). But studies on the nature of time in relation to history are few (Barnes, 1896a, 1896b; Jahoda, 1963; Oakden & Sturt, 1922). Thus, even though we have limited knowledge of this topic, it looks like adolescents have difficulties in precisely estimating the time between two historical periods (Carretero et al., 1991). For example, in this study they estimated the durations of prehistorical periods as much briefer than they really were. Probably this is because they established some kind of intuitive relationship between amount of time and important events presented in the textbooks for any historical period. Of course, in this sense many more things "happened" in this century than in any prehistorical period. In this study it also was found that it is rather difficult for adolescents to use chronological measurement tools concepts such as "before Christ" and "after Christ" in order to determine how recent some historical facts are. Thus, it can be concluded that both the representation of history as a content that is represented by concepts that do not exist at the present time and the quantitative estimation of past times constitute specific difficulties in the understanding of history as an inferential process that is being applied.

HISTORY AS A REASONING PROCESS

In previous sections we examined a number of issues related to the influence of values and political attitudes in historical knowledge. There is no doubt that in order to generate and understand historical contents, subjects are influenced by those issues. But they also have to go through a reasoning process. In this section we examine some controversial features of this process.

As in other parts of this chapter, we consider two types of contributions that can be helpful to this respect. On the one hand, in the philosophy of history, ideas have been tested to capture the reasoning processes used by historians. On the other hand, there have been cognitive studies that have analyzed adolescents' and adults' performance on reasoning about historical and social tasks.

At the present time probably many historians would agree with Collingwood's (1946) assumption that history is not simply a matter of classifying events in chronological order, but a cognitive activity in which logical inferences are commonly used. But the problem appears as soon as those logical inferences have to be defined and analyzed.

Collingwood (1946) compared historical knowledge to detective activity in the sense of being something directed to get evidence and test theories. Unfortunately Collingwood did not provide more precise details about how historical inferences could be described. He insisted on the importance of not accepting historical documents uncritically, especially testimonies that already appeared in past books, such as in his criticism of "cut and paste history." Therefore, he strongly recommended a critical analysis of historical sources. But beyond that, few concrete details about the process of how historical inferences are drawn and conclusions are founded were established. In this sense, Kuhn, Weinston, and Flaton (this volume) established a comparison between historical and juror reasoning. Both situations are considered to be postdictive in the sense of not being directed to predict the future but to determine causal processes in the past. Their research permits us to know more precisely how inferences are established in historical reasoning. From this point of view, as these authors suggested, historical reasoning can be considered to be theory-evidence coordination. But what are the subjects' theories about historical phenomena? How do they influence subjects' inferences and conclusions?

If we take into consideration what historians think about this matter, at least some of them hold the idea that in history there are no pure facts. Fact selection depends on the historians' theories. This idea was pointed out some time ago by an excellent historian. To put it in his own words:

> According to the common-sense view, there are certain basic facts which are the same for all historians and which form, so to speak, the backbone of history . . . [but] the necessity to establish these basic facts rests not on any quality in the facts themselves, but on *a priori* decision of the historian. The historian is necessarily selective. The belief in a hard core of historical facts existing objectively and independently of the interpretation of the historian is a preposterous fallacy, but one which it is very hard to eradicate. (Carr, 1961, p. 10)

Thus, it can be shown that there is an interesting coincidence between history and natural science methodologies, in the sense of a common position against some radical positivist ideas. In fact, the quotation from Carr (1961) is similar to some authors' ideas such as Hanson or Kuhn, who also criticize the existence of pure facts in any scientific activity. In this respect, it should not be disregarded that at present there are a number of historiographical approaches that are based on very distinct theories. As it is well known by historians and philosophers of history, an important historiographical renovation started in France at the beginning of the century when the Annales school emerged as a reaction against the positivist approach in history. This school strongly criticized historical research as simply being focused on empirical data and the role of great historical figures. Thus, the Annales school defended a historical view based on the interactions of economic and social structures in which particular persons do not play a crucial role. The Marxist theory of history held a similar but not identical position because of its emphasis on the existence of materialistic dialectical laws based on Hegel's philosophy of history. On its side, the recent approach of History of mentalities mainly focuses its research activity on ideological and private-life events of the past (i.e., history of the family or history of pleasure activities) because it is considered that this facet of history has not been taken into account by previous approaches. Therefore, when studying any specific topic in history, any of these approaches will select its data according to its more general theories.

Thus, from an instructional point of view, it would be important to insist that historical data such as battles, documents, or monuments have no meaning in themselves but only in the context of a theory. This point is related to the research carried out by Shemilt (1987), in which it was found that young adolescents usually tend to consider that historical data are objective data that exist independent of the historian. Also Leadbeater and Kuhn (1989) analyzed how historical reasoning can be influenced by different epistemological beliefs and theories.

It is generally considered that experiments are the standard procedure to test scientific theories. In fact, most of the cognitive contributions about how scientists or lay subjects verify or falsify their theories of any kind have been based on the use of scientific thinking skills. History, however, does not allow experiments because it is not possible to repeat any historical phenomena. This means that a reasoning strategy such as the control of variables cannot be applied to historical problems in the same way as in both scientific and everyday problems. For example, if a comparison between the First and the Second World Wars is established in order to determine their respective causes, the influence of a specific social, economic, and political variable cannot be isolated because the rest of them were not the same in the two wars. In fact, in general, it can be said that complex historical explanations can be characterized by the attempt to establish the interaction of multiple factors instead of isolating the influence of each of them. For example, we could compare the way a student solves a flotation problem to an immigration movement that occurred centuries ago. In the first case, the student could compare objects of different weights and sizes with respect to their flotation properties. As in numerous natural science situations, he or she has to apply a control of variables strategy, in which the perfect physical separation of variables is possible. In the case of the immigration situation, the solving method is rather different. The variables would be social, economic, and political factors. For example, a decreasing average income or the appearance of frequent political instability may be observed. These variables cannot be totally and physically separated, as with the case of weight and size. Instead the subject has to look for similar situations in the past that can be compared to the one being explained, such as a period of time in which an immigration was also produced, but in which there was no decrease in the average income of the population.

However, there are also a number of scientific activities in which reasoning strategies such as the control of variables cannot be perfectly applied, as what happens in geology or paleontology. And it is also true that basic scientific reasoning skills, as they are generally considered, only partially characterize scientific activities. For example, they are essential in order to understand most of the Newtonian physics taught in high schools, but there is an important part of modern physics that is based more on theory than on experiments. Due to these reasons, we think that even though some straightforward differences between historical and scientific reasoning abilities exist, probably there are also some similarities. There is no doubt that historical reasoning has its specific features, but we agree with Kuhn et al. (this volume) and Voss et al. (this volume) with respect to the usefulness of applying some concepts from logical reasoning and problem-solving research to the analysis of historical reasoning, because it might be that a number of common reasoning skills are used in different domains. Of course, this issue needs much more empirical research. But we think that some of its theoretical issues can be better understood if we examine more in depth some of the controversies about causal explanations in history. After all, reasoning processes are established in order to provide explanations about different phenomena. In natural sciences the variables used in explanations have no intentions or motives because they are impersonal, but this is not the case of historical explanations in which human agents are always present.

CAUSAL EXPLANATIONS IN HISTORY

One of the fundamental problems in the philosophy of science has been to determine what is the nature of scientific explanations. Some of the questions posed have been: What conditions must scientific explanations satisfy? Are they the same for all the sciences, or do they differ, depending on which science is being considered? Or, indeed—What is the relationship between the models of explanation conceived for the natural sciences and those proposed for the social sciences?

Such questions have been discussed at length by philosophers and social theorists throughout the history of sciences, so that the two sides of this debate have come to be represented by important philosophical schools of thought. Furthermore, they have formulated different theories with regard to the type of explanatory schemes proposed for social sciences and history. On the one hand, the positivist approach takes the view that the explanatory schemes or procedures used in natural sciences are identical to those used in the social sciences. The cause-effect model of natural sciences is considered as the ideal explanatory model for all sciences. On the other hand, there is another line of thinking that draws a distinct line between the approach to the explanation in the natural sciences and that of the social sciences.

The emergence and development of the teleological or intentionalist models proposed for history and the social sciences are presented as an alternative position, in view of the problems created by the use of the traditional causal model in this area of study. The intentional approach is in opposition to the explanation of historical events in strictly causal terms. It is based on the assumption that the methods of natural sciences cannot be transferred to social sciences, given the different nature of the two types of science. This leads to the establishment of fundamental differences between causal explanations advanced in natural sciences and intentional explanations—focusing fundamentally on human actions—proposed as being suitable for the study of history (Collingwood, 1946; Dray, 1957). History, from this perspective, is defined as the study of human or individual actions, that is, it is concerned with the reconstruction of the lives of people in other times and places. Thus, for Collingwood (1946), "the object of history is the study of the actions of human beings which took place in the past" (p.19). For this reason, and for some authors, historical explanations are of a different type from those in the natural sciences (Dray, 1957). Thus, we commonly find the distinction, established by Windelband in 1894, between nomothetic sciences, referring to those sciences whose objective is the production of general and invariable laws, and ideographic or historical disciplines, which concentrate on the study of particular entities or the individual. With regard to this distinction, Megill (1989) pointed out that, at least for Windelband, both disciplines were considered as scientific, whereas the logical positivist reserved the status of "science" for nomothetic studies.

One of the most complex and developed theoretical models for explanation in the social sciences and history is the teleological or intentional model of explanation proposed by von Wright (1971, 1974). This author argued for an intentional theory of action as an explanatory model for the social sciences and history. To explain an action teleologically implies the understanding of a particular intention in the actor who performs it, such that the intention constitutes its most characteristic feature.

Von Wright (1971) also stated that the explanation of historical facts involves taking into account the occurrence of one or more prior events that can be considered as "contributory causes." In order to illustrate his model, von Wright considered, as an example, that the assassination of the Archduke of Austria in Sarajevo was one of the causes of World War I. In this case, the incident at Sarajevo can be considered as one of the contributory causes of the historical fact we are trying to explain. But how does this action (the assassination) relate to the historical fact being studied (World War I)? The connection between the antecedents or contributory causes and the historical event that is to be explained is not formulated in terms of general laws or causal relationships or in terms of necessary and sufficient conditions as would be the case of the natural sciences. The connection is revealed through the generation of a series of inferences, which together provide the contextual background for the motives underlying the actions. In this example, one starts from the assumption that World War I was the result of a complex network of actions. Each one of these actions in turn helped to pave the way, in motivational terms, for subsequent actions, and these led finally to the particular historical event. This means that an action or event (the assassination in Sarajevo) provides a motive for realization of a series of subsequent events (for example, Austria's ultimatum to Serbia, the mobilization of the Russian army, Austria's declaration of war on Serbia, etc.) until one arrives finally at the historical event to be explained.

AN EMPIRICAL STUDY ABOUT CAUSAL EXPLANATIONS

In the previous sections we examined some of the theoretical issues on historical causality. But, what type of causal explanation do subjects tend to formulate in order to explain historical events? For example, are their explanations more deterministic as in the case of natural sciences? Are specific individuals, such as leaders or other prominent figures, considered as important as more abstract causes such as economic or political forces? We have been working on a research project about causal explanations in history using different tasks (Carretero & Jacott, 1992; Carretero, López-Manjón, & Jacott, 1994; Jacott & Carretero, 1993). In this chapter we present some data concerning to what extent adolescents as well as novice and expert adult subjects consider intentional causes, involving specific actors, to be more or less important than structural causes, such as political or economic forces.

Method

Subjects.   One hundred subjects participated in this study; 20 in each of five groups. Three groups were adolescents of the following grades: 6th (11–12-year-olds), 8th (13–14-year-olds), and 10th (15–16-year-olds). All of them came from two public schools in Madrid. The other two groups were university graduates, one in psychology and the other one in history and both from the Autonoma University of Madrid.

Procedure.   Participants in the investigation were interviewed individually. The interview began with the question: "What caused the discovery of America?" In an effort to obtain a precise answer to this question, subjects were told that they would be presented with a set of six cards to be used to explain what caused this historical event and that each card could be considered as one of the possible causes of the discovery of America (see Table 15.1). Subjects were asked to rank the six cards in order of the importance each one had in the production of this historical event, ranking the most important card first and the least important sixth. The six cards contained basic information about the main causes of the discovery of America. They were based on the main political, economic, ideological, scientific-technological, foreign affairs, and intentional issues presented in textbooks as explanations of this historical event. In this occasion we present only the data concerning the ranking of causes, but subjects were also asked to give a narration of how America was discovered. These more qualitative data appear elsewhere (Jacott & Carretero, 1993), but some comments about them can be found in the discussion of this chapter.

Results

The results are presented in two parts. In the first, results related to the ranking of the causal factors obtained between groups are presented. And

TABLE 15.1
Contents of the Six Cards Presented to Subjects (Different Types of Causes)

Intentional: Columbus's and Spanish King and Queen's motives: curiosity, desire of adventure and ambition, and desire to be rich
Political: The formation of a national and powerful state in Spain during 1492. Territorial, political, and religious unification had been achieved.
Economic: The need for a new commercial route.
Scientific-technological: Scientific knowledge of the earth at that time. Instruments and means of navigation: caravel, compass, astrolabe.
Ideological: Legends, myths, and tales about the existence of remote lands.
Foreign affairs: The previous trips of Portuguese to Africa.

second, those related to the ranking of the causal factors obtained within groups are considered. Table 15.2 shows subjects' rankings of the importance of the causes. An analysis of variance (ANOVA) revealed a significant effect of Group x Causal factor interaction ($F(4,95) = 40.7$, $p = 0.0001$).

A Kruskal-Wallis test indicated that significant differences were found among the groups for the following causal factors: intentional (Columbus's and Spanish King and Queen's motives) ($p < 0.01$), political (the formation of a national and powerful state in Spain) ($p < 0.05$), and foreign affairs (the previous trips of Portuguese to Africa) ($p < 0.01$).

Additional analysis revealed that history graduates differed significantly from sixth and eighth graders with respect to the intentional factors ($p < 0.05$). The data indicated that the sixth and eighth graders ranked this factor as the most important cause in their hierarchy, whereas history graduates ranked it as the second lowest cause. The results suggest that these adolescent subjects, as opposed to history graduates, considered as fundamental the motives of Columbus and the Spanish King and Queen in the explanation of the discovery of America. Thus, intentional elements had an important role in historical explanations in the case of young adolescents, but not for those subjects who were experts in history domain.

In the case of the political cause, history experts differed significantly from sixth graders ($p < 0.05$), but their answers are opposite to that of the intentional cause. The history group ranked the political factor as the second most important cause, whereas the sixth graders ranked it as the least important one. Thus, the data suggest that historians considered the relevance of more abstract and complex factors as the political context when they explain this historical event. On the contrary, sixth graders gave much less importance to this cause in their explanation. The results obtained in relation to the foreign affairs cause indicated that history experts differed significantly from sixth and eighth graders ($p < 0.05$), with

TABLE 15.2
Group Mean Ranks of Importance Assigned to Each Cause in the
Explanation of the Discovery of America (1 is Most Important and 6 is
Least Important)

Causes	Groups				
	6th	8th	10th	Psycho.	History
Intent.	1.65	2.20	2.55	2.65	4.15
Politic.	4.50	3.60	3.70	3.55	3.00
Econom.	3.05	2.45	1.75	2.25	2.10
Scienti.	2.65	3.10	3.55	3.70	3.15
Ideolog.	4.20	4.75	5.25	5.15	5.10
Foreign Affairs	4.95	4.90	4.20	3.70	3.50

the experts giving a higher level of importance to the international context than young adolescents.

Until now, we have described the significant differences between the groups in the level of importance given to the different causes presented in this study. But what are the similarities among the groups? These are related to the remaining causes. Thus, there were no significant differences between groups with respect to the following causes: economic (the need of a new commercial route), scientific-technological (scientific knowledge of the earth at that time), and ideological (legends, myths, and tales about the existence of remote lands). It can be observed that all the groups attributed a rather intermediate level of importance to the scientific-technological and economic causes. In the case of the ideological cause, all the groups considered it to have a very low level of importance.

If we consider the findings as a whole in relation to the causal order generated for each group, we find that sixth, eighth, and tenth graders presented almost the same pattern of responses. These subjects considered intentional, scientific-technological advances, and economic causes in the three first places of their causal order, with intentional aspects the most important to sixth and eighth graders. It is very interesting to observe that psychology graduates considered intentional cause in the second level of importance. To the contrary, however, historians considered this cause as having almost no importance. Thus, these results seem to show that subjects not trained in history tend to consider the intentional aspects as essential to the explanation of the discovery of America.

The data were also analyzed in relation to the differences generated within groups. A Tukey test revealed that sixth graders ranked the intentional cause significantly different with respect to the ideological, political, and foreign affairs causes. The results indicated that the intentional cause was the most important cause, whereas the ideological, political, and the international were the lowest causes in their explanation of the discovery of America.

The results obtained in the case of eighth and tenth graders and also psychology graduates indicated that these subjects ranked the intentional and economic causes significantly different than ideological and foreign affairs ones. Thus, the data showed that the former causes were considered as the two most important causes in their explanations, whereas the latter were the lowest ones.

The answers of the history group were quite different from the other groups. History experts ranked the economic and political causes significantly different from the intentional and ideological ones, ranking them as the two most important causes, whereas the latter causes were ranked as least important.

To summarize, the data obtained in this study show that different age and expertise groups tend to provide different types of historical explanations. In the case of historians, the data suggest that the causal explanation formulated by them could be considered as a structural explanation. This is due to the fact that these subjects established intentional factors as having a very low level of importance in their causal order, whereas at the same time they maintained that political context was an essential cause in order to explain the historical event studied. However, the other groups seemed to combine both types of explanation — intentional and structural — with intentional being more frequent with sixth and eighth graders.

Discussion

The results obtained in this study suggest that historical explanations generated by adolescents and also by adults, except for experts in history, considered the role played by intentional factors as quite important when they try to explain a historical event. On the contrary, historians tend to generate structural explanations, establishing a set of economic, political, scientific, and social factors as the main causal elements of the social reality in relation to the event. In this case, human actions are located in the context of particular social conditions that constitute the historical reality under which events happen (Carretero & Jacott, 1992).

One possible question that can be considered in relation to these data is to what extent similar results could be obtained in the case of different groups and different historical facts. For this reason, we presented a very similar task to various groups of eighth and tenth graders, and psychology and history students (Carretero et al., 1994). In this occasion, the historical facts selected were the French Revolution and World War II, as well as the discovery of America. Also, six causes of the same types were elaborated for each fact and presented to the subjects in order, to be ranked according to their importance. The results indicated a number of differences on the subjects ranking, depending on the facts. For example, ideological cause was considered as having more importance in the case of World War II than in the case of the French Revolution. On the other hand, economic cause was more important in the case of the French Revolution than in World War II. With respect to the subjects' explanations of the discovery of America, we found similar pattern of responses in the two studies.

These results suggest that subjects do not give the same importance to one type of cause when they have to explain the production of different historical facts. That is, economic cause is not always the most important one in the explanation of the three historical events considered. Thus, research on the understanding of historical causality should take into account the characteristic of the historical events under study. But on the other hand, as in the study presented in this chapter, adolescents and adults tended to consider the role of personal agents as being much more important than did history experts.

Also, a more qualitative approach could be fruitful in this kind of research. For this reason, we also present some comments about a study (Jacott & Carretero, 1993) in which a narration about the discovery of America was asked of subjects. We established a number of categories in order to analyze the subjects' narrations. Two of them were the type of agents and the type of motives mentioned, that is, who was mentioned spontaneously by subjects as the agents of the discovery of America and what kind of motives they had in order to be involved in that historical fact. Younger students only mentioned personal agents (Columbus, King and Queen, etc.) and motives (i.e., desire to explore new territories). Adult nonexperts in history mentioned both personal and social agents and economic motives. Finally, most of the history experts mentioned only social and political agents (Monarchy, Spain, Crown, etc.) and abstract motives, mainly political, such as the rivalry between Spain and Portugal at those times.

Thus, these data are congruent with those presented in this chapter. It can be observed that in the spontaneous explanation of the discovery of America, subjects considered aspects such as agents and motives, which match with the ranking of the causes. For example, the consideration of personal agents and personal motives such as ambition, desires, and need of exploration agree with the importance given to the intentional cause in the study presented here by younger subjects.

On the other hand, it is also possible to interpret our results in terms of a personalized understanding of history, as Halldén (1986) maintained is common among many adolescents. That is, adolescents and adults, except experts in history, tend to consider the influence of specific persons in historical events to be much more important than abstract and nonpersonalized factors, such as the case of political and social structures. Of course, the main reason for this would be that those abstract issues would imply a much more in-depth knowledge about social and historical processes.

CONCLUSIONS

As was mentioned in the first part of this chapter, cognitive and instructional research on the understanding of historical contents is a rather recent endeavor, especially as compared to other domains. For this reason, we presented a general overview of the main theoretical issues implied in this research as an attempt to provide some basis for future research. Along with those aspects, an empirical study about causal explanations in history was also included.

In this section some general comments about the close relationship among the different issues included in this chapter is presented, and lastly a number of instructional implications are also discussed. Our claim is that the theoretical aspects presented here not only have importance by themselves, but also in relation to the rest of the mentioned characteristics of historical knowledge. Thus, we think that the influence of values and ideological attitudes is essential to study complex processes in the understanding of history. For example, in the task used in our study, historians considered intentional or personalistic causes as having almost no importance on historical causation. Would we have obtained the same results in the case of North American or Russian historians? Maybe not. In Spain, Marxist and Annales historiographical ideas, both of them paying little attention to personal agents in history, have been very popular among historians and social scientists, but it might not be the case in other countries. In addition, as has been pointed out previously, historiographical ideas also have a strong influence on the selection and testing of different theories through an inferential process.

On the other hand, it seems clear that some of the controversies among different approaches in history during this century are useful in order to understand how lay subjects understand historical contents. Most of the theoretical issues presented in this chapter can be related to the distinction between a structural and paradigmatic approach in history and a narrative one. In the first case, personal agents have almost no influence, and the most influential variables are political, economic, and social structures. In this case, these variables can be considered as similar to the physical variables in the sense of producing some type of historical regularities. In the second case, history is seen as a narrative enterprise that is based on a different type of logic. As a matter of fact, the comparison between history and stories has been an important issue in the philosophy of history (Danto, 1985; Gallie, 1964). It is in this sense that Ricoeur (1983) considered the relevance of the narrative nature of history: "If history would break out the link established with the basic human skill to follow a story and also with the cognitive operations of narrative comprehension, its distinctive condition in the concert of historical sciences would be lost: it would not be historical" (p. 133).

We think that, at the present, most historians would agree with the idea of both of these approaches, the structural and the narrative ones, as being necessary in order to fully understand historical processes (Rodrigo, this volume). In addition, the distinction between these two approaches is not a dichotomous one, because historical structures can be seen in a narrative way, and any historical narration can contain structural elements. The instructional implication of this would be that the teaching of history should foster the understanding of both approaches.

As has been pointed out, ideological and social values play an important role in how historical contents are selected and taught in the schools. On the other hand, even historians' theories are based on the historiographical perspective each historian holds. Thus, the instructional implication of these aspects is that students' development of critical thinking should be an important goal of history instruction. For instance, it would be useful to promote students' comparisons of different versions of historical events (as suggested by Hahn, this volume). These types of activities could help students to develop a relativistic conception of historical knowledge (Kuhn, Weinstock, & Flaton, this volume), may lead them to a better understanding of historical causal explanations, and may be useful for promoting the learning of some basic ideas about how historians build historical knowledge.

Narration plays an important role both in history and how history is taught in schools. Very often the way history is taught consists of offering the "story of the past." This could partly explain some of results. Do students and adult nonexperts in history generate intentional explanations partly because of this widespread conception of history as a "story of the past"? If instruction is oriented in a different way, would these subjects be able to generate different explanations? These are interesting questions opened to future research. Furthermore, by being intentional explanations based on personal agents – the starting point in students' explanations – the teacher could use them as a first step in helping students to develop more elaborated explanations.

On the other hand, another important issue from an instructional point of view is the complexity of students' historical explanations. Independent of students' causal explanations in history being more based on political and abstract factors or on personalized ones, it is essential to consider their complexity. In this respect, it is interesting to consider that most of the adolescent explanations do not take into account the political and foreign affairs context of the discovery of America. We think that to offer and emphasize that context should be an important goal of history instruction.

ACKNOWLEDGMENTS

This research was supported by grant (PB91-0028-C03-03) from DGCYT, Spain, to the first author. This chapter was written during a sabbatical leave of the first author at LRDC, University of Pittsburgh (scholarship from Spanish Ministry of Education). We thank J. F. Voss and D. Resnick for his very valuable comments on a first draft of this chapter. Carmen Vizcarro and Iris Berent also provided useful suggestions. Saul Bitran gave us the first notice about the Mexican history textbooks case.

REFERENCES

Barnes, M. S. (1896a). The development of the historical sense in children (I). *Studies in Education, I*(2), 43-52.

Barnes, M. S. (1896b). The development of the historical sense in children (II). *Studies in Education, I*(3), 83-93.

Carr, E. H. (1961). *What is history.* New York: Random House.

Carretero, M., Asensio, M., & Pozo, J. I. (1991). Cognitive development, causal thinking and time representation in adolescence. In M. Carretero, M. Pope, R. J. Simons, & J. I. Pozo (Eds.), *Learning and instruction* (pp. 27-48). Oxford: Pergamon Press.

Carretero, M., & Jacott, L. (1992). The development of problem solving and causal explanations in history domain. *International Journal of Psychology, 27*(3-4), 150.

Carretero, M., López-Manjón, A., & Jacott, L. (1994). *Causal explanations about different historical events.* Submitted for publication.

Carretero, M., Pozo, J. I., & Asensio, M. (1983). Comprensión de conceptos históricos durante la adolescencia [The understanding of historical concepts in adolescence]. *Infancia y Aprendizaje, 23*, 55-74.

Collingwood, R. G. (1946). *The idea of history.* London: Oxford University Press.

Danto, A. C. (1985). *Narration and knowledge.* New York: Columbia University Press.

Dewey, J. (1915). The aim of history in elementary education. In J. Dewey, *The school and society.* Chicago: The University of Chicago Press.

Dray, W. H. (1957). *Laws and explanation in history.* Oxford: Oxford University Press.

Ferro, M. (1981). *Comment on raconte l'Histoire aux enfant à travers le monde entier* [How history is told to children of different parts of the world]. Paris: Payot.

Friedman, W. J. (Ed.). (1982). *The developmental psychology of time.* New York: Academic Press.

Gallie, W. B. (1964). *Philosophy and historical understanding.* London: Chatto and Windus.

Habermas, J. (1970). *Zur Logik der Sozialwissenschaften.* Frankfurt: Suhrkamp Verlag. (English translation published as *On the logic of Social Sciences.* Cambridge, MA: MIT Press, 1988.)

Halldén, O. (1986). Learning history. *Oxford Review of Education, 12*, 53-66.

Jacott, L., & Carretero, M. (1993). Historia y relato. La comprensión de agentes históricos en el "descubrimiento" de ("encuentro" con) América [History and narrative. The understanding of historical agents in the "discovery of" ("meeting with") America]. *Substratum, I*(2), 21-35.

Jahoda, G. (1963). Children's concept of time and history. *Educational Review, 15*(2), 87-104.

Kuhn, D. (1991). *The skill of argument.* Cambridge, England: Cambridge University Press.

Kuhn, D., Amsel, E., & O'Loughlin, M. (1988). *The development of scientific thinking skills.* Orlando, FL: Academic Press.

Leadbeater, B., & Kuhn, D. (1989). Interpreting discrepant narratives: Hermeneutics and adult cognition. In J. Sinnot (Ed.), *Everyday problem-solving: Theory and application* (pp. 155-179). New York: Praeger.

Leinhardt, G. (1993). Weaving instructional explanations in history. *British Journal of Educational Psychology, 63*, 46-74.

Marrou, H. I. (1959). *De la connaissance historique.* Paris: Seuil. (English translation published as *The Meaning of History.* Baltimore: Helicon, 1966.)

Megill, A. (1989). Recounting the past: Description, explanation and narrative in historiography. *American Historical Review, 94*, 627-653.

Mink, L.O. (1973). The divergence of history and sociology in recent philosophy of history. In P. Suppes et al. (Eds.), *Logic, methodology and the philosophy of science* (Vol. 4, pp. 725-742). Amsterdam: North-Holland.

Minstrell, J. A. (1989). Teaching science for understanding. In L. B. Resnick & L. E. Klopfer (Eds.), *Towards the thinking curriculum: current cognitive research* (pp. 129–149). Washington, DC: Association for Supervision and Curriculum Development.

Oakden, E. C., & Sturt, M. (1922). The development of knowledge of time in children. *British Journal of Psychology, 12*, 309–336.

Piaget, J. (1933). Psychologie de l'enfant et enseignement de l'histoire [Developmental psychology and teaching history]. *Bulletin Trimestriel de la Conférence Internationale pour l'Enseignement de l'Histoire, 2*, 8–13.

Piaget, J. (1946). *Le developpment de la notion du temps chez l'enfant.* Paris: Presses Universitaires de France.

Resnick, L. B., & Klopfer, L. E. (1989). *Toward the thinking curriculum.* Washington, DC: Association for Supervision and Curriculum Development.

Ricoeur, P. (1983). *Temps et Récit* [Time and narrative] (Vol. I). Paris: Seuil.

Shaver, J. P. (Ed.). (1991). *Handbook of research on social studies teaching and learning.* New York: Macmillan.

Shemilt, D. (1987). Adolescent ideas about evidence and methodology in history. In C. Portal (Ed.), *The history curriculum for teachers* (pp. 39–61). Londres, UK: Falmer Press.

von Wright, G. H. (1971). *Explanation and understanding.* Ithaca, NY: Cornell University Press.

von Wright, G. H. (1974). Replies. In J. Manninen & R. Toumela (Eds.), *Essays on explanation and understanding* (pp. 371–413). Dordrecht: Reidel.

Voss, J. F. (1991). Informal reasoning and international relations. In J. F. Voss, D. N. Perkins & J. W. Segal (Eds.), *Informal reasoning and education* (pp. 37–58). Hillsdale, NJ: Lawrence Erlbaum Associates.

Wineburg, S. S. (1991). Historical problem solving: A study of the cognitive processes used in the evaluation of documentary and pictorial evidence. *Journal of Educational Psychology, 83*, 73–87.

16 Historical Reasoning as Theory-Evidence Coordination

Deanna Kuhn, Michael Weinstock, and Robin Flaton
Teachers College, Columbia University

Despite enormous growth in the study of thinking, we still know relatively little about how people reason about the social phenomena and issues involved in disciplines such as history, sociology, and political science. Yet such reasoning abilities could hardly be more important. They are fundamental to participation in a democratic society and arguably, therefore, should hold a privileged place as a focus of education. To become able to engage in effective debate of the serious social issues that arise in the collective life of a society is a potentially unifying goal of education in an increasingly pluralistic culture (Kuhn, 1993a). Social science topics, moreover, may provide an optimum context for developing reasoning skills, because the average person finds them more accessible than topics in most areas of science.

The nature of historical reasoning, as a particular type of social science reasoning, is even less well understood, and the various contributions to this volume are all addressed to better understanding the cognitive demands and challenges that historical reasoning poses. Historical reasoning focuses on analysis of particular events in the past. One question that needs to be asked is how it differs from analysis of particular events in the present or the future. In both cases, the individual brings to bear a wide range of general knowledge of how social variables function and interrelate in order to interpret the specific events under consideration.

A contrasting form of reasoning that we have studied extensively with both social and nonsocial content is inductive inference. In this case, reasoning is from particular to general—specific instances are evaluated as a basis for drawing general conclusions. In this chapter, we claim that historical reasoning (which is largely postdictive and particularized) and inductive causal inference (which is predictive and general) require some common cognitive skills and can usefully be regarded in a common conceptual framework of social science reasoning. We begin with a review of some of our work on inductive social science reasoning and then proceed to work on historical reasoning.

INDUCTIVE CAUSAL INFERENCE IN SOCIAL SCIENCE DOMAINS

One line of work (Kuhn, 1991, 1992) examined people's argumentive reasoning skills with respect to real social issues such as children's school failure and criminal recidivism. We asked subjects from adolescence through late adulthood to give evidence to describe and justify their views regarding the causes of these problems. Following the framework of a dialogic argument, we also asked them to generate alternative theories, counterarguments, and rebuttals, as well as presenting some evidence of our own for them to evaluate.

Overall, people described their causal theories readily and expressed considerable certainty that these theories were correct. Yet they showed surprising variability in the argument skills that would enable them to justify this certainty. No systematic differences in skill emerged as a function of sex or age group, but there were consistent differences as a function of education level (college vs. noncollege). In a word, poorly performing subjects did not regard their theories in the framework of alternative possibilities and could not conceive of evidence that would disconfirm them. Instead, these theories regarding why children fail in school or prisoners return to crime when they are released seemed to simply tell a story — "this is the way it happens" — with little conception that it could be otherwise. Theories are not reflected on as objects of cognition — as claims needing to be evaluated in light of alternatives and evidence. Moreover, the new evidence that we presented to subjects — whether it was minimally informative or suggestive of multiple causes — tended to simply assimilate to their own theories. "This pretty much goes along with my own view" was the typical response. We saw this finding as further indication of the difficulties people have in reflecting on their own thought, in a way that would allow them to clearly distinguish and coordinate theories and evidence. If new evidence is simply assimilated to a theory, any potential for constructing relations between the two is lost.

In another series of studies (Kuhn, Garcia-Mila, Zohar, & Andersen, forthcoming; Kuhn, Schauble, & Garcia-Mila, 1992), we further probed the difficulties that social science reasoning poses, by comparing it with reasoning in physical science domains. In each domain, we asked subjects to generate and interpret evidence involving a multivariable set of potential causes that might be implicated in an outcome. The content of one of the two problems in the social science domain, for example, was children's school failure. The subject was presented a "file cabinet" of student records, each containing a summary evaluation of a student's school performance in terms of one of four outcomes (ranging from "excellent" to "poor"). Also included was information regarding five factors that were the subject of a study being done on factors that might affect school performance. The subject was asked to examine the records to find out which factors do and do not make a difference. In a parallel problem, subjects were asked to investigate factors that do and do not make a difference in the popularity of children's TV programs. In two corresponding problems in the physical science domain, subjects investigated the effects of various factors on the speed at which model boats traveled across a tank of water and the speed at which cars traveled along a microcomputer racetrack. In all four problems, the causal structure was the same. Two of the five factors were noncausal, one had a simple causal effect, one had an interactive causal effect, and one had a curvilinear effect. Prior to investigating the evidence, subjects' own theories about effects of the factors were assessed, enabling us to examine how these theories affect strategies of investigation and inference.

The research design was a microgenetic one, in which subjects repeatedly engaged these problems over 10 weeks. During the first 5 weeks, each subject worked on one problem in the physical domain and one in the social domain, each once a week. During this time we observed gradual improvement in most subjects, both in their knowledge of the causal effects that were operating and in the strategies they used to acquire that knowledge. At the sixth week, we substituted new problem content in both domains. Knowledge of the causal effects, of course, showed a temporary decline, until the new content was mastered; but the critical outcome is that there was no decline in the level of strategies used to generate and interpret evidence. In the framework of a classical transfer design, the newly developed skills transferred to new content.

This very important result establishes that we are dealing with some *forms* of thinking—thinking strategies—that are distinguishable from the content in which they are embedded. It is a notable result in a climate in which domain specificity has been the ascendant view and demonstrations of domain-specific effects have been impressive. It enables us to probe more deeply exactly what the challenges are that such thinking poses and how they are met in ways that lead to improved thinking.

The microgenetic method is very powerful in this respect, allowing us to examine closely patterns of change over time. The method has told us first of all what people definitely do *not* do, and that is to simply access and gradually accumulate evidence until enough is obtained to draw conclusions. Instead, the investigative process is clearly theory directed. Subjects' theories influence the evidence that is generated, as well as how it is interpreted, and subjects are reluctant to acknowledge evidence without a compatible theory in place to explain it. The challenge, then, is not simply one of correctly "reading" the data, but of coordinating theories and evidence.

The multivariable problem format is a particularly rich one for observing this process, because it contains high degrees of freedom with respect to causal attribution. If an outcome appears to conflict with expectations with respect to one variable, these implications can be avoided simply by shifting to other variables to do the explanatory work. A frequent cost of such freedom, however, is in the validity of the inferences that are drawn. The resulting variability in validity is exactly what the microgenetic data show. People explain events by drawing from a repertory that includes both valid and invalid inference strategies, and this mixture of the two is maintained over an extended period of time.

As an example, consider Geoff, a young adult who was one of our community college sample. In the social science domain, Geoff for the first 5 weeks worked with the TV content. His task was to make inferences about the effects of five factors on the popularity ratings given by a group of children to different TV programs. These factors were whether or not the show had music, whether it had commercials, whether it had humor, whether it was shown on Tuesday or Wednesday, and its length (1 half hour, 1 hour, or 2 hours). After his own theories about the effects of these factors were assessed, Geoff was asked to choose a record from our file cabinet. He said he was going to "pick just any program." The record he chose to see was of a program with commercials but without music or humor, 2 hours long and on Tuesday. (A summary of the problem structure and the evidence Geoff generated at the first two sessions is shown in Table 16.1.) After making a prediction, he was allowed to examine the record, and he learned that the outcome was a rating of "fair." He was asked what he had found out, and his interpretation was as follows: "You see, this shows you that the factors I was saying about . . . that you have to be funny to make it good or excellent and the day doesn't really matter, and it's too long." Geoff's inference was slightly more complex than many because he interpreted a negative instance—absence of one or more things leads to a poor outcome. Yet his was nonetheless a classical false inclusion inference, in which one or more variables were causally implicated in an outcome simply because they co-occurred with it.

When asked to choose a second record, Geoff added humor and music and changed the length to 1 half hour and the day to Wednesday (see Table 16.1). The outcome this time was "excellent," which he interpreted as

TABLE 16.1
Illustrative Evidence Generated in the TV Problem

True Effects for the TV Content (Social Domain)

Music (M or -)	Simple causal effect
Commercials (C or -)	Interactive causal effect (causal only in absence of music)
Length (0, 1, 2)	Curvilinear causal effect (0 > 1 = 2)
Day (t or w)	Noncausal
Humor (f or s)	Noncausal

Evidence generated by Geoff

Session 1		
instance 1	-C2ts	fair
instance 2	MC0wf	excellent
instance 3	M-1wf	good
Session 2		
instance 4	MC0wf	excellent
instance 5	M-2wf	good
instance 6	--2ws	poor
instance 7	MC2ts	good
instance 8	MC2tf	good
instance 9	MC2wf	good

Note. For length, 0 = 1/2 hr, 1 = 1 hr, 2 = 2 hrs; for day, t = Tuesday, w = Wednesday; for humor, f = funny, s = serious.

follows: "It has basically what I thought. It does make a difference when you put music and have commercials and the length of time and the humor. Basically the day is the only thing that doesn't really matter."

So, the two initial pieces of evidence Geoff chose provided him the opportunity to confirm all of his initial theories. Three of the factors that covaried with outcome (music, humor, and length) he interpreted as causal. The commercials factor, despite the fact it did not vary, he also included as causal, whereas day, which did vary, he nonetheless excluded as noncausal. None of these inferences, of course, is valid.

Yet, before the end of the second session, Geoff has generated and intends to interpret a potentially valid comparison (instances 7 and 8). In generating instance 8, he predicted: "I know that if we make it funny, it will be even better. (How do you know?) Because we've seen records with funny and it was excellent." The outcome, however, remained the same ("good"), providing the opportunity for a valid exclusion strategy, that is, to conclude that humor in fact does not make a difference. But Geoff shied away from this conclusion and instead made this interpretation: "It [the rating] was less than I expected. This brings me back to what I thought . . . it's rated less because it's too long." We know, furthermore, that Geoff understood and could use the valid exclusion strategy, because the very next instance he generated (instance 9) enabled him to achieve his stated intent of "finding out that the day doesn't make a difference." The outcome was again "good" and he concluded: "The day doesn't make a difference, because the previous one was a different day and it still was good."

What we see here is the difficulty Geoff has in relinquishing a causal theory (that humor affects outcome), even though he must compromise the validity of his inference strategies to save the theory. This challenge was the most difficult one for all of our subjects; they had much less difficulty in detecting covariation where they did not anticipate it and constructing a causal theory to explain it.

Although this difficulty was evident in both domains, it was more pronounced in the social than in the physical science domain. Inference validity was lowest when an initial theory was causal, the true effect was noncausal, and content was in the social domain. In these cases, no more than one third of the subjects in the community college sample ever discovered the true effect when the content was social, compared to about five sixths who eventually discovered it when the content was in the physical science domain. A similar difference appeared when subjects had to reverse the direction of a causal theory (e.g., from believing that commercials made a program less popular to concluding that it made a program more popular). In the physical domain, the large majority of subjects eventually did so when the evidence required it, whereas in the social domain no more than one third did.

Of particular interest are two strategies that subjects showed for "saving" their incorrect causal theories. The first was to particularize an inference ("In this particular class, having a teaching assistant didn't help"), with the implication that the theory was by no means dead and might well apply elsewhere. The second, more common strategy was to particularize the theory, by linking the factor to another one with perceived causal power (humor makes a difference because "every time humor was with music, they rated it excellent"). Our subjects' efforts in this respect were many and varied – commercials make a difference in longer programs although not in shorter ones, presence of a teaching assistant makes a difference if the class is large, and so forth.

Thus, in both this work and the research on argumentive reasoning described earlier, people show a tendency to particularize their social science reasoning – to attach it to a particular scenario or instance or configuration of other factors. We were therefore curious about the reasoning people would show if they were asked to reason about a particular event or phenomenon. This, of course, brings us to historical reasoning, which we turn to shortly.

We conclude the present section by noting that the significance of the skills in theory-evidence coordination considered here lies in the concept of control. For individuals lacking in these skills, beliefs come into contact with new evidence in an unstable way. Evidence is either ignored or distorted to protect the belief, or the individual is unduly swayed by it, leaving beliefs at the mercy of transitory, unpredictable external influence over which the individual exercises no control. In contrast, those who have achieved control of the interaction of theory and evidence in their own thinking are able to distinguish what comes from their own thought and what comes from external sources (Kuhn, 1989). They exercise this control because they are able to think *about* their theories, not merely *with* them. If these skills are recognized as important, we next want to ask what determines people's disposition to develop and exercise them. Here, it becomes important to examine epistemologies.

EPISTEMOLOGICAL ASPECTS OF SOCIAL SCIENCE REASONING

Epistemology and Argumentive Reasoning Skills

Based on several questions of an epistemological nature included in our interview in the argumentive reasoning research (Kuhn, 1991) — questions such as whether experts know for sure the answers to these questions or anyone's answer could be proved right or wrong — we observed the same general progression noted by other researchers who have investigated naive epistemologies. It begins with the most prevalent stance of absolutism, in which knowledge is regarded as a free-standing attribute of the environment (Chandler, Boyes, & Ball, 1990) that accumulates toward certainty, without connection to the human minds that do this knowing, and proceeds to an also prevalent stance of multiplism or relativism. Multiplists descend the slippery slope of observing that even experts disagree, going on to infer that therefore nothing is certain. From there, it is only a short distance to the conclusion that all opinions are of equal validity. Beliefs or opinions are the possessions of their owners, freely chosen according to the owner's tastes and wishes, and accordingly not subject to criticism. In the words of one of the adolescents in our sample, "You can't prove an opinion to be wrong because an opinion is something somebody holds for themselves." And so (in the final step down the slope), because everyone has a right to their opinion, all opinions are equally right. Only about 15% of the adolescents and adults in our sample had progressed to what we called an evaluative epistemology, in which knowing is understood as a process that entails judgment, evaluation, and argument. They have reconciled the idea that people have a right to their views with the understanding that some views can nonetheless be more right than others.

This lack of epistemological understanding may be an important factor in the limited argumentive reasoning ability that people display. People must see the point of argument if they are to engage in it. If knowledge is entirely objective, certain, and simply accumulates, as the absolutist believes, or if knowledge is entirely subjective, subject only to the tastes and wishes of the knower, as the multiplist believes, critical thinking and judgment are superfluous. An individual who has not reached the evaluative level of epistemological understanding does not conceive of any basis for judging the strength of an argument beyond its power to persuade. There is no need nor place for the comparative weighing and evaluation of alternative views that are the heart of skilled debate. Empirical findings from the argument research are consistent with this association (Kuhn, 1991). Those subjects who espoused an evaluative epistemology were more likely to exhibit the key argumentive skills of counterargument and generation of alternative theories. These findings thus point to the relevance of epistemological understanding to sound reasoning. In sum, they suggest that both skill and disposition are important if people are to acquire the critical habit of thinking about their own thought.

Epistemological Underpinnings of Historical Reasoning

In initial studies of historical reasoning (Kuhn, Pennington, & Leadbeater, 1983; Leadbeater & Kuhn, 1989), we focused on its epistemological aspect, clearly a key dimension in how people conceive of history. Is historical knowledge regarded as absolute and accumulative or relative to the interpretation and reinterpretation of observers? To investigate this question, a range of subjects was presented the Livia task, having to do with two historians' conflicting accounts of the fictitious "Fifth Livian War" (see Table 16.2). Subjects were asked to "describe what the war was about and what happened" and were probed regarding the differences between the two accounts.

The progression in epistemological understanding that we observed resembles in many ways the one described earlier. Initially, the historians' accounts of the events are not distinguished from the events themselves. The narrative does not exist as relative to an observer. Accordingly, metastatements (about the accounts) are rare, and the subject focuses on statements about the events themselves. No differences in the accounts may be noted, or, if they are, they are explained as omissions or additional information in one of the accounts. The two accounts can thus be "added together" to provide a more complete version.

At a subsequent level, the two accounts are seen as genuinely different. Initially, however, differences are attributed to willful misrepresentation or bias on the part of one of the historians. A neutral, third party is seen as

TABLE 16.2a
A Brief Account of the Fifth Livian War
by J. Abdul (National Historian of North Livia)

On July 19th 1878, during a period set aside by North Livia to honor one of their national leaders, the ceremonies were interrupted by a sneak attack from the South Livians, beginning the Fifth Livian War. Because the North Livians were caught by surprise, they were unprepared at first and the South Livians won a few early battles. But then the tide turned heavily in favor of the North Livians. Before the North Livians could reach a final victory, however, a neighboring large country intervened to prevent further bloodshed.

Despite their early setbacks, the later sweeping victories of the North Livians showed that they would have won, had the fighting continued. As a result of this war, the South Livians finally recognized that anything they gained from the North Livians would have to be worked out through peaceful negotiations. Thus ended the Livian Wars.

TABLE 16.2b
A Brief Account of the Fifth Livian War
by N. Ivan (National Historian of South Livia)

In the last war, North Livia had beaten South Livia, taken some of its land and refused to leave. South Livia could no longer tolerate this situation and spent large sums of public funds to strengthen its military defenses. On July 20th 1878, the Fifth Livian War began. The war took place with rapid, dramatic victories for South Livia, resulting in great national celebration. After these dramatic victories, the South Livians suffered some minor losses. But then a neighboring large country intervened to prevent further blood shed.

Despite their later setbacks, the final victory of South Livia seemed assured because of its overall position of strength. As a result of this war, the South Livians felt a new self-respect. They had always felt embarrassed by their previous defeats, but now they had proven that they were the equals of the North Livians on the battlefield. Because the South Livians had achieved military respect, they were willing to work out future differences through peaceful negotiations, thus ending the Livian Wars.

capable of discerning the "true facts." Only one quarter of the sixth graders in our sample showed reasoning at this level, and none exceeded it (Leadbeater & Kuhn, 1989).

At the next level we see emerge the multiplism that was so common in the epistemological stances observed in the argument research. Recognition of the subjective at least temporarily obliterates any objective component. In contrast to the preceding level, subjects now maintain that both accounts could be right, because "everyone sees things from their own point of view." The accounts are regarded as devoid of facts, as is almost all opinion. This level first appeared among ninth graders and became the most frequent stance by the twelfth grade.

What remains debatable is the endpoint of this progression, especially as relatively few adolescents or even adults exhibit the higher levels. Among our sample, which included both student and nonstudent adults, two further levels were observed. At both, two realms of discourse were recognized: one of subjective perspective and one of objective fact. At one level, an objective reality is regarded as ultimately knowable, through critical evaluation of multiple accounts. At the other, the realm of facts exists only as interpreted by human observers. These interpretations are subject to critique and comparison but do not yield a single reality. Common to both levels, however, is the recognition of the relevance of critical evaluation, conspicuously missing at the earlier levels.

These results suggest significant differences in the epistemological understanding that individuals bring to an historical reasoning task. For many, historical accounts simply portray reality, detached from any human knowing system; for others they are reduced to mere "opinion." Only among some are they seen as subject to critical evaluation. As Wineburg (1991, this volume) and other contributors to this volume also suggest, one cannot investigate historical reasoning very deeply without taking such differences in epistemological perspective into account.

JUROR REASONING AS AN HISTORICAL REASONING TASK

In recent work, we have investigated historical reasoning skills in the context of juror reasoning. A number of factors influenced our choice of the juror task as an historical reasoning task. First, and most essential, the reasoning a juror engages in shares key features of historical reasoning. Both juror and historian have the goal of reconstructing a past event and making decisions about the role of human action and intention in the event. Both start with events that are known to have occurred and then construct an argument to explain what happened. The reasoning is "postdictive," because the reasoner is "predicting the past" (Hexter, 1971). Both juror and historian rely on evidence that is incomplete, uncertain, often inconsistent, context-specific, and mediated through other people.

Research indicates that both historians (Leinhardt, Stainton, Virji, & Odoroff, this volume) and jurors (Pennington & Hastie, 1993) approach their tasks through the construction of narratives. To carry out their tasks competently, however, neither juror nor historian can be satisfied with constructing a single narrative. If all of the available evidence fit a single narrative construction, we would not need historical inquiry or judicial trials. The incomplete, uncertain, and inconsistent nature of evidence about past events inevitably leads to alternative constructions, which both juror and historian must examine as multiple theories of "what happened." The existence of multiple theories demands an evaluation of evidence—its source, its credibility, and the relation it bears to each of the theories, which must be explicitly compared to one another. (We say more shortly about the cognitive skills that are entailed in this effort.)

If we accept the juror task as an historical reasoning task, it offers several important advantages as a tool in investigating historical reasoning, particularly of nonexperts. One is that it equates the main information base that subjects draw on. Each subject is presented exactly the same trial testimony and asked to reach a verdict choice. Thus, any differences in reasoning that may be observed cannot be explained by differing degrees or kinds of knowledge about the specific events to be explained. Historical reasoning tasks, of course, also may be based on specific texts (e.g., Perfetti, Britt, Rouet, Georgi, & Mason, this volume), but these texts describe real historical events that subjects have (differing) prior knowledge and understanding of.

Another advantage of the juror task as an historical reasoning task is that it provides the subject with a clear, practical goal (deciding a verdict), one that the subject is familiar with and can readily understand. It is now widely recognized, within both the formal and informal reasoning literature, that how subjects construe the meaning and purpose of a task significantly affects their performance. One of the challenges in studying historical reasoning is the fact that nonexperts asked to reason historically lack a context for approaching the task. If subjects interpret what they are being asked to do as a school task, it is likely to invoke a whole "school learning" context, focusing on right answers and encompassing a complex body of tacit knowledge regarding expected behavior in this context (Krechevsky & Gardner, 1990; Okagaki & Sternberg, 1990). If subjects do not interpret the task as a school task, they are left with little alternative basis for interpreting the meaning and purpose of what they are being asked to do.

The juror task thus offers an alternative to the school learning context as a means of investigating the cognitive processes involved in historical reasoning. Also, as an informal reasoning task, it provides a bridge between the investigation of historical reasoning and the rapidly growing literature on informal reasoning, much of which is concerned with reasoning skills, such as evaluation of evidence and construction of narratives that are salient to historical reasoning.

A final point bears mentioning. In regarding the juror task as a task in informal or everyday reasoning, it is necessary to keep in mind that individual cognitive processes are only one component of the actual jury process (Hastie, 1993). They are nonetheless an essential one. Without their contribution, no social exchange among the members of a jury would occur. As we attempt to establish in our research, the skill with which these cognitive processes are executed is a matter of critical significance to the jury process.

Models of Juror Reasoning

Pennington and Hastie's story model is the most explicit cognitive model of juror reasoning available (Pennington, 1992; Pennington & Hastie, 1986, 1993), in addition to being well supported empirically. It stipulates a three-phase process. In the initial, evidence evaluation phase, the juror draws on evidence to construct a plausible narrative structure (story) of what happened. Second, the juror must learn the set of verdict alternatives (including multiple criteria associated with each), and, finally, the juror compares the story representation to representations of the verdict category features to find an acceptable match. Most of Pennington and Hastie's research addresses the initial, story-construction phase of their model, and they are able to show substantial correspondence between the story a subject constructs and verdict choice.

In seeking to identify dimensions of individual variation, we focus on the latter two phases to a greater extent. Even the first phase, however, suggests a largely unexplained dimension of individual variation, given that jurors construct different stories based on identical evidence. We propose individual differences at all three phases, although the latter two phases, as Pennington and Hastie (1993) acknowledge, are less well specified, and it is here especially that the possibility arises of different ways of executing the task.

In our work, we undertook an initial conceptualization of this potential variability by identifying two alternatives representing contrasting extremes of a competence-related continuum, with numerous intermediate positions clearly possible. The difference between the two begins with the first phase—story construction—and a dimension that Pennington and Hastie (1993) identified as unresolved in their work—whether the juror integrates presented evidence into a single plausible story or whether multiple stories (presumably of varying degrees of plausibility) are constructed.

In what we label a *satisficing* model, the juror draws on the presented evidence to construct a single plausible story, omitting from further consideration any evidence that resists integration into this scenario. This story is then compared to representations of one or more of the verdict categories. If a satisfactory match exists between the constructed story and a verdict category, that verdict is chosen and the task is completed.

At the other end of this continuum is a model of optimal performance that can be termed a *theory-evidence coordination* model. According to this model, the juror draws on the conflicting evidence to construct multiple stories. Different stories correspond most closely to different verdict categories, as Pennington and Hastie (1993) have shown. However, the trial evidence remains differentiated from the stories in the sense that the juror recognizes that not all of the presented evidence fits any one story. For each story (and corresponding verdict), there exists some evidence that is consistent and some that is discrepant with that story.

To reach a verdict decision, according to this model, the juror's task is one of evaluating each story/verdict constellation — or theory — both (a) against the evidence, and (b) against the alternatives. In contrast to the satisficing model, then, the juror is not satisfied simply to identify a verdict that adequately matches a constructed story. Instead, theories are evaluated, with respect to both the evidence consistent with them and the evidence discrepant with them. These are then compared against one another, and the one having the most consistent and least discrepant evidence associated with it is the verdict chosen. (Although clearly more cognitively demanding than the satisficing model, this model, it should be noted, still falls short of the "beyond a reasonable doubt" standard associated with ideal performance from a legal perspective.)

The contrasting satisficing and theory-evidence coordination models were derived jointly from consideration of the juror task itself and from our work on argumentive reasoning more broadly (Kuhn, 1991). In that work, as we noted, substantial individual variation was found, with some subjects able to reflect on their theories in a framework of alternative theories and pertinent evidence capable of disconfirming them. Others, in contrast, were satisfied simply to tell a story — "this is the way it happens" — with little conception that it could be otherwise.

The Juror Task

We administered a juror reasoning task developed and used extensively by Pennington and Hastie (1986, 1993) to the same subjects who participated in our argument research — adolescents and young, middle, and older adults of two education levels (basically college and noncollege, with the difference prospective among the adolescents). In addition to examining individual variation in performance of the task — a topic that has received little attention in research on juror reasoning — we were therefore able to explore the generality of such differences, that is, do they extend beyond the juror task?

The task involved audiotaped presentation of the short (25 min) version of the case of *Commonwealth v. Johnson*, reenacted by actors based on the transcript of an actual trial (Pennington & Hastie, 1986). Presentation of the trial information was followed by an individual interview eliciting a verdict decision and probing the subject's reasoning. Included in the presentation were attorneys' opening statements, direct and cross-examinations of witnesses and the defendant, attorneys' closing statements, and the judge's instructions to the jury. Subjects also received a written copy of the judge's instructions to refer to (although this is not the practice in real trials). The judge's instructions included an explanation of reasonable doubt and of the criteria defining each of four verdict choices — first-degree murder, second-degree murder, manslaughter, and self-defense.

In *Commonwealth v. Johnson*, the defendant Frank Johnson was charged with first-degree murder. The undisputed background events included a quarrel between Johnson and the victim, Alan Caldwell, early on the day of Caldwell's death. At that time, Caldwell threatened Johnson with a razor. That evening they were at the same bar, went outside together, got into a fight, and Johnson knifed Caldwell, resulting in Caldwell's death. Matters under dispute included whether Caldwell pulled a razor, whether Johnson actively stabbed Caldwell or merely held his knife out to protect himself, how they got outside together, whether Johnson intentionally went home and got his knife, and why Johnson returned to the bar.

After the subject listened to the tape and was offered the opportunity to look over the written version of the judge's instructions, the following questions were asked:

1. If you were one of the jurors, what verdict would you choose? Why?
2. What other factors went into your decision to choose that verdict?
3. Was there any other evidence that influenced you?
4. How certain are you that the verdict you chose is the right one?
5. Was there anything in the trial that suggested this was not the right verdict? (If not already answered) Why didn't this information lead you to rule out this verdict?
6. I'd like to ask about each of the verdicts you didn't choose. What about _____ ? Why didn't you choose this verdict? (question repeated for each alternative verdict).

The first three questions were designed to elicit as full a justification as possible of the subject's verdict choice, and the purpose of the fourth question was to assess the subject's certainty regarding the choice. The fifth question probed the subject's awareness of counterevidence or counterarguments (in the event these had not been raised previously) and how the subject dealt with them. Finally, the sixth question assessed whether the subject could discount alternative verdicts with justification.

Even in the short version we used, the subject was presented with a large quantity of detailed evidence and must select among four verdicts defined by complex criteria. It is improbable that many, if any, untrained jurors would be able to execute the task perfectly as characterized by the theory-evidence coordination model. We therefore looked for evidence of any of the various reasoning processes entailed in the model. In addition to examining correspondences with argumentive reasoning in another domain, we also related subjects' use of these processes in the juror task to two outcome variables — verdict choice and the certainty subjects attach to that choice. Our argument research showed that subjects who reasoned more adequately — who contemplated their theories in the framework of alternatives and evidence — were *less* certain that these theories were correct than were subjects who constructed a single scenario. We therefore predicted the similar result in the juror task that more adequate reasoning would be associated with lower certainty. Along the same line, we hypothesized that more adequate reasoning, in particular, the recognition of alternative possibilities and conflicting evidence, would be associated with more moderate verdict choices (in this case, second-degree murder or manslaughter, in contrast to first-degree murder or self-defense).

Summary and Illustration of Findings

Transcripts of the juror interviews were divided into units that were coded according to quality, function, and type (see Kuhn, Weinstock, & Flaton, in press, for additional details). To be coded as sufficient (vs. deficient) in quality, a unit had to relate relevant and legitimate evidence to one of the verdict categories. To be legitimate, the evidence must either be drawn directly from testimony or constitute a reasonable inference drawn from testimony. To be relevant, the evidence must either increase or decrease the probability that the criteria associated with the verdict in question are met.

Supporting Arguments.   The function of a unit can be either to support or discount a particular verdict. Four subtypes of units that function to support a verdict were identified; the first two being nonjudgmental and the other two judgmental. The two nonjudgmental subtypes are factual and narrative. In the factual subtype, the subject refers to pieces of evidence drawn directly from testimony, without elaboration, to support the verdict choice. In the narrative subtype, testimony is drawn on to construct an explicit narrative that is consistent with testimony but elaborates on it. In the two judgmental subtypes, the subject reflects on the evidence, evaluating it rather than merely drawing on it uncritically. This evaluation functions to enhance the value of particular evidence as supportive of the verdict choice. In the importing subtype, the subject imports real-world knowledge that the evidence is compared against,[1] with the outcome that the evidence is judged more likely to be accurate (and therefore supportive of the verdict choice). For example, a subject justified the second-degree

---

[1]All jurors, of course, interpret testimony in terms of their real-world knowledge. The dimension identified here is whether a subject does so in an explicit way, indicating that he or she is aware of its application and can reflect on its relevance.

murder verdict (which includes the criterion of intent) as follows: "He intended to fight. If he were intending to just talk, he could have talked inside just as easily." In the credibility subtype, the subject evaluates the source of the evidence, that is, the witness who provided the testimony, again with the outcome that this evidence is judged more likely to be accurate (and therefore supportive of the verdict choice). For example, a subject justified a self-defense verdict by stating: "I thought that Johnson's testimony was very clear and very lucid and it seemed there was nothing hazy about it."

Discounting Arguments.   Two major ways of discounting a verdict are possible: (a) evidence inconsistent with that verdict can be noted, or (b) evidence alleged to support that verdict can be discounted. Within each type, further subdivisions can be identified, based on distinctions similar to those made among subtypes of supporting units. Evidence inconsistent with a verdict can be noted in two ways, one nonjudgmental and one judgmental. In the nonjudgmental factual case, the subject refers to pieces of direct testimony that are alleged to be discrepant with the verdict being discounted. In the judgmental importing case, the subject imports real-world knowledge to support the argument that the particular evidence is discrepant with the verdict. For example, to discount first-degree murder (which requires premeditation), a subject stated, "If it actually was premediated and he actually wanted to kill the guy, he would probably have brought something bigger and more effective than just a little fishing knife." Thus, the subject drew on real-world knowledge to assert the presence of the fishing knife as inconsistent with the first-degree murder verdict category.

The second way of discounting a verdict — by discounting evidence alleged to support it — also can be divided into two subtypes. Both of these are judgmental, requiring reflection on the evidence. In the importing subtype, the subject imports real-world knowledge that the evidence is compared against, with the outcome that the evidence is judged as less likely to be accurate (and therefore supportive of the verdict choice). For example, a subject stated: "Another witness said that he probably had time to put the razor back in his pocket. If he has been stabbed in his heart, I don't think he would really . . . think about putting the razor back in his pocket." In the credibility subtype, the subject evaluates the source of the evidence, that is, the witness who provided the testimony, again with the outcome that this evidence is judged less likely to be accurate (and therefore supportive of the verdict choice). One subject, for example, discounted particular testimony, stating: "The officer said he raised the knife but his view was obstructed by the car and it was dark . . . I don't think his testimony can be relied on too much."

Summary Dimensions. Application of the coding system yielded a database amenable to a variety of potential analyses. In initial analysis, we focused on several summary dimensions most relevant to the theory-evidence coordination model. Story/verdict constellations can be thought of as theories, one of which the subject endorses as the chosen verdict. The model stipulates that the endorsed theory be evaluated (a) against alternative theories, and (b) against evidence. To evaluate the theory against alternatives means that these alternatives are recognized and addressed. To evaluate theories against evidence implies recognition of their falsifiability, that is, of the potential for evidence that does not fit the theory. The recognition of multiple theories and the multiple relations that evidence can have to these theories implies that evidence must be reflected on and evaluated, rather than merely assimilated, in order to determine these relations.

In analysis of the coded data, we thus looked for indications of these two broad dimensions of what the model specifies as competent performance. First, are there indications that the theory is considered in light of alternatives? The most obvious indicators in this respect are coded units devoted to the function of discounting alternatives. Another indicator that the theory is considered in the light of alternatives is the production of counterarguments (either during the main portion of the interview or in response to question 5); these are in effect alternatives to the subject's theory, whether they take the form of arguments in support of an alternative theory or arguments against the subject's theory (the two types of counterarguments we observed). The second broad dimension we examined is the extent to which the subject reflects on the evidence, evaluating it rather than merely drawing on it uncritically. The two specific indicators in this respect are the judgmental evidence subtypes described earlier — importing and credibility.

Results. A majority of subjects (84%) showed some discounting of alternative verdicts during the initial (open-ended) portion of the interview. The remaining 16% offered only supportive arguments in favor of the chosen verdict — hence showing no evidence of having considered any verdicts other than the one they chose. Among the majority, however, there was further variation, because 26% of the total sample offered *only* discounting arguments (leaving 58% who offered both supporting and discounting arguments). Those offering only discounting arguments in effect argued for their chosen verdicts by eliminating alternatives, without providing any direct argument in support of the verdict that was chosen. The 58% majority who showed both supporting and discounting arguments can thus be regarded as fulfilling the task in the most competent way, the 26% who showed only discounting as fulfilling it in a less competent way, and the 16% who showed no indication of considering alternatives as fulfilling it in the least competent way.

A slightly greater proportion of subjects (87%) showed at least some discounting of alternative verdicts when this discounting was elicited (question 6). Only a minority (13% of the total sample), however, successfully discounted all three alternative verdicts. Two of the three verdicts were successfully discounted by 40% of the sample, one of the three by 35%, and none of the three by 13%. The spontaneous discounting indicator thus provides some indication of the subject's disposition to discount as an argumentive strategy, and the elicited discounting indicator provides an indication of the subject's skill in doing so.

Either spontaneously (in the initial portion of the interview) or in response to question 5, only slightly more than half of the sample—56%—were able to generate a successful counterargument. Furthermore, only a minority—35%—of the counterarguments coded as successful were genuine counterarguments in the sense of being arguments against the chosen verdict. The remaining 65% of subjects coded as successful responded to question 5 by noting the presence of evidence supporting an alternative verdict (in contrast to evidence against the chosen verdict).

Whether the function was supporting or discounting, credibility inferences were displayed by 40% of the sample and importing inferences by 63%. The percentage of subjects showing no judgmental use of evidence was 20%. These subjects showed only the factual subtype or some combination of factual and narrative. (No subject showed exclusive use of the narrative subtype.)

Associations among these dimensions provide some evidence of an overall pattern of reflection on evidence to weigh and discount alternatives. Counterargument success was empirically related to success in elicited but not spontaneous discounting. Importing was related to spontaneous and elicited discounting but not counterargument. No associations involving credibility were significant.

Are the individual differences that have been described here confined to the juror task, or do they reflect differences in argumentive reasoning strategies more broadly? To address this question, we focused on two major dimensions in the argumentive reasoning research in which these subjects had participated—generation of genuine evidence and generation of alternative theories. Only about 40% of the subjects offered genuine evidence for their theories, defined simply as evidence differentiated from the theory and bearing on its correctness. As noted in our earlier description of these findings, subjects frequently responded to the request for justification by elaborating the theory, that is, describing a story or scenario of how the phenomenon occurs. Subjects who offered this "pseudoevidence" (or nonevidence, such as merely restating the outcome) to support their theories, we found, were less likely than others to be able to offer an alternative theory of how the phenomenon might occur (Kuhn, 1991).

Both of these dimensions were related to corresponding dimensions in the juror domain. Most relevant to the alternative-theory dimension is whether jurors consider (and discount) alternative verdicts (spontaneous discounting) and whether they can offer counterarguments to their own theories (especially as the majority of these, recall, consisted of evidence to support an alternative verdict, rather than evidence against the chosen verdict). Although the association with discounting did not reach statistical significance, the association with counterargument was significant: Subjects largely successful (for two or more of three topics) in producing an alternative theory in the argument research were more likely to produce a successful counterargument in the juror domain.

Production of genuine evidence in the argument research was significantly related to counterargument, as well as discounting, in the juror domain (although not to judgmental evidence). Thus, both dimensions from the argument research — generation of genuine evidence and alternative theories (dimensions that are themselves related) — are indicative of the extent to which the subject is likely to regard a verdict choice in a framework of alternatives.

With respect to the outcome variable of verdict choice, results supported our predictions. Those subjects who exhibited what was regarded as more competent reasoning were more likely to choose an intermediate (second-degree murder or manslaughter) than an extreme (first-degree murder or self-defense) verdict. For example, among subjects showing no spontaneous discounting of alternative verdicts, 75% chose one of the extreme verdicts, compared to 48% among remaining subjects.

Associations were also significant for the certainty attached to verdict choice. Subjects overall showed inappropriately high certainty (less than half said they were not certain that their choice was correct), with less competent reasoners the most likely to express very high certainty. For example, subjects showing no spontaneous discounting of alternative verdicts, that is, those who showed no indication of considering verdicts other than the one they chose, were most likely to be highly certain that this verdict was correct — 59% of these subjects indicated high certainty. Among the remaining subjects, those who showed only discounting of alternative verdicts were least likely to show very high certainty (12% did so), compared to 38% among subjects who showed both supporting and discounting.

Case Study Excerpts. To provide a qualitative sense of the individual variation observed, we present here excerpts from the protocols of subjects who represent contrasting ends of the continuum that has been examined.

The first subject, S16, was highly certain of the verdict choice of self-defense. She justified this verdict with some simple factual evidence, but the evidence cited was largely elaborated into a narrative form (see earlier list of questions):

(Q1) Because they say that Caldwell first hit him in the face and he [Johnson] fell to the floor and then Caldwell took out his razor. So he [Johnson] thought he [Caldwell] would stab him, so he had to take out his fishing knife to defend himself. (Q2) Because Johnson was home with his wife and his two kids and if somebody came over and asked him if he wants to go to the restaurant and have a drink, he says sure, because he didn't think Caldwell was going to be there, but he went anyway. When Caldwell walked in, you know, Caldwell was very nice and friendly and he said he wanted to talk. So Johnson says sure. So they went outside and when Caldwell hit him in the face, he had to defend himself.

In response to the request for a counterargument (Q5), S16 was able to contrast her own conclusion to a different one, but offered no arguments on either side: "Well, they said that he did it deliberately, but in my opinion he didn't do it deliberately—he did it just to protect himself." Nor, in response to probing (Q6) was she able to justify discounting any other verdicts based on the criteria stipulated in the judge's instructions. In attempting to discount first-degree murder, for example, she stated: "He didn't want to do that because he has a wife and children to support; so he probably would not just kill a man."

Another subject, S149, similarly was highly certain of the verdict choice of self-defense and similarly did not consider alternatives. The evidence offered, however, was largely drawn from the testimony, with lesser indication of being knitted into a narrative like that of S16:

(Q1) Because Caldwell was threatening him before and later during the day and attacked him in the evening. So what he was trying to do was to defend himself from that. He just walked with the knife like he was going fishing or something like that. So, since he drew out the razor from his pocket and started to . . . you know, he was trying to defend himself so he takes a knife to defend himself. (Q2) Because the guy was threatening him with the razor.

In response to the counterargument question (Q5), S149 denied there being anything that "suggested this was not the right verdict." "No, not to me," he replied. Nor was he able to discount any alternative verdicts, justifying the discounting of first-degree murder, for example, as follows: "No, I don't think first-degree murder would be right because he was trying to defend himself, so he can't be charged for first-degree murder."

In contrast to S16 and S149 stands a subject, S69, who chose the manslaughter verdict, based on a combination of supportive evidence for this verdict (focused on the criterion of reasonable provocation) and discounting evidence against other verdicts — both self-defense (focused on the criteria of reasonable fear of great bodily harm and exhausts all means to avoid confrontation) and first- and second-degree murder (focused on the criterion of intent). In addition, he showed frequent use of importing of real-world knowledge to make judgments about the evidence:

(Q1) There are several things. I find it incredible that a man who is dying would put a razor back in his pocket and they did find it in his pocket. He may never have taken it out at the time he was seen attacking Johnson. I do believe in those circumstances. As one who has spent a good part of my life on 149th Street and 8th Avenue [in New York City], I have lived through things like this. I have actually seen fights among people and I have seen the razors and I have seen terrible slashing and under those circumstances I would say that probably 85 to 90 percent of the people carry some kind of a weapon. They are afraid of being mugged. They are afraid of being attacked. Life is filled with fear. So I can understand both of them carrying weapons.

The other part is that several saw Johnson being hit in the face and the instinct is to respond with a weapon, especially as he knows that the other one has a weapon which he saw earlier in the day. He had been threatened earlier in the day with it.

I would not put it as murder in the first or second because he was in an area where he goes all the time. He was there first. Caldwell came in afterwards. Apparently, they were talking in a fairly friendly fashion when they went out. Of course in the back of his mind might have been the fact that a battle might ensue, but there was a possibility that it would end up calmly.

(Q2) I would not call it an out-and-out self-defense because he did return to a scene where he had been threatened earlier. If he wanted to avoid violence entirely he would have stayed away from that area. He would not have been in that place, and when he was invited to go outside, he would either have refused or literally run away, assuming that he saw that something was about to happen. Therefore I cannot say it is strictly self-defense because when he went back to the place and when he went outside, there was a possibility of a physical confrontation.

S69 at this point introduced a spontaneous counterargument against his own argument supporting manslaughter, but incorporated with it a spontaneous rebuttal: "I do believe that the main attack came from Caldwell, in spite of the fact that he [Caldwell] did not have his razor out, because he was seen . . . whatever was seen . . . the first violence was his punching

Johnson." After offering a further argument, one against the first- and second-degree murder criterion of malice (focusing on testimony that Johnson was a peaceful man and that no comparable testimony was presented regarding Caldwell), and repeating an argument against self-defense (regarding the plausibility of a dying man returning a razor to his pocket), S69 concluded his justification of the manslaughter verdict by saying: "I do not believe that Caldwell ran onto the knife. I believe he was stabbed, but I believe that this was because Johnson had been attacked and the instinct is to use whatever weapon you have, knowing that the other one has a weapon."

S69 was able to offer justification for discounting each of the three alternative verdicts, but expressed low certainty regarding the chosen manslaughter verdict, going on to note: "With all the evidence we really do not know who was the real aggressor outside. It might have been Johnson but there is no visual evidence of that."

In sum, in contrast to S16 and S149, who appeared to construct a single story of what happened with no evidence of considering alternatives, S69 clearly construed the task as one of evaluating and weighing evidence for and against a set of alternatives, a process that left him with less certainty that his chosen verdict was correct. This individual variability, we claimed, is related to argumentive reasoning skill more broadly, rather than idiosyncratic to the juror domain. For example, when asked to justify her theory that rejection by the criminal's family causes return to crime, S16 (quoted earlier) elaborated a scenario in which the criminal felt that there was no one outside that cared about him and that prison was the only place where he belonged, leading him to want to return there after he was released. Pressed further for evidence of the correctness of her theory, S16 cited the case of an uncle whose experience followed this scenario. When asked for an alternative theory, she was unable to generate one. Exemplified here, then, is an argumentive approach that extends at least across the two contexts involved in our research.

CONCLUSIONS

Our research on juror reasoning extends Pennington and Hastie's (1993) work by identifying different ways in which a story model might operate — most notably whether stories are considered in a framework of alternatives, but also in the ways in which evidence is processed, particularly when it is not readily assimilable into a story the subject has constructed. Our work indicates substantial individual variation in the manner in which the juror task is approached. This variation, moreover, is readily conceptualized along a competence dimension — considering alternatives and reflecting on evidence is clearly more competent than not doing so. Finally, and perhaps most significant, the individual differences we identified both make a difference in the outcome of the juror task itself and relate to argumentive reasoning more broadly.

A majority of our subjects showed inappropriately high certainty regarding their verdict choices. This certainty is suggestive of the epistemological stance of "absolutism" discussed earlier, with the subject conceiving of the task as one of identifying a single truth, rather than a probabilistic task of weighing alternatives. Those who construe the juror task as one of identifying a single truth will be less disposed to contemplate the evidence in a framework of alternatives. Instead, they are more likely to search for a plausible scenario of "what happened"—the story central to Pennington and Hastie's model—and to seek evidence allowing them to attach certainty to this story. Such an approach establishes optimum conditions for the "biased assimilation" (of evidence) that has been found prevalent in research on reasoning (Baron, 1988; Kuhn, 1993a; Kunda, 1990).

Rather than integrating evidence uncritically into a plausible scenario, ignoring any that resists integration, the competent juror needs to critically evaluate evidence in a framework of its bearing on multiple theories of "what happened." The relation between epistemological understanding of the juror task and exercise of these reasoning skills warrants investigation in future research. A sophisticated "evaluative" epistemology (Kuhn, 1991, chap. 7) most likely promotes use of the more competent reasoning skills. At the same time, considering alternatives and reflecting on evidence may promote more sophisticated epistemological understanding.

We earlier made a case for the potential of the study of juror reasoning in providing insight into historical reasoning. This potential, we believe, extends to the issues surrounding history education addressed by many of the contributors to this volume. The aims of education are a subject of continuing debate (Kuhn, 1993b), and history is one of the disciplines in which goals are particularly ill specified. Most of the contributors to this volume share the view that a focus on historical method—indeed on the epistemological foundations of the discipline of history (Baron, 1993)—holds the promise of enhancing the coherence of history education. Most would endorse the claim made by Perfetti et al. (this volume) that, "there is value to acquainting students with the use of evidence and argument in history learning." If this view is taken, the kinds of psychological data described in the present chapter become particularly important. We need to understand how students come to be able to exercise the coordination of theories and evidence involved in skilled argumentation—certainly before we can educate them regarding these skills as they are practiced by professional scholars in history or other disciplines (Baron, 1993; Kuhn, 1993c).

Both historical reasoning, which is largely postdictive and particularized, and inductive causal inference, which is predictive and general, we claim, can be regarded in a common conceptual framework of social science reasoning. The challenges that social science reasoning poses, we also claim, are largely metacognitive. They require thinking about one's own thought — evaluating one's ideas in a framework of alternatives that compete with them and evidence that bears on them. They lead to the important achievement of knowing what and how one knows.

Both a richer knowledge base and greater affective investment most likely contribute to making the challenge of skilled reasoning greater when the content is in the social, as compared to the physical, domain. In thinking about such topics, people have a wealth of personal experience and accrued information to draw on and many ideas, but exactly for these reasons they are likely to be attached to these ideas and find it hard to revise them. Both the advantages and the obstacles that familiarity affords make social science reasoning worthy of our close attention. Social science topics are likely both to engage people and to challenge them. This is exactly the combination that gives them such great potential as vehicles for improving thinking.

REFERENCES

Baron, J. (1988). *Thinking and deciding.* New York: Cambridge University Press.

Baron, J. (1993). Why teach thinking? *Applied Psychology, 42*(3), 191–237.

Chandler, M., Boyes, M., & Ball, L. (1990). Relativism and stations of epistemic doubt. *Journal of Experimental Child Psychology, 50,* 370–395.

Hastie, R. (1993). Introduction. In R. Hastie (Ed.), *Inside the juror* (pp. 3–41). New York: Cambridge University Press.

Hexter, J. (1971). *The history primer.* New York: Basic Books.

Krechevsky, M., & Gardner, H. (1990). Approaching school intelligently: An infusion approach. In D. Kuhn (Ed.), *Developmental perspectives on teaching and learning thinking skills. Contributions to human development* (Vol. 21, pp. 79–94). Basel: Karger.

Kuhn, D. (1989). Children and adults as intuitive scientists. *Psychological Review, 96,* 674–689.

Kuhn, D. (1991). *The skills of argument.* New York: Cambridge University Press.

Kuhn, D. (1992). Thinking as argument. *Harvard Educational Review, 62,* 155–178.

Kuhn, D. (1993a). Connecting scientific and informal reasoning [Special Issue]. *Merrill-Palmer Quarterly, 39*(1), 74–103.

Kuhn, D. (1993b, March). *Missing links in the IQ equation.* Paper presented at a symposium at the biennial meeting of the Society for Research in Child Development, New Orleans.

Kuhn, D. (1993c). Thinking as an epistemological enterprise (reply to Baron). *Applied Psychology, 42*(3), 226–228.

Kuhn, D., Garcia-Milla, M., Zohar, A., & Andersen, C. (forthcoming). Strategies of knowledge acquisition. *Monographs of the Society for Research in Child Development.*

Kuhn, D., Pennington, N., & Leadbeater, B. (1983). Adult thinking in developmental perspective: The sample case of juror reasoning. In P. Baltes & O. Brim (Eds.), *Life-span development and behavior* (Vol. 5, pp. 158–197). New York: Academic Press.

Kuhn, D., Schauble, L., & Garcia-Mila, M. (1992). Cross-domain development of scientific reasoning. *Cognition and Instruction, 4,* 285–328.

Kuhn, D., Weinstock, M., & Flaton, R. (in press). How well do jurors reason?: Competence dimensions of individual variation in a juror reasoning task. *Psychological Science.*

Kunda, Z. (1990). The case for motivated reasoning. *Psychological Bulletin, 108,* 480–498.

Leadbeater, B., & Kuhn, D. (1989). Interpreting discrepant narratives: Hermeneutics and adult cognition. In J. Sinnott (Ed.), *Everyday problem-solving: Theory and application* (pp. 175–190). New York: Praeger.

Okagaki, L., & Sternberg, R. (1990). Teaching thinking skills: We're getting the context wrong. In D. Kuhn (Ed.), *Developmental perspectives on teaching and learning thinking skills. Contributions to human development* (Vol. 21, pp. 63–78). Basel: Karger.

Pennington, N. (1992). Explaining the evidence: Tests of the story model for juror decision making. *Journal of Personality and Social Psychology, 62,* 189–206.

Pennington, N., & Hastie, R. (1986). Evidence evaluation in complex decision making. *Journal of Personality and Social Psychology, 51*(2), 242–258.

Pennington, N., & Hastie, R. (1993). The story model for juror decision making. In R. Hastie (Ed.), *Inside the juror* (pp. 192–221). New York: Cambridge University Press.

Wineburg, S. (1991). Historical problem solving: A study of the cognitive processes used in the evaluation of documentary and pictorial evidence. *Journal of Educational Psychology, 83*(1), 73–87.

17

The Collapse of the Soviet Union: A Case Study in Causal Reasoning

James F. Voss, Mario Carretero, Joel Kennet,
and Laurie Ney Silfies
University of Pittsburgh

This chapter is concerned with how people perceive historical causation: What do people believe to be the causes of historical events? We chose to study the issue of historical causation primarily because it is one of the most fundamental topics of historical understanding, and therefore also one of the most important aspects of history instruction. Moreover, the study of historical causation also is related to other fundamental questions of understanding history, questions of historical explanation, historical narrative, the role of the historian, and the mental representations of historical events.

We addressed the question of historical causation by asking individuals to write an essay on what produced the collapse of the Soviet Union. Subsequently we asked them to rate the importance of a number of potential causes of the collapse and show how at least some of these causes produced it. In the first part of this chapter we discuss the nature of causal reasoning, especially as related to the topic of history, and in the second part we describe the study that was conducted. The third and final section contains a discussion of the findings with respect to history-related causal reasoning.

PERCEIVED CAUSATION IN HISTORY

Preliminary Considerations

Historical causation is a complex topic, and we want to emphasize that our concern is with how individuals perceive causation with respect to an historical event. The extent to which such reasoning about causation maps onto what historians or philosophers have said about the topic was not the major thrust of the work, although we do consider this general issue. We especially draw on the work of Topolski (1991), who has written about narrative structure and causation in history.

In the present section we address four topics related to historical causation, namely, the concepts of sufficiency and necessity, the idea of causal fields, the delineation of causal contents and structures, and the concepts of historical causation and historical explanation. As these topics are developed, seven questions are raised regarding reasoning about causation in history, the questions subsequently being considered in relation to the results of the study.

Sufficiency and Necessity

Causal relations are frequently considered in relation to the concepts of sufficiency and necessity. To help consider these concepts, Fig. 17.1 presents a diagram of the relations of a possible cause A and a possible effect B. The "1" cell indicates the occurrence of both A and B. The "2" cell indicates that when A occurs, B does not occur. The "3" cell indicates that A does not occur, but B occurs, whereas the "4" cell indicates the nonoccurrence of both A and B.

Sufficiency.   Sufficiency refers to the idea that whenever A occurs, B occurs. Thus, to assert that A is a sufficient cause of B, we need to determine that every occurrence of A produces B. In Fig. 17.1, cell "1" events would support the sufficiency of A, but cell "2" events, with A occurring but B not occurring, would disconfirm the sufficiency of A as a cause of B.

When considering sufficiency in the context of history, a particular difficulty is that an event A and the related A-B contingency occurs only once, and it is typically impossible to arrange for it to occur again. The Japanese attack on Pearl Harbor, one could argue, was a sufficient condition for the United States to enter World War II. But if we wanted to provide a test of this hypothesis, we would not be able to produce another Japanese bombing of Pearl Harbor, much less produce a bombing under the same set of world conditions that existed in 1941. Thus, in order to maintain the sufficiency hypothesis, we would need to provide an argument supporting the bombing as a sufficient condition for U.S. entrance into the war. We may want to state an empirical generalization such as "If one country attacks another, the countries go to war," even though this is not always true. Given these considerations, our first question (Q1) is: Did individuals identify any sufficient conditions with respect to the collapse of the Soviet Union?

Effect

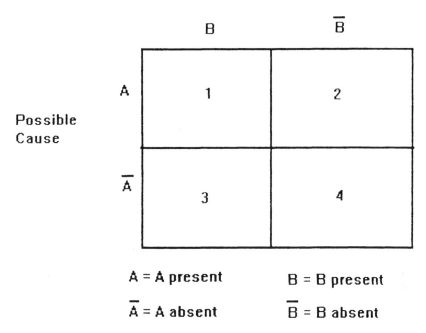

B   B̄

A | 1 | 2 |

Possible
Cause

Ā | 3 | 4 |

A = A present   B = B present

Ā = A absent   B̄ = B absent

FIG. 17.1.   Diagram of relations of a possible cause and a related effect.

Necessity.   The idea that A is a necessary cause of B requires that A be present whenever B occurs. One can test for necessity by determining whether if B has occurred, A has also occurred. In Fig. 17.1, this means given that B has occurred (Column 1), an instance of cell "1" supports the necessity of A, whereas an instance of cell "3," B occurring but A not occurring, would disconfirm the necessity of A in producing B.

But what about historical events? Was the Japanese bombing of Pearl Harbor a necessary condition for American entrance into World War II? We cannot, of course, have America enter World War II again and ascertain whether the Japanese did indeed bomb Pearl Harbor. Instead, to hold that A was necessary for B to occur, we need to ask whether other events, for example, the German invasion of Great Britain, could have produced American entrance into the war. This consideration leads to our second question (Q2): Did individuals assert the necessity of any conditions with respect to the collapse of the Soviet Union?

As suggested in the immediately preceding paragraph, the question of necessity raises the possible role of counterfactuals in reasoning historically. This issue requires closer examination, especially because some historians have stated that historians, in general, use counterfactuals to establish causation.

Ringer (1989) used the example of an automobile accident to examine the role of counterfactuals in historical causation. Assume, he essentially asserted, that an accident has occurred in which a car, going at an appropriately slow rate of speed, has gone around a curve, hit an ice patch, and slid into a tree. What caused the accident? Ringer's argument is that one arrives at the conclusion that the ice patch caused the accident because, the reasoning goes, had the ice patch not been there, the accident would not have happened. Similarly, Ringer argued, historians use counterfactual reasoning to determine causation in historical events. Or, to use an example from the history literature (cf. Dray, 1957), if Cleopatra's nose had been only a bit longer, thereby making her less attractive, would the course of history have been changed?

Similarly, MacIntyre (1976) stated that for counterfactual reasoning to be legitimate, four conditions need to be met. First, a "normal" course of events needs to be determined. Second, the likely outcome of that course of events needs to be established. Third, an intervening event needs to be defined, and fourth, it needs to be shown that the intervening event produced a different outcome than would otherwise have occurred. Indeed, both MacIntyre (1976) and Ringer (1989) placed strong emphasis on the intervening event and its producing the outcome change. In terms of Fig. 17.1, counterfactual reasoning asks if A had not occurred (the second row), would B have occurred? If A did not occur and yet B occurs (cell "3"), then one may conclude that A is not necessary for B to occur; if, however, A does not occur and B does not occur (cell "4"), then the counterfactual provides support for the necessity of A. Interestingly, using counterfactuals provides support for the necessity of A by the nonoccurrence of both A and B. Thus, a cell "4" instance—the nonoccurrence of two events—supports a cell "1" occurrence with respect to the necessity of A.

The cell "3" versus cell "4" test for counterfactuals is different from the necessity test of Q2. Q2 refers to looking at an event such as entrance into World War II (B) and asking whether other conditions could have produced American entrance into the war (cell "1" vs. cell "3"); counterfactual reasoning asks if the bombing had not occurred, would America have entered the war (cell "3" vs. cell "4"). The consideration about counterfactuals then leads to our third question (Q3): Did people use counterfactual reasoning in their account of the Soviet collapse?

Causal Fields, Conditions, and Causes

Perhaps the most difficult issue of causal reasoning in history, one discussed by a number of writers, involves the specification of an antecedent condition, a, as the cause of the particular consequent, c. The problem involves the fact that a large number of antecedents can usually be identified, thereby raising the question of what is the "cause" or what are the "causes." In the previously mentioned Ringer example, was the taking of the trip a "cause" of the accident? Was the fact that the person had learned to drive a "cause?" Was the Peace Treaty of World War I a "cause" of the 1991 Gulf War? One could suggest that "Had the Ottoman Empire not been divided as it was, the Gulf War would not have occurred." Nevertheless, in considering causes of the Gulf War, what we usually think of are factors such as Iraq's invasion of Kuwait, Hussein's motives, and American Middle East policy, especially as related to Israel and as related to oil. How then from all of the possible antecedents of a given consequent does one select the cause or causes?

A number of answers to this question have been advanced and we consider two of them (the reader is referred to Fischer, 1970, for a list of eight). First, there is the position of John Stuart Mill who argued that you must consider all of them: "The real cause is the whole of these antecedents, and we have, philosophically speaking, no right to give the name of cause to one of them, exclusively of the others" (Mill, 1843/1950, p. 196). The second position has been termed the abnormal conditions model, described by MacIver (1964) and subsequently considered by others (e.g., White, 1965). The model subscribes to the idea that we think of a cause as something that occurs that is abnormal relative to the normal course of events. Other antecedents that are related to the consequent in question are then referred to as conditions.

Mackie (1965) delineated causes and conditions in the following way. Assume that there is a fire "caused" by a short in an electric circuit, but the short-circuit only causes the fire under a particular set of conditions, such as the short occurring with flammable material surrounding the wire, and with the lack of a working sprinkler system. Thus, the short-circuit in itself is not a sufficient cause, but a given set of conditions, which includes the short-circuit, constitute a sufficient cause. (The set of conditions is not necessary, however, because different sets of conditions could cause the fire.) However, if a person is asked what caused the fire, the answer is quite likely to be that it was caused by a short-circuit, the answer not including other conditions that in fact needed to exist for the fire to occur. The so-called other conditions have sometimes been referred to as enabling conditions, that is, conditions that "enabled" the given outcome to occur, in this case a fire, but that in themselves are not regarded as having "caused" it.

As noted by Einhorn and Hogarth (1986), such "enabling" conditions are often standing, that is, they exist for a period of time without producing an outcome for which a person seeks a cause. We do not think of what causes us to be healthy, but we think of what causes us to become ill. But if a person's system is deteriorating with terminal cancer and there suddenly is a period of remission, we want to determine what caused the period of relative health rather than the illness.

Einhorn and Hogarth (1986) have suggested that conditions and causes can be distinguished by three criteria. One is that over time conditions usually show little change, whereas causes occur with relative suddenness. The second, in agreement with MacIver (1964), is that causes are often unexpected and often abnormal, in the sense that one does not expect them in the normal course of events (cf. Hart & Honoré, 1959; Hilton & Slugoski, 1986). The third is that causes are usually intervening, in the manner described previously in this chapter.

Although the issue of delineating causes and conditions constitutes one problem, a second, related problem is introduced when the issue of context is considered. To address this issue, Einhorn and Hogarth (1986) used the following example. A person hits his watch crystal with a small mallet and the crystal cracks. What caused the cracking? Most people would say that the person was the agent that caused the crystal to break with the mallet serving as the instrument. But assume that instead in a watch factory crystals are tested on an assembly line by having a small mallet tap each crystal as it moves on the line, and assume further that a given crystal breaks. What caused this break? Most people would likely say it was a defective crystal that caused the cracking. The point then is that what constitutes a perceived cause is a function of the causal field, the general context of the situation.

Another interesting example (Einhorn & Hogarth, 1986) of how causal fields can provide shifts in the idea of what constitutes a cause and what constitutes a condition assumes that a person working for an asbestos company develops lung cancer and sues the asbestos company, showing that the incidence of lung cancer is significantly higher for workers in that factory than for workers in other factories. But the company's lawyers argue that the particular worker smokes over two packs of cigarettes a day and that the incidence of lung cancer is higher for such people than for those not smoking or smoking less. Thus, the question of the likely "cause" of the cancer is rendered ambiguous. We thus are left with the idea that causes and conditions can be delineated by their perceived differences in normality and abnormality, which in turn, however, are related to context. But to press the issue further, White (1965), in a history context, noted that two historians could consider the same situation and set of facts and yet provide different accounts of the causative factors, and both could provide strong cases for their position. This argument thus emphasizes the orientation and background of the historian in developing a causal structure. Furthermore, the position underscores the idea that for a given historical consequent, there is no single cause, no "the" cause (Shope, 1967). This brings us to our fourth question 4 (Q4): To what extent did individuals distinguish causes and enabling conditions in reasoning about the Soviet collapse?

Causal Structures and Contents

Causal Structures.   For the sake of the present work, we assumed that historical analysis usually involves one or both of two types of text structure (see Rodrigo, this volume). One is the narrative, in which an account is provided of conditions, actions, and/or events that lead to a given event (Mink, 1987). Usually there are causal links built into the narrative, either explicitly or implicitly. The other structure is expository, in which what produced a given event is described in an expository or quasi-expository manner. Such structure typically has a hierarchical organization, developing issues such as "There were four factors that produced the American Civil War." In this format, arguments are developed to express a point of view regarding the causes of the given event. A third possibility is the combination of the two forms, a narrative with some expository sections elaborating on the narrative, or an expository analysis containing narrative elements.

We also assumed that within each type of structure the account provided could vary in a simple-to-complex manner. In the case of a narrative, there may be only a relatively few steps provided or, at the other extreme, there may be a long string of events. A simple expository format would be a short and simple listing of causes, whereas a more complex expository format would consist of the delineation of causal relations and considerable development and/or argumentation justifying the analysis. These considerations lead to the fifth question 5 (Q5): To what extent did individuals use narrative and/or expository structures in reasoning about the Soviet collapse, and what was the level of complexity of such accounts?

Contents.   We initially felt that for our purposes or causes in history could be regarded as being of four types, namely, conditions, actions, events, and the operation of a law. Figure 17.2 presents a summary of the categories and subcategories that were employed. By condition we mean a state of affairs that has generally been in existence in a relatively stable form for a reasonable period of time. On a priori grounds we delineated four types of conditions: geographical, cultural, political, and economic, with structural and institutional causes included in these categories. In the course of analysis, however, we delineated another category, namely, psychological conditions. By this we mean a state of mind of an individual or group of individuals. Thus, a "dissatisfaction" with current economic conditions or a "fear" of the KGB were regarded as psychological conditions, even though the psychological states were generated by economic and political factors, respectively.

By an action we mean that a given person or group did something that produced a change in conditions. Gorbachev's initiating Glasnost and the attempted coup of the hard-liners to remove Gorbachev constitute actions. Actions were classified by their source, that is, an action could be performed by an individual, a small group such as the Politburo, an organized unit such as the Red Army, or a general population such as the people of the Republics of the Soviet Union.

An event, although admittedly difficult to define (Pachter, 1974), was considered as a specific occurrence that had, at least to the subject, some type of impact on the Soviet collapse, such as "the collapse of the Berlin Wall." In contrast to actions, events did not have an identified source that "produced" them. A law was taken to be a statement that depicted the occurrence of some underlying regularity or theme that acted to produce a change in conditions, as the use of a Marxian explanation, or stated the idea that the Soviet Union would inevitably collapse due to the nature of its economic system or stated that the collapse occurred because it was God's plan.

Analyzing essays and classifying the various stated causes was more difficult than expected. Classifying causes in relation to the subcategories was relatively simple; determining which of the major categories a cause belonged in was at times difficult because a number of statements could fit more than one category. For example, was the shooting down of the KAL airliner an action or an event? Nevertheless, rules were established for coding, and an 87% level of scoring agreement was obtained.

Conditions
    Political
    Economic
    Cultural
    Geographical
    Psychological
Actors
    Specific agents (Gorbachev)
    Groups (Politburo)
    Units of Government (Red Army, KGB)
    Global Units Government, collectively or specific populations
    as citizens of a Republic)
Event
Law or Scheme

FIG. 17.2. Classification taxonomy of statement contents.

To identify the type of causes that were stated was taken as one of the most important aspects of the study. Previous research (Hallden, 1986; Shemilt, 1987), using adolescents, had indicated that at least those populations considered history to be personally driven, that is, the actions of individuals were considered as the critical causes of history, with relatively little emphasis being given to economic, political, and cultural conditions. Our causal analysis was considered important in determining whether the essays we collected would again favor personal action.

These categories thus constituted a more-or-less working model of possible elements found in the accounts of historical causation. The model leads to our sixth question 6 (Q6): To what extent did individuals use each of these factors on a relative as well as absolute basis in their essays on the Soviet collapse, and how were the various causes interrelated?

Causation and Explanation

The issue considered in this section is the possibility that, related to the idea of laws, individuals use explanation as part of their historical causal account. During the development of the field of history, various types of explanations have been set forth to explain historical events, and for our purposes we briefly consider three of them.

First, there is what Mink (1987) called the Universal Scheme. This view holds that there is a general underlying single theme that provides an explanation for history. In the Greek period, according to Collingwood (1946/1980), there was relatively little effort to explain history in a broader theoretical sense; Thucydides, for example, while analyzing the reasons for the Peloponnesian Wars, did so in the context of local events. But in the Middle Ages, the underlying theme was God's plan (Collingwood, 1946/1980). Finally, as noted by Mink (1987), the most recent incarnation of a general orientation or framework has been Marxism and neo-Marxism, the explanation based on the unfolding of broad-based, sociopolitical-economic factors.

A second, and somewhat related, explanatory idea is that there exist laws of history, and that these function in establishing causal relations. The issue of historical laws has been controversial, with Hempel's Covering Law (1942) postulating the existence of such laws. A number of other writers (e.g., Dray, 1957; Reisch, 1991; Scriven, 1959) have denied the existence and/or usefulness of laws. Our interest is not to analyze this issue, but to recognize that our subjects could state that the collapse of the Soviet Union was caused by operations of the laws of history.

The third view of explanation considered here is essentially that there are no laws, and that each historical situation is unique. Explanation then involves constructing a reasonable causal analysis of the situation and event in question. Ringer (1989), for example, argued that explanation relates directly to the causal relationships that are established in a given situation. These considerations thus lead to our seventh question 7 (Q7): Did individuals use explanations in providing causal accounts? Did they, for example, state that a particular historical event occurred due to operation of a historical law or an underlying theme?

STUDY ON THE COLLAPSE OF THE SOVIET UNION

Procedure

The study had four parts. Thirty-two individuals were asked to write an essay in which they were to describe "what they think produced the downfall of the Soviet Union." After completing this essay, they were asked to indicate "why, with the riots in Tiananmen Square, did the collapse of the People's Republic of China not occur." (Results involving the latter essays are not considered in the present chapter.) Third, subjects were given a list of 40 possible causes of the downfall of the Soviet Union and were asked to rate each with respect to its importance to the collapse. The list was determined with the help of two Soviet experts, political scientists specializing in the Soviet Union. The experimenters added some factors to those indicated by the experts. (The views of each expert are considered later in this chapter.) Fourth, the subjects were asked to draw a causal map of the collapse of the Soviet Union, using as many of the 40 Part III causes they chose to, and adding any other factors they thought appropriate. This condition was included to determine the extent to which providing possible causes of the collapse to the subjects would enhance their performance relative to their respective essays.

The 32 participants were undergraduate students, graduate students, and a few individuals not enrolled in college. The subjects were paid for their participation.

Experimental Findings

Essay Structure. The statements of each essay were extracted and diagrammed in the manner shown in Figs. 17.3, 17.4, and 17.5. Two individuals had a reliability of 92% agreement in producing the diagrams.

Figure 17.3 presents a diagram of the contents of a simple expository essay. The causes listed included various conditions and a single action. Although the essay was basically a listing of causes, there was one narrative-like step in which Gorbachev took action on his belief, at least as the essay author perceived it.

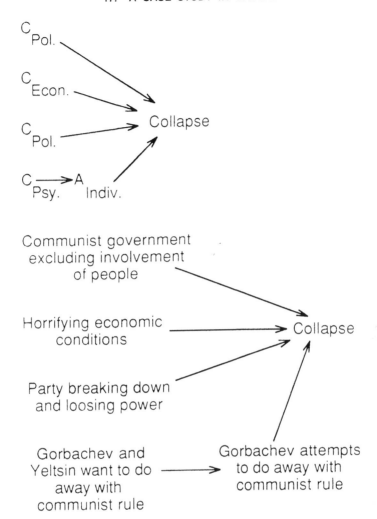

FIG. 17.3.   Diagram of a simple expository essay (S#23).

Figure 17.4 presents the diagram of an essay classified as having an intermediate narrative structure. This diagram is typical of the narrative essays we obtained in that there is not a single step-by-step chain providing the narrative structure. Instead, there are two or more branches, each involving steps that lead to the collapse. In other words, narratives were often similar to expository accounts in that a number of different causes were delineated, the narrative component emerging in one or more of the branches.

Figure 17.5 presents a diagram of one of the three most complex

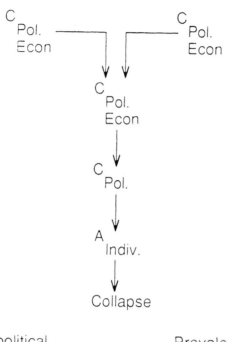

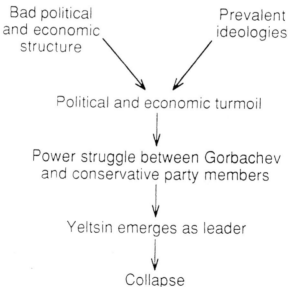

FIG. 17.4. Diagram of intermediate narrative essay (S22).

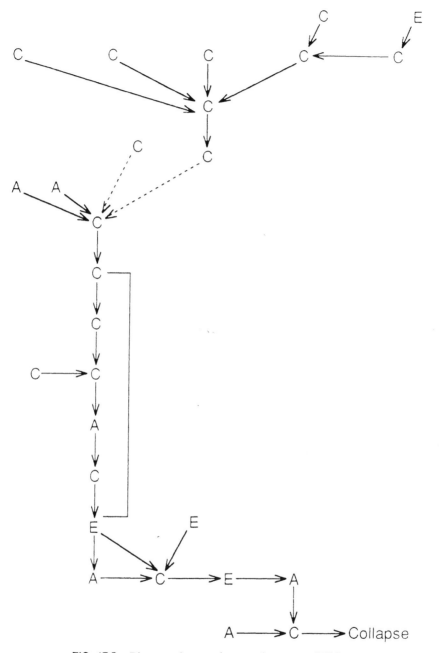

FIG. 17.5.   Diagram of a complex expository essay (S#20).

structures we obtained. Although classified as complex expository, it also clearly has a highly developed narrative component. The upper part of the figure shows that the subject provided a general background of the issue, and although the essay contained no direct statement linking the top part to the bottom part, what S#20 apparently did was to show that Gorbachev responded to the conditions of the upper part. The bottom part then essentially provides a narrative account of events leading to the collapse. Figures 17.6a and 17.6b describe the contents of the Fig. 17.5 diagram. One thing particularly impressive about S#20's essay is how readily the various components of the collapse are woven into the account, factors such as economic conditions, political problems in the Kremlin, and problems in the Republics.

Each of the 32 essays was classified as primarily narrative or primarily expository, although, as noted, the essays usually had elements of both. Within each type the essays were also classified as simple, intermediate, or complex. Of the 32 essays, 14 were classified as narrative and 18 as expository. Of the 14 narrative, 2 were simple, 11 were intermediate, and 1 was complex. For the 18 expository, 5 were regarded only as simple listings, 10 had listings with some further development, and 3 were regarded as complex, with highly developed explanations. Taken as a whole, the essays were not of a high quality, but a few such as that of S#20 were well developed. Furthermore, some of the essays contained statements of questionable accuracy, reflecting what appeared to be oversimplification.

Contents.   Table 17.1 presents the mean frequencies of occurrence for the four types of causal statements. As shown, the most frequently stated factors were conditions, with statements about actions occurring next in frequency.

Table 17.2 presents the frequency of occurrence of the different types of condition statements. Psychological statements were the most frequent, followed equally by political and economic factors. Examples of the items include: (a) psychological: "People realize that reforms can't take place in a totalitarian system" (S#1), or there was "dissatisfaction with repercussions of disobedience" (S#5); (b) political: "power struggle between Gorbachev and the party members" (S#22); and (c) economic: "a lagging economy" (S#1). As presented in Table 17.2, some conditions were counted twice.

TABLE 17.1
Frequency and Mean Occurrences of Four Types of Casual Statements

	Conditions	Actions	Events	Laws
Frequency	189	73	25	2
Mean	5.91	2.28	0.78	0.6

TABLE 17.2
Frequency and Mean Occurrences of Different Types of Causal Conditions

	Economic	Political	Psychological	Cultural
Frequency	62[a]	82[b]	90[c]	9[d]
Mean	1.94	2.56	2.81	0.28

[a]Includes 13 also classified with other categories.
[b]Includes 32 also classified in other categories.
[c]Includes 27 also classified in other categories.
[d]All classified in other categories.

Table 17.3 presents the mean frequency of occurrence of actions for each of the four types of causal actors. Reference to specific individuals was most common, followed by reference to global units. Specific individuals mentioned included Gorbachev and Yeltsin, whereas global units included citizens of the Republics.

Conditions and actions were tabulated separately for those essays classified as narrative and those classified as expository, testing the idea that narrative essays should have a higher proportion of actions and expository essays should have a higher proportion of conditions. The differences of type of cause within each essay type did not approach significance however.

Returning to Table 17.1, there was a relatively low frequency of events, as we defined the term. Examples include the "collapse of the Berlin Wall" (S#6). Laws or schemes also were not frequently mentioned. One example was "Communism is incompatible with human nature" (S#11).

Overall, the essays on the Soviet Union collapse provided an array of conditions and actions that were shown to interact in a causal manner. Subjects often initially stated conditions and then indicated that these produced actions of individuals or groups of individuals. Subject #20, as shown in Fig. 17.6, provided this type of account. Or, the conditions were shown to give rise to other conditions, and sometimes an action was stated. A few subjects began with an action such as Gorbachev instituting Glasnost or Perestroika, although this was relatively infrequent and occurred in the less sophisticated essays. The picture that emerges then is that in the more sophisticated essays, conditions were described that included or led to psychological, political, and economic conditions, with conditions then giving rise to actions or possibly other conditions.

TABLE 17.3
Frequency and Mean Occurrences of Types of Causal Actions

	Person	Group	Government Unit	Global Unit
Frequency	35	13	7	18
Mean	1.09	0.41	0.22	0.56

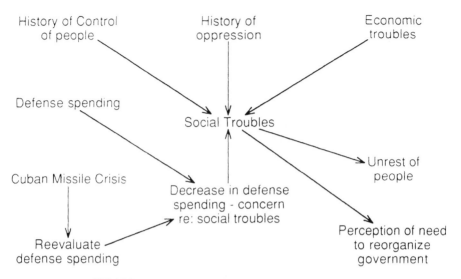

FIG 17.6a.   Diagram of contents of Figure 5 essay (S#20).

Ideas about Causation.   The analyses described thus far provide tentative answers to the seven questions developed in the introductory section. Q1: The data show no overt attempts by subjects to consider sufficiency, in the usual sense. However, results of other studies at least suggest that subjects may well have considered their essays reasonably sufficient with respect to describing the Soviet collapse. Shaklee and Fischhoff (1982), as well as Hansen (1980) and Major (1980), provided evidence indicating that subjects attempt to simplify their attributions of causation, following a specific line of causation with other possible causes being excluded. In other words, in the present context, individuals may generally have presumed sufficiency in providing their account of the collapse, at least to some degree, because many seemed to limit the possible exploration of additional factors, factors they presumably were aware of. Q2: The data show subjects rarely dealt with the question of necessity, except in the use of counterfactuals (Q3) and in a few instances described later in the chapter. Q3: Four cases of counterfactual reasoning were observed, these being by subjects who generated more sophisticated causal accounts. The use of counterfactuals was thus not extensive.

Q4: This question refers to whether individuals distinguished causes and conditions, a question that raises an important consideration. The data are clear in that many times subjects delineated conditions, defining conditions in the sense that the given factor was relatively long-standing and showing little change, as well as not being sudden or intervening. Thus, there were frequent references to "economic conditions," "political conditions," or "political oppression." However, the nature and context of these statements

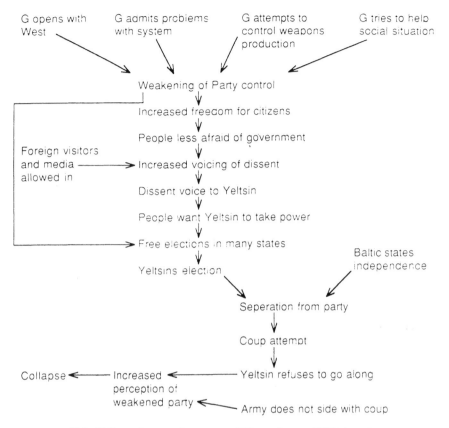

FIG 17.6b.   Diagram of contents of Figure 5 essay (S#20) (cont.).

also made it clear that people generally regarded such conditions as causes, not contextual or enabling conditions. The "economic conditions" produced "dissatisfaction," a psychological condition, and this led to action on the part of Gorbachev, for example. Subjects thus used "conditions" in the sense of an economic or political-social state of affairs that produced an effect and did not employ conditions as a context in which the "causes" operated. Only in rare cases did subjects mention what apparently was an enabling condition, as one subject did in mentioning the Soviet Revolution of 1917. The data therefore do not support an "abnormal conditions" view of causation.

Q5: Subjects provided both narrative and expository accounts, each of which varied in complexity, although the essays reflected more a combination of both types of contents. It is interesting to note that the two Soviet experts, when asked to indicate why the Soviet Union collapsed, provided different types of accounts. One expert, a person who closely observed

Kremlin activities and political moves, used a general narrative account. The other, who was an international relations expert, used an expository format, stating the reasons that produced the collapse and why they did.

Q6: Taken as a whole, the data indicate that most subjects delineated both conditions and actions as causes, with conditions employed more frequently. Overall, a composite set of reasons for the collapse was that a combination of economic and political-social conditions produced a need for a change, and that Gorbachev therefore instituted a set of actions that produced yet other conditions and other actions that produced the collapse. Gorbachev, for example, decreased party power and increased the power of the Republics, and this led to the Republics disregarding Kremlin control. The protocols thus do not personalize in the sense that the collapse could simply be attributed to Gorbachev. On the other hand, there was the relatively frequent personalization that occurred via the operation of "dissatisfaction" or other personal "states of mind."

The frequent number of statements involving psychological conditions seemed to suggest something not quite true. As the actual scenario of the collapse unfolded, there was not really a clash between large segments of the population and the government. In Lithuania, there was some unrest, but overall the people's dissatisfaction with the status quo did not produce a revolution. Gorbachev and others in the party recognized the existence of serious economic problems and in trying to deal with them produced political changes, probably considerably beyond Gorbachev's intentions. Some of the protocols seem to give the idea that the subjects felt the general population played a larger role than it really did.

Q7: Although a few subjects made statements such as "The collapse was inevitable," thereby suggesting the operation of laws, the data are marked by the absence of statements depicting any explanatory laws or schemes underlying the collapse.

Data Analyses of Parts III and IV

As previously mentioned, subjects were provided with 40 possible causes of the Soviet collapse and asked to rate each for importance. Three aspects of the Part III data are discussed. First, with respect to contents of the items, the data indicate that the more immediate potential causes with respect to time and place were rated as more important than causes that were more remote. Specifically, the four highest rated causes referred to the economy of the Soviet Union, the 5th to the loss of power of the Communist Party, the 6th to the lack of consumer goods, again an economic factor, and the 7th and 8th reasons referred to Gorbachev's leadership. Soviet military spending was rated 15th, and nationalism in the Republics rated 16th. The American strategy of an arms race was rated 29th, and Reagan's policies early in his term was rated 36th. In addition, the 1917 Soviet Revolution was rated 31st, the shooting down of the KAL airliner was rated 39th, and the Cuban Missile Crisis 40th. The writings of Karl Marx were rated 37th. The clear message then is that the subjects regarded the collapse as due to the economic conditions and political changes that took place in the Soviet Union, and regarded as least important the more remote possible causes, in time, as well as factors external to the Soviet Union, such as U.S. influence.

The second result noted is that subjects demonstrated considerable variability with respect to how many of the 40 possible causes they regarded as important. The mean rating on a 5-point scale of the 40 potential causes for the subject giving the highest ratings over all 40 items was 3.32. This subject thus felt that a number of the causes were relatively important. The lowest mean rating for a given subject was 1.23, this subject not considering many of the causes to be very important.

Third, the data were examined to determine whether those subjects that generated more causes in their essays rated the causes given in Part III as more important than subjects who stated fewer causes in their essays. The correlation of mean causal rating with number of causes generated in the Part I essay was not significant, $r(30) = .18$. However, there was a nonlinear tendency in the relationship in that when the 32 subjects are divided into fourths, the 8 subjects having the highest average ratings over all 40 items in Part III generated an average of 12.6 causes in their Part I essays, whereras those having the second, third, and fourth highest fourths in their mean ratings of Part III had mean numbers of causes in their essays of 6.4, 7.6, and 8.5, respectively. Similarly, although the correlation of mean rating in Part III only approached significance with the number of causes selected in Part IV (see later, $r(30) = .30$, $p > .05$, the 8 subjects having the highest mean rating in Part III selected an average of 26.1 causes in Part IV, whereas the remaining groups selected an average of 20.3, 20.0, and 20.6. Thus, there was a tendency for the subjects who thought that a relatively large number of the Part III causes were important to have more causes in their essay and to select more causes in the Part IV task.

Number of Factors Generated and Selected.   With respect to the Part IV data, the mean number of causes stated per subject in the essays was 8.78(4.72) as opposed to a mean of 21.75(8.00) selected in the Part IV task, a significant difference ($t(31) = 9.81$, $p < .001$). Moreover, of the 40 Part III causes, the subjects rated a mean of only 1.94 causes as unfamiliar. These findings suggest that although the Part I essay data demonstrated that a number of the subjects did not seem to know much about the collapse, stating an average of only 8 causes, in Part IV they selected on the average almost 22 potential causes, a result suggesting that the subjects had a greater knowledge of the collapse than shown in the Part I essay, and that they were not able to retrieve the information and/or organize their knowledge for their essay.

Ratings of Factors Selected.   The mean importance rating for Part III causes selected in Part IV was 3.21(0.44), whereas for items not selected, the mean was 2.14(0.75), $t(30) = 9.55$, $p < .001$. This result indicates that in providing the graph for Part IV, the causes subjects selected from the Part III list of 40 were regarded as more important by each respective person than were the causes not selected.

Part IV Diagrams.   The causal maps drawn in Part IV were considerably more developed than those of Part I, as one could surmise from the greater number of factors employed in Part IV. Figure 17.7 presents the graph constructed by S#23, the same subject who constructed the simple expository graph of Figure 17.3. The difference is rather apparent.

The graphs of Part IV took various forms, but almost all of them were more complex than the essay diagrams. With few exceptions, sequential accounts were provided, with a number of branches converging on the collapse.

DISCUSSION

Causation and the Essays

Narrative Structure.   Although many of the essays of Part I were sparse in content and at best only touched on the causal complexities of the Soviet collapse, a rather important finding is that, in principle, historical accounts are often similar to the more complex essays we obtained. Specifically, Topolski (1991) delineated two types of narratives: structural and dynamic. The former refers to narratives in which one is not especially interested in constructing a particular course of events, but instead attempts to construct sequences of events that tend to be recurrent, often dealing with institutions, for example. Dynamic narratives are much more explicit with respect to cause-effect relations, motives, and the interaction of motives and external events. Indeed, Topolski quoted a specific dynamic historical account and showed how the causes considered are interwoven, with conditions and actions interacting.

The more sophisticated essays looked reasonably like such an account, with even the less sophisticated essays portraying some sense of the interaction of conditions and actions in producing a given outcome. There was a sense of multiple causes portrayed in the essays, with the more sophisticated essays showing how the different causes led to the collapse. At the same time, arguments for specific causes were not extensively devel-

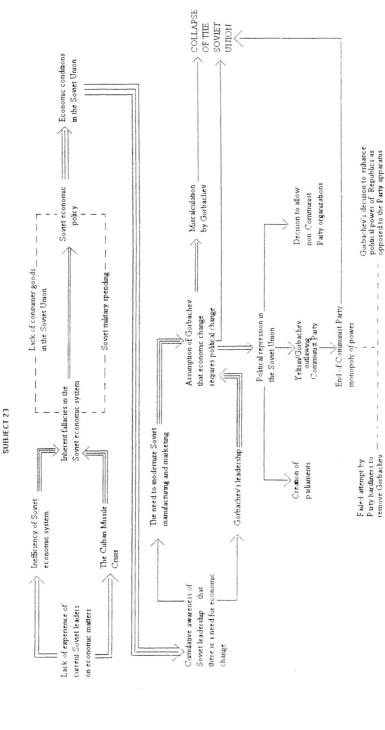

SUBJECT 23

FIG. 17.7. Part IV diagram of (S#23).

423

oped. Subjects did not evidently see their task as "defending" their position, that is, subjects provided very little justification for their causal claims (see Kuhn, Weinstock, & Flaton, this volume). With perhaps a little imagination, the essays could also be viewed in relation to von Wright's (1971) distinction of teleological and Humean causation, the former involving goals and motives of an individual or group and the latter involving causation as found in the physical world.

Whether most of our protocols qualify as "real" narratives could be debated, because in many cases the "narrative" component consisted of a few causal contingencies. Nevertheless, the data do suggest that a history narrative is not simply the telling of a story (see Perfetti, Britt, Rouet, Georgi, & Mason, this volume), but instead subjects, in telling the "story" of the Soviet collapse, felt the need to consider a number of causes and how each led to the collapse, without being able to weave these factors into a single, coherent, narrative account. Such a finding is similar to that found with novice social science problem solvers, who referred to isolated causes and solutions in solving ill-structured problems, as opposed to experts, who subsumed such causes within a more abstract context (Voss, Greene, Post, & Penner, 1983). Historians, in other words, may be able to generate historical accounts that tell a more abstract, yet more coherent, story.

Abnormal Conditions.   Earlier in this chapter we discussed the concept of causal field and the distinction of causes and conditions. Of particular interest to these concepts are two findings. First, there is no evidence from the present data supporting the idea that individuals viewed abnormal conditions as the causes of the Soviet collapse. Instead, as previously noted, the essays indicated that subjects viewed the collapse as the outcome of a series of interactive conditions and actions.

An important question raised by the finding that the subjects did not perceive causes as abnormal conditions or intervening events in the MacIntyre and Ringer sense is whether, in a complex domain such as history, there is any event that may be taken to be abnormal? "Act of God" perhaps? Using MacIntyre's previously mentioned criteria, it seems that determining what a normal nonintervening event would be and how it would differ from what a more unexpected "intervening" event would be a quite difficult task, as would it be to determine the "normal outcome" of a set of events. (Was Hitler's rise to power an "abnormal" event?)

The second finding noted is that although subjects considered both conditions and actions as causes, they also did not state general enabling conditions. Thus, the responses were like the Mackie "starting of the fire" example in that individuals did not state the existing standing conditions, that is, the present subjects did not state the world conditions that existed at the time of the collapse, but instead viewed stated conditions as causes.

Necessity and Sufficiency. In considering causation, Topolski (1991) described five ways in which causes and conditions are found in historical narratives: (a) as necessary conditions for an event being explained, (b) as sufficient conditions for it, (c) as necessary conditions only in the situation being described by the historian, (d) as conditions conducive to the occurrence of an event, or (e), as conditions preventing its occurrence. Topolski, incidentally, also noted that in a discussion of sufficient and necessary conditions, the terms *often* or *usually* are used rather than strict necessity or strict sufficiency.

The essays we obtained clearly demonstrated the fourth use and in a few cases the fifth use. The first three of these causal types were generally not employed in the present essays. Moreover, these three uses of causation tend to occur when an historian states that "for such-and-such an outcome to occur, you need to have two conditions satisfied, X and Y. However, in this situation one did not have X." In this case the historian sets up necessary conditions, then shows that the conditions were present or at least one of the needed conditions was not present. Possibly, the closest essay example to Topolski's account was a subject who stated that Gorbachev realized that economic change required political change, thereby suggesting that political change was a necessary condition for economic change. In addition, it is easy to see that our subjects' knowledge of history was such that they were unable to define the "necessary conditions" for given outcomes to occur. It seems then that given Topolski's delineation of five uses of causation, our subjects responded in a not unreasonable way, given their limited knowledge.

With respect to sufficiency, as previously noted, there was little evidence concerning whether subjects viewed their respective accounts as sufficient. However, future work may indicate that individuals do in fact presume their accounts to be sufficient.

With respect to explanations of the Soviet collapse that involved theoretical factors or the operation of laws, little was found in the essays except a few statements to the effect that the collapse of the system was inevitable. Our subjects thus looked like individuals providing accounts most closely related to the dynamic narratives described by Topolski (1991), with conditions playing a major role, interacting with actions.

Personalization of History

With respect to the personalization of history found by Hallden (1986) and Shemilt (1987), our subjects generally thought that particular economic and political conditions existing in the Soviet Union were critical to the downfall of the Soviet Union and that Gorbachev, and in some essays Yeltsin, contributed toward the collapse by the actions they took. But as previously noted, it was not believed that the collapse occurred solely because of the actions taken by one or more individuals. So, history was thus not personalized in the essays in the sense that the collapse was due almost solely to the actions of specific individuals.

On the other hand, there was personalization of a different type. Topolski (1991) argued that individual motives found in historical accounts are of two types: goals and emotional states. In the essays provided in the present study, a number of the causes classified as psychological states were of the emotional variety, "fear" of the KGB, "dissatisfaction" over economic conditions, feeling "repressed," and on the positive side, obtaining an "increased sense of independence." But goals were also stated, such as "desire to emulate non-communist countries," "people want to try a new form of government," "democracy is better for the people," and people "wish to be more like Americans." There is then in the essays a type of personalization, but it involves the perceived reactions and motives of people to the economic and political conditions and the goals or desires they have in attempting to alleviate these conditions. Such types of people-based contents, moreover, also were found not only for "people," but for individual leaders, especially Gorbachev. The personal factor is thus found in ascribing in goals and emotions.

Topolski (1991) also pointed out that the goals being sought are usually related to one or both of two origins, namely, the person's knowledge and the person's (or group's) values. Insofar as the current essays are concerned, the goals stated in most cases were based on values. These values, as they are explicitly stated or strongly implied, included better economic conditions and standard of living, generally as found in democracies, as well as freedom, independence (Republics), and alleviation from fear of government. Thus, values were perceived by the subjects to be important factors in producing the goals involved in the collapse. At the same time, knowledge was a major factor in establishing goals, with references being made, for example, to Gorbachev's and the people's awareness of the need for change and Gorbachev's initiation of Glasnost and Perestroika. Also, and quite importantly, the people's awareness of the corruption and favored lifestyle of the leaders was mentioned as well as an awareness or perception of how things are better in other countries, how the solidarity movement led to change, and how at a given point in time the people were able to voice dissent. The essays thus indicated that values and knowledge were important factors in providing goals for individuals or groups. Thus, in an interesting way, the subjects as a whole took an American perspective (see Wertsch, this volume) and employed their own values projecting them into what they saw were the values of the Soviet Union (see von Borries, this volume, for ideas regarding the projection of values).

Instructional Issues

We feel the results of this study have at least three points to make regarding instruction. One is that instruction should include emphasis on the idea of multiple causation and indicate how the different causative factors lead to a given outcome. But given the differences in the initial essays and the causal structures of Part IV found in this study, it would seem to be of critical importance instructionally for individuals to receive practice in generating such essays, drawing extensively on what they know. This matter, moreover, involves an important psychological phenomenon, namely, that individuals can apparently know quite a bit about a topic, but if the information is not organized in memory a priori, they have trouble retrieving it and providing a coherent essay (cf. Prawat, 1989). Apparently, it is only when they are given the causal events that they can meaningfully organize them. Psychologically, in this regard, the limitations of working memory may be an important factor, along with one's underlying knowledge organization.

Second, the quality of the essays was such that individuals apparently did not have a very strict criterion regarding what constitutes an acceptable answer as to why the Soviet Union collapsed. As noted, many of the answers, given by people of college age and older, were rather simplistic, and although such simplicity might be explained by knowledge and/or processing inadequacies, the fact that simplistic accounts were obtained suggests that many of the participants had a rather low or mediocre criterion of acceptability for an adequate historical account. Perhaps instruction could produce a better idea of a quality explanation.

Third, the finding that causes were perceived as involving both actions and conditions as important is encouraging. Although historians may not agree on the nature of causal explanation, the "intuitions" of the novice individuals of this study seemed to show awareness of personal actions and policies as well as the cultural, social, and political factors of society. At the same time, the subjects did apparently not have much of a sense of more remote causal factors, emphasizing actions and conditions immediately before the collapse. There would appear to be a need then to develop a better sense of distant causes.

ACKNOWLEDGMENTS

The research reported in this chapter was supported by a grant of the National Research Center for Student Learning, awarded to the Learning Research and Development Center of the University of Pittsburgh by the

Office of Educational Research and Improvement of the United States Department of Education and the Mellon Foundation. The contribution of the second author was made possible by a grant from the DGCYT of Spain (PB-91-0028-C03-03) and a scholarship from the Spanish Ministry of Education.

REFERENCES

Collingwood, R. G. (1980). *The idea of history*. Oxford, England: Oxford University Press. (Original work published in 1946)

Dray, W. (1957). *Laws of explanation in history*. London: Oxford University Press.

Einhorn, H., & Hogarth, R. M. (1986). Judging probable cause. *Psychological Bulletin, 99*, 3-19.

Fischer, D. H. (1970). *Historians' fallacies. Toward a logic of historical thought*. New York: Harper & Row.

Hallden, O. (1986). Learning history. *Oxford Review of Education, 12*, 53-66.

Hansen, R. D. (1980). Commonsense attribution. *Journal of Personality and Social Psychology, 39*, 996-1009.

Hart, H. L. A., & Honoré, A. M. (1959). *Causation and the law*. Oxford, England: Clarendon Press.

Hempel, C. G. (1942). The function of general laws in history. *The Journal of Philosophy, 39*, 40-52.

Hilton, D. J., & Slugoski, B. R. (1986). Knowledge-based causal attribution: The abnormal conditions focus model. *Psychological Review, 93*, 75-88.

MacIntyre, A. (1976). Causation and history. In J. Manninen & R. Tuomela (Eds.), *Essays on explanation and understanding* (pp. 137-158). Boston: D. Reidel.

MacIver, R. M. (1964). *Social causation*. New York: Harper & Row.

Mackie, J. L. (1965). I. Causes and conditions. *American Philosophical Quarterly, 2*, 245-264.

Major, B. (1980). Information acquisition and the attribution process. *Journal of Personality and Social Psychology, 39*, 1010-1023.

Mill, J. S. (1950). *John Stuart Mill's Philosophy of scientific method*. New York: Hafner. (Original work published in 1843)

Mink, L. O. (1987). *Historical understanding*. Ithaca, NY: Cornell University Press.

Pachter, H. M. (1974). Defining an event: Prolegomenon to any future philosophy of history. *Social Research, 44*, 439-466.

Prawat, R. S. (1989). Promoting access to knowledge, strategy, and disposition in students: A research synthesis. *Review of Educational Research, 59*, 1-41.

Reisch, G. A. (1991). Chaos, history, and narrative. *History and Theory, 30*, 1-20.

Ringer, F. K. (1989). Causal analysis in historical reasoning. *History and Theory, 28*, 154-172.

Scriven, M. (1959). Truisms as the ground for historical explanations. In P. Gardiner (Ed.), *Theories of history* (pp. 443-475). New York: Macmillan.

Shaklee, H., & Fischhoff, B. (1982). Strategies of informal search in causal analysis. *Memory and Cognition, 10*, 520-530.

Shemilt, D. (1987). Adolescent ideas about evidence and methodology in history. In C. Portal (Ed.), *The history curriculum for teachers* (pp. 39-61). Philadelphia: The Falmer Press.

Shope, R. K. (1967). Explanations in forms of "the cause." *Journal of Philosophy, 64*, 312-319.

Topolski, J. (1991). Towards an integrated model of historical explanation. *History and Theory, 30*, 324-338.

Voss, J. F. Greene, T. R., Post, T. A., & Penner, B. C. (1983). Problem solving skill in the social sciences. In G. H. Bower (Ed.), *The psychology of learning and motivation: Advances in research theory* (Vol. 17, pp. 165–213). New York: Academic Press.

von Wright, G. H. (1971). *Explanation and understanding.* Ithaca, NY: Cornell University Press.

White, M. (1965). *Foundations of historical knowledge.* New York: Harper & Row.

Discussion of Chapters 13-17 The Cognitive Construction of History

Angel Rivière
Autonoma University of Madrid

From some philosophical perspectives, history is a construction deeply rooted in the human cognitive system. In the philosophy of José Ortega y Gasset, for example, the activity of making stories is an act almost as natural and as necessary as breathing, in that it constitutes a basic function of what he calls "vital reason." This is not a secondary function, still less a by-product of Reason with a capital 'R," that is, paradigmatic reason as conceived by the Rationalists, as a universal instrument, that conceives of objects independently of time and perspective. On the contrary, historical reason, inevitably subject to conditions of time and perspective, is the most primary reason of people, which they employ to do something inevitable: interpret their own lives as they unfold. Thus, to conceive of life in terms of stories is to perform a cognitive activity so fundamental that, without it, human life would be merely a series of events, not just a biography with meaning.

History with a capital "H" cannot, of course, be reduced to that other much more fundamental, although less eminent and complex activity, of constructing one's own and others' lives as history with a small "h" — as stories (this chapter was written in Spanish and in that language, *history* and *story* are expressed by the same word, *historia*). However, as Wertsch notes in this volume, the two activities are closely related. The former can be considered, in part, a scientific elaboration of so natural a function as storytelling (see also White, 1981, 1987). Thus, although history is a construct of a superior order, it is based on lower or more basic activities in human cognitive functioning. It could be expected, then, that the cognitive processes related to history would be one of those principal areas of educational psychology, but, as Carretero et al. (this volume) point out, this has not been the case. This is an anomaly that demands an explanation. Why, in spite of its cognitive importance, has history scarcely appeared on the agenda of those working in the cognitive psychology?

As on many occasions, we may turn to "history" in order to explain this apparent anomaly. In the history of cognitive psychology itself, we must look for the underlying causes of this seeming lack of interest in history as a knowledge construct. To explain these causes, we can turn to Bruner's (1986) distinction, already mentioned in this volume, between the "paradigmatic" and "narrative" modes of thinking as they are related to those made previously by philosophers such as Windelband or Dilthey between ideographic and nomothetic sciences, or between sciences of nature and sciences of the spirit.

The distinction (apart from the doubtfulness of its clarity) is of great interest for two reasons: the first is that it helps us to understand better both the cognitive specificity of history and its "epistemological drama." The second reason is that it allows us to throw some light, from a historical perspective, on the reasons why history itself has not been given the attention it deserves by psychologists of knowledge. The drama and the specificity derive from the very definition of history, as it can be made from Bruner's distinction between the two modalities, for history is precisely that knowledge construct that consists in integrating the narrative modality with the paradigmatic one, submitting the former to the criteria of verification and explanation that are normally applied to the latter. The possibility of combining these modalities is part of the epistemological drama of history, to which I refer latter. I now turn our attention to another "drama": that of cognitive psychology itself.

In *Acts of Meaning*, Bruner (1990) himself referred, with a certain bitterness, to this other drama. It consists, essentially, in the predominance, from the beginning, of explanatory models related to the idea of information processing. From a historical perspective, the conception of the cognitive system as a computational system has involved logistic connotations and a conception of human reason closely linked to the functioning and criteria of justification of the so-called "paradigmatic modality."

Processes of formulation and contrasting of hypotheses, differentiation and control of variables, formalization, discovery of causes (not of "reasons," but of "causes," in accordance with the traditional distinction) thus become the essential foci of interest. Some of the chapters in this section are good examples. For instance, the works by Voss et al. and Kuhn et al. are related to the paradigmatic and not the narrative component of history. This is not a negative feature (given that history as a discipline, in contrast to stories, does indeed have this paradigmatic component), nor does it prevent the narrative modality from making its presence felt, sometimes unexpectedly (for example, in the "psychological conditions," which Voss et al. found it necessary to include in order to account for their subjects' causal explanations).

The problem is that, from a unilaterally paradigmatic perspective (which is not that of the authors quoted above), history is not satisfactory as a knowledge construct, although it includes components from the other modality. In reality, the production and comprehension of "stories," as with history as a discipline, present the cognitive psychologist with a problem that is difficult to approach from the computational perspective: the problem of *meaning*.

The question is, however, important and urgent. At the least, historians appear to see it that way. In recent years, history as a discipline has been going through a crisis affecting its very foundations. The social and human sciences have for so long now been considered to be in crisis that the announcement of a crisis in history may appear scarcely newsworthy. Is it perhaps more serious now than it was 50 or 100 years ago? Is the investigation of historical knowledge more urgent now? I believe, as do many historians, that the answer to these questions is affirmative. It seems that professional historians perceive the existence of a crisis of sense that goes beyond the chronic problems of the social sciences.

The perception of a crisis is the reflection, among other things, of the end of the "dreams of Reason" as conceived by idealistic philosophers (having been preceded by the "dream of Faith" of Christian or Islamic thought). These positions were based on two suppositions: (a) that history is shaped by some kind of universal explanatory principle or scheme (dialectical laws, Providence, etc.); and (b) that history is, essentially, progressive or, at the very least, that it has a sense, a direction (meeting of the Idea with Itself, classless society, the Kingdom of God on Earth, etc.). Postmodern people perceive of neither sense, nor direction, nor, in many cases, progress, in history. They are acutely aware of experiencing "the death of capital letters" of "isms," ideologies and religious doctrines, as they relate to history. Some of the data presented by von Borries (this volume) reflect fairly clearly these features of the mentality that is characteristic of the postmodern era: German students are openly skeptical about progress in history, with respect to both the future and to important aspects of the recent past, even if they have a "hidden tendency" to be more positive about it. It is significant that this tendency is greater the higher the student's level. Taken together, these results show, if nothing else, an implicit conflict between, on the one hand, the hope for progress in history and, on the other, a pessimistic and, above all, "disorientated" (nondirectional) version, characteristic of the end of the great ideologies in history. Although the idea of progress is preserved at a nonconscious level, knowledge of history as a discipline leads to the interiorization of a nonvectorial conception of it.

The old models that tried to "bridle" history having failed, the current historiographical view tends to be totally removed from all directional concepts and is, moreover, pluralist. The refinement of historical knowledge does not consist in the imposition of one method or one conception, but rather in the recognition of this plurality of alternatives. The criterion of "epistemological sophistication" in history, employed in their empirical work by Kuhn et al. and Wertsch, and the acknowledgment that there exist alternative forms of explanation or narration for the same sequence of events, are thus quite in accordance with that of the new historiography.

The crisis of history is accompanied by a certain skepticism about the possibility of objectivity. This skepticism has been strongly influenced by recent analyses concerning the narrative nature of history and the similarity between the cognitive processes implied in historical reasoning and those in the production of fictional narratives. In any case, there is a process going on, within history, of a heightening of epistemological sensibility, a process that is easy to explain: a "metacognitive" consciousness (to use Kuhn's terminology) of the epistemic nature of a form of knowledge that tends not to be clear when scientists feel themselves to be mirrors of an objective world, in this case of an objective history, but it becomes clearer as uncertainty about the sense and status of scientific constructs increases.

Uncertainty, moreover, revives old antagonistic questions concerning conceptions of history, some of which have been referred to by Carretero et al., in their work: Is history essentially explanatory or interpretive? Is it determined by suprapersonal factors, or does it depend on the rational actions of people? Above all, does it consist in narration or analysis?

Underlying these questions, as valid today as a century ago, we find a concern for the objectivity of history. It is not possible to approach this complex question about objectivity from the object itself, as a completed "thing," but rather it must be done from an examination of the processes of construction of the object, and this is where cognitive psychology plays a decisive role. Thus, it is noteworthy that the chapter by Carretero et al. concerning "historical knowledge" begins with a presentation of matters closely related to the concern about the objectivity and specificity of historical objects. The following questions appear repeatedly in this volume.

History is knowledge of the past and possesses, in an inherent and specific form, a note of temporality. This has been analyzed, in a careful and thorough manner, by Ricoeur (1981, 1984). Yet, is it possible to know about the past in an objective way? Moreover, is it possible to understand it? This is a question that was also raised both by von Borries' data about "lack of empathy" with the past, and by Wineburg's reflections in this volume. Is the radical discontinuity between present and past irreconcilable? Are we necessarily cut off from the past, or is it possible for us to comprehend it?

On the other hand, is it possible to give historical explanations without understanding, in Dilthey's sense of the word, that is, without any kind of "shared life experience," outside of particular times and situations? The affirmation, in current historiography, of the narrative element inherent in history is difficult to reconcile with the assumption that the past is radically incomprehensible, unless we accept the pessimistic and absurd conclusion that history constructs fictional narratives from which it can, by some strange kind of transmutation, explain the past.

The second question raised by Carretero et al., and one that crucially affects the possibility of objectivity in history, refers to the decisive influence, in any historical narration, of ideological pressures and dominant values. How is it possible, under these conditions, to have scientific treatment of an object of study? The mask of neutrality in history has been stripped away and at this moment it is clear that often historical explanations conceal an inevitable influence in terms of values and ideologies. Historians themselves have shown, for example, that the appearance and development of the profession of historian in the 19th century was partly a result of the necessity to justify the development and consolidation of nation states, as they are now conceived. However, if history is inevitably subject to values and ideological pressures, its only possible path to objectivity involves explicit recognition of this. This, again, leads to the prescription of a relativist epistemology, to the necessity for historians to make their own position when "making" history, and to the need to recognize the possibility of alternative narrations subject to different pressures and value systems.

A third type of question relates to the role of inferences, variables and "facts," and the very notion of "historical fact." The concept of "fact" in history does not conform to the positivist notion of "fact." Historical facts are unrepeatable, the result of a complex web of selections, determined by historiographical conceptions, visibly or invisibly, depending on the present. Variables are not physically differentiable. Inferences deal with intricate material, unable to be subjected to any axiom, and inevitably imply an interpretive component. For this reason, the comparison made by Collingwood, and quoted by Carretero et al., between the activity of the historian and the detective, seems particularly apt. Although, from the classical positivist view of objective knowledge, these characteristics of historical facts, inferences, and variables constitute important defects, this is not necessarily an obstacle to accepting the possibility of objectivity in history.

Lastly, history constitutes, as already mentioned, an attempt to combine the paradigmatic modality of thinking with the narrative. In this latter modality, the use of intentional vocabulary is inevitable. Here we face again the problem of objectivity and sense. We can talk of narratives as making or not making sense, but to make claims of objectivity is more problematical. Intentional language is apparently divorced from any pretension of objectivity, in the classical sense of the word, due to the inevitable involvement of a component of interpretive inference, which always goes beyond the facts themselves. It refers to reasons, not causes. Nevertheless, even in books by historians for whom intentional language is, ostensibly, alien, we can find a proliferation of intentionalist interpretations. The attempts of the Annales school or some Marxists, or the efforts of certain structuralists, to eliminate intentional vocabulary from history have resulted in failure.

The problem lies in the fact that, without intentional imputations, narration is not possible, and without narration, neither is history. Narratives are always articulated around a central column, constituted by the intentions, beliefs, and desires of men and women. As von Wright (1971) stated, and Carretero et al. refer to, the basis of narration is a different form of inference to that employed in the paradigmatic modality of thinking: practical inference. In history and in teleological explanations, moreover, this form of inference operates "in the opposite direction," in a postdictive form, which raises again the complex problem of objectivity, in the broad sense of the constitution of epistemic objects that conform "history."

This observation has led some pessimistic epistemologists to seriously question any claim to objectivity by history. In this connection, however, the notion of "evaluative epistemology" employed by Kuhn et al. in their chapter can be useful. History is an analyzed and evaluated narration that, as such, involves a self-consciousness of its epistemic nature.

On the other hand, the character of "situated" interpretation that all historical narratives possess follows inevitably from its narrative nature. As Wertsch notes in this volume, all narration stems from someone telling the story. Wertsch employs Bakhtin's powerful metaphor when he refers to the voices that echo through the narrative. It is inevitably a matter of situated voices, and for this very reason, all historical phenomena are susceptible to alternative narrations. On this idea is based Wertsch's elegant study on the accounts produced by North American students about the origin of their country. What are the voices they echo? His subtle analysis of the linguistic resources employed in their accounts (of the events mentioned in them, the representation of agency and the patterns of propositional referentiality) is a good example of the fertility of the analysis of historical descriptions and explanations as narratives. Moreover, it demonstrates the need for a perspectivist epistemology of history, which breaks definitively with the illusory claim of objectivity understood as impersonality.

If there is any field of knowledge in which this perspectivist version of objectivity is applicable, it is in history. In fact, this type of ideas are mentioned by the students in Wertsch's study who recognized the Eurocentric nature of their accounts of the origin of their country, and by those studied by Kuhn et al., who were able to evaluate alternative accounts and whose narrative constructions were accompanied by a greater degree of uncertainty. These subjects possessed a more elaborated epistemology and, at the same time, developed more objective constructions, in the historical sense, than the others. The difficult exercise of distancing oneself from one's own perspective (not to deny it, but to see it) is the first condition of historical objectivity.

I have thus noted a first important consequence of the narrative nature of history: the difficult problem of its objectivity. In contrast to arguments in the paradigmatic modality, which have limits and can frequently be subjected to some axiomatic system (e.g., a logical or mathematical one) in order to determine their formal validity, narrative constructions lack precise limits. They are inexhaustible. They always admit alternative interpretations, given that interpretation, in contrast to explanation, is a "situated" activity. Thus, in a "double-sided" activity such as history, a peculiar situation occurs: Insofar as history lies within the paradigmatic modality of thinking, it is evaluated in accordance with the norms of that modality. Consequently, it is possible and permissible to say that there are "better and worse histories" and, above all, better and worse analyses of history. The pluralist and perspectivist perception of the construction of history does not by any means lead to the supposition that "anything goes" as a historical construct. On the other hand, however, and insofar as history is also an hermeneutic activity, strongly conditioned by its historicality, submission to its disciplinary or paradigmatic conventions never "shuts off" the construction of historical objects of study.

In the same way that the hermeneutic nature of history derives from its narrative character, a second feature also stems from it, as mentioned by Wertsch, namely, all history as narration has an end, is shut off. The temporality of history, cannot be expressed in terms of a linear succession of instants in an imaginary straight line; quite the contrary, it is best represented as "woven" time, as time "with a plot" (Ricoeur, 1981).

In this way, histories are defined as narrations insofar as they possess a plot and an end. If indeed historians generally disdain philosophical conceptions such as that of Hegel, that conceive of history as consisting in an epiphenomenic manifestation of an underlying abstract plot (and hence of a Sense, with a capital letter), they can nevertheless not avoid that their own cognitive productions also have a plot, whose necessity is determined, to a large extent, by a need for "moral significance," as White (1981) has clearly pointed out.

If we accept the principles established up to now, that is, that all history possesses a narrative component, that it is defined by the significant "closure" of the narration, and that the necessity for closure derives from a moral demand, then we must also admit some important consequences that follow and that give a special significance to research such as that of von Borries (this volume). There are two obvious conclusions that have been formulated, in one way or another, by different contributors to this volume (such as Carretero et al., Kuhn et al., Wertsch, and von Borries).

First, all that history, insofar as it is history, contains, outside of its plot and as a support for it, is some implicit or explicit moral foundation to hold it together. It is no coincidence that history has developed, to a large extent, attempts to develop people's moral and social consciousness, or to influence it. As is clearly perceived by Carretero et al., this peculiar and inevitable "moral substance" that history possesses explains both its very origin and its propensity for exerting political and ideological pressures, and constitutes, at the same time, an inevitable quality of history and a powerful obstacle to its objectivity. It does, however, confer on history a particular importance for education, such as a basic instrument of socialization and interiorization of moral norms.

That second consequence is as evident from the earlier premises as it is, at first sight, surprising. Imagine history, for a moment, as a kind of epistemic-construct in layers that contain from inside to outside, a plot, a narration, a collection of analyses, justifications, and validations of it. Although, this is not all. In its very interior, there is a nucleus, not epistemic but axiological, of moral values. This may lead to a conclusion worthy of discussion: All history contains, in a sense, an anachronic nucleus, if we accept (as seems logical from relativist and perspectivist approaches) the "situated" and "historical" nature of norms and moral judgments themselves. This would be, in turn, a basic argument justifying the "inexhaustible" character of history, in terms of both narration and hermeneutics.

The findings of von Borries are revealing, and his chapter most eloquent. The students tended to apply "universal moral principles," and "the ethics of human rights" to historical accounts. They showed no signs of situating themselves in the ethics of "the others," who continued to be, for them, "radically others." They were incapable of putting themselves "in the shoes" of historical agents, of empathizing with their intentions, plans, and moral values. What is surprising is that this same tendency also appears in teachers of history. In spite of proclaiming the need for historical relativism as a desirable attitude for the teaching and learning of history, teachers are even more rigid than students when it comes to condemning certain actions of historical agents based on ethical norms that are, in themselves, historically determined and delimited.

The problem in question is, in reality, to what extent and in what conditions, a true moral relativism in history, similar to that required, for example, in anthropology or ethnography, is possible. The application of moral consequences to intentional plots is probably as inevitable as it is inescapably mediated, knowingly or unknowingly, by one who judges. Is history, then, unavoidably anachronic, at least in this moral aspect? What course of action can the historian take in order to treat his or her epistemic products for this "anachronic disease" so potentially dangerous? Is it possible to achieve a "historical empathy," as called for in his article by von Borries?

Probably, none of these questions has a conclusive or radical answer. There are, or there can be, various degrees of historical anachronisms, empathy, and "estrangement." If, in history, explanation requires comprehension (to use Dilthey's distinction between these two forms of epistemic penetration), and comprehension requires the transmission or, at least, reconstruction of life experiences, then von Borries is completely right when he claims "empathy" should be the goal of history teaching. However, we must recognize that historiographical criticism of this possibility of empathy is overwhelming, and the position of Wineburg (this volume) is a good demonstration of this. Nevertheless, if we assume the inevitable "estrangement" of all historical objects of study, we arrive at the strange situation of "having to establish the conditions of a dialogue, between the present and the past, that can never occur." The conditions of an impossible and infinite *dialogue des sourds*.

The problem is that narration is only able to make sense if this dialogue exists in some way. Some of the most promising and fruitful ideas about history have resulted from the awareness of the necessity for a rigorous reconstruction of the mental worlds of historical agents, in order to be able to understand the unfolding of history. This is the intention, for example, of the "history of mentalities," which, interestingly, has grown in importance at the very time when any possibility of historical empathy is being questioned, and the radical estranged nature of any explanation of the past affirmed. In many cases, *mentality*, that is, the abstraction of socially common aspects of the mental content of a period, is indeed an advantageous concept for the study of causes and conditions of historical phenomena.

This leads to one of the central problems raised in the chapters by Carretero et al. and Voss et al. in this volume: the problem (mentioned briefly earlier) of the role of intentional vocabulary in historical explanations. In our view, intentional vocabulary is, as it were, the "machine language" of history, that is, that language to which all other language must be reduced in order for history to "run" as a meaningful narrative situated in time, in the same way that computer programming languages have to be compiled in more molecular language for the programs to "run." Thus, the understanding of the dynamism of history and the construction of history as narrative are made possible by the task of "compilation," accomplished by historians using the suprapersonal vocabulary and the more molecular "machine language" of history, which, paradoxically, is intentional vocabulary.

This vocabulary is the expression of a conceptual system (that which cognitive psychology calls "Theory of Mind") that appears to possess properties, the knowledge of which is important for the understanding of the cognitive implications of the "double modality" (paradigmatic and narrative) concept of history. I am referring to a conceptual system whose basic elements are propositional attitudes (beliefs, intentions, desires) and that carries out with extreme efficiency tasks of inference and prediction of specific human actions, about a universal and precocious system, specialized in interaction with members of the species, and apparently not reducible to the conceptual systems on which the "paradigmatic modality" of thinking is based. It is, finally, the system that allows us to "make sense of" and "impute with moral responsibility" human actions, and which makes it possible to give accounts of them.

If history is, then a form of narration that cannot avoid the use of a basic language of intentional vocabulary, this helps to explain some of the findings in the studies mentioned earlier: (a) the peculiar "familiarity" of historical and social explanations that, at the same time as apparently facilitating them, tends to simplify them and make them difficult, in comparison to natural explanations (Kuhn et al., this volume); (b) the propensity for "personalizing" suprapersonal factors; (c) the inevitable bond between history and moral judgments (permitted by the imputation of intentional states to individuals and groups); (d) "humanization" and the tendency to accentuate the role of psychological conditions in history (Voss et al., this volume); and (e) the higher incidence of these aspects, the more naive and "primitive" the historical explanations are.

History is not, however, only narration, nor is it written only in the language of intentions (although it tended to be only this for a very long time). Attention to the paradigmatic component is just as important as the understanding of the narrative aspect, in order to give an account of the epistemic construction of historical objects of study, hence, the importance of the research of Kuhn et al., on the one hand, and of Voss et al. on the other. They raise questions related to those traditions of the subject that allow history to exist as an analyzed narrative, with claims to truth and evaluability. They also raise, as I understand, two fascinating, but enormously complex questions: Is it possible, strictly speaking, to talk of "variables" and "control of variables" in history? Second, what is historical causation, and how is it understood by individuals?

As Carretero et al. point out, historical variables are not able to be physically discriminated, although, occasionally, they can be differentiated conceptually. It is not possible to "control" them. The conditions of historical explanations are unavoidably complex and difficult to simulate in simplified and analytical contexts, in which time does not play the same role as it does in history and in which the causal rules are known in advance, in contexts where, moreover, narrative aspects, essential in history, are excluded. All of this represents a warning to be cautious when extrapolating to the domain of history findings that refer to other social sciences or simplified conditions, such as those of a jury, which was used by Kuhn et al.

The jury situation is, indeed, an ingenious idea for the analysis of aspects common to history and other narrational modalities. It includes components of closedness, sense, and moral evaluation that, as we have seen, are of great importance in the construction of historical objects. At the same time, however, it lacks much of the "ecology of history," an ecology with components of complexity and temporality and which refers to social, political, and economic, even mental, processes of a supranatural character. Thus, the findings from the tasks of inductive causal inference and judicial reasoning presented by Kuhn et al., although of great interest for the explanation of aspects of reasoning in the social sciences, has only an indirect significance for history.

There are other aspects of Kuhn et al.'s article of great importance for the understanding of how historical reasoning develops, on its most paradigmatic side. On the one hand, there is the fact that history demands reasoning about proof, data, and evidence. This capacity appears to depend on two interrelated factors: the degree of elaboration of the epistemologies underlying the reasoning processes, and the level of metacognitive consciousness of the epistemic, constructive, and alternative nature of the historical narratives. In my opinion, both the suggestive sequence of epistemological levels indicated by Kuhn et al. (which goes from ingenuous realism to evaluative epistemology, passing through relativist pluralism) and the important findings in relation to this sequence and to the degrees of certainty in historical explanations are theoretically and practically highly significant: theoretically, because they allow the establishment of some kind of order in the development of the comprehension of history, and practically, because they have obvious implications for its teaching, in terms of both methodology and content. The findings suggest a critical and pluralist teaching of history; of a teaching centered, at the same time, on the development of ordered and intelligent processes of evaluation of alternative narrations and explanations, situating them in relation to the framework of historical documents.

Evaluation is a difficult task, and this is one of the reasons why the job of the historian is also difficult. Given the strongly reconstructive and inferential character of history, the combination in it of practical inferences and others more akin to the paradigmatic mode, and the extreme complexity of the causes and conditions of history, the relationship between inferences and "data," is frequently and typically quite indirect at the moment of the construction of historical objects. In their interesting article, Voss et al. present in a clear fashion some of the complex problems that affect historical causality: the possibility of establishing necessary and sufficient causal relations; the special role of conterfactuals; the distinction between causal fields, conditions, and causes; the types of causal structure; and so on. The question raised in this case is whether it is possible, in the strict sense, to make causal inferences in history. In recent years, the use of models that deal with complex systems has permitted the development of a version of interactive relations in these types of system that is moving further and further away from the classical and determinist models of causation. To what extent would these models be useful in the explanation of forms of influencing (rather than strict determination) that characteristically occur in history? We are still a long way from being able to respond to this important and open question.

Conterfactuals in history are as dangerous as they are inevitable (and although infrequent in Voss et al.'s research, they are, at times, more daring than is desirable among professional historians themselves). Let that serve as an excuse to use one myself: If psychologists had studied historical knowledge, our contribution to clearing up the epistemological crisis in history and improving its teaching would currently have been far more advanced. The first efforts are now producing important results for the field of education. The chapters discussed here give definition to some important aspects that should be taken into account in the teaching of history: (a) the narrative modality should probably be given most importance in the teaching of young children; (b) history should, from the first moment, pursue moral and socialization objectives and favor ethical perspectives and relativist and "historicist" epistemologies; (c) an essential objective of teaching should consist of the development of the capacity to recognize, respect, and evaluate alternative accounts of the same events and also to choose between them; (d) history is also invaluable as an instrument for helping to understand human actions, without divesting them of moral responsibility, but neither naively reducing them to their personal components and recognizing inevitable suprapersonal conditioning and influences; and (e) history may continue to be considered as human responsibility, despite any influence to which it is subject.

REFERENCES

Bruner, J. (1986). *Actual minds, possible words*. Cambridge, England: Cambridge University Press.

Bruner, J. (1990). *Acts of meaning*. Cambridge, MA: Harvard University Press.

Ricoeur, P. (1981). *Hermeneutics and the human sciences*. Cambridge, England: Cambridge University Press.

Ricoeur, P. (1984). *Time and narrative* (Vol. 1). Chicago: University of Chicago Press.

White, H. (1981). The value of narrativity in the representation of reality. In W. J. T. Mitchell (Ed.), *On narrative*. Chicago: University of Chicago Press.

White, H. (1987). The content of the form. Narrative discourse and historical representation of reality. In W. J. T. Mitchell (Ed.), *On narrative*. Chicago: Chicago University Press.

von Wright, G.H. (1971). *Explanation and understanding*. Ithaca, NY: Cornell University Press.

Author Index

A

Abramovitch, R., 24, *44*
Adelson, J., 31, 33, *45*, 93, *100*
Ajello, A. M., 49, 50, *75*
Alexander, A., 238, *255*
Almond, G., 205, *217*
Amsel, E., 315, *319*, 358, *375*
Andersen, C., 378, *400*
Angell, A., 215, *217*
Arons, A. B., 159, *181*
Asensio, M., 257, *283*, 361, 362, *375*
Atkinson, R. F., 189, *199*
Avery, P. G., 207, *218*

B

Bakhtin, M. M., 324, *337*
Ball, D. L., 159, *181*
Ball, L., 383, *400*
Barber, B. R., 215, *217*
Baron, J., 399, *400*
Barnes, J., 170, 171, *182*
Barnes, M. S., 362, *375*
Barroso, R., 99, *100*
Bartlett, F. C., 223, *232*
Bauer, P. J., 311, *319*
Baughman, J. E., 205, 207, *217*
Baur, M., 25, *46*
Bean, T. W., 132, *157*

Beck, I. L., 49, 50, 72, *74*, *75*, 106, *121*,
    132, *157*, 160, *182*, *183*, 237, 239, 240,
    241, 244, 251, 254, *255*, *256*
Bennett, J. M., 268, *283*
Bennett, L., 285, 304, *306*
Berger, P. L., 93, *100*
Bern, H., 238, *255*
Berti, A. E., 17, 22, 23, 25, 27, 44, *45*, 50,
    74, 77, 78, 93, 100, *101*, 106, *121*
Birkey, C., 19, *46*
Black, J. B., 238, *255*, 258, *282*, 315, *319*
Blankenship, G., 207, *217*
Bombi, A. S., 17, 22, 23, 25, 27, 44, *45*,
    49, 50, *74*, *75*, 77, 78, 93, 100, *101*, 106,
    121
Booth, W. C., 159, *182*
Borries, B. V., 339, 347, 354, 355, *355*
Boutilier, R. G., 98, *101*
Bower, G. H., 258, *282*, 312, *319*
Boyes, M., 383, *400*
Bradley Commission on History in Schools,
    203, *217*, 286, *306*
Branch, T., 169, *182*
Brewer, W. F., 103, *122*
Britt, M. A., 260, 262, 263, 272, 279, 281,
    282
Britton, B. K., 315, *319*
Brophy, J., 215, *217*
Brown, J. I., 268, *283*
Brown, K., 224, 230, 231, *232*

Bruner, J., 310, 312, *319*, 432, *442*
Burgard, P., 35, *45*, 95, *101*
Burke, K., 310, *319*, 328, *337*
Burris, V., 19, *45*

C

Calvani, A., 49, 74, *75*
Campbell, M., 36, 37, 38, *46*
Caravita, S., 189, *199*
Carey, S., 51, *75*
Carpenter, P. A., 238, *256*
Carr, D., 325, *337*
Carr, E. H., 172, *182*, 363, *375*
Carretero, M., 257, *283*, 361, 362, 367, 368, 371, 372, *375*
Center for Strategic Studies, 263, *283*
Chafe, W. L., 332, *337*
Champagne, A. B., 159, *182*
Chandler, M. J., 98, *101*, 383, *400*
Cheyne, W., 35, *45*, 95, *101*
Chi, M. T. H., 104, 105, *121*
Chiesi, H. L., 238, *255*
Chizmar, J., 41, *45*
Cleare, A., 25, *45*
Clement, J., 159, *182*
Cohen, D. K., 180, *182*
Cole, M., 286, *306*
Collingwood, R. G., 139, 140, *157*, 172, *182*, 222, *232*, 363, 366, *375*, 411, *428*
Coltham, J. B., 50, *75*
Connell, R. W., 34, *45*, 50, 73, *75*, 93, *101*
Cook, T. D., 81, *101*
Correa, N., 317, *319*
Cram, F., 27, *45*
Crane, P. M., 264, *283*
Croce, B., 172, *182*
Cuban, L., 202, 209, 210, 214, *217*
Cubero, M., 230, *232*
Cummings, S., 22, *45*

D

Danto, A. C., 225, *232*, 373, *375*
Danziger, K., 18, 20, *45*, 93, *101*
Davidson, D., 40, *45*
Davis, O. L., Jr., 202, 204, 216, *219*
Daza, D., 78, 99, *101*
de Beni, R., 25, *45*
de Certeau, M., 231, *232*, 324, 336, *337*
DeFleur, L. B., 80, *101*

DeFleur, M. L., 80, *101*
del Barrio, C., 97, 98, *101*
Delval, J., 78, 79, 97, 99, 100, *101*
D'Emilio, J., 137, *157*
Dennis, J., 31, *45*
de Vega, M., 312, *320*
Dewey, J., 357, *375*
Díaz-Barriga, F., 78, 99, *101*
Dickinson, A. K., 286, *307*
Dickinson, J., 35, 36, *45*, 95, *101*
Donald, D., 171, *182*
Downey, M., 203, 215, *217*
Dray, W. H., 366, *375*, 406, 411, *428*
DuBois, W. E. B., 170, *182*
Dunkin, M. J., 170, 171, *182*

E

Easley, J. A., Jr., 204, *219*
Easton, D., 51, *75*
Echeita, G., 78, 97, *101*
Edgar, R., 28, *47*
Education Development Center, 212, *217*
Edwards, A. D., 190, *199*
Edwards, D., 223, *232*
Ehman, L. H., 204, 205, 207, *217*
Ehrlich, M. F., 316, *320*
Einhorn, H., 407, 408, *428*
Elbow, P., 159, *182*
Emler, N., 35, 36, *45*, 95, *101*
Engestrom, R., 224, 230, 231, *232*
Engestrom, Y., 224, 230, 231, *232*
Engle, S. H., 204, *217*
Ericsson, K. A., 290, *307*
Evans, R., 135, *157*
Evans, R. W., 213, *217*

F

Farnen, R. F., 206, *219*
Fehrenbacher, D. E., 292, *307*
Fernandez-Armesto, F., 164, 165, *182*
Ferro, M., 359, *375*
Finn, C. E., Jr., 168, *183*, 202, *219*
Fischer, D. H., 289, 306, *307*, 407, *428*
Fischhoff, B., 418, *428*
FitzGerald, F., 132, *157*, 238, *255*
Flaton, R., 391, *401*
Foner, E., 170, *182*, 183
Fox, K., 40, *45*
Frazee, C., 132, *157*

Frederiksen, J. R., 238, *255*
Fredrickson, G., 297, 299, *307*
Freedman, J., 24, *44*
Friedman, W. J., 89, *101*, 362, *375*
Furby, L., 28, 35, *45*
Furnham, A., 17, 21, 25, 27, 29, 30, 32, 37, 44, *45*, *46*, 93, *101*
Furth, H. G., 24, 25, 33, *46*, 50, *75*, 78, 89, 93, *101*

G

Gagnon, P., 132, *157*, 166, *182*
Gal, R., 50, *75*
Gallie, W. B., 310, *319*, 373, *375*
Garcia-Mila, M., 378, *400*, *401*
Gardiner, P. L., 225, *232*
Gardner, H., 387, *400*
Garrow, D., 169, *182*
Gelman, S., 104, *122*
Genovese, L., 50, *75*
Georgi, M. C., 260, 262, 263, 279, 281, 282, *283*
Gerace, W. J., 159, *182*
Gergen, K. J., 226, *232*
Gergen, M. M., 266, *232*
Gernsbacher, M. A., 312, *319*
Geyl, P., 172, *182*
Gibbon, E., 138, *157*
Giesse, J. R., 208, *217*
Gilligan, C., 216, *217*
Girardet, H., 50, 74, *75*
Glenn, C. G., 258, 279, *283*
Goldmann, L., 88, *101*
Goldsmith, H. H., 312, *319*
Goodlad, J. I., 202, 204, *217*
Goold, G. P., 137, *157*
Gordon, C., 238, *256*
Gottschalk, L., 298, *307*
Grant, L., 31, *46*
Gray, R., 24, *46*
Green, B., 93, *100*
Greene, T. R., 424, *429*
Greenspan, S. L., 312, *319*
Griffin, A. F., 204, 216, *217*
Gromoll, E., 72, *74*, 160, *182*, 237, 239, *255*
Guarracino, S., 49, 51, *75*
Gunstone, R. F., 159, *182*
Gunter, B., 32, *45*
Gyselinck, V., 316, *320*

H

Habermas, J., 361, *375*
Hacking, I., 229, *232*
Hahn, C. L., 205, 206, 207, 209, 210, *218*
Halinski, R., 41, *45*
Halldén, O., 106, *121*, 188, 189, 196, 198, 199, 372, *375*, 411, 425, *428*
Halliday, M. A. K., 332, *337*
Handlin, O., 172, *182*
Hanna, G., 268, *283*
Hansen, H., 41, *46*
Hansen, J., 238, *256*
Hansen, R. D., 418, *428*
Harcourt Brace Jovanovich, Inc., 244, *256*
Harris, D. E., 213, *218*
Hart, H. L. A., 408, *428*
Harwood, A. M., 206, 207, *218*
Haste, H., 17, 31, 44, *46*, 104, *121*
Hastie, R., 386, 387, 388, 389, 398, *400*, *401*
Helburn, S. W., 202, 204, 216, *219*
Hempel, C. G., 139, *157*, 310, *319*, 411, *428*
Herman, W. L., Jr., 165, 166, *182*
Herodotus, 137, *157*, *158*
Hertzberg, H. W., 203, *218*
Hess, R., 106, *121*
Hexter, J., 386, *400*
Hilton, D. J., 408, *428*
Himmelfarb, G., 324, *337*
Himmelweit, H., 31, *46*
Hinojosa, M. L., 78, 99, *101*
Hirsch, J., 108, *121*
Hofstadter, R., 294, *307*
Hogarth, R. M., 407, 408, *428*
Holt, T., 159, *182*, *232*, 324, *337*
Honoré, A. M., 408, *428*
Hook, J., 81, *101*
Horton, R., 42, *46*
Humphreyes, P., 31, *46*
Hunt, M. P., 204, 216, *218*

I

Ingels, S., 37, 39, *46*
Inhelder, B., 82, 86, *101*
Irving, K., 28, *46*

J

Jackson, R., 31, *46*
Jacott, L., 367, 368, 371, 372, *375*

Jaeger, M., 31, *46*
Jahoda, G., 19, 24, 25, 26, 35, *45*, *46*, 49, 50, 75, 78, 80, 93, 95, 99, *101*, *102*, 362, *375*
Jaros, D., 31, *46*
Jeismann, K. E., 347, *355*
Jennings, M. K., 204, *218*
Johansson, M., 190, *199*
Johnson, D. W., 216, *218*
Johnson, N. S., 258, 279, *283*
Johnson, R. T., 216, *218*
Jones, S., 27, *46*
Jordan, W. D., 302, *307*
Judd, C. H., 286, *307*
Jurd, M. F., 49, 50, 73, *75*
Just, M. A., 238, *256*

K

Katz, M., 31, *46*
Keil, F., 51, *75*
Kermode, F., 325, *337*
Kilgore, J., 40, *45*
Kintsch, W., 291, *307*
Klopfer, L. E., 159, *182*, 358, *376*
Kluger, R., 169, *182*
Koistinen, K., 224, 230, 231, *232*
Kosthorst, E., 347, *355*
Kourilsky, M., 36, 37, 38, 39, *46*
Krechevsky, M., 387, *400*
Kuhn, D., 315, *319*, 358, 364, *375*, 377, 378, 383, 384, 385, 389, 391, 395, 399, *400*, *401*
Kunda, Z., 399, *401*

L

Landress, C., 207, *218*
Langton, K. P., 204, *218*
Lansdale, D., 206, 207, *219*
Lare, J., 50, *75*
Lastrucci, E., 49, 50, *75*
Lave, J., 119, *121*, 286, *307*
Leadbeater, B., 364, *375*, 384, 385, *400*, *401*
Leahy, R. L., 29, 30, *46*, 77, 80, *102*
Lee, P. J., 286, *307*
LeFeber, W., 263, *283*
Leinhardt, G., 132, 133, 134, 145, 155, *158*, 358, *375*
Leiser, D., 19, 35, *46*
Leming, J. S., 210, 213, 216, *218*
Leontiev, A. N., 223, 224, 230, *232*
Levstik, L., 203, 215, *217*, *218*

Levy, D., 35, *46*
Lincoln, A., 285, 291, 293, 296, 298, 301, 307
Lis, A., 27, *45*
Litt, E., 204, *218*
Lochhead, J., 159, *182*
Lockwood, A. L., 213, *218*
López-Manjón, A., 367, 371, *375*
Lowenthal, D., 302, *307*
Loxterman, J. A., 160, *183*, 237, 240, 241, 254, *255*, *256*
Luckmann, T., 93, *101*

M

Macaulay, T. B., 138, *158*
MacIntyre, A., 406, *428*
MacIver, R. M., 407, 408, *428*
Mackie, J. L., 407, *428*
Madaras, L., 212, *218*
Maestre, J. P., 159, *182*
Major, B., 418, *428*
Mallon, F., 137, *158*
Mandler, J. M., 258, 279, *283*, 311, *319*
Marrero, J., 318, *319*
Marrou, H. I., 361, *375*
Mason, M., 209, *218*
Mason, R. A., 272, 281, *283*
Mathien, T., 224, 226, *232*
Mattingly, G., 164, 165, *183*
McConville, K., 33, *46*
McCrone, D., 31, *45*
McDermott, L. C., 159, *183*
McDiarmid, G. W., 133, *158*, 160, 161, 162, 166, *183*
McGrath, P., 221, *232*
McKenzie, R., 41, *46*
McKeown, M. G., 49, 50, 72, *74*, *75*, 106, 121, 132, *157*, 160, *182*, *183*, 237, 239, 240, 241, 244, 251, 254, *255*, *256*
McNeil, L. M., 202, 204, 209, 213, 216, *218*
Means, B., 286, *252*
Megill, A., 366, *375*
Merryfield, M. M., 211, *218*
Metcalf, L. E., 204, 216, *218*
Middleton, D., 223, *232*
Mill, J. S., 407, *428*
Mink, L. O., 304, *307*, 325, *337*, 361, *375*, 409, 411, *428*
Minstrell, J. A., 358, *376*
Monk, G. S., 159, *182*
Montangero, J., 89, *102*

Moore, W. M., 50, *75*
Morrisett, I., 203, *218*
Morrow, D. G., 312, *319*
Moscovici, S., 95, *102*

N

National Archives and Records Administration, 212, *218*
National Center for Research on Teacher Learning, 305, *307*
National Council for the Social Studies, 212, 216, *218, 219*
Newmann, F. M., 204, 213, 216, *219*
Ng, S. H., 26, 27, 30, 38, *45, 46*, 78, *102*
Nisbett, R. E., 290, *307*
Noddings, N., 216, *219*
Novick, P., 177, *183*

O

Oakden, E. C., 362, *376*
O'Brien, M., 37, 39, *46*
Ochoa, A. S., 204, *217*
O'Connor, K., 327, 335, *337, 338*
Ohana, J., 95, *101*
Okagaki, L., 387, *401*
Oliver, D. W., 204, *219*
O'Loughlin, M., 315, *319*, 358, *375*
Omanson, R. C., 258, *283*
O'Neil, R., 31, 33, *45*
O'Neill, R., 93, *100*
Onosko, J. J., 213, *219*
Oppenheim, A. N., 206, *219*
Oxford Universal Dictionary Illustrated, 225, *232*

P

Pachter, H. M., 410, *428*
Palmer, J. R., 238, *256*
Pandel, H. J., 347, *355*
Pascarella, E. T., 159, *183*
Pearson, P. D., 238, *256*
Peel, M., 49, *75*
Penner, B. C., 424, *429*
Pennington, N., 384, 386, 388, 389, 398, *400, 401*
Perfetti, C. A., 238, *256*, 260, 262, 263, 272, 279, 281, *282, 283*
Perkins, D. N., 289, *307*
Perry, S., 28, *47*

Pettersson, K. A., 189, *200*
Piaget, J., 79, 82, 86, 89, 92, *101, 102*, 332, *337*, 357, 362, *376*
Pietras, M., 30, 36, 38, *47*
Pliner, P., 24, *44*
Poggi, G., 51, *75*
Polic, M., 22, *47*
Pollio, H., 24, *46*
Pongratz,, L. H., 226, *232*
Porter, D., 310, *319*
Post, T. A., 424, *429*
Pozo, J. I., 257, *283*, 361, 362, *375*
Prawat, R. S., 427, *428*
Project 30, 181, *183*

R

Radley, A., 224, *232*
Ragazzini, D., 49, 51, *75*
Ramsett, D., 41, *46*
Ravitch, D., 168, *183*, 202, *219*
Reisch, G. A., 411, *428*
Resnick, L. B., 132, *158*, 358, *376*
Ricouer, P., 325, 326, *337*, 373, *376*, 434, 437, *443*
Ringer, F. K., 406, 412, *428*
Robertson, E., 215, *219*
Robertson, R. R. S., 312, *319*
Robertson, W. C., 290, *307*
Robinson, J. B., 302, *307*
Rodrigo, M. J., 317, 318, *319*
Rodriguez, A., 318, *319*
Rogoff, B., 95, *102*
Rosenberg, M., 80, *102*
Rouet, J.-F., 260, 262, 263, 272, 279, 281, *282, 283*
Rumelhart, D. E., 258, *283*
Rüsen, J., 347, 355, *355*

S

Santayana, G., 174, *183*
Schafer, B., 347, *355*
Schauble, L., 378, *401*
Schloder, B., 347, *355*
Schmitt, C., 51, *75*
Schoenfeld, A., 159, *183*
Schug, M., 19, *46*
Schwab, J. J., 140, *158*
Scott, K. P., 215, *219*
Scriven, M., 411, *428*
Searle, J., 197, *200*

Secco, T., 238, *256*, 258, *283*
Seixas, P., 215, *219*
Sevon, G., 19, 29, 35, *46*, *47*
Shafer, R. J., 260, *283*
Shaklee, H., 418, *428*
Shantz, C. U., 92, *102*
Shaver, J. P., 202, 204, 216, *219*, 358, *376*
Shemilt, D. J., 286, *307*, 364, *376*, 411, 425, *428*
Shope, R. K., 409, *428*
Siegal, M., 28, 29, *46*, *47*
Silverstein, M., 329, 331, 332, *337*
Simmons, R., 80, *102*
Simon, H. A., 290, *307*
Sinatra, G. M., 160, *183*, 237, 240, 241, 254, *255*, *256*
Singer, H., 132, *157*
Singer, M., 29, *47*
Slotta, J. D., 104, 105, *121*
Slugoski, B. R., 408, *428*
Smith, E. L., 314, *320*
Smith, J., 25, *46*
Smith, P., 159, *183*
Social Issues Resources Series, 212, *219*
Social Science Education Consortium, 213, *219*
Solomon, J., 198, *200*
SoRelle, J. M., 212, *218*
Sorter, J., 132, *157*
Sperry, L., 312, *320*
Spilich, G. J., 238, *255*
Stacey, B., 17, 21, 29, *46*, *47*, 93, *101*
Stake, R. E., 204, *219*
Stampp, K., 170, *183*
Stein, N. L., 258, 279, *283*
Sternberg, R., 387, *401*
Stewart, D., *183*
Stone, L., 5, *14*, 310, *320*
Stradling, R., 31, *47*
Strauss, A. L., 18, 23, *47*, 93, *102*
Sturt, M., 362, *376*
Sutton, R., 19, *47*

T

Taebel, D., 22, *45*
Takaki, R., 288, *307*
Tardieu, H., 316, *320*
Task Force on Curriculum of the National Commission on the Social Studies, 203, *219*
Taylor, C., 324, *337*

Teppe, K., 347, *355*
Terenzini, P., 159, *183*
Thompson, D., 197, *200*
Thorndyke, P. W., 258, *283*
Thucydides, *158*
Tierney, D. S., 133, *158*
Tocci, C., 205, *218*
Topolski, J., 404, 422, 425, 426, *428*
Torney, J. V., 106, *121*, 206, *219*
Torney-Purta, J., 17, 31, 44, *46*, 104, 107, 108, *121*, 206, 207, *219*
Törnkvist, S., 189, *200*
Trabasso, T., 238, *256*, 258, 259, *283*, 312, *320*
Tranströmer, G., 189, *200*
Triana, B., 317, *319*
Tulving, E., 223, *232*
Tyler, S., 107, *122*

V

van den Broek, P., 238, *256*, 258, 259, *283*, 312, *320*
van Dijk, T. A., 291, *307*
Verba, S., 205, *217*
Vinten-Johansen, P., 160, 161, 162, 166, *183*
von Ranke, L., 139, *158*
von Wright, G. H., 139, 140, *158*, 366, 367, *376*, 424, *429*, 436, *443*
Vosniadou, S., 51, *75*, 103, *122*
Voss, J. F., 107, *122*, 238, *255*, 358, *376*, 424, *429*
Vygotsky, L. S., *232*, 324, 332, *337*

W

Wagner, K. A., 50, *75*
Waite, P., 41, *47*
Walsh, W. H., 135, 137, *158*, 172, *183*, 197, *200*
Walstad, W., 41, *47*
Wasna, M., 347, *355*
Watts, M., 41, *47*
Weaver, R., 296, 297, *307*
Webley, P., 21, 30, *47*
Weckstrom, S., 19, 29, *47*
Weidenaar, D., 42, *46*
Weinstock, M., 391, *401*
Weiss, I. R., 204, *219*
Wellman, H., 104, *122*
Wenger, E., 119, *121*

Wertheimer, M., 226, *232*
Wertsch, J. V., 95, *102*, 230, *232*, 323, 324, 327, 329, 331, 332, 334, 335, *338*
White, H., 225, 226, *232*, 310, *320*, 325, *338*, 431, 438, *443*
White, J. J., 238, *256*
White, M., 407, 408, *429*
Whitehead, D., 38, *47*
Wiley, K. B., 204, *219*
Wilson, M., 215, *219*
Wilson, S. M., 132, 133, 134, *158*, 209, *219*, 286, 305, *307*, *308*
Wilson, T. D., 290, *307*
Wineburg, S. S., 113, *122*, 132, 133, 134, *158*, 160, *183*, 209, *219*, 231, *233*, 261, 262, 268, 281, *283*, 286, 289, 290, 298, 305, *307*, *308*, 311, *320*, 334, *338*, 358, *376*, *401*

Winocur, S., 29, *47*
Wistedt, I., 198, *200*
Woerdenbagch, A., 78, *102*
Woodward, C. V., 170, *183*
Wosinski, M., 30, 36, 38, *47*

Y

Yengo, L., 107, *122*

Z

Zabucovec, V., 22, *47*
Zevin, J., 205, 207, *219*
Zinchenko, P. I., 223, 230, *232*
Zinser, O., 28, *47*
Zohar, A., 378, *400*

Subject Index

C

Causal models, 258-260
Classroom climates, 204-207
  creation of, 212
Colligatory concepts, 197-199
Conceptual change, 104-120
  in physics, 104-106
  in social studies, 104, 106-107
  role of development vs. instruction in,
    116-120, 125-126
Conceptual development, 18-22, 32-43,
    72-74, 88-89, 124
  class differences, 35-36
  cross-cultural studies, 35-36, 77-88, 99,
    205-206
  experience and, 99-100
  gender differences, 36-37
  model of, 43
  stages in, 18-22, 88-89, 124-128
Contextualized thinking, 285-306
  of teachers, 290-306
Current events, understanding of,
    66-72
  Germany, unification of, 67
  European union, 68
  Kuwait, annexation of, 68
  Soviet Union, collapse of, 412-422
  Yugoslavia, secession in, 70-72

E

Economic concepts, 18-30, 35-40, 77-88,
    107-109
  banking, 26
  explanation of, 77-79, 124
  international debt, 107-109
  money, 23-24
  possession and ownership, 26-28, 35
  poverty and wealth, 28-30, 80-88
  prices and profit, 24-25
Economic values, 37-39
Economics instruction
  attitudes and, 38-39
  goals for, 42-43
  in primary grades, 39-42

H

Historical accounts by students, 325-336,
    403-427
  alternative perspectives in, 333-336
  causal fields in, 406, 424
  contents of, 327-336, 409-411, 416-422
    agents, 328-333
    events, 327-328
  explanations in, 411-412, 416, 420, 427
  neccessity and sufficiency of causes in,
    404-406, 425
  personalization in, 425-426
  structures of, 235-236, 409, 412-416, 422

Historical concepts, 361
 in college students, 169-171
 in novices, 107, 123-124
Historical documents
 detecting author bias in, 263-265, 277
 detecting incompleteness in, 265-266,
  277-278
 evaluation of, 272-276
 resolving conflict in, 265-267, 278
 use of, 260-278, 280
Historical knowledge
 of college students, 167-169
 confusions in, 250-252
 loose ends in, 252-253
 of school children, 240, 244-253
 uses of, 221-223
Historical literacy, 260-262, 313-315,
  317-319
Historical topics, understanding of
 American Revolution, 240, 244-253
 the Crusades, 341-345
 formation of Egypt, 60-64
 the Holocaust, 109-110
 Spain in 1492, 110-114
Historical views
 of classical historians, 135, 137-141,
  363-364
 of college students, 171-176, 333-336
 history as different from sociology,
  361-362
 history as experimental science, 139-141,
  143-144
 history as interpretive, 139-140, 143-144,
  207-208
 history as mediated action, 323-325
 history as narrative, 137-143, 188-190,
  310-311, 325-326, 373, 431-442
 history as purposive, 141
 of history teachers, 176-178
 of school children, 339-355, 364
Historiography learning, 161-166
History of history, 4-7
History instruction, 375-379, 427
 assignments, 188
 as citizenship training, 203-207
 controversial issues, use of, 201-216
 evaluation of, 316-317
 goals for, 14-15, 120-121, 131-134,
  155-157, 166-167, 199, 208, 311-315,
  373-374, 427
 in high school, 201-208
 multiple texts, use of, 317-319
 narratives, use of, 190-199, 315-316

 practices of successful teachers, 145-155,
  209-214
History learning
 longitudinal study of, 244-245
 as story understanding, 257-260,
  279-282, see also Historical views,
  history as narrative
 study of, 7-9
 from text, 241-244, 262-263
Historical reasoning
 causal reasoning, 364-372, see also
  historical accounts
 in classrooms, 136-137, 145-155, 190-197
 epistemology and, 383-386
 about evidence, 260-262
 and inductive inference, 377-383, 400
 and juror reasoning, 386-399, 441
 with multiple documents, 280-281
History and memory, 223-225
History, meanings of, 225-228
History and moralization, 345-355

N

Narratives, see Historical accounts;
  Historical instruction; Historical
  views
Narrative literacy, 311-313, 315-317

P

Political concepts, 31-32, 49-74
 colony, 57-58
 democracy, 53-54, 56
 global environments, 114-115
 government, 53, 55-56
 human rights, 107-109
 kingdom, 60-66
 law, 53, 56
 Pharoah, 56
 political parties, 31-32
 political symbols, 31
 state, 52-55
 state formation, 55, 60-72
 war, 59
Political understanding, 30-34, 70-72, 125
 development of, 32-34
 in a real vs. imaginary context, 70-72,
  125
 sources of, 31-32, 58-59
Problem solving, 107-109

S

Social knowledge, 89–98
  mental models, 91–92
  open systems view, 97–98
  theories of acquisition, 89–96
Social mobility, 82–88
Social models, 96–97
Social organization, 79–80
Social stratification, 80–82
Supplementary materials, 212–213

T

Teacher education, 159–161, 176–181, 213
Textbooks, 49–54, 58–59, 72, 125, 237–242, 254–255, 359–361
  contents of, 359–361
  influence of, 58–59
  problems with, 49–54, 72, 125, 237–241, 254–255
  revision of, 240–242, 254–255